The Art of Accommodation

Russian Transformations: Literature, Thought, Culture

Series Editor:
Andrew Kahn, University of Oxford

Volume 5

PETER LANG
Oxford · Bern · Berlin · Bruxelles · Frankfurt am Main · New York · Wien

Leon Burnett and Emily Lygo (eds)

The Art of Accommodation

Literary Translation in Russia

PETER LANG
Oxford · Bern · Berlin · Bruxelles · Frankfurt am Main · New York · Wien

Bibliographic information published by Die Deutsche Nationalbibliothek.
Die Deutsche Nationalbibliothek lists this publication in the Deutsche National-
bibliografie; detailed bibliographic data is available on the Internet at
http://dnb.d-nb.de.

A catalogue record for this book is available from the British Library.

Library of Congress Control Number: 2013933469

ISSN 1662-2545
ISBN 978-3-0343-0743-7

© Peter Lang AG, International Academic Publishers, Bern 2013
Hochfeldstrasse 32, CH-3012 Bern, Switzerland
info@peterlang.com, www.peterlang.com, www.peterlang.net

All rights reserved.
All parts of this publication are protected by copyright.
Any utilisation outside the strict limits of the copyright law, without the
permission of the publisher, is forbidden and liable to prosecution.
This applies in particular to reproductions, translations, microfilming,
and storage and processing in electronic retrieval systems.

Printed in Germany

Contents

Note on Transliteration   vii

Acknowledgements   ix

Notes on Contributors   xi

LEON BURNETT AND EMILY LYGO
The Art of Accommodation: Introduction   1

ALEXEI EVSTRATOV
Drama Translation in Eighteenth-Century Russia:
Masters and Servants on the Court Stage in the 1760s   31

BRIAN JAMES BAER
Vasilii Zhukovskii, Translator:
Accommodating Politics in Early Nineteenth-Century Russia   55

NATALIA OLSHANSKAYA
Turgenev's Letters on Translation   77

LEON BURNETT
Turgenev and the Translation of the Quixotic   97

KATHARINE HODGSON
Heine and Genre: Iurii Tynianov's Translations of Heine's poetry   117

SUSANNA WITT

Arts of Accommodation:
The First All-Union Conference of Translators, Moscow, 1936,
and the Ideologization of Norms　　　　　　　　　　　　　141

ELENA ZEMSKOVA

Translators in the Soviet Writers' Union:
Pasternak's Translations from Georgian Poets and the
Literary Process of the Mid-1930s　　　　　　　　　　　　185

ALEKSEI SEMENENKO

Identity, Canon and Translation:
Hamlets by Polevoi and Pasternak　　　　　　　　　　　　213

PHILIP ROSS BULLOCK

Not One of Us?
The Paradoxes of Translating Oscar Wilde in the Soviet Union　　235

EMILY LYGO

Free Verse and Soviet Poetry in the Post-Stalin Period　　　　265

Select Bibliography　　　　　　　　　　　　　　　　　　285

Index　　　　　　　　　　　　　　　　　　　　　　　　303

Note on Transliteration

The transliteration of Cyrillic characters has followed the Library of Congress system, without the use of diacritics. Russian surnames established in English usage, where they differ significantly from the transliterated form, have been preserved, e.g. Herzen, instead of Gertsen. The names of tsars are given in their customary English form, e.g. Alexander, instead of Aleksandr.

Acknowledgements

The editors wish to acknowledge financial assistance from the British Association for Slavonic and East European Studies (BASEES) in support of the conference *Pushkin's Post-Horses: Literary Translation in Russian Culture*, held at the University of Exeter, on 14–15 April 2008, which brought together many of the contributors to this volume. Research funding from the Department of Literature, Film, and Theatre Studies at the University of Essex and the School of Arts, Languages and Literatures at the University of Exeter enabled the publication to proceed to its conclusion.

Angela Livingstone was consulted in the course of the preparation of this collection of essays and her helpful comments are gratefully acknowledged. Maia Burnett and Karin Littau assisted with particular details of translation, and Ben Pestell with compilation. We thank them also.

Some of the material that is included in the chapter on 'Identity, Canon and Translation: *Hamlets* by Polevoi and Pasternak' first appeared in Aleksei Semenenko, *Hamlet the Sign: Russian Translations of Hamlet and Literary Canon Formation* (Stockholm: Almqvist & Wiksell International, 2007).

Notes on Contributors

BRIAN JAMES BAER is Professor of Russian and Translation Studies at Kent State University, Ohio. He is the author of *Other Russias: Homosexuality and the Crisis of Post-Soviet Identity* (2009). His most recent publications include the edited volume *Contexts, Subtexts, Pretexts: Literary Translation in Eastern Europe and Russia* (2011) and *No Good without Reward: The Selected Writings of Liubov Krichevskaya* (2011). His anthology, *Russian Writers on Translation*, co-edited with Natalia Olshanskaya, is forthcoming.

PHILIP ROSS BULLOCK is University Lecturer in Russian at the University of Oxford. He is the author of *The Feminine in the Prose of Andrey Platonov* (2005) and *Rosa Newmarch and Russian Music in Late Nineteenth and Early Twentieth-Century England* (2009), and the editor and translator of *The Correspondence of Jean Sibelius and Rosa Newmarch, 1906–1939* (2011). He is currently co-editing *Russia in Britain: From Melodrama to Modernism* with Rebecca Beasley.

LEON BURNETT is Reader in Literature and Director of the Centre for Myth Studies at the University of Essex. His research interests and publications are mainly in comparative and Russian literature of the last two centuries, with particular attention to the place of poetry, literary translation, fantasia and myth in modern culture. He has edited *F. M. Dostoevsky (1821–1881): A Centenary Collection* (1981) and *Word in Time: Poetry, Narrative, Translation* (1997).

ALEXEI EVSTRATOV holds a two-year postdoctoral assistantship at the University of Oxford, working on the project 'The Creation of a Europeanized Elite in Russia: Public Role and Subjective Self', directed by Andreas Schönle and Andrei Zorin. His recent publications include '"Ad Urbanitatem informare": la langue et l'éducation dans les comédies de Catherine II (exemple de *O temps!*)', in *Histoire. Epistémologie. Langage* (2010).

KATHARINE HODGSON is Associate Professor in Russian at the University of Exeter. Her chief research interests lie in the field of twentieth-century Russian poetry, in particular the development of the poetry canon in the post-Soviet period. She has published a study of the poet Ol'ga Berggol'ts, *Voicing the Soviet Experience* (2003), as well as articles on the translation and reception of English and German poetry in Russia.

EMILY LYGO is Lecturer in Russian at the University of Exeter. Her research interests are mainly in twentieth-century Russian poetry, translation in the USSR, and Anglo-Soviet cultural relations. Her publications include *Leningrad Poetry 1953–75: The Thaw Generation* (2010), and articles on Russian poetry and cultural history.

NATALIA OLSHANSKAYA is Professor of Russian in the Department of Modern Languages and Literatures at Kenyon College, Ohio. She has taught courses in translation studies at several universities. Her publications include numerous articles on the theory and practice of translation, such as 'Ukraine: Translating the Wars', 'Translating Political Discourse' and 'After [Isaac] Babel: Teaching Communicative Competence for Translation'.

ALEKSEI SEMENENKO is a Research Fellow in the Slavic Department at Stockholm University. He is the author of *Hamlet the Sign: Russian Translations of Hamlet and Literary Canon Formation* (2007), *The Texture of Culture: An Introduction to Yuri Lotman's Semiotic Theory* (2012), and articles on Russian culture, translation and semiotics. He is also a co-editor (with Lars Kleberg) of *Aksenov and the Environs* (2012).

SUSANNA WITT is Associate Professor at the Uppsala Centre for Russian and Eurasian Studies. She specializes in twentieth-century Russian literature, Russian translation history and Stalinist culture. Recent publications include 'Between the Lines: Totalitarianism and Translation in the USSR' in *Contexts, Subtexts and Pretexts* (2011), 'Epistemologiia poetiki (Neskol'ko nabliudenii nad "Okhrannoi gramotoi" Pasternaka)' in *Iazyk kak mediator mezhdu znaniem i iskusstvom* (2009), and '"Nature" in *Doctor Zhivago*' in *The Life of Boris Pasternak's Doctor Zhivago* (2009).

ELENA ZEMSKOVA is Associate Professor in the Department for Translation Studies, Institute of Philology and History, Russian State University of the Humanities. She is a specialist in Russian–German literary and cultural relations and the history of literary translation in Russia and the USSR, and wrote a doctoral thesis entitled 'The Russian Reception of German Views of the Nation in the Late Eighteenth and Early Nineteenth Centuries'.

LEON BURNETT AND EMILY LYGO

The Art of Accommodation: Introduction

Literary translation refers to a process by which a work of foreign origin is accommodated within a host culture. As such, it is part, but always only part, of the process of cultural assimilation. Translation does not occur in a vacuum. In all countries and cultures and, indeed, in all literary periods within cultures, there are local variations in the ways that the process of literary translation and consequently its product may be regarded. Russia is no exception to the rule. The assimilation of the literary works of other nations has been, and continues to be, an essential element in the establishment of its national identity, politically, socially and culturally. In Russia, works of foreign literature have, at times, been taken as models and, at other times, been used as a foil to demonstrate the undesirable, but however viewed, the act of receiving and responding to foreign texts has been integral to the literary process. No comprehensive study of Russia can afford to ignore the contribution made by translators and translation in the development of its literature, and concomitantly in the evolution of its cultural and social identity.

The volume does not present a chronological account of literary translation in Russia: this has already been established. Iurii Levin's *Istoriia russkoi perevodnoi khudozhestvennoi literatury* and *Russkie perevodchiki XIX veka i razvitie khudozhestvennogo perevoda* cover the period up to the end of the nineteenth century, and Maurice Friedberg's *Literary Translation in Russia* provides an historical introduction to translation in the eighteenth and nineteenth century as background to his study of literary translation in the nineteenth century and especially the Soviet period.[1] Friedberg's study

---

[1] Iurii Levin, ed., *Istoriia russkoi perevodnoi khudozhestvennoi literatury. Drevniaia Rus'. XVIII vek. Tom I: Proza. Tom II. Dramaturgiia. Poeziia.* (St Petersburg:

addresses not only the development and chronology of literary translation, but also the theoretical perspectives on translation and the practicalities of being a translator, in general and specifically in Russia and the Soviet Union. At the close of his study, he touches upon the mutual interdependence of translations into Russian and the status of Russian literature and culture:[2] this is the departure point for the present study.

The essays in this volume are linked by the central underlying assumptions they share: that literary translation is a process that entails the accommodation of a new text by a host culture, and that this involves an accompanying adjustment to prevailing conventions within the culture. The idea of accommodation, then, resonates with two primary implications: on the one hand, it acknowledges the fact that a foreign text is housed by a new culture, and, on the other hand, it asserts that the text is manipulated in the process of translation to accommodate the particular conditions of that culture – Russian culture in the current study – at any given moment.

Literary translations, whether they reinforce the cultural norms that obtain within the society at the time of their publication or serve as vehicles to engender new and radical expectations, are subject to a process of accommodation. This process necessarily involves both *adaptation* – the adjustment that has to be made to the text to render its existence meaningful in a second language – and *reception* – the provision of a place for it to reside. These are the two fundamental senses in which the concept of accommodation is applied in this volume, but the dictionary furnishes further nuances that are equally applicable. Thus, we find in the *Oxford*

Russian Academy of Sciences Institute of Russian Literature, 1995); Iurii Levin, *Russkie perevodchiki XIX veka i razvitie khudozhestvennogo perevoda* (Leningrad: Nauka, 1985); Maurice Friedberg, *Literary Translation in Russia: A Cultural History* (Pennsylvania: Pennsylvania State University Press, 1997). Other works on the history (as opposed to the theory) of literary translation in Russian include Andrei N. Girivenko, ed., *Iz istorii russkogo khudozhestvennogo perevoda pervoi poloviny XIX veka: Epokha romantizma* (Moscow: Nauka, 2002); Iurii Levin, ed., *Na rubezhe XIX i XX vekov: iz istorii mezhdunarodnykh sviazei russkoi literatury. Sbornik nauchnykh trudov* (Leningrad: Nauka, 1991).

2   Friedberg, *Literary Translation in Russia*, 207–10.

English Dictionary ascriptions such as 'assimilation', 'conformity to circumstance', 'compromise', 'anything which supplies a want, or affords aid', and, interestingly, 'the action or power of adapting the eyes to view objects at various distances'; this reminds us that the proximity, or otherwise, of translation to text – geographically, historically, linguistically, or culturally – is an important factor. The translator always works with the material at hand, but the way in which this material is put to use is sometimes at a far remove from its function in another culture. Thus, accommodation can also conform to the *OED* sense of the 'adaptation of a word, expression, or system to something different from its original purpose'.

In the field of Translation Studies, a preoccupation with the concepts of 'source text' and 'target text' has become ingrained, and the abbreviations 'ST' and 'TT' are adopted without interrogation in critical articles. Aleksei Semenenko observes in his contribution to this volume that 'in the field of literary translation the most common practice of a reviewer or a critic is to compare a translator's work with the source text and indicate "right" and "wrong" renditions of the original'. As he points out,

> this seemingly natural approach does not take into account the actual process of reception and adaptation of a foreign text to the national culture, and demonizes the original as the source of imaginary truth.

The metaphor of accommodation proposes that a translation may be regarded more as an arrival than a departure: the emphasis is not so much upon its 'source' in the donor language as in the *resources* of the recipient culture – and the resourcefulness of the translator.

The study of translation has evolved towards an understanding of it as an activity integrated into broader literary and social processes, which enable us to conceive of translation as far more than a linguistic exercise. Since Susan Bassnett and André Lefevere's assertion that the unit of translation studies is culture,[3] the field has broadened to encompass the examination of not only the process of translating, but also the effects of

---

3   Susan Bassnett and André Lefevere, eds, *Translation, History and Culture* (London: Pinter, 1990), 8.

a translation. Emphasis has shifted towards the receiving culture, which is to say towards the processes of assimilation, the ripples caused by a literary text that is plunged – via translation – into a new cultural setting. Theorists of culture have approached the process of translation from various angles, but largely concur that the focus for the study of translation should lie at the endpoint of the process: the culture that receives a new text.

Iurii Lotman has sketched out five stages in the process of translation from the perspective of the recipient culture. After an initial phase in which foreign works of literature are highly valued and considered superior to anything that has been achieved in the native language, there follow phases of transplantation and assimilation. It is during these two phases that the imported text and the home culture restructure each other as the latter proceeds to appropriate the ideas and ideology expressed in the former. Thereafter, in the final two phases, the host culture becomes increasingly equipped to take on the role of a transmitter itself.[4]

In his understanding of the process of translation, Wolfgang Iser points to the interaction of the two cultures involved in the process. In his conception, translation is not a linear process, but one which involves mutuality, which brings about change for both cultures involved:

> a foreign culture is not simply subsumed under one's own frame of reference; instead, the very frame is subjected to alterations in order to accommodate what does not fit. Such a transposition runs counter to the idea of the hegemony of one culture over the other, and hence the notion of translatability emerges as a counter-concept to a mutual superimposing of cultures.[5]

He sees the experience of another culture that is gained through translation as the introduction of one culture to the 'otherness' of one alien to it;

---

4   Yuri M. Lotman, *Universe of the Mind: A Semiotic Theory of Culture*; trans. Ann Shukman (London: Tauris, 1990), 146–7.
5   Wolfgang Iser, 'On Translatability', *Surfaces*, IV (1994). *Surfaces* is an Electronic Review published by Les Presses de l'Université de Montreal and is available at <http://www.pum.umontreal.ca/revues/surfaces/index.html>. The essay was published as 'On Translatability: Variables of Interpretation' in *The European English Messenger* 4 (I): 30–8 (1995).

though he argues that 'otherness' is a quality that 'becomes tangible only in individual manifestations', he nevertheless illustrates the point with examples of what this encounter might involve: a duality which results in an experience of difference; an exploration of difference that raises the question of why there are such disparities; assimilation, which leads to a politics of cultural relationships; appropriation; and heightened self-awareness, which leads to self-confrontation.⁶ The confrontation of otherness, for Iser, is a productive and transforming encounter for both sides.

Russia's geographical and historical position at the edge of Europe and on the border of Asia means that both East and West have been perceived, at various times in its history, as close relation and alien other. In this exploration of affinities – whether Slavophile or Westernizing – translation has played a key role, and thus contributed to the evolution of Russian identity. Lawrence Venuti has referred perceptively to this identity-forming power of translation in the life of a culture. In *The Scandals of Translation*, he writes:

> A calculated choice of foreign text and translation strategy can change or consolidate literary canons, conceptual paradigms, research methodologies, clinical techniques, and commercial practices in the domestic culture. Whether the effects of a translation prove to be conservative or transgressive depends fundamentally on the discursive strategies developed by the translator, but also on the various factors in their reception [...] and the uses made of the translation in cultural and social institutions, how it is read and taught.⁷

The privileged place of literature in Russian culture, and in particular its well-established, central role in political and social debate, has meant that literary translation has played a leading role in the processes of identity negotiation. From the theatre of Catherine's court to post-Soviet publishing, the accommodation of foreign literature has sometimes strengthened, sometimes weakened Russia's sense of its distinctive path of development, its Eastern affinities, or its congruence with the West.

---

6   Ibid.
7   Lawrence Venuti, *The Scandals of Translation: Towards an Ethics of Difference* (London: Routledge, 1998), 68.

The metaphor of accommodation, then, challenges the traditional evaluation of the success of a translation on the basis of a comparison of a translator's work with the source text. Translation is seen as an activity which applies to texts but also to cultures. Translations are cultural events with prehistories and consequences; they influence the history of the text translated, but also produce profound changes in the course of a culture's development. The question arises, then, whether or not we can speak of a successful or unsuccessful translation in this broadened sense of the word. David Damrosch has discussed what makes a bad translation, with reference to translation strategy and accommodation within the receiving culture. He acknowledges Lefevere's point that translations are '"good" only with respect to a certain place and a certain time, in certain circumstances,'[8] but he maintains that sometimes a translation 'can produce potentially unreadable texts, and [...] can create a separatist mode of translation that undermines the reader's sense of connection to a common human experience' while at other times it 'gets us to no common ground beyond our own local cultural position'.[9] Damrosch is arguing, then, for a balanced accommodation of a text that manages conflicting pulls upon the text's potential meanings and status. He suggests that, for a translation to be successful, it must contribute to the identity of the receiving culture, neither losing its distinctiveness nor remaining too foreign to have relevance. John Johnston's study of 'Translation as Simulacrum' points to Ezra Pound as having achieved such an accommodation within English poetry by producing accessible versions of unfamiliar poems, which nevertheless breathed new life into the English literary language: 'Pound never translated "into" something already existing in English ... [his] translations are really reconstructions or re-inscriptions intended to expand the expressive possibilities of the English language'.[10] To be successful, the translator needs to have mastered the challenge of adapting the existing idiom to accommodate works that

---

8   David Damrosch, quoting Lefevere, in *What is World Literature?* (Princeton: Princeton University Press, 2003), 167.
9   Damrosch, *What is World Literature?*, 168.
10 John Johnston, 'Translation as Simulacrum' in Lawrence Venuti, ed., *Rethinking Translation: Discourse, Subjectivity, Ideology* (London: Routledge, 1992), 42–56 (45).

are being introduced into the language to such an extent that the readership comes to consider itself as a partner in the enterprise.

To see translation as an event that happens to texts and cultures, to identify the translator as the agent of accommodation who masters the adaptation of a text, is to envisage a trajectory of movement from origin to new culture, to see the literary work impelled *from* a source outside into the receiving culture. But translation can often also be a return *to* a different source, a gravitational pull that draws it in to the recipient culture at a particular historical period. Lefevere has discussed how the degree to which a foreign writer is accepted in a recipient culture, and therefore how successful a translation is, is determined by that native system's need for such a text.[11] The arrival of a text in the host language may seem like the end of a journey, but it can also partake of the nature of a homecoming in response to a philological imperative that restores to the nation something it had temporarily lost. In an essay on 'Word and Culture', in which he remarked famously that poetry is the plough that turns up time, Osip Mandel'shtam, poet and translator, referred metaphorically to that imperative:

> The silver trumpet of Catullus – *Ad claras Asiae volemus urbes* – alarms and excites us more forcefully than any Futurist riddle. Such poetry does not exist in Russian. Yet it *must* exist in Russian. I chose a Latin line because it is clearly perceived by the Russian reader as a category of obligation: the imperative rings more vividly in it.[12]

At its most accomplished, and that is what Mandel'shtam is interested in, a poetic translation may serve as plough or trumpet, in the temporally instrumental and existential sense he intends, when an additional resource is perceived at the same time as both a recovery and a restoration: it *must*

---

11   André Lefevere, 'Mother Courage's Cucumbers: Text, System and Refraction in a Theory of Literature' in Lawrence Venuti, ed., *The Translation Studies Reader* (Abingdon: Routledge, 2004), 239–55 (243).
12   Osip Mandelstam, *The Complete Critical Prose and Letters*; ed. Jane Gary Harris (Ann Arbor: Ardis, 1979), 114.

exist in Russian. Otherwise, as he writes in another essay, 'translation is merely interpolation'.[13]

Mandel'shtam's sense of the imperative for a text to enter a language and a culture is intimately bound up with the timeliness of a translation: that a text or writer is needed at a given cultural moment, contributing foreign ideas, forms or traditions that stimulate the evolution of the native system. Other texts, however, are received successfully into a culture not just at one pivotal moment, but repeatedly, in the different guises of multiple translations. Such texts, commonly referred to as classics, are not timely but timeless: their appeal and relevance seem inexhaustible. With each re-translation, new elements of the classics are revealed that are successfully accommodated within the recipient culture. As Frank Kermode has remarked, '[t]he books we call classics possess [...] an openness to accommodation which keeps them alive under endlessly varying dispositions'.[14] Venuti sees this as true not only for classics within their own language and culture, but also for translated classics accommodated within other systems. The acts of translation and of re-translation serve to refresh and re-cast the text, uncovering and creating new meanings:

> [I]n contributing to the canonicity of a foreign text, the translation leaves neither that text nor the receiving situation unaltered. The foreign text undergoes a radical transformation in which it comes to support a range of meanings and values that may have little or nothing to do with those it supported in the foreign culture. And the linguistic choices, literary traditions and cultural values that comprise the translator's interpretation may reinforce or revise the understanding and evaluation of the foreign text that currently prevail in the receiving situation, consolidating readerships or forming new ones in the process.[15]

---

13   See Leon Burnett, 'The Survival of Myth: Mandel'shtam's "Word" and Translation' in Theo Hermans, ed., *The Manipulation of Literature: Studies in Literary Translation* (London: Croom Helm, 1985), 164–97 (175).
14   Quoted in Lawrence Venuti, 'Translation, Interpretation, Canon Formation' in Alexandra Lianeri and Vanda Zajko, eds, *Translation and the Classic: Identity as Change in the History of Culture* (Oxford: Oxford University Press, 2008), 27.
15   Ibid.

To see translation as the art of accommodation means to understand that the significance of any act of translation is found in the interplay of text, time and place. Gabriel Rockhill asserts that '[t]he conceptual network defining the basic elements and modalities of what is generally understood as translation is necessarily dependent on a historical situation,'[16] and that '[i]n order for a translation to be recognized as such and considered worthy of the name, it has to abide by the broad parameters operative in a particular community'.[17] Thus, two essential, and inter-related, criteria, central to the idea of accommodation, provide a framework for thinking about translation: the historical situation and the social context.

> Communities do, of course, come into conflict – both with themselves and with other communities –, but the basic point remains unchanged: just as the translator never works in a historical vacuum, *translation is never an isolated soliloquy uninformed by a community*.[18]

From the eighteenth century to the twentieth the engagement of the literary community in Russia with questions of translation formed and changed, reflecting historical and social concerns that contributed to the shaping of Russian culture at large. It was not always a case of 'reflection', however, for some of the most significant translation projects of the last two and a half centuries may be regarded as salient interventions in the nation's literature affecting its historical development. The following survey of literary translation in Russia is seen through the prism of translation as accommodation, and seeks to foreground the interactions and interdependencies that exist between literary translation in Russia and Russian literature and culture. The chapters in this collection develop in detail case studies which belong to this history.

Aleksandr Pushkin once remarked that 'we have no ancient literature': 'Our literature appeared suddenly in the eighteenth century, like

---

16   From the 'Translator's Preface', in Jacques Ranciére, *The Politics of Aesthetics: The Distribution of the Sensible*; translated with an introduction by Gabriel Rockhill (London: Continuum, 2004), vii.
17   Ibid., viii.
18   Ibid., italics added.

the Russian nobility without ancestors or a pedigree.'[19] In the absence of any national pedigree, letters patent (to extend Pushkin's metaphor) were granted in what Pushkin dubbed the 'Age of Encouragement' to books of foreign provenance, especially works emanating from France. In conjunction with the import of foreign ideas, came the translation of literary and philosophical texts into Russian. In this way, translation acquired in the second half of the eighteenth century a strategic importance for the first time in Russia, when Catherine the Great indicated the appropriateness of accommodating major works of the Enlightenment within the purlieus of the Russian court.[20] The establishment of the Society for the Translation of Foreign Books in 1768, under her patronage, was symptomatic both of an engagement with Western thought and of an ambition to expedite the development of an indigenous literature. Within four years, the Society had published more than forty titles. The success of the enterprise was so great that, as has been wryly noted, 'Moscow reported an epidemic as deadly as the recent outbreak of plague – the spurning of Russian scholars, artists and artisans in favour of foreigners.'[21]

The initial phase of translation during Russia's Enlightenment prepared the ground for a Golden Age of translation that ran in parallel, in the first half of the nineteenth century, with the Golden Age of literature when the emergence of a succession of authors marked the arrival of Russian literature on the world stage. Recognition of the achievements of Pushkin, Lermontov and Gogol' in the West, however, was slow in coming. In 1840, Thomas Carlyle, concluding his third lecture 'On Heroes and Hero-Worship', lamented the fact that, unlike Italy which had 'produced its Dante', Russia lacked a 'voice of genius, to be heard of all men and times.'[22]

19 Tatiana Wolff, ed., *Pushkin on Literature* (London: Methuen, 1971), 272. Pushkin made an exception of *The Lay of Igor's Campaign*.
20 Catherine also promoted the development of Russian drama through the introduction of foreign models; see the chapter by Aleksei Evstratov in this volume.
21 W. Gareth Jones, *Nikolay Novikov: Enlightener of Russia* (Cambridge: Cambridge University Press, 1984), 82.
22 Thomas Carlyle, *Works (The Ashburton Edition) in Seventeen Volumes. Volume III, On Heroes, Hero-Worship and The Heroic in History* (London: Chapman and Hall, 1889), 94.

In this assertion, he was, of course, mistaken. With the benefit of hindsight, the explanation as to why the voice of Russia had not at that time been heard in England is obvious: if Russian literature did indeed lack a voice, as Carlyle asserted, it was the voice of a translator equal to the occasion. The absence of a translator 'of genius', rather than of a poet-hero, rendered the nation 'dumb'. In contrast, Russia possessed one of the most able and assiduous translators of the period, Vasilii Zhukovskii, who stands out in the history of its literature for his work as a creative translator. His translations were considered to be on a par with their foreign models and, in their sheer range, they answered the need for the kind of cultural enlargement that the assimilation of foreign works brings and which paves the way to the establishment of a national literature.

Zhukovskii regarded the translator's task as one demanding creativity equal to, but not identical with, that of the original poet.[23] He justified his own practice by reference to the re-creative power of the imagination. In this he had the approbation of Pushkin, who referred to imitation as 'a hope of finding new worlds, following in the steps of genius, or the experiencing, even more lofty in its humility, of a desire to study one's model and thus give it a second lease of life'.[24] Zhukovskii endorsed a view of the *poetic* translator as a rival, rather than a slave.[25] In his choice of Western models, he reacted against French poetry, which he regarded as having had a debilitating effect on Russian literature. His first translation from the literature of Western Europe, completed in 1802, was of Thomas Gray's 'Elegy, written in a Country Churchyard',[26] but it was to the poetry of

23 V. A. Zhukovskii, *Sobranie sochinenii v chetyrekh tomakh* (Moscow, 1960), IV, 410.
24 Wolff, ed., *Pushkin on Literature*, 401.
25 'Without fear of contradiction, we allow ourselves to insist that it is possible for the verse-imitator to be an *original* author, even though he has written nothing of his own. The translator *in prose* is a slave; the translator *in verse* – a rival.' V. A. Zhukovskii 'O basne i basniakh Krylova', *Vestnik Evropy* (1809), No. 9. See V. A. Zhukovskii, *Sobranie sochinenii v chetyrekh tomakh: tom chetvertyi* (Moscow and Leningrad: Gosudarstvennoe izdatel'stvo khudozhestvennoi literatury, 1960), 402–18 (410).
26 Zhukovskii made a second translation of the elegy in 1839. All his translations of English poetry are printed, with the originals on facing pages, in V. A. Zhukovskii, *Angliiskaia poeziia v perevodakh V. A. Zhukovskogo: Sbornik*; sostavl. K. N. Atarovoi

German Romanticism that he devoted his main attention. His first translated ballad was 'Liudmila' (1808), a free version of Bürger's 'Lenore', in which the heroine's eventual fate is to accompany her dead lover on a final ride, not to a blissful life together, but to the burial chamber. The ballad's narrator asks rhetorically: 'Where is your bridal crown? A grave – your house, a corpse – your groom'. Liudmila's fate, as the conclusion to the ballad makes clear, is recompense for a life in which she refused to accept in her heart that love is immortal. The change of title and the change of narrative location from medieval Germany to medieval Russia gave notice of an incipient nationalism that was to play a significant part in the development of Russian Romanticism. Zhukovskii returned to the theme of Bürger's 'Lenore' in his third ballad translation in 1812.[27] On this occasion he gave the heroine the name Svetlana and the ballad the happy ending that the first version (and the original) lacked. In 'Svetlana', the heroine achieves a victory over the dream-death that is Liudmila's. Zhukovskii set out the moral of the tale in a postscript: 'Here unhappiness is a false dream; happiness – an awakening'.[28]

The absence of a strongly developed national literature at the end of the eighteenth century explains to a large extent Zhukovskii's life-long engagement as a translator of foreign poetry, an occupation that extended from the early translations of works of contemporary or near-contemporary German and English poets to the late translations, in the 1840s, of epic works from Ancient Greece and the Orient.[29] His translation of the

and A. A. Gugnina (Moscow: Izd. Rudomino/ OAO Izd. Raduga, 2000). For an examination of Zhukovskii's translations of English romantic poets and his accommodation of their politics, see Brian James Baer's chapter in this volume.

27 Zhukovskii had translated Schiller's 'Kassandra' in the interval.

28 Pavel Katenin produced a version of the same ballad. His renaming of the heroine as Ol'ga was motivated by a preference similar to Zhukovskii's for a euphonious Russian name. Pushkin preferred Katenin's 'remarkable' translation to Zhukovskii's 'inaccurate but charming imitation, which changed it in the way that Byron changed *Faust* in *Manfred*, weakening the spirit and form of its original'. Quoted from Wolff, ed., *Pushkin on Literature*, 335.

29 Between 1809 and 1833 Zhukovskii translated all of Schiller's ballads. During this period he also translated ballads by Goethe, Uhland and Bürger. From 1834 to 1852,

Odyssey, however, was not the first, nor necessarily the most esteemed, version of a Homeric epic to appear in Russia in the first half of the nineteenth century. Nikolai Gnedich's version of the *Iliad*, 'the *magnum opus* which established his reputation as a literary figure',[30] was a landmark translation of the romantic period. When Gnedich's translation, on which he had first embarked in 1807, was finally published in 1829, Pushkin wrote a short notice, printed in the second issue of *Literaturnaia gazeta* for 1830, in which he referred to it as a 'book which is bound to exercise [...] an important influence on our native literature.'[31] At the same time, Pushkin wrote to Gnedich praising the work as 'good for Russia', but apologising for his lack of knowledge of the Greek language that 'prevents me from undertaking a full-scale analysis of your *Iliad*'.[32] Nevertheless, this reservation did not stop him from penning a tribute in verse in which, employing an unusual analogy for the translation process, he likened the translator to Moses on Mount Sinai and thus, by implication, Homer to God. 'To Gnedich' commences with the line 'With Homer long you conversed alone'[33] and proceeds to express the fear that Gnedich would

---

he showed greater interest in the composition of large narrative works – *poemy* and tales in verse – than in shorter, lyrical forms. In this period, he adapted the Indian tale 'Nala and Damayanti' (1841) and 'Rustam and Sohrab' (1847) – both from German versions – and he translated the *Odyssey* (1842–8) from a German interlinear text.

30   Alessandra Tosi, 'At the Origins of the Russian Gothic Novel: Nikolai Gnedich's *Don Corrado de Gerrera* (1803)', in Neil Cornwell, ed., *The Gothic-Fantastic in Nineteenth-Century Russian Literature* (Amsterdam and Atlanta: Rodopi, 1999), 59–82 (59). Tosi lists excerpts from Thomson's *The Seasons*, Young's *Night Thoughts*, and an incomplete translation of Gray's 'Elegy, written in a Country Churchyard' as being among his translations. For a fuller account, see I. I. Tolstoi, 'Gnedich kak perevodchik *Iliady*', in Gomer, *Iliada*, perevod N. I. Gnedich (Moscow and Leningrad, 1935), 101–12 and A. N. Egunov, *Gomer v russkikh perevodakh XVIII–XIX vekov* (Moscow and Leningrad, 1964), 147–295.

31   Wolff, ed., *Pushkin on Literature*, 232.

32   Letter to Gnedich, 6 January 1830. Ibid., 278.

33   Compare Exodus 24:18: 'And Moses went into the midst of the cloud, and gat him up into the mount: and Moses was in the mount forty days and forty nights.' As Michael Wachtel points out, the opening is reminiscent of Gnedich's own poem, 'To my Foreign Guests', which includes the line: 'I conversed with Homer and Nature'.

smash his 'tablets' in frustration at the sight of the frivolous behaviour of his 'senseless children', that is to say, of the reading public. It concludes by reassuring the reader that the peaceful, nature-loving poet did not, in fact, repeat Moses' angry act of destruction.

Pushkin, as is well known, took a lively interest in all aspects of literary production, from the source of the poet's creativity to the business of the bookseller's trade. A significant part of his deliberations on the current state of literature was concerned with the reception of foreign works, especially the translation and imitation of influential models. Although his most-quoted remark on the topic of translation is the aphoristic statement that translators are 'the post-horses of enlightenment',[34] his letters and jottings afford manifold examples of the close attention he gave to a critical – and often polemical – analysis of individual authors and literary works, particularly in the 1830s, when, as one biographer has commented, he 'was minded, while not abandoning literature, to refashion himself as a historian'.[35] Typical was his rounding on Samuel Johnson ('an exceedingly rude man') for his vituperations against the author of *The Poems of Ossian*. Ahead of his time, Pushkin recognized that quibbling over whether Macpherson's work was 'a translation, an imitation, or his own composition' was an issue of secondary importance to a consideration of the work's accommodation right across Europe, where 'everybody read and re-read [the poem] with delight'. Nevertheless, despite his rebuke of Johnson, Pushkin concluded his remarks on the literary controversy with a call for the emergence in Russia of critics of the stature of a Johnson or an Addison.[36]

Pushkin's most remarkable venture into translation criticism, however, was an article on which he had been working at the time of his death and

---

See Michael Wachtel, *A Commentary to Pushkin's Lyric Poetry, 1826–1836* (Madison: University of Wisconsin Press, 2012), 242. Pushkin was less kind in an unpublished epigram where he contrasted Gnedich, who had had only the use of his left eye since his youth, with blind Homer, and his 'one-eyed' translation with the original epic.

34 Wolff, ed., *Pushkin on Literature*, 277.
35 T. J. Binyon, *Pushkin: A Biography* (London: Harper Collins, 2002), 365–6.
36 Pushkin's comments were published anonymously in *Literaturnaia gazeta*, No. 5 (1830). See Wolff, ed., *Pushkin on Literature*, 276–7.

The Art of Accommodation: Introduction

which, edited by Zhukovskii, was published posthumously in *Sovremennik* in 1837. In 'On Milton and on Chateaubriand's translation of *Paradise Lost*', Pushkin displayed a familiarity with current theoretical debates about literary translation as well as an awareness of the practice of *les belles infidèles* in France, as the following extract demonstrates:

> Now (an unheard-of precedent) the leading writer in France translates Milton *word for word* and announces that line-by-line translation would have been the consummation of his art, had he been able to achieve it! Such humility in a French writer, the prime master of his trade, must have greatly astonished the champions of *improved translations* and will probably have an important influence on literature.[37]

His favourable critique of Chateaubriand's translation, a work which, it is to be noted, had appeared in print only in 1836, had an assurance and authority to it that came from a well-informed reading of contemporary French literature which enabled him to contrast the latest interpretation of Milton with earlier attempts.[38]

Concerned that 'of late its influence has been slight [...] confined only to translations and some imitations', Pushkin did much, in a series of critical pieces that he wrote in the 1830s, to reinstate French literature as a model worthy of emulation.[39] There were dissenting voices to this view, Gogol' and Belinskii in particular, who, from different perspectives and for different motives, took pride in a home-grown nationalism and resented what they regarded as interference from the outside. Nevertheless, the tide was turning: the influence of Byron and Scott was on the ebb, while the

---

37 Ibid., 453.
38 'Of all great foreign authors Milton was the most unfortunate as far as France was concerned. [...] What was done to him by Alfred de Vigny, unceremoniously placed by French critics on a level with W. Scott? How was he presented by Victor Hugo, another favourite of the Parisian public? Maybe readers have forgotten both *Cinq-Mars* and *Cromwell* and are therefore unable to judge of the absurdity of Victor Hugo's pictures.' Ibid., 453–4.
39 Ibid., 397. His critical observations on foreign works were not, however, limited to French literature. He wrote, for *Sovremennik*, a review of a new translation of a book by Silvio Pellico and a lengthy account of John Tanner's narrative, based on the French translation (Paris, 1835).

reception of Eugene Sue and George Sand could be said by the 1840s to be in full flood. The works in translation of the latter pair would retain their popular appeal for the remainder of the nineteenth century. Turgenev's love affair with French literature (as well as with one of its most famous opera singers) ensured that translations and imitations from that source, especially given the increasing respect accorded to the genre of realism, would enjoy the recommendation of one of the most prominent novelists of the age.[40] It is hardly surprising, in this context, to learn that Théophile Gautier, when he attended a ball in Moscow in the late 1850s, had his own verse quoted to him by a masked lady. As Gautier reminded himself, in resisting the charms of the mysterious figure, 'the Russians read a great deal, and [...] the least French authors have a larger circle of readers in St. Petersburg and Moscow than in Paris itself'.[41]

Dostoevskii's debut on the literary scene came with his translation of Balzac's *Eugenie Grandet* in 1844, two years before his own *Poor Folk* and *The Double* were published, and, despite (or, perhaps, because of) a strong inclination to Slavophile ideology, he continued to the end of his days to entertain a conviction that Russia would benefit from works of foreign provenance. In his last public pronouncement on Russian literature, he praised Pushkin for his universal sympathy, which 'makes him a national poet'. His 'Pushkin speech', delivered on 8 June 1880 at a meeting of the Society of Lovers of Russian Literature, offered an indirect riposte to Carlyle's accusation that Russia was a nation of 'dumb greatness': its 'genius', as evidenced in its hero-poet, lay in a capacity, unparalleled even by 'creative geniuses of immense magnitude', such as Shakespeare, Cervantes and Schiller, for accommodating the creations of other nations:

---

40   On Turgenev's importance for literary translation in Russia, see the chapters by Leon Burnett and Natalia Olshanskaya in this volume.
41   Théophile Gautier, *Voyage en Russie*, 2 vols (Paris: Charpentier, 1867). The English translation is from vol. 7 (*Travels in Russia. Belgium and Holland: A Day in London*) of *The Complete Works*; trans. and ed. S. C. de Sumichrast (London: Athenaeum Press, 1900–3, 12 v.), II, 83.

The very greatest of these European poets could never exemplify as intensely as Pushkin the genius of another people – even a people that might be near at hand – the spirit of the people, all the hidden depths of that spirit and all its longing to fulfill its destiny. On the contrary, when the European poets deal with other nationalities they most often instilled in them their own nationality and interpreted them from their own national standpoint. Even Shakespeare's Italians, for instance, are almost to a man the same as Englishmen. Pushkin alone, of all the poets of the world, possesses the quality of embodying himself fully within another nationality.[42]

Elsewhere, Dostoevskii proposed a model for translation that was consistent with the central idea expressed in the 'Pushkin speech', namely that 'the capacity to respond to the whole world' – or the art of accommodation – was 'the principal capacity of our nationality'.[43] His view of translation was based on a fundamental asymmetry in which '[o]n the one hand, Russia displayed an ability to *absorb* (or assimilate) the genius of other languages; but, on the other, the material of Russian literature was *resistant* to any accommodation in other languages'.[44]

If the literary history of Russia (as indeed of many other European countries) is notable, in the first half of the nineteenth century, for the enthusiastic accommodation of two British authors with titles of nobility to their names – Lord Byron and Sir Walter Scott, then the second half of the century is marked by a comparable phenomenon involving a professional writer from further afield whose credentials were democratic in the extreme. The coming of Edgar Allan Poe helped to prepare the way for the transition from an era steeped in compendious works of heart-rending realism to one susceptible to the more recondite nuances of symbolism, decadence and degeneration. The first substantial attempt to introduce the American author to the Russian reading public was made by Dostoevskii, who, in 1861, published three of Poe's tales in a translation by Mikhailovskii,

---

42 Fyodor Dostoyevsky, *A Writer's Diary*; trans. Kenneth Lantz (London: Quartet Books, 1995), 1292.
43 Ibid., 1291.
44 See Leon Burnett, 'Dostoevsky's "New Word": A Short and Curious Note on Language Acquisition', *New Comparison*, 29 (2000), 81–6 (82).

from Baudelaire's French version.[45] Dostoevskii wrote a foreword to the tales that in retrospect reads like an early manifesto for his own brand of 'fantastic realism'. In it, he argued for Poe's importance and individuality as a writer who 'puts his hero into the most exceptional external or psychological position' in order to 'tell the condition of that man's soul'.[46] It was not this Poe, however, who captured the Russian imagination, as it had the French. It was, rather, Poe the poet, who made an impression. Three Russian translations of 'The Raven' – by Andreevskii, Obolenskii and Kondrat'ev – appeared between 1878 and 1880. There followed, in 1892, a version by Dmitrii Merezhkovskii, and, in 1894, the version by Konstantin Bal'mont which was to establish itself as the canonical translation.[47]

Joan Delaney Grossman introduced the concept of the 'propitious moment' into her study of the reception of Poe in Russia.[48] She dates the accommodation ('an epiphany paralleling his renewed reputation in France') to 1895. In her view, neither the two anonymous translations of Poe's collected works, which were published in 1885–6 but attracted little critical interest, nor Valerii Briusov's belated translation of *The Complete Collection of Poems and Verses of Edgar Poe* in 1924 came at a sufficiently 'propitious' time to establish (or re-establish) his name in Russian letters. She notes that '[c]hanged esthetic concepts, new social and intellectual concerns, and finally a sparking point of some sort were needed to propel Poe into real importance'.[49] The 'sparking point' was the debate that took place in Russia over European Symbolism and its literary Doppelgänger,

---

45   The tales ('The Tell-Tale Heart', 'The Black Cat' and 'The Devil in the Belfry') appeared in the January issue of *Vremia*.
46   See Leon Burnett, 'Dostoevsky, Poe and the Discovery of Fantastic Realism' in Leon Burnett, ed., *F. M. Dostoevsky (1821–1881): A Centenary Collection* (Colchester: University of Essex, 1981), 58–86.
47   See Joan Delaney Grossman, *Edgar Allan Poe in Russia: A Study in Legend and Literary Influence* (Würzburg: Jal-Verlag, 1973), 191–200, for a list of translations of Poe's works into Russian.
48   Ibid., 66, 159.
49   Ibid., 67.

Decadence.[50] As Tamara Bogolepova maintains, it was in the 'atmosphere of [the] poetic flourishing [of Russian Symbolism] that Poe's poetry became *necessary* for Russian culture'.[51] The themes of the double, composition (and decomposition), and life after death that are found in Poe's *oeuvre*, as well as the notoriety of the author as *poète maudit* and transcendental dreamer, germane in any consideration of the transmigration of his works into another culture, saw the nineteenth century out and lingered on long enough into the first decade of the next for Aleksandr Blok still to avow in 1906 that '[t]he works of Poe are as if written in our times'. By the 1920s, however, when Briusov turned his attention in earnest to the American writer, the 'propitious moment' had passed and his new translation did nothing to revive interest in the 'cult of Poe' which, according to Bogolepova, had 'led Russian intellectuals and artists to serious and profound studies, as well as to a high level of translation of his writings'.[52]

Two factors coalesced to ensure that the practice of literary translation remained high on the agenda for Russian poets of the Silver Age. The first was an appreciation of the richness of the literary legacy bequeathed by leading practitioners of French Symbolism and the second was an attraction to aesthetic theories of transformation or transcendence. It is possible to trace these two aspects, prominent in the poetics of early twentieth-century Russian authors, back to a common origin in Baudelaire's idea of *correspondences*. Translation as a symbolic activity could thus be regarded as a kind of metamorphosis of the body of the text or even a reincarnation of the spirit of the original impulse that gave rise to it. The sense of an 'elective affinity' between author and translator that this generated reached its apogee in the coining of the name 'Shel'mont' in response to

---

50   The first Russian edition of Cesare Lombroso's *Genio e follia* came out in 1885 and of Max Nordau's *Entartung* in 1892 (ibid., 70–1).
51   Tamara Bogolepova, '"A Cooperation of Souls": Edgar Allan Poe's Poetry translated by Russian Symbolists', <http://spintongues.msk.ru/bogolepova3eng.htm> accessed 17 May 2012.
52   Ibid.

the 'unwarranted liberties' that Bal'mont took with Shelley's poetry.[53] Osip Mandel'shtam, reacting against what he regarded as the excesses of Russian Symbolism ('a workshop producing scarecrows'), applied an extra twist to the knife in commending Bal'mont's translations of Shelley and Poe as having left more of a trace than his own verse, which 'forces one to believe in the existence of highly interesting originals'.[54]

Like Mandel'shtam, Nikolai Gumilev was an acmeist: both were members of a new school of poetics that challenged the tenets of its predecessor, Russian Symbolism, whose international outlook, however, it shared. Acmeism's 'nostalgia for world culture', though, was based on an ideology of identities rather than of correspondences, on the craft and graft of a Salieri rather than the indolent genius of a Mozart.[55] Gumilev took the principle of identity further than Mandel'shtam in promulgating 'The Translator's Nine Commandments' (1919), in which the translator is expected to follow the original poet in his adherence to form and function. Gumilev insisted that in a translation it was obligatory to observe:

> 1) the number of lines, 2) the meter and measure, 3) the alternation of rhyme, 4) the nature of the *enjambement*, 5) the nature of the rhyme, 6) the nature of the vocabulary, 7) the type of similes, 8) special devices, 9) changes in tone.[56]

---

[53] The phrase 'unwarranted liberties' is taken from Oleg A. Maslenkov, *The Frenzied Poets: Andrey Biely and the Russian Symbolists* (Berkeley: University of California Press, 1952), 22. Maslenkov (ibid.) does, however, acknowledge that Bal'mont 'more than anyone else, was responsible for popularizing in Russia Oscar Wilde, Walt Whitman, Edgar Allan Poe, and Shelley, to say nothing of Rosetti [sic], Blake, Coleridge, and Tennyson'.

[54] Mandelstam, *The Complete Critical Prose and Letters*, 126. For Mandel'shtam, Bal'mont was 'a translator by calling, by birth, even in his most original works', ibid., 125. Mandel'shtam had high praise in the same essay ('On the Nature of the Word') for Innokentii Annenskii as a translator.

[55] The definition of Acmeism as a 'nostalgia for world culture' is attributed to Osip Mandel'shtam by his wife in Nadezhda Mandelstam, *Hope Against Hope: A Memoir*, trans. Max Hayward (London: Collins Harvill, 1989), 246–7. Pushkin contrasted the two eighteenth-century composers in his 'little tragedy', 'Mozart and Salieri' (1830).

[56] 'On Translations of Poetry', in Nikolai Gumilev, *On Russian Poetry*, ed. and trans. David Lapeza (Ann Arbor: Ardis, 1977), 34–8 (38).

Pushkin had earlier invoked the memory of the Jewish Patriarch in reference to the topic of translation. Gumilev does the same, but he concludes his appeal in an altogether different register by noting: 'These are the translator's nine commandments: since there is one less than those of Moses, I hope that they will be better observed'.[57]

Gumilev's advice was directed at a new generation of translators who would become active in the early years of the Soviet period. The October Revolution of 1917 had brought wholesale changes to the former Empire which were to have a profound effect on how literary works written in languages other than Russian would be accommodated within the USSR. An early manifestation of these changes was the establishment, under the directorship of Maksim Gor'kii, of a new publishing house called World Literature (*Vsemirnaia literatura*), whose aim was to publish classics of world literature in translation. This project, even though it underwent a series of alterations to its name, was to become the main conduit through which the state sought to enforce its monopoly in controlling access to foreign literature for most of its citizens.[58] World Literature, which remained in existence for six years from 1918 to 1924, was succeeded by Academia, which published a series of translations under the general rubric of 'Treasures of World Literature' before it was merged, by 1938, with the State Publishing House (*GIZ*), which continued to publish translations of the classics. In 1929, Mandel'shtam, frustrated by the economic exploitation of translators, bemoaned a decline in the general standard of translation ('one of the most difficult and responsible aspects of literary work')[59] that was the direct result of this venture, which, as he saw it, rewarded quantity rather than quality. Once again, we encounter a notable analogy for the act of translation:

---

57   Ibid., 38.
58   As Mandel'shtam had noted acerbically in his essay 'On Translations', '[t]he main consumers of translated literature were the philistines who did not know any foreign languages' (Mandelstam, *The Complete Critical Prose and Letters*, 290).
59   Ibid., 284.

The translation itself is treated as if one were pouring grain from one sack into another. To prevent the translator from concealing or stealing any grain while he is transferring it, he is paid for the Russian text, and not for the original, as a means of grain control. Thus, for this seemingly insignificant reason, books swell from year to year and fall ill with dropsy. Translators add to the number of pages in order to make ends meet somehow.[60]

Nevertheless, many of the finest authors in Russia worked at this time as translators. They included, in addition to Mandel'shtam himself, Evgenii Zamiatin, Iurii Tynianov,[61] Nikolai Zabolotskii, Mikhail Zoshchenko, Anna Akhmatova and Boris Pasternak.

Pasternak's interest in the translation of poetry was already evident in the 1920s, but as a translator he is best known for his versions in the 1930s and 1940s of Georgian poetry and Shakespeare's plays, made at a time 'of unprecedented interference in literature by the ruling Communist Party and of damaging pressures from Party-influenced critics and editors'.[62] With regard to Georgian poetry, it is important to bear in mind that encouragement by the Soviet state of the production of literary translations from the 'internal' national languages of the peoples of the USSR, in addition to any 'external' ones, constituted part of a larger plan intended to impose a unitary

---

60 Ibid. The inclusion of additional material by translators was nothing new. Vilen N. Komissarov cites the case of Irinarkh Vvedenskii who, in the nineteenth century, introduced his own texts into the translation of *David Copperfield*, which he justified 'by the desire to please the reader, claiming that the translator had the right to freely recreate the spirit of the source text, to give new life to the ideas of the author in a new situation – "under another sky", as he put it'. Quoted from Mona Baker, ed., *Routledge Encyclopedia of Translation Studies* (London: Routledge, 1998), 545.
61 On Tynianov's translation's of Heinrich Heine, see Katharine Hodgson's chapter in this volume.
62 Boris Pasternak, *The Marsh of Gold: Pasternak's Writings on Inspiration and Creation*; selected, translated, edited, introduced, and provided with commentaries by Angela Livingstone (Boston: Academic Studies Press, 2008), 2. The plays of Shakespeare that Pasternak translated in the 1940s were *Romeo and Juliet*, *Antony and Cleopatra*, *Othello*, *King Henry IV* (Parts I and II), *Hamlet*, *Macbeth* and *King Lear*. On Pasternak's translations of Shakespeare, see Aleksei Semenenko's chapter in this volume.

literary and cultural identity on creative works through an adaptation to an aesthetic canon consistent with the definition of Socialist Realism. In this respect, Pasternak found himself at odds with Soviet orthodoxy in both theory and practice. In 'Notes of a Translator', he explained his idea of what the relation between an original work and a translation (as base to derivative) should be:

> Translations are conceivable because ideally they too have to be works of art, and, by virtue of their own unrepeatability, must stand on the same level as the originals, while sharing their text. Translations are conceivable because, for centuries before our time, whole literatures translated one another, and translation is not so much a method of becoming acquainted with individual works as a medium for the age-old communion of cultures and peoples.[63]

At the height of Stalinism, then, Pasternak's statement aligned the poet more with Zhukovskii (whom he mentions – together with Bal'mont – in the article) than with any state-sponsored ideology. His approach to translation was somewhat unorthodox, but his stature and talent gave him leeway to diverge from the standard model.[64] In general, however, the translation of foreign literature presented difficulties to the authorities in the USSR and never ceased to be a source of anxiety.

Whereas the Soviet literary process evolved to ensure that Soviet writers' work was written, edited and re-written to meet as far as possible the demands of the dominant methodology of Socialist Realism, foreign literature had not been subject to the processes of internal and then state-imposed censorship. The simplest resolution of the problem would have been not to translate foreign works at all and the authorities came closest to adopting this path during the anti-cosmopolitan post-war years of Stalinism. Maurice Friedberg explains that 'the low ebb in the fortunes of West European and American literature in the USSR was reached in the later 1940s [...] The "anti-cosmopolitan" campaign with its bitter denunciations of "servility to the West" all but destroyed any serious study of

---

63 Ibid., 229–30. This piece was first published in *Znamia* I (1944), with Pasternak's translation of four poems by Shelley.
64 See the chapter by Elena Zemskova in this volume.

Western writing and could not fail to affect the publication of translated Western literature'.[65] For most of the Soviet period, however, the internationalist agenda of bolshevism and the desire not to be seen as parochial or oppressive led the authorities into negotiations over the accommodation of foreign literature within Soviet culture. This resulted in a skewed, Soviet version of various national literary canons that prioritized authors seen as politically sympathetic or appropriate, but could take in a surprising range of authors, including those who might have been seen as inimical to Soviet values.[66]

As the methodology of Socialist Realism took hold and the breadth of published Soviet literature diminished, the scope for variety and diversity in translation also narrowed. The school of literal translation became increasingly associated with the proscribed *formalism*, or excessive attention to form in literature, and 'free' translation was adopted as the official methodology.[67] In practice, this method was advantageous to the state in that it allowed the text to be interpreted, to be moulded to express correct attitudes and opinions through appropriate register, vocabulary and imagery. The process of translation thereby allayed some of the anxieties about introducing foreign literature to Soviet readers; this was further dealt with by direct censorship of the translations.[68] Another, unintentional advantage of 'free' translation emerged for the translators, however: for those creative writers, such as Pasternak, working in translation during the Stalin period when their original works were proscribed, it offered the opportunity to work creatively.

---

65 Maurice Friedberg, *A Decade of Euphoria: Western Literature in Post-Stalin Russia, 1954–64* (Bloomington: Indiana University Press, 1977), 5.
66 Oscar Wilde, for example, was consistently translated and published in the USSR. For a history of his accommodation in Soviet culture, see the chapter by Philip Ross Bullock in this volume.
67 On the debates between literalists and realists, see: Friedberg, *Literary Translation in Russia*, especially 76–93; Susanna Witt and Elena Zemskova in this volume.
68 On the censorship of foreign literature, see Friedberg, *Literary Translation in Russia*, 139–40.

The debate over 'literal' or 'free' translation in Russian literature was not confined to the USSR: questions of translation were a matter of importance for émigré writers forced to negotiate the problem of reception for their works outside the Russian-speaking world. The first wave of émigrés in the 1920s and 1930s tended to write in Russian for a select Russian audience, and as a result in many cases became increasingly depressed about the possibility of existing as a Russian writer outside Russia.[69] Starting with Nabokov and continuing with writers of the Third Wave emigration, authors paid attention to questions of translation, the translatability of texts and, in the extreme, resorted to writing in English rather than Russian, in order to circumvent the problems of translation. Nabokov, the first Russian émigré to write novels in English, took an extreme 'literalist' approach in his infamous translation of *Evgenii Onegin*: the notes are far longer than the text, aiming to plumb the depth of meaning to be read in Pushkin's work.

Nabokov's project defiantly rejected the Soviet-adopted method of 'free' translation, and assumed an elitist, uncompromising attitude toward the understanding and interpretation of a text in translation. The notes accompanying the translation seek to render the whole of the text without losing any shade of meaning or allusion. The Soviet approach to translation contrasts with this: texts were shaped not only by 'free translation', but also by introductions, criticism and notes that pointed towards the correct reading. Thus editors sought to mitigate the potential subversive effects of texts. To cite one example, the works of Jack London that were hugely popular in the USSR as they had been in pre-revolutionary Russia, were framed by commentaries about the writer as 'a socialist enemy of bourgeois America and a friend of the oppressed'.[70] This device for controlling literature was employed beyond the Stalin period; indeed, it became especially important when the impetus to accommodate more translated literature in the USSR grew under Khrushchev.

---

69 Khodasevich's essay of 1933 'Literatura v izgnanii' is a famous expression of the failure of Russian literature in emigration, reprinted in *Literaturnye stat'i i vospominaniia* (New York: Izdatel'stvo imeni Chekhova, 1954), 255–72.
70 Friedberg, *A Decade of Euphoria*, 123.

When Stalin died in 1953, a new anxiety about literature, and in particular foreign literature in the USSR, surfaced for the authorities: that the country had become backward as a result of the recent xenophobic decades. Soviet readers and specialists knew far too little about the development of world literature, and this isolation had exacerbated the damage done to Soviet literature by purges and terror; even Soviet writers who survived physical assault had been cut off from modern developments and their works were now seen as backward.[71] The Khrushchev era was characterized by attempts to rehabilitate Soviet literature, and the nervous adoption of foreign literature within Soviet culture was an important development. The significance that translations of foreign literature had for the writers of the Thaw was evinced by the writers themselves: in answers to a questionnaire about influences upon them they named, alongside Russian classics such as Tolstoi and Chekhov, foreign writers including Böll, Salinger, Neruda, Whitman and Hemingway.[72]

Of these and other names mentioned, Ernest Hemingway was far and away the most significant for Soviet literature and culture during the Thaw. Genis and Vail' assert that 'from 1959, when the two-volume [Hemingway] came out in Moscow, America and Hemingway became synonymous'.[73] Hemingway's works were subject to the usual 'free' translation, censorship, and simplistic interpretation.[74] However much the Soviet authorities may have desired to cast Hemingway and other writers as socialist and anti-capitalist in tune with the USSR, their popularity as romantic others indicate that the authorities struggled to control their reception and influence. In fact, Genis and Vail' argue that Hemingway was important for the culture of the 1960s, which took from him a more informal mode

---

71   Emily Lygo, *Leningrad Poetry 1953–75: The Thaw Generation* (Oxford: Peter Lang, 2010), 15.
72   Friedberg, *A Decade of Euphoria*, 298–9.
73   Aleksandr Genis and Petr Vail', *60-e: mir sovetskogo cheloveka* (Ann Arbor: Ardis, 1988), 64.
74   Friedberg gives an account of the deletions made in the Russian version of *For Whom the Bell Tolls*, published in 1968, which avoided mention of Soviet interference in the Spanish Civil War (*A Decade of Euphoria*, 44–6).

The Art of Accommodation: Introduction

of behaviour, the cult of friendship groups and an emphasis on leisure.[75] Hemingway's works seem to have chimed with the Thaw era's keynote of sincerity and the rejection of false notes in official culture: they provided the cultural and literary models that the post-Stalin era needed in its quest to redefine Soviet society.

In a similar way, the works of Kafka translated during the Thaw apparently voiced something that Soviet readers could understand and wanted expressed. The Soviet authorities published him reluctantly; he was too important to be ignored, but introductions described the limitations of his works and attempted to pigeonhole him as a bourgeois writer. The response to his works was not so muted, however: although he was virtually unknown in the USSR, when a volume of his works was published in April 1965 it sold out very quickly and was worth a huge thirty-five roubles on the black market.[76] Friedberg suggests that this reception was in part because of the relevance of his subject matter to recent Soviet experience:

> Kafka's tales of the futility of human efforts to avert the wrath of omnipotent authorities whose cruel whims are unpredictable must have struck many Soviet readers as fantasy that was also – as attested by multitudes of eye-witnesses – documented truth.[77]

The reassessment of the Stalinist past that took place during the Thaw, its effect upon social discourse, and the emergence of a new youth culture, called for new literary modes. Both Hemingway and Kafka are examples of the way that foreign literature provided models which helped to break the mould of Stalinist Socialist Realism and open the way to a wider range of voices and forms in prose. While Hemingway's works offered a new voice for the present, Kafka's conveyed a sense of terror and horror that could play a role in the attempts to understand the Stalinist past. Each was discovered and taken up at a time when it was needed within Soviet Russian literature.

Translations also played a role in invigorating Soviet poetry during the Thaw. Joseph Brodsky's work as a translator brought him into contact

---

75   Genis and Vail', 66–9.
76   Friedberg, *A Decade of Euphoria*, 274.
77   Ibid., 278.

with poetry that fed into his own work, enriching its range of forms and poetic voice. In particular, he was influenced by Anglo-American poetry: John Donne and W. H. Auden are two of the most important poetic interlocutors that he discovered though his study of English and experience of translation. Brodsky's own subsequent influence as the major poet of his generation has ensured that this influence has been amplified in Russian poetry.[78] As Soviet publishing tried to catch up on what had been missed during the Stalin years, there was a good deal of modern poetry to be translated. The emphasis tended to be on left-wing, sympathetic foreign poets. The translation of such works presented a problem, however: they were often written in modernist or free verse forms which had remained conspicuously absent from Soviet poetry as a result of their censure as *formalizm*. The task of translating such verse prompted much soul-searching about the form of Soviet poetry and the Soviet canon.[79]

The Thaw era saw the return to a dialogue with foreign literature, but anxiety about the effect that it might have in the USSR persisted; censorship and proscription, therefore, also persisted. During the 1970s, works of foreign literature continued to be translated and published in the USSR, and slowly but surely the boundaries of what could be published in the USSR broadened. There were many translations from fellow socialist countries including the new socialist allies emerging in Latin America, Africa and the Far East. In the era of *glasnost'* and *perestroika*, censorship relaxed much more quickly, and translations of Western literature formerly proscribed flooded into the USSR and, after 1991, Russia. This inundation included literary writers whose works had been excluded from the USSR on the grounds of ethics, ideology, and aesthetics, such as Henry Miller, Milan Kundera and William Burroughs. The phenomenon most remarked upon, however, in the field of translation during this era, was the translation of pulp or genre fiction: horror, detectives, thrillers and romance that had

---

78   See Yasha Klots, 'The Poetics and Politics of Joseph Brodsky as a Russian Poet-Translator' in Brian James Baer, ed., *Contexts, Subtexts, and Pretexts: Literary Translation in Eastern Europe and Russia* (Amsterdam: John Benjamins, 2011), 187–204.
79   See the chapter by Emily Lygo in this volume.

not been publishable under Soviet censorship found an eager readership in Russia. Since there had been no Soviet production in these genres, the market was initially dominated by translations. During the 1990s, Russian originals began to appear, profoundly shaped by the Western examples that were the first to be made available to Russian readers.[80]

The approach presented in this volume sees translations as events with consequences for both the work translated and the host culture that receives the new work. Translations are seen as a further stage in the life of a text: set in a new context, the text reverberates with new, and perhaps renewed, meanings. It acquires a different resonance when transposed from its original language, intersecting with the politics and ideologies operative in the new environment. With its arrival in a new language, a translation reconfigures the native literary process, bringing about reconsideration of the shape of the existing tradition and influencing its future course of development. The view of translation as an art of accommodation insists upon regarding translations as interconnected with the literary process of the receiving culture. In this respect, translations become the conduits for cross-currents between native and foreign traditions, whose influence and interaction shape, renew, re-focus and refresh the literary traditions that receive them.

---

80 Stephen Lovell, *The Russian Reading Revolution* (Basingstoke: Macmillan, 2000), 134–5.

ALEXEI EVSTRATOV

Drama Translation in Eighteenth-Century Russia: Masters and Servants on the Court Stage in the 1760s

In the age of Russian modernization, translation was the leading tool of cultural transfer. It was so central to the project of modernization, that to give a detailed account of the translation theory and practice in eighteenth-century Russia would mean to write a cultural history of the epoch. Many translators were prominent writers (including Vasilii Trediakovskii and Vladimir Lukin, whose work is the subject of this chapter), and many writers considered translation as a major literary experiment very close to original writing.[1] Literary scholars of the eighteenth century have sought to recover what was translated, who was translating, and how and why they approached their work.[2] And while we have now sufficient data about the questions 'who' and 'what', the existing general interpretations of 'how' and 'why' are still wanting. Iurii Levin, for instance, describes the translations made during the period in predominantly negative terms: they are not accurate, they demonstrate a lack of style, and there is a gap between translation theories and practice.[3] In comparison with translation in later

1   Grigorii Gukovskii, in a well-known article, bases his definition of Russian classicism on a study of the translation practice of such writers as Trediakovskii, Lomonosov, and Sumarokov. 'K voprosu o russkom klassitsizme. (Sostiazaniia i perevody)', *Poetika*, vyp. IV (Leningrad: Academia, 1928), 126–48; see the recent edition in G. A. Gukovskii, *Rannie raboty po istorii russkoi poezii XVIII veka* (Moscow: Iazyki russkoi kul'tury, 2001), 251–76.
2   For the most recent historical account, see: Iurii Levin, ed., *Istoriia russkoi perevodnoi khudozhestvennoi literatury: Drevniaia Rus': XVIII vek*, 2 vols (St Petersburg: Russian Academy of Sciences Institute of Russian Literature, 1995).
3   Iurii Levin, 'Khudozhestvennyi perevod v literaturnoi kul'ture XVIII veka', *Russko-evropeiskie literaturnye sviazi. XVIII vek* (St Petersburg: Fakul'tet filologii i iskusstv

periods, these criticisms may be true. What is also true is that the translations were completed in response to different pragmatics and a different set of objectives. The latter may give us the key to understanding translations of this period better.

The significance of translation in eighteenth-century Russia needs to be understood for political, cultural and literary spheres. It was, first of all, a state-sponsored enterprise, as was the creation of a new Europeanized literature in general. Peter I ordered the most important works to be translated,[4] and did some translating himself.[5] Under his successors, governmental control probably diminished, but the authorities and the sovereigns themselves still encouraged translators' work. In 1767, Catherine II took part, with her close entourage, in the translation of Marmontel's *Bélisaire*, a moralistic novel censured in France. A year later, she ordered a working group for the translation of foreign books to be founded, and financed its activities until 1783.[6] Due to the coincident emergence of translation and publishing, the most important texts of many world civilizations, from Homer to *Bhagavad Gita* and *The Quran*, and from Cicero to Goethe, became available in Russian translation in a relatively short period of time.[7]

SPbGU, 2008), 297–306 (298–302). This article is a part of Levin's earlier work on the evolution of translation theory, from the eighteenth century to the 1920s. See 'Ob istoricheskoi evoliutsii printsipov perevoda', in M. P. Alekseev, ed., *Mezhdunarodnye sviazi russkoi literatury. Sbornik statei* (Moscow and Leningrad: Izdatel'stvo Akademii nauk SSSR, 1963), 5–63.

4 Levin, ed., *Istoriia russkoi perevodnoi khudozhestvennoi literatury*, vol. 1, 76–7.

5 See, for instance, Nikolai A. Kopanev, 'Petr I – perevodchik', *XVIII vek*, vol. 16 (Itogi i problemy izucheniia russkoi literatury XVIII v.) (Leningrad: Nauka, 1989), 180–3. For details of the development of the printing industry, see Gary Marker, *Publishing, Printing and the Origins of Intellectual Life in Russia, 1700–1800* (Princeton: Princeton University Press, 1985).

6 V. P. Semennikov, *Sobranie, staraiushcheesia o perevode inostrannykh knig, uchrezhdennoe Ekaterinoi II: 1768–1783: Istoriko-literaturnoe issledovanie* (St Petersburg: Sirius, 1913).

7 See *Svodnyi katalog russkoi knigi grazhdanskoi pechati XVIII veka, 1725–1800*, 5 vol. (Moscow, 1962–7).

Translation was not seen as markedly distinct from original literature, and the nature of the relationship between the two was the subject of polemics and frequently redefined.[8] Trediakovskii's famous phrase, 'the only difference between the translator and the author is his name' (переводчик от творца только что именем рознится),[9] reminds us that the distinction between the two was not clear within the Russian language at this point; the language and these terms became standardized only in the nineteenth century. Both translators and authors were engaged in the task of linguistic creation. At the centre of their experiments was the translation of poetry, since poetic language was considered the essence of the language which defined the range of possibilities within Russian in general.[10] From the 1760s, however, the rise of theatrical institutions stimulated both reflection and practice in the field of drama translation. Catherine herself tried to bring about the creation of a 'genuinely Russian' comedy using the system of patronage and the social connections of the Russian court and state administration.[11]

The case-study below examines a text that, without being a translation *strictu sensu*, is an example of the kind of intellectual and creative work that was understood to constitute translation in eighteenth-century Russia. It examines its treatment of the master-servant theme, which was explored in many of the plays of the period. By placing this in the literary

---

8   For a collection of writers' reflections on translation, see Iurii D. Levin, A. V. Fedorov, eds, *Russkie pisateli o perevode, XVIII–XX vv.* (Leningrad: Sovetskii pisatel', 1960).
9   Quoted in Levin, ed., *Istoriia russkoi perevodnoi khudozhestvennoi literatury*, vol. 1, 11. For a defence of this point of view, see Trediakovskii's note to the reader which opens his *Sochineniia i perevody*, vol. 1 (St Petersburg: Pri Imperatorskoi Akademii Nauk, 1752), i–xxvi (and its recent reprint: St Petersburg: Nauka, 2009, 7–17).
10 Viktor M. Zhivov, *Iazyk i kul'tura v Rossii XVIII veka* (Moscow: Iazyki russkoi kul'tury, 1996), 263–4. See also its English version in Marcus Levitt, *Language and Culture in Eighteenth-century Russia* (Boston: Academic Studies Press, 2009).
11 Alexei Evstratov, 'K voprosu o genezise "teorii skloneniia na russkie nravy": literatura i gosudarstvennyi zakaz v nachale tsarstvovaniia Ekateriny II', *Russkaia filologiia 19: Sbornik nauchnykh rabot molodykh filologov* (Tartu: Tartu Ülikooli Kirjastus, 2008), 29–34.

and social context of the 1760s, the chapter will clarify the purposes of the early Russian stage and elucidate the ideological origins of translation theory and practice in eighteenth-century Russia.

I

After many months of mourning, first for Elizaveta Petrovna, then for Peter III, in the autumn of 1762 Catherine II's coronation celebrations brought fireworks, balls and theatrical performances back to Russia. In 1763, the court company of Russian actors gave eighteen performances, many of which were composed of two plays. In the New Year, after the court's return to St Petersburg, the number of Russian performances reached twenty-eight. This rhythm led to an attempt to create a repertoire on the basis of a sufficient number of plays in Russian that could be regularly performed in the court theatre and which could satisfy court audiences. Several authors, such as Vladimir Lukin and Denis Fonvizin, invested in the production of the repertoire as translators or adapters of foreign plays in Russian: one may say that the Russian comedy of the eighteenth century was founded by such translators.[12]

On 19 January 1765, the Russian company staged Lukin's comedy *Mot liuboviiu ispravlennoi* (*Spendthrift reformed by love*, hereafter – *Mot*) at the court theatre. This performance was followed by *Boltun* (*Tattler*), a one-act comedy by the same author. There are several indications that these comedies by Lukin were a success. Semen Poroshin, one of Grand Duke Paul's teachers, wrote in his journal on the same day:

---

12 Il'ia Serman, 'Russkaia literatura XVIII veka i perevod', *Masterstvo perevoda: Sbornik 1962* (Moscow: Sovetskii pisatel', 1963), 337–72 (338); Pavel N. Berkov, 'O iazyke russkoi komedii XVIII veka', *Izvestiia AN SSSR: Otdelenie literatury i iazyka*, t. VIII, vyp. 1 (1949), 34–49.

Both these plays are original works by Mr Lukin, secretary to Ivan Perfil'ich Elagin. Both were very much applauded. Her Majesty was not present. After the grand play had finished, His Highness deigned to request the author to attend him in his box; he permitted him to kiss his hand and praised him for his work. After the comedy, His Highness deigned to attend Her Majesty. [...] At the table we spoke mostly about today's comedy.[13]

On the following day the plays were again discussed around Pavel Petrovich's table.[14] Five days later, the Empress, absent from the first performance of the comedies, ordered a second performance; she attended it and was well satisfied.[15] Most significantly, in the summer of 1765 the publishing house of the Academy of Sciences printed two volumes of Lukin's works.[16] On 24 August, Lukin presented the first volume to the Grand Duke Paul, and the gift was the subject of conversation at Paul's the same evening.[17] A striking novelty of the young author's work was the long forewords to the plays.[18] In these texts, Lukin criticized the existing dramatic repertoire (especially

---

13   Semen A. Poroshin, 'Zapiski', in *Russkii Gamlet* (Moscow: Fond Sergeia Dubova, 2004), 164. Translations are my own, unless indicated otherwise.
14   Poroshin, 'Zapiski', 165.
15   *Sochinenii i perevody Vladimira Lukina*, vol. Ia (St Petersburg: [tipografiia Akademii nauk], 1765), XXVIII. I have no evidence of other performances of *Mot*, but the *Dramatic Dictionary* states that the comedy was often played in Russian theatres (*Dramaticheskoi slovar', ili Pokazaniia po alfavitu vsekh rossiiskikh teatral'nykh sochinenii i perevodov* [Moscow: tipografiia A.A., 1787], 83).
16   In the 1760s not many plays were printed; therefore every edition should be studied carefully. Apart from Lukin's works, ten dramas were published in 1765, only two of them were presented as original works: a comedy *Opekun* (*Tutor*) by Sumarokov and a tragedy *Plamena* by Kheraskov (see *Svodnyi katalog russkoi knigi grazhdanskoi pechati XVIII veka, 1725–1800*).
17   Poroshin, 'Zapiski', 262–3.
18   Lukin, *Sochinenii i perevody* 1765, II, iii–iv; *Truten' N. I. Novikova, 1769–1770* (St Petersburg: tipografiia I. I. Glazunova, 1865), 20. There are two published variants of the foreword to Lukin's comedy *Mot*: a shorter one (29 pages) and a longer one (31 pages) (*Svodnyi katalog russkoi knigi grazhdanskoi pechati XVIII veka, 1725–1800*, II: 183). The former (Ia) was reprinted in Efremov's edition of Lukin and Elchaninov's works in 1868 and is usually quoted in the studies. The latter (Ib) gives some additional data concerning the origins of Lukin's project.

comedies, and particularly Sumarokov's) and proposed a new technique for adapting foreign plays to the Russian stage. In his foreword to the comedy *Nagrazhdennoe postoianstvo (Rewarded constancy)*, published in the second volume of his works, he set out his approach:

> More than once I have heard from some members of the audience that both their hearing and understanding is offended when characters, even if their mores are somewhat like ours, bear stage names such as *Clitandre, Dorante, Tsitalinde* and *Claudine*: and they utter speeches that are not in tune with our ways [...] if *Timandre* [...] were to say '*I've only just arrived from Flanders, and my old acquaintances have already asked me to ruin a new comedy that was brought from Lyon and is ordered to be staged at the Royal Theatre.*' If he were to say in the presence of connoisseurs, that he would this time move them from Petersburg to Paris, and perhaps he would annoy them so much, that they would withdraw from the theatre.[19]

Paris is not an accidental example here. The courtiers' taste was formed by the French companies, the first of which arrived in Russia in 1742, and the Comédie Française had been a subject of general admiration since Elisabeth's reign.[20] During the season of 1764–5, a new company of French actors recently arrived in Russia performed twice a week. Consequently, the influence of the French repertoire on the early Russian productions was immense. Lukin himself debuted with traditional translations of French comedies in 1763. In 1765, however, he emphasized the importance for the audience of the connection between the performance and national mores, thus demonstrating his belief that the French model needed to be accommodated to Russian conventions. In the history of Russian drama, Lukin's forewords to his several comedies are considered an important theoretical innovation of the period.[21] His method, however, was largely derived from European

19   Ibid., v–vii.
20   Poroshin, 'Zapiski', 69; Vsevolod G. Vsevolodskii-Gerngross, *Teatr v Rossii pri Elisavete Petrovne* (St Petersburg: Giperion, 2003), 133.
21   See special studies of Lukin's dramatic theory and practice: Pavel N. Berkov, *Vladimir Ignat'evich Lukin, 1737–1794* (Moscow and Leningrad: Iskusstvo, 1950); Pavel Berkov, *Istoriia russkoi komedii XVIII veka* (Leningrad: Nauka, 1977), 71–82; and Hugh McLean, 'The Adventures of an English Comedy in Eighteenth-Century Russia: Dodsley's *Toy Shop* and Lukin's *Shchepitil'nik*', in *American Contributions to the*

aesthetic theory and drama practice of the eighteenth century: Lukin knew both French and German, and a study of his translation theory and practice needs to take the sources from both these traditions into account.

Jean-Baptiste Du Bos, in his famous treatise, *Réflexions critiques sur la poésie et sur la peinture* (*Critical Reflections on Poetry and Painting*, 1719), wrote about national character as crucial for theatrical creation. In the comic genre, for instance, he asserts that the mores of a nation should provide a plot and its temperament should generate a style of performance (the gestures, etc.): 'les personnages de Comédie – doivent être taillés [...] à la mode du pays pour qui la Comédie est faite'.[22] This theory spread quickly over eighteenth-century Europe and guided the practice of different writers, such as Holberg and Goldoni.[23] A collection of the dramatic texts in German published by Johann Christoph Gottsched from 1741 to 1745, titled *Die deutsche Schaubühne nach den Regeln der alten Griechen und Römer eingerichtet* (*German Theatre Arranged According to the Rules of Ancient Greeks and Romans*), became an authoritative model for the translation and adaptation of drama in Russia. According to Gottsched, German dramatic writers should imitate French plays, which had incorporated the principles of classical theatre in the best way possible.[24] His concept

---

Fifth International Congress of Slavists, Sofia, September 1963 (The Hague: Mouton, 1963), 201–12. The principle of adaptation had already been practised, in poetry by Kantemir and in prose by Elagin (A. A. Deriugin, 'Soderzhanie perevodcheskogo priema *sklonenie na nashi (russkie) nravy*', *Izvestiia RAN. Seriia literatury i iazyka*, vol. 54, 5 (1995), 61–4 (61); David J. Welsh, *Russian Comedy 1765–1823* (The Hague and Paris: Mouton, 1966), 15).

22 Jean-Baptiste Du Bos, *Réflexions critiques sur la poésie et sur la peinture* (Paris, 1770; reprint: Geneva and Paris, 1993), 165. '[T]he personages of comedy ought to be cut out [...] after the fashion of that country, for which the comedy is written' (*Critical Reflections on Poetry, Painting and Music* by the Abbé Du Bos, translated by Thomas Nugent, vol. I (London: John Nourse, 1748), 132).

23 Gina Maiellaro, 'Lo "sklonenie na russkie nravy" nelle commedie di Vladimir Lukin', *Europa Orientalis*, vol. 15 (1996), 25–49.

24 For a detailed discussion of Gottsched's method, see Roland Krebs, *L'Idée de 'Théâtre National' dans l'Allemagne des Lumières: Théorie et Réalisations* (Wiesbaden: Otto Harrassowitz, 1985), 93–116.

of imitation assumed that there would be an adaptation of the original to the German reality. In the foreword to the second volume of *Die deutsche Schaubühne* (which was published before the first), Gottsched expounded these principles of translation:

> Throughout the entire play we have, however, taken liberties that would doubtless be of no little advantage to all comedies imported from foreign tongues into ours. I have, that is, simply changed all those French names which sound so repugnant to our German ears and that give such translated comedies an alien appearance, into German. Accordingly, the play acquires a wholly native and German appearance; and a German reader or spectator takes greater part than were it got up in so strange a form.
> Now on this basis, and following the same rule, I have made the Parisian into the Hamburg Opera, and the City of Lyon, where the whole story takes place, into Lübeck.[25]

The practices of the accommodation of drama were to be found in other countries as well, including France. 'I have taken the liberty of mangling the names a little to make them easier to pronounce for the French reader',[26] wrote the translator of Lillo's *London Merchant*, changing, for instance, a character's name from 'Thorowgood' to 'Sorogoud'. Still, Gottsched's writings were particularly relevant to such Russian writers as Lukin and Elagin.[27]

---

25 See *Die deutsche Schaubühne nach den Regeln der alten Griechen und Römer eingerichtet*, 6 vols (Leipzig, 1741–5), 2: 35–6, 39, 41; see also Krebs, *L'Idée de 'Théâtre National' dans l'Allemagne des Lumières*, 98–9.

26 *Le marchand de Londres, ou l'Histoire de George Barnwell; tragédie bourgeoise*, traduite de l'Anglois de M. Lillo, par M. 'Pierre Clément' (S.l., 1748), 4.

27 Lukin's patron, Ivan Elagin, appreciated German literature and was a member of Leipzig's Savant Society (headed by Gottsched). See an anonymous epigram directed at Elagin from 1753: 'A avtorov za to nemetskikh pochitaesh,/ Chto po-frantsuzski ty ni slova sam ne znaesh' (And you appreciate German authors, / Because you do not know a word in French) (*Russkaia epigramma vtoroi poloviny XVII – nachala XX v.* (Leningrad: Sovetskii pisatel', 1975), 169, 678. For more details on Gottsched and Russia, see Ulf Lehmann, *Der Gottschedkreis und Russland, deutsch-russische Literaturbeziehungen im Zeitalter der Aufklärung* (Berlin: Academie-Verlag, 1966).

While these principles and practices were common in European literature, the quantity and the quality of modifications made to original texts differed from one author to another. The translator of Lillo's play wanted to make the pronunciation of the characters' names simpler for French readers. In original French dramas Gottsched replaced French names by German ones. The Russian writer Sergei Glebov, translating Diderot's *Le Père de famille* (1758), decided it was appropriate to change the title of the play to *Chadoliubivoi otets* (*Philoprogenitive father*) and explained it by the absence of the social phenomenon of 'starshii v rode' (as Glebov translated the French title) in Russia.[28] On the other hand, he did not really russify the characters' names, modifying only some and translating two of them (Le Bon and Papillon) in the footnotes.[29] He left the location of the action the same as in the original text, which is Paris. A similar approach was adopted in an anonymous translation of another of Diderot's plays, *Le Fils naturel* (1757), which stressed the necessity of changing the servants' names – Karl and Justina – since they were considered unattractive to the Russian ear, but retained all the other names such as, for instance, Rosalie or Constance (neither of which sounds Russian).[30]

The difference in the translation approaches is explained by the variety of the translators' tasks. Lukin, in order to justify his work, stressed the theatre's importance for the development of moral awareness (thus

28 *Chadoliubivoi otets: komediia v piat' deistvii*: sochinenie G. Diderota; perevedena s frantsuzskago (St Petersburg: [tipografiia Sukhoputnogo kadetskogo korpusa], 1765), [6].

29 Didro, *Chadoliubivoi otets*, 7–8; see also Piotr Zaborov, 'Le théâtre de Diderot en Russie au XVIIIe siècle', *Colloque international Diderot (1713–1784)* (Paris: Aux amateurs de livres, 1985), 493–501 (494); cf. Levin, ed., *Istoriia russkoi perevodnoi khudozhestvennoi literatury*, vol. 2, 31.

30 *Pobochnyi syn ili iskushenii dobrodeteli komediia v piati deistviiakh i prostoiu rech'iu pisannaia*. Sochinenie G. Diderota [St Petersburg: tipografiia Sukhoputnogo kadetskogo korpusa, n.d.]. For hypotheses concerning the date of printing, see *Svodnyi katalog russkoi knigi grazhdanskoi pechati XVIII veka, 1725–1800*, I: 290–1. For more details of this translation, see Andrew Kahn, '*Le Fils naturel* et la réforme de la comédie russe', *Etudes sur Le Fils naturel et les Entretiens sur le Fils naturel de Diderot*, ed. Nicholas Cronk (Oxford: Voltaire Foundation, 2000), 159–70.

repeating the arguments of his European colleagues).³¹ In the foreword to *Nagrazhdennoe postoianstvo* quoted above, the Russian author explains:

> I will as far as possible adapt all comic works for theatre to our habits, because many members of the audience do not receive any moral correction from comedies staging foreign mores. They think that the comedy is making fun not of them, but of foreigners. It happens because they hear, as I said before, *Paris, Versailles, Tuileries* and so on, which for many of them belong to an unknown language; besides, they notice that the types who are treated comically, it turns out, not only speak not in our manner, they also wear unfamiliar clothes. *The French, the English, the Germans* and other nations who possess Theatres always keep to their own types, and portray them: they rarely present foreigners, and when they do they are only minor characters; why shouldn't we stick to our own too?³²

Thus, the characters have to be recognizable in order to give a play didactic value.³³ According to different theorists of drama and aesthetics in general, such as Du Bos, the didactic function of a comedy can be effective only if it accommodates itself to the context in which it is to be performed.³⁴ In a similar vein Luigi Riccoboni, an Italian actor working in France, wrote in his influential work on the comic genre, *Observations sur la comédie, et sur le génie de Molière* (*Observations on Comedy and on Molière's Genius*, 1736):

> Although as its objective it has the correction of manners, it must always represent men as they are, and that fundamentally passions or characters do not change at all: however the mores, or the habits particular to each nation make a character, which per se is the same one, not show itself in France as it does in Spain or in England.³⁵

---

31   See, for instance, Louis Bourquin, 'La controverse sur la Comédie au XVIIIe siècle et la *Lettre à d'Alembert sur les Spectacles*', *Revue d'histoire littéraire de la France*, vol. XXVI (1919), XXVII (1920), XXVIII (1921).
32   Lukin, *Sochinenii i perevody* 1765, II: xv–xvi; partially translated in Welsh, *Russian Comedy 1765–1823*, 15.
33   Welsh, *Russian Comedy 1765–1823*, 63.
34   See, for instance, Du Bos, *Réflexions critiques sur la poésie et sur la peinture*, 48 (and its English translation in Du Bos, *Critical Reflections on Poetry, Painting and Music*, I, 131–2).
35   Louis Riccoboni, *Observations sur la comedie, et sur le genie de Molière* (Paris: Chez la Veuve Pissot, 1736), 1–2.

According to Lukin, adaptation is especially important for the stage performance to accomplish its moral task (whereas books can provide readers with an accurate translation of a play).[36]

2

Mot, liuboviiu ispravlennoi is the most important and well-known play of Lukin's 1765 *Sochinenii i perevody*. The plot of the comedy provides a moral lesson. Dobroserdov has been a spendthrift, but before the play begins he has completely changed his conduct because of his love for Kleopatra. He lives at the house of Kleopatra's aunt, the Princess, and the lovers can see each other freely. The Princess has a passion for Dobroserdov and she is jealous, so, being Kleopatra's tutor, she wishes to see her niece married as quickly as possible to another man. Dobroserdov's old creditors want to recover their money, and because the young man cannot give it to them, they try to have him sent to gaol. His friend Zloradov hopes to marry the rich Princess and intrigues against Dobroserdov thinking the latter to be his rival. Only their servants are willing to help Dobroserdov and Kleopatra to be together, but it is the unexpected arrival of Dobroserdov's brother that saves the ex-spendthrift from prison. The play ends with the moral that is to be taken from the play, pronounced by Vasilei, Dobroserdov's servant. He wishes his master,

> May all maidens be like your lover; and the old coquettes, who take their coy manners to their graves, receive, like her Excellency, distaste from it. May all spendthrifts turn to the true path, according to your example, and servants and servant-girls, like *Stepanida* and me, serve their masters faithfully. Lastly, may the ignoble and cunning, in horror of their low vices, leave these and remember that God does not leave ill-doings unpunished.[37]

---

36   Lukin, *Sochinenii i perevody* 1765, II: xvi–xvii.
37   Lukin, *Sochinenii i perevody* 1765, I: 150.

Thus, closing the play, Vasilei comments on the moral lesson offered by every character in the comedy. The vices represented in the play are not confined to gambling.[38] Moreover, this vice is not represented directly in the comedy, because the moral transformation of Dobroserdov is accomplished *before* the action begins; he has already been 'corrected by love (*liubov'iu ispravlennoi*)' as the title puts it.[39] In this, *Mot* differs from its main source indicated by Lukin in the preface to the play – Destouches's comedy *Le Dissipateur, ou l'Honnête friponne* (*Spendthrift, or Honest Rascal*, first edited in 1736 and performed for the first time at the Comédie Française in 1753). *Le Dissipateur* was the kind of comic play which emerged in France in the 1730s, traditionally called a *comédie larmoyante* or moralizing comedy.[40] Compared with other popular plays such as Regnard's or Lesage's comedies, Destouches's play is striking for the novelty of a happy ending: the spendthrift at the centre of the play was saved in both a financial and a moral sense by his beloved. In contrast to other plays concerned with morals and social mores of the period, this comedy does not show a vicious character being punished at the end, but rather his reformation through love. In the final scene of *Le Dissipateur*, the protagonist wants to kill himself because he has lost all his money and, as a result, all his friends, but his beloved Julie stops him. She restores to Cléon his lost property which she had saved, and agrees to marry him. In this way, the play achieved the moral aim of demonstrating

---

38 In the foreword, however, the author relates his own experience as a gambler. At the beginning of Catherine the Great's reign this topic appeared very frequently in the repertoire of the court's French company. See such examples as *Le Joueur* (*The Gambler*, 1696) by Regnard (performed in 1764, on 1 October, in 1765, on 10 February, 29 April, 10 and 21 November), and Lesage's *Turcaret* (1709) (performed in 1764, on 27 January and 1 October).

39 Lukin, *Sochinenii i perevody* 1765, I, 21. See also Dobroserdov's soliloquy in the first scene of the second act.

40 Gustave Lanson, *Nivelle de La Chaussée et la comédie larmoyante*, 2nd edn (Geneva: Slatkin Reprints, 1970 [1903]). See John Dunkley, 'Destouches and Moralizing Comedy: The Defining of a Genre' in Derek Connon and George Evans, eds, *Essays on French Comic Drama from the 1640s to the 1780s* (Oxford: Peter Lang, 2000), 153–70.

the correction of mores.⁴¹ Lukin adopted this type of comic scheme with a happy ending, describing the comedies of character as 'pathetic and filled with noble thoughts'. The Russian writer calls Destouches a 'great author' and describes his plays as being worth imitating.⁴²

The French dramatist and his play about a spendthrift were much appreciated by Russian court society. *Le Dissipateur* was in the repertoire of the court company,⁴³ and later was even performed, at least once, by the nobility, which indicates the highest degree of success.⁴⁴ We have some idea of the reactions of court spectators of the 1760s to the French *comédies larmoyantes* from Poroshin's *Notes*. Poroshin attended, among others, Destouches's *Le Dissipateur*, performed by the French company on 4 October 1764:

> His Highness was not at the comedy. I went. They performed the grand comedy very well: in the last scene I was moved to tears. On my return, I told His Highness about it. He deigned to say to me: *I think that if I had been there, then I would have shed tears.*⁴⁵

Destouches depicted the moral transformation of his characters in several *scènes pathétiques*, and it was such scenes in the French plays which made

---

41   See Destouches's preface to the comedy *Le Glorieux* (1732). For commentaries on it see McLean, 'The Adventures of an English Comedy in Eighteenth-Century Russia', 204–6. Lukin's foreword to *Mot* bears some resemblance to that of Destouches.
42   Lukin, *Sochinenii i perevody* 1765, Ib, xiv. Many of the comedies of French writers named by Lukin in this preface formed part of the Russian court theatre repertoire of the 1760s. Destouches was also much appreciated in the Germanies. *Le Dissipateur*'s translation was published in *Die deutsche Schaubühne* (Jacques Lacant, *Marivaux en Allemagne, Reflets de son théâtre dans le miroir allemand*, t. 1, L'Accueil (Paris: Klincksieck, 1975), 27–9; Krebs, *L'Idée de 'Théâtre National' dans l'Allemagne des Lumières*, 100–2).
43   On 4 October and 4 July 1764 (Poroshin, 'Zapiski', 31, 223).
44   On 11 January 1769 (*Deux astronomes genevois dans la Russie de Catherine II* (Ferney-Voltaire: Centre national d'étude du XVIIIe siècle, 2005), 135–6, 267).
45   Poroshin, 'Zapiski', 31.

the courtiers weep.[46] Poroshin shed tears at the repentance of the hero who, thanks to the virtuous and sensible mistress, is reunited in a touching scene with his father. When Cléon has lost all he had and all his servants are discharged, his valet Pasquin is the only one who remains with him:

> PASQUIN: Je ne sais point ce que l'on me destine;
> Mais, qu'on me chasse ou non, mon pauvre cœur s'obstine
> A ne vous point quitter; et, jusques à la mort,
> Je suis bien résolu de suivre votre sort.
> CLÉON: Que feras-tu de moi? Je suis un miserable.
> PASQUIN: Le peu que je possède ...
> CLÉON: Ah! ce trait-là m'accable.
> Voilà le seul ami qui me demeure. Ingrats!
> Et cet exemple-là ne vous confondera pas!
> Va-t'en; laisse-moi seul au fond du precipice.
> Donne-moi ce fauteuil; c'est le dernier service
> Que j'exige de toi.
> PASQUIN *(lui baissant la main):* Mon cher maître![47]

---

46 According to Poroshin's notes, tears were not only permitted in a comic performance, but were a conventional way of showing one's pleasure in the theatre (see Poroshin, 'Zapiski', 319–20). The history of public emotions proposes different explanations for this phenomenon, see, for instance, Anne Vincent-Buffaut, *Histoire des larmes, XVIIIe–XIXe siècles* (Paris: Payot & Rivages, 2001), 415.

47 *Le Dissipateur ou l'Honneste friponne*, comédie, par M. Néricault Destouches (Paris: Prault père, 1736), 137. Cf.:

> PASQUIN. I do not know how they intend to dispose of me, sir. But be it as it may, I am determin'd, while I have life, never to quit you, but follow your fortunes all the world over.
> CLEON. What can'st thou expect of me? I am a beggar.
> PASQUIN. The small matter I am master of, as it was got in your service, shall be spent in it.
> CLEON. Ah! this is too much. I now feel all my misery. Behold the only one left me of all my friends! Ungrateful wretches! let this example make you blush, if you are yet capable of it – Go, Pasquin, leave me alone to my fate – Give me that chair; it is the last service I shall require at thy hands.
> PASQUIN. [Kneels, and kisses his hand.] My master! oh, my dear master! ...

The servant offers his savings to his master, thus showing the highest degree of *fidelité*, which was not found in any of the noble, but immoral friends of Cléon. Thus, the comedy places moral qualities beyond social distinctions such as money or titles, and makes of the patriarchal household a social utopia.

The *scènes pathétiques*, which involved the valet and the master and reappraised the social distance between them, presented a different view of the character of the valet, who in many French comedies of the early eighteenth century had ruled the intrigue, with the masters being passive observers of the servants' artful actions.[48] In 1736, Riccoboni in his *Observations sur la comédie* remarks that the demonstration of a vice in comedy, such as was often found in the character of the valet, contributed to the moral corruption of the spectators:

> I do not disagree that as there are in one and the other sex of the masters, those whose character it is to use everything to satisfy their passions, so there are also valets who are naturally deceitful and without honour; but I also think that it would be much wiser to embarrass each of them with their vices, and correct them of these faults, than to confirm them, by making them happy in a theatrical action.[49]

Destouches's faithful servant Pasquin is typical of the reaction to the deceitful, Figaro-like servant characters, which began as early as the 1730s.[50] Lukin, too, criticized the existing dramatic use of servants who appear as

---

('The Spendthrift. A Comedy', in Samuel Foote et al., *The Comic Theatre being a Free Translation of all the Best French Comedies*: vol. I (London: Dryden Leach, 1762), 109–236 [233–4]).

48 Guy Spielmann, *Le jeu de l'ordre et du chaos. Comédie et pouvoirs à la fin de règne, 1673–1715* (Paris: Honoré Champion, 2002), 227–31. Spielmann sees a hint of social destabilization in the rising importance of the dramatic action of the servant personae towards the end of Louis XIV's reign. Later, indeed, this tradition will produce the servants of Marivaux and, finally, Beaumarchais, whose Figaro very quickly became the personification of social transgression in pre-revolutionary France.

49 Riccoboni, *Observations sur la comédie, et sur le genie de Molière*, 113.

50 The enterprising valets appeared on the stage of the Russian court theatre in such plays as *Les Fourberies de Scapin* (1671) by Molière, *Crispin rival de son maître* (1707) by Lesage and *Légataire universel* (1708) by Regnard.

'deceitful' ('*bezdel'niki*') and chose as a model comedies which had devoted and sensible servitors.[51] In general, Lukin's characters eventually achieve happiness because they are virtuous (which is not the case of the French comedy and its protagonist Cléon). In *Mot* the valet represents an ideal version of social order, and the author justifies the gap between the social reality and its representation in his comedy in these terms:

> I have created a wholly virtuous servant, and some critics who attacked me said that we have never had such a servant here. Perhaps, I said to them, but that is why I created *Vasilei*, in order to create others like him, so that he can serve as a model. I used to be ashamed, my dear sirs, I continued, to see that in all translated Comedies the servants were dreadful layabouts, and that at the denouement almost all of them remained without punishment for their roguery, and some even gained some reward.[52]

Lukin, like Destouches, stresses the importance of an accurate depiction of the country's mores in his declarations,[53] but at the same time he justifies the representation of idealized characters. The theatrical performances obviously had a purpose beyond simply mirroring social reality. Both the French and Russian authors changed the established structures of the comedy to achieve a declared moral purpose and to stage the social ideal of master-servant relations.

Lukin responded to the commentaries on his play concerning the *vraisemblance* of the character of the loyal servant by arguing that his character was not intended to be an accurate portrayal of a typical Russian servant, but a model of what one should be. Clearly, however, the idealized servant character could not act as a model for Russian *servants*, since, according to the court theatre regulations, no man in livery could attend a

---

51   According to Gustave Lanson, this type of domestic was Destouches' invention (*Nivelle de La Chaussée et la comédie larmoyante*, 41–2).
52   Lukin, *Sochinenii i perevody* 1765, Ib, xvi–xvii.
53   Destouches declared his intention in *Le Dissipateur* as follows: 'représenter le monde tel qu'il est, & non pas tel qu'il devroit être. [...] Peindre est l'objet de la Comédie' ['to represent the world as it is, and not as it should be. [...] Painting is the object of Comedy'] (Destouches, *Le Dissipateur*, viii–x).

performance.⁵⁴ Nevertheless, the scene between the master and the servant in Lukin's play is the central one, full of social symbolism.

3

Lukin said that he wanted to avoid (*'ubegat"*) imitating Destouches, and in order to show his creative independence, he compared the scenes of a discussion between the spendthrift and his servant in Destouches's play and his own:

> I think that I did not copy Destouches, and it is not possible to consider me a thief, who has stolen his beauties. Our final scenes are similar, when his *Spendthrift* converses with *Pasquin*, and my *Dobroserdov* with *Vasilei*, but, on this point, anyone who knows theatre will see that mine is the opposite of his. The servant of Destouches's *Spendthrift* is free, but *Vasilei* is a serf. Being free, that servant gives his master money when he is in dire straits, and I accept that this good deed from such a lowly person is great; but *Vasilei's* is greater. He attains freedom and receives his reward, but he accepts neither. Let us suppose that he does not care for money; but freedom, that is the precious thing that they covet more than anything, and for the sake of which the good ones serve us zealously all their youth, so that in old age they can be released; however, *Vasilei* scorns freedom and remains with his master. There you have exemplary virtue! which cannot be called common in our Boyars.⁵⁵

It seems that the foregrounding of the relations between master and servant in Lukin's play and their idealized representation are related to the broader social programme of the comedy. The final comment in the paragraph quoted above widens the range of possible social meanings of a play that staged basic social categories and placed them in a sentimental context.

---

54 Nikolai V. Drizen, 'Liubitel'skii teatr pri Ekaterine II (1761–1796 gg.)', in *Ezhegodnik Imperatorskikh teatrov, Sezon 1895–1896*, Prilozheniia, kn. 2 (1897), 77–114 (84).
55 Lukin, *Sochinenii i perevody* 1765, Ib, xviii–xix.

The character of the virtuous serf (*krepostnoi*) has given rise to numerous modern readings.[56] The author of the academic history of translated literature in Russia, for instance, asserts that Lukin destined his comedies for people of the lower classes and that his orientation towards 'democratic' tastes should be explained by the low social origins of the writer.[57] According to Il'ia Serman, on the contrary, the views of Lukin need to be analysed in the context of the philosophy of the Enlightenment, and the criticism of vices in Lukin's works has, as Serman maintained, a general moral – and not social or class-oriented – sense.[58]

None of these interpretations foregrounds the fact that *Mot* was designed to be performed on the court stage, since, in seeking to understand the significance of the master-servant relationship, one should take into consideration the audience of this theatre, its tastes and the moral issues

56 Pavel Berkov found that Lukin was incoherent in his ideology: the writer defended 'good-hearted peasants', and at the same time he propagandized the 'slave's morality' by representing 'artificial' Vasilei as a model (Berkov, *Vladimir Ignat'evich Lukin: 1737–1794*, 48; cf. Welsh, *Russian Comedy 1765–1823*, 41). Liudmila Kulakova remarked, on the contrary, that Lukin's position was well-articulated and close to that of the Empress: Liudmila I. Kulakova, 'Neizdannaia poema Ia. B. Kniazhnina (Epizod iz istorii literaturnoi polemiki 1765 goda s prilozheniem teksta poemy *Boi stikhotvortsev*)' in *Russkaia literatura i obshchestvennaia bor'ba XVIII–XIX vekov* (Leningrad: Leningradskii gosudarstvennyi pedagogicheskii institut im. A. I. Gertsena, 1971), 73–93 (78). Kulakova proposed changing Aleksandr Pypin's formula concerning Lukin from 'partisan of the national spirit in literature' (*partizan narodnosti v literature*) to 'partisan of the official populism' (*partizan ofitsial'noi narodnosti*). See Aleksandr N. Pypin, 'V. I. Lukin', in *Sochineniia i perevody Vladimira Ignat'evicha Lukina i Bogdana Egorovicha El'chaninova* (St Petersburg: Izdaniia Ivana Il'icha Glazunova, 1868), lix, and Kulakova, 'Neizdannaia poema Ia. B. Kniazhnina', 78.
57 Levin, ed., *Istoriia russkoi perevodnoi khudozhestvennoi literatury*, 35. Giovanna Moracci uses the same opposition and writes of Lukin's comedies: 'The comedy required the verisimilar representation of the epoch's reality: the life of the streets and not that of the court'. Giovanna Moracci, 'Gallomania, società e morale nella commedia russa fra il XVIII e XIX secolo', *Ricerche slavistiche*, 43 (1996), 381–416 (384).
58 Il'ia Z. Serman, *Russkii klassitsizm (Poeziia. Drama. Satira)* (Leningrad: Nauka, 1973), 235–6.

that the spectators saw resolved in the plays. Elise Kimerling Wirtschafter, in her study of a large corpus of drama published in Russian, treats the master-servant pair as a part of a larger theme, that of the patriarchal household.[59] It constituted, indeed, the organizing principle of social relations in Russian society.[60] The paternalist society of the *Ancien Régime* organized itself using several major couples, such as *father – son* and *master – servant* (even the most powerful aristocrats were, finally, servants of their sovereign and of God).[61] Since the Petrine reforms, patronage and master-servant (or chief-executor) dialectics had organized the working relations in the state administration.[62] Lukin's patron Ivan Elagin, for example, described his disposition in one of his letters to Count Aleksandr Vorontsov as follows: 'Having served my country for thirty years, I have got used to giving and following orders'.[63] The family was the most widespread symbol in the description of the connections between different levels of the social hierarchy and a common metaphor for the monarchy. In 1759, the political writer Friedrich Karl von Moser discussed the relations between a sovereign and his ministers and likened the sovereign to the father and his or her subjects to the children:

59 Elise Kimerling Wirtschafter, *The Play of Ideas in Russian Enlightenment Theater* (DeKalb: Northern Illinois University Press, 2003), 80. There are some common points between this book and my study, namely certain texts and the interest in social history. However, I do not share Wirtschafter's approach to Russian drama as a tool of social critique nor her conclusion on the common idea expressed by Russian playwrights: 'that the individual [...] held the key to social progress'.
60 See, for instance, Walter Gleason, 'Political Ideals and Loyalties of Some Russian Writers of the Early 1760s', *Slavic Review*, vol. 34, 3 (1975), 559–75 (566).
61 Iurii M. Lotman, 'Ocherki po istorii russkoi kul'tury XVIII – nachala XIX veka', *Iz istorii russkoi kul'tury*, vol. IV (Moscow: Iazyki russkoi kul'tury, 2000) 13–346 (34). On the coupling 'tsar-Bog' see the classical study, Viktor M. Zhivov and Boris A. Uspenskii, "Tsar' i Bog: Semioticheskie aspekty sakralizatsii monarkha v Rossii, in *Iazyki kul'tur i problemy perevodimosti* (Moscow: Nauka, 1987), 47–153.
62 David L. Ransel, *The Politics of Catherinian Russia: The Panin Party* (New Haven and London: Yale University Press, 1975); Anna Joukovskaïa-Lecerf, 'Hiérarchie et patronage: Les relations de travail dans l'administration russe au XVIIIe siècle', *Cahiers du monde russe*, 47 (2006), 551–80.
63 *Arkhiv kniazia Vorontsova*, kniga IV (Moscow, 1877), 337.

One good word from the Prince makes the subject give him everything, to the last kopeck; but that is not all; he also gives him what he has kept in reserve, in case his wife should be widowed or his children orphaned.'[64]

Lukin's comedy gives a perfect illustration of this thesis on the lower social level. The audience, it was assumed, would guess that the master equals the prince and the servant equals the prince's subjects.

In general, the relations between the master and the servant were a key topic of European literature of the modern period.[65] For instance, Lesage's novel *Histoire de Gil Blas de Santillane* (1715–35), published in Grigorii Teplov's translation in 1754–5,[66] was a kind of guide to social

64 *Gosudar' i ministr kniga, sochinennaia gospodinom Mozerom, s nemetzkago iazyka perevedena Artillerii Kapitanom Iakovom Kozel'skim* (St Petersburg, 1766), 20. The Russian translation was published in 1766 with a dedication to the Empress, who had read the book or at least said she had (A. F. Walther, ed, *Briefwechsel der 'Grossen Landgräfin' Caroline von Hessen. Dreissig Jahre eines Fürstlichen Frauenlebens*, Bd. 2 (Vienna: Wilhelm Braumüller, 1877), 414). Iakov Kozelskii's translation of the German title as 'sovereign and minister' ('gosudar' i ministr') comes from the contents of the book. Russian noblemen read the French translation of the work. In October 1760, Count Mikhail Vorontsov, sending the book to Count Kirill Razumovskii, wrote: 'considering its good content, you will certainly like the book' (*Arkhiv kniazia Vorontsova*, kniga IV, 46).

65 The plays of Molière, Marivaux and Beaumarchais are often explored from this perspective: see, for example, Jean Emelina, *Les Valets et les servantes dans le théâtre comique en France de 1610 à 1700* (Cannes: C.E.L.; Grenoble: Presses Universitaires de Grenoble, 1975). As for English literature, there are many studies dedicated to the Renaissance drama and, particularly, Shakespeare. See Mark Thornton Burnett, *Masters and Servants in English Renaissance Drama and Culture: Authority and Obedience* (Basingstoke: Palgrave, 2001), 2–5, 11–12 for bibliography.

66 Seventy-five copies were distributed among the *znatnye persony*, or noblemen (see Database *Russkaia kniga grazhdanskoi pechati XVIII v. v fondakh bibliotek RF*, available as online at <http://www.nlr.ru/rlin/ruslbr_v2.php?database=RLINXVIII>). Poroshin read the novel in Russian translation to the Grand Duke in 1765 (Poroshin, 'Zapiski', 250–2). Catherine II herself had apparently read the novel (see *Dnevnik A. V. Khrapovitskogo. 1782–1793* (St Petersburg: A. F. Bazunov, 1874), 301, 408 and 'Vospominaniia i dnevniki Adriana Moiseevicha Gribovskago, stats-sekretaria imperatritsy Ekateriny Velikoi', *Russkii arkhiv*, 1 (1899), 27).

mobility for masters and servants.[67] The protagonist, a Spanish countryman, has become the favourite of the powerful minister, having changed his social status many times meanwhile. In the ninth book Gil Blas loses his place and fortune because of an intrigue and finds himself in gaol. His servant Scipion's fidelity goes beyond words; he does not accept half his master's savings, but wants to be imprisoned with him.[68] The situation in Lukin's comedy is close to that of the French novel, but Lukin stresses the importance of a specifically Russian social reality in his play. Vasilei is a serf, and he is not legally free (which was not the case of the servant in Destouches's play). Therefore the Russian author chooses to present the servant's readiness to decline a proposition of freedom;[69] ultimately, however, the scene in his comedy forms part of a tradition representing the social ideal of loyalty in theatre and fiction, and brings this tradition into Russian literature

This case-study of Lukin's most famous play illustrates the way that the early Russian court theatre adapted the moral lessons of foreign comedies in order to accommodate the audience of the Russian court. That Russian dramatic translators of the time laid emphasis on master-servant relations is also evident in a play translated by another secretary of Elagin's, Denis Fonvizin. On 10 November 1764, the court company performed his translation in verse of Gresset's comedy *Sidney* (*Korion* in the Russian version). In the denouement of the plot, Sidney, the protagonist, has retired to the country feeling guilty and disillusioned and decides finally to commit suicide. But his devoted valet Dumont exchanges a glass of poison for a glass of water and thanks to his vigilance his master remains alive. Saved,

---

67   See, for instance, *Vsiakaia vsiachina* (St Petersburg, 1769), 115.
68   *Pokhozhdeniia Zhilblaza de Santillany, opisannyia g. Le Sazhem, a perevedennyia Vasil'em Teplovym*, vol. III (St Petersburg, pri Imperatorskoi Akademii Nauk, 1754), 299–301.
69   A hypothesis concerning the allusions in the comedy is proposed in Aleksei Evstratov, 'K semantike siuzheta pridvornoi komedii 1760-kh gg. (*Mot, liuboviû ispravlennyi* V. I. Lukina)', *Russkaia filologiia*, 20. *Sbornik nauchnykh rabot molodykh filologov* (Tartu: Tartu Ülikooli Kirjastus, 2009), 18–26 (24–5).

Sidney makes a marriage proposal to his beloved Rosalie, thus returning to social life too. He wants to reward his valet for the service,

> Vivez, je suis payé;
> Les gens de mon pays font tout par amitié;
> Ils n'envisagent point d'autre reconnaissance;
> Le plaisir de bien faire est notre récompense.[70]
>
> [Be alive, I am rewarded;
> People of my country do everything for friendship's sake;
> They do not expect another acknowledgement;
> Pleasure of good action is our reward.]

In Gresset's original play the valet's deed demonstrates his moral qualities. Dumont talks about his master in terms of friendship and Sidney embraces his servant in this touching scene. In Fonvizin's translation Andrei (the Russian Dumont), in contrast to the French valet, stresses the importance of the category of service:

> Не требую награды.
> Я вам из одного усердия служу
> И в том одном свое веселье нахожу.
> Я жизни счастливой усердно вам желаю
> И с днем рождения нижайше поздравляю.[71]
>
> [I do not demand reward.
> I serve you from zeal alone
> And in this only I find my joy.
> I wish you heartily a happy life
> And I wish you humbly a happy birthday.]

He explains his action by his zeal, and the last line of the quoted extract lays emphasis on the social distance between master and servant ('I wish

---

70 Gresset, *Sidney, comédie* (The Hague, 1745), 45.
71 Fonvizin, *Sobranie sochinenii* I: 41–2. The last line could be addressed to a nobleman who assisted at the first performance of *Sidney* in the court theatre on 10 November 1764 (Poroshin, 'Zapiski', 87). Ivan Elagin's birthday was on 30 November.

you humbly'). In this way, the adaptation and accommodation of foreign drama by Russian writers went beyond simple modifications of names. Their purpose was to build a relevant representation of the social order and its hierarchies.

Thus, my conclusion contrasts with those of researchers who find an opposition between democratic and aristocratic tendencies in the dramas of Lukin and other writers of the period. The opposition itself was, obviously, relevant to contemporary society. My aim, however, has been to show that although Lukin's message was clearly a didactic one, to speak in the name of serfs was not his purpose. Using topical metaphors in his comedy *Mot*, Lukin represented moral standards of the noble elite as universal ones. Once approved by the court and the Empress herself, his comedies could be printed and staged in the public theatre. This 'new theatre' as a form of entertainment spread from the political centres (capitals and royal residences) to the periphery (provincial towns, fairs), where it saw a change in audience, language (from foreign to vernacular) and aesthetic (from *opera seria* and tragedy as the major, 'noble' genres to comedy, comic opera and *proverbe*). Thus, once approved at court, the performative models of dominance and submission formulated in court drama were diffused throughout the polity, so that their message might reach all subjects and social strata. The plays became a tool in the outreach of the values of Russian 'paternal autocracy', based, as Lotman has shown, not on the idea of contract and laws, but on family love between the monarch and the people.[72]

Court theatre was the site of the initial reception of original dramatic texts. A number of plays performed in a foreign language at court had never been translated into Russian, and a large part of the translations performed by the Russian company at court had never been published. But when they were, between Russian society's first encounter of a foreign play (usually in French, and in the form of a performance) and the publication or performance of that work in Russian, one can discern the kind of modifications that were considered significant when a play went before a

---

72 See Lotman, 'Ocherki po istorii russkoi kul'tury XVIII–nachala XIX veka', 196.

larger audience.[73] The translator was obviously a major figure in this process of accommodation of a text to the country's social norms, even if these were not necessarily its real social conditions. As demonstrated by the case study of Lukin's comedy, the translator-writer could go further: as well as shaping his own translation, he might use translation as an instrument to try to shape the social reality in his own culture.

73   In a wider context, one can also discover which plays were judged suitable for popular audiences and which were never performed outside the court.

BRIAN JAMES BAER

Vasilii Zhukovskii, Translator: Accommodating Politics in Early Nineteenth-Century Russia

Introduction

The current focus on questions of power and authority in Translation and Interpreting Studies and attendant calls for greater activism among translation and interpreting professionals is reflected in the attention paid to acts of resistance, that is, on the ways translators and interpreters have used their position to critique – in more or less covert forms – the powers that be.[1] Because of its reliance on translation, on the one hand, and censorship restrictions, on the other, Russia – from the eighteenth century to the Soviet period – offers a wealth of examples of how translation has functioned as an act of resistance. Such acts involved not only translations themselves but also critical literature on translations and translators, through which emerges a discourse of heroic resistance to fate and, very often, by extension, the regime. Less attention, however, has been paid to those translators who attenuate the political implications of foreign works through a variety of strategies and for a variety of reasons. I will examine

---

1 See Maria Tymoczko and Edwin Gentzler, eds, *Translation and Power* (Amherst: University of Massachusetts Press, 2002); Mona Baker, *Translation and Conflict: A Narrative Account* (London and New York: Routledge, 2006); Maria Tymoczko, *Translation, Resistance, Activism* (Amherst: University of Massachusetts Press, 2010); Julie Boéri and Carol Maier, *Translation/Interpreting and Social Activism* (Manchester: St Jerome, 2010); and Moria Inghilleri and Sue-Ann Harding, 'Special Issue: Translation and Violent Conflict', *The Translator* 16.2 (2010).

these strategies and the motivations behind them in the work of Russia's arguably best-known translator-poet Vasilii Zhukovskii (1783–1852) as an example of how translators accommodate literary works to the political realities of the target culture.

The illegitimate son of a Russian nobleman, I. A. Bunin, and a Turkish slave, Zhukovskii was sent to the newly opened Moscow University Gentry Pension, which had a strong focus on literature. He made his reputation more as a translator than as an original writer, although many writers and critics remarked that his translated works read 'like originals.'[2] A friend and confidant of many of the progressive-leaning writers of the Golden Age of Russian literature – Aleksandr Pushkin described him as a 'genius of translation' (genii perevoda)[3] – Zhukovskii was the private tutor to the Russian Royal Family, educating the man who would become Russia's tsar-liberator, Alexander II. As a rule, Slavists have refrained from exploring Zhukovskii's politics, focusing instead on his contribution to Russian literature in terms of aesthetics – he introduced new genres into Russia's fledgling literature (such as the German ballad) and popularized certain

2   The influential critic and social commentator Vissarion Belinskii expressed his views on Zhukovskii's genius in the following way in his review of Russian literature in 1841: '*Undine*, this sweet, melodic and fantastic tale of the heart, this is Zhukovskii's *original translated* work which can explain, best of all, why critics do not want to call him a translator but view him as an independent poet. One definitely cannot label Zhukovskii merely a translator. When selecting plays to translate he did not follow a single uncontrollable impulse but, rather, the source. He searched everywhere for *his own* and, finding it, translated it. All of his translations possess some kind of general mark; all together they form a particular world of poetry – *Zhukovskii's poetry*' (Iurii Levin and Andrei Fedorov, *Russkie pisateli o perevode* (Leningrad: Russkii pisatel', 1960, 218; trans. A. Wesolowski). Nikolai Gogol' shared this point of view in his essay of 1846, 'What is the Ultimate Essence of Russian Poetry?', writing: 'that inner yearning that is imprinted on [Zhukovskii's] translations lends them such vitality that even Germans who have mastered the Russian language acknowledge that the originals seem like copies and the translations like true originals. You don't know what to call him – a translator or an original poet. A translator loses his own individuality, but Zhukovskii revealed his more than all our other poets' (ibid., 188).
3   A. S. Pushkin, *Polnoe sobranie sochinenii v 16-i tomakh*. Vol. XIII (Moscow-Leningrad: AN SSSR, 1937–1959), 183.

verse forms.⁴ Scholars also point to the great liberties taken by Zhukovskii, in particular, his russifications in renderings of contemporary German and English poetry, in which he would often change foreign names to Russian ones and paint landscapes with a distinctly Russian geography.

Belonging to a generation older than the Decembrists, Zhukovskii was raised in elite company heavily influenced by the masonic beliefs of Ivan Turgenev, the father of Zhukovskii's closest childhood friend, Andrei Turgenev. Zhukovskii was one of the founders of the Literary Friendship Society, which was 'interested in German and English pre-romantic literature and occupied itself with translations'.⁵ Zhukovskii was a friend to many of the future Decembrists and to Decembrist sympathizers such as Pushkin, and a courtier in the capacity of both reader and, from 1825, tutor to the future Tsar Alexander II. For the most part, he moved deftly among these political camps, although he was not immune to censorship. In Zhukovskii's translation of Sir Walter Scott's lyrical ballad 'On the Eve of St. John', the censor objected to the decision to translate the English word *monk* with the Old Russian word *chernets*, suspecting that the archaic word might serve as a cue to readers to find in Scott's ballad historical parallels with contemporary Russia.⁶ In the early 1820s, his translation of Schiller's 'Maid of Orleans' was banned from performance by the Minster of Internal Affairs, V. P. Kuchebei, who found it 'dangerous'.⁷

Zhukovskii's views on translation evolved in the course of his long career. In the early period, he appeared willing to take enormous liberties in his translations – going so far as to remove the three witches from

---

4   For more on Zhukovskii's contribution to the formation of modern Russian literature and a modern Russian identity, see David L. Cooper, *Creating the Nation: Identity and Aesthetics in Early Nineteenth-Century Russia and Bohemia* (DeKalb: Northern Illinois University Press, 2010).
5   Antonia Glasse, 'Zhukovskii, Vasily Andreevich' in Victor Terras, ed., *Handbook of Russian Literature* (New Haven: Yale University Press, 1985), 531–3 (531).
6   Charles A. Rudd, *Fighting Words: Imperial Censorship and the Russian Press, 1804–1906* (Toronto: University of Toronto Press, 2009), 43.
7   A. A. Gugnin, 'Introduction' in V. A. Zhukovskii, *Zarubezhnaia poeziia v perevodakh V. A. Zhukovskogo v dvukh tomakh*, vol. 1 (Moscow: Raduga, 1985), 9–14 (14).

Shakespeare's *Macbeth*, despite the urgings of his friend Andrei Turgenev to 'let Shakespeare remain Shakespeare'.[8] He would over the course of time adopt what Susan Bernofsky referred to as a 'service translation' point of view, seeking to achieve greater accuracy without entirely sacrificing 'originality'.[9] In a letter written on September 12 (24), 1847 to Sergei Uvarov, which he would later use as the introduction to his translation of Homer's *Odyssey*, he described his approach to translation as breathing life into an interlinear translation prepared by a German philologist:

> beneath every Greek word he placed a German word, and beneath every German word – the grammatical meaning of the original. In this way I was able to have before me the entire literal meaning of the *Odyssey* and had before my eyes the entire sequence of words; in this chaotically faithful translation, inaccessible to the reader, were assembled before me, so to speak, all the building materials; only beauty, proportion and harmony were lacking. And this is what my own labors consist in: I had to find proportionality hiding in the lack of proportionality I was given, to use my poetic feeling to seek out beauty in ugliness and to create harmony from sounds that pain the ear; and all this not to the detriment of the original, faithfully retaining its ancient physiognomy. For this reason my translation itself might be seen as an original work.[10]

Here Zhukovskii evokes a rather modern notion of scholarly fidelity in translation that differs markedly from his earlier, 'freer' approach.

The translations examined below, however, are from his earliest period, when Zhukovskii took great liberties – aesthetically and thematically – in translating contemporary poetry. They date from a time when translation was one of the principal vehicles for the introduction of progressive political ideas into Russia. Zhukovskii's use of translation contrasts with this

---

8   Andrei Turgenev, 'Pis'ma Andreia Turgeneva k Zhukovskomu' in V. E. Vatsuro and M. N. Virolainen, eds, *Zhukovskii i russkaia kul'tura: Sbornik nauchnykh trudov* (Leningrad: Nauka, 1987), 350–430 (407).
9   Susan Bernofsky, *Foreign Words: Translator-Authors in the Age of Goethe* (Detroit: Wayne State University Press, 2005).
10 Vasilii Zhukovskii, 'Gomerova 'Odisseia'. Vmesto predisloviia' in *Polnoe sobranie sochinenii V. A. Zhukovskogo v 12-ti tomakh*, vol. VI (St Petersburg: 1902), 56–8, (58), translated by James McGavran.

prevailing trend, however: his translations of English poems attenuate the political import of the subject matter, and advance instead a religious and ethical position influenced by the mystical side of freemasonry and pietism.

Translation and Politics

Translation in eighteenth-century Russia was a driving force in what would be, until 1917, the greatest cultural transformation in Russian history, and was seen by many as 'service to the state', lending it a political hue. Peter the Great issued an *ukaz* in 1723, instructing translators on how to go about the task of translation; he also initiated a new translation of the Slavonic Bible into contemporary Russian. Catherine the Great, herself a translator, established the Society for the Translation of Foreign Books in the late eighteenth century to support translation into Russian. In the early nineteenth century, especially following Russia's victory over Napoleon, issues related to translation – what to translate and how to translate it – were seen as closely tied to the problem of Russian national identity and those questions were debated in Russia's own version of the quarrel between the Ancients and Moderns.[11]

The immense quantity of translated works offered a 'mediated' – and so, relatively safe – venue for the expression of political views and social protest under conditions of censorship. Already in the eighteenth century, translation was involved in the anti-feudal and anti-clerical debates. Numerous free translations from Horace, describing idyllic scenes of pastoral life were often ironically reinterpreted by Russian poets to provide a striking contrast to Russia's feudal reality. In several Russian translations of Horace's ode *Beatus ille, qui procul negotiis*, known as *Pokhvala sel'skoi zhizni* (*In Praise of Rural Life*), the reference to *verna*, the slave born and raised in Horace's house, was eliminated, since Russian poet-translators

---

11   For more on this, see Cooper, *Creating the Nation*.

viewed this image as a possible argument in favour of serfdom in Russia.¹² Translations were in fact one of the only public venues for the discussion of serfdom. Consider Andrei Turgenev's decision to translate August von Kotzebue's play *Die Negersklaven* (*The Negro Slaves*) (1796) as *Negry v nevole* (*Negroes in Captivity*) (1803). While the politics of Kotzebue's play was obvious – Jenna Marie Gibbs describes it as 'a didactically anti-slavery play in which Kotzebue drew from the French *philosophes* and the precept of freedom as a birthright stated in the *Declaration of the Rights of Man* to argue that "no man can be born a slave"'¹³ – Turgenev avoids the use of *rab*, or 'slave', in the Russian title, perhaps because it would have drawn too close a parallel with the Russian tradition of serfdom and therefore risked censorship.

And so, while translation offered a venue to comment on the burning political issues of the day in Russia, it was always to some extent mediated by its very status as a translation, lending the translator a certain degree of safety. After all, it was always someone else's words. The eighteenth-century playwright Denis Fonvizin's translation into Russian of the Confucian text *Ta Hsüeh* (from a French translation), for example, 'provided a language in which to articulate the reflections on imperial legitimacy and political opposition that had preoccupied him since the late 1760s'.¹⁴ One of the early acts of civic courage in translation practices was Aleksandr Radishchev's translation of an excerpt from Voltaire's anti-clerical *Poème sur la loi naturelle* (*A Poem on the Natural Law*). Some of Radishchev's other translations, including those from Horace and Ewald Christian von

---

12 P. N. Berkov, 'Rannie russkie perevodchiki Goratsiia', *Izvestiia AN SSSR. Otdelenie obshchestvennykh nauk* 10 (1935), 1039–56 (1044).

13 Jenna Marie Gibbs, *Performing the Temple of Liberty: Slavery, Rights, and Revolution in Transatlantic Theatricality (1760s–1830s)* (University of California: Proquest, 2008), 285.

14 Jeffrey D. Burson, 'Mandate of the Fatherland: Denis Fonvizin's Translation of Neo-Confucianism into the Politics of Enlightened Absolutism under Catherine the Great', *Vestnik. The Journal of Russian and Asian Studies* (12 Dec. 2005) <http://www.sras.org/denis_fonvizin_s_translation_of_neo-confucianism> accessed 31 January 2012.

Kleist, could also be interpreted as early attempts at promoting freedom of speech.[15]

The politics of translation was intensified in the generation of writers and poets who arrived on the literary scene following the Napoleonic Wars (1803–15), about a decade after Zhukovskii had made his debut. Their experience of war and their time spent in Europe, and especially Paris, after Napoleon's defeat, produced idealistic, civic-minded poets and authors for whom Byron was a revolutionary hero and the struggle for independence in Greece a rehearsal for Russia's own struggle for freedom. The obvious subtext to Decembrist Vil'gelm Kiukhel'beker's poems dedicated to Greece or to Byron ('Grecheskaia pesn'' ('Greek Song') or 'Smert' Bairona' ('The Death of Byron')) was the cause of liberty.[16] Many educated Russians who had been exposed to the freedom of Western Europe in the course of the Napoleonic Wars returned to Russia with a liberal political agenda. Writers sought to contribute to that agenda by developing a civic or civic-minded literature in Russia, one that raised various political issues and asserted the existence of a civil society, separate from the control of the state. Translation was an important tool in their arsenal.

In their search for a civic literature, Russian writers looked to foreign models. As Leighton notes, '[f]or political idealists like the Decembrists the impetus came from the French revolution as one model, the American as another. For the literary romantics, dreams of freedom were aroused by Lamartine, Chénier, Schiller, especially by the verse tales of Byron, and even more by the liberating effects of the free romantic imagination.'[17] Translations and imitations of French literature and, in particular, the literature of the French Revolution, were especially important to Russians attempting to develop a civic literature.[18] Consider Pushkin's reference to 'vozvyshennaia Galla' ('sublime Gaul') in his 1820 ode 'Vol'nost'' ('Liberty'),

---

15   Iurii Lotman, 'Radishchev – poet-perevodchik' in Iurii Lotman, *O poetakh i poezii* (St Petersburg: Iskusstvo-SPB, 1996), 279–84 (280–2).
16   All translations are mine unless otherwise indicated.
17   Lauren Leighton, *The Esoteric Tradition in Russian Romantic Literature* (University Park: Pennsylvania State University Press, 1994), 71.
18   Iu. Danilin, *Beranzhe i ego pesni* (Moscow: Khudozhestvennaia literatura, 1973), 319.

the poem that led to his internal exile. Mikhail Zetlin explains the special relevance of eighteenth-century France to early nineteenth-century Russians:

> While in the West the romantic era was coming into its own, in Russia Pushkin still read Voltaire's *La Pucelle* and the sentimental poems of Parny. Whereas Paris raved about Chateaubriand and de Maistre, St. Petersburg was only just beginning to discover Adam Smith and Montesquieu. At a time when throughout the Western world people were seeking to adjust themselves to post-Napoleonic reaction, in Russia there was growing up a generation kindred in spirit to that which, a score of years earlier, had made the French Revolution.[19]

The association of French literature – and poetry, in particular – with politics is obvious in Prince Viazemskii's survey of contemporary French poetry, published anonymously in the journal *Moscow Telegraph* in 1826: 'You ask what poetry is doing in France? It is doing politics.'[20] He then goes on to offer a definition of civic literature as 'any popular or civic poetry that contains lofty, social truths', which he then promotes: 'And why shouldn't the poet be the equal of the orator as the guardian of popular interests and the public welfare?'[21]

Three French poets were especially popular among Russian translators and poets: André Chénier (1762–94), Pierre-Jean de Béranger (1780–1857), and Antoine-Vincent Arnault (1766–1834). All were caught up in the politics of the revolutionary period and, among liberal Russian writers, served as models of the civic-minded poet. Through translations and imitations of these authors' works, Russian writers and translators introduced a civic-minded literature into Russian letters. Because such literature was especially suspect in the eyes of the autocratic regime, writers and translators developed unwritten codes to allow for the circulation of texts and paratextual materials that were available to unofficial, often oppositional,

---

19 Mikhail Zetlin, *The Decembrists*; trans. George Panin (Madison, CT: International Universities Press, 1958), 14.
20 Quoted in Zoia Staritsyna, *Beranzhe v Rossii. XIX vek* (Moscow: Vyshshaia Shkola, 1969), 16.
21 Ibid.

interpretation. The charged political environment forms the backdrop of Zhukovskii's greatest works as a translator, which, significantly, were to go against the progressive, political grain.

The Politics of English Poetry

Eighteenth-century English poetry with its focus on the countryside and its inhabitants was inevitably shaped by the shifting politics of land ownership. Two pre-romantic English poems that were especially popular in the Russian literary circles of the time were Thomas Gray's 'Elegy Written in a Country Churchyard' (1751) and Oliver Goldsmith's 'The Deserted Village' (1773). Gray's elegy was written on the eve of the industrial revolution and the land enclosure policy that would change the landscape of Britain. Goldsmith's 'The Deserted Village' was composed in the midst of the land enclosures that would force great numbers of peasant farmers to leave the countryside. The poems would be translated in earnest in Russia in the late eighteenth and early nineteenth centuries, decades after their original publication, with the belated arrival of Romanticism.

While the politics of Gray's 'Elegy' is less pointed than that of Goldsmith's 'The Deserted Village', contemporary readers were not oblivious to the political implications of Gray's moving description of the rural poor. As John Quincy Adams observed, referring to Gray's deep empathy for the peasantry, 'No land of slavery could ever have produced Gray's *Elegy*'.[22] Western critics continue to point out the political aspects of the 'Elegy'. Empson describes the Elegy as 'an odd case of poetry with latent political ideas',[23] while Richard Sha acknowledges the compassion for the

---

22   Quoted in James D. Garrison, *A Dangerous Liberty: Translating Gray's Elegy* (Newark: University of Delaware Press, 2009), 23.
23   Ibid., 116.

poor on the part of Gray's narrator but argues that such compassion 'is contingent upon the silent and cheerful penury of the lower classes'.[24]

Goldsmith's 'The Deserted Village' has a sharper political point of view, dealing head-on with the more brutal aspects of the land enclosure policy. As Gilbert Slater explains, 'Early in the eighteenth century there begins the great series of private acts of enclosure, of which 4,000 in all, covering some 7,000,000 acres were passed before the General Enclosure Act of 1845. During the same period it is probable that about the same area was enclosed without application to Parliament'.[25] The policy of enclosure allowed landlords to usurp lands once held in common by the villagers in order to turn them into pasture lands for sheep and to enlarge their own farms. The effects on villagers – and on rural villages – were devastating. As Slater points out, 'The majority of the small tenant farmers had to choose between migrating elsewhere, or becoming landless labourers'.[26] Controversy surrounding the Enclosure Acts brought issues of class that were latent in Gray's 'Elegy' to the forefront. The presence of debated political issues in these poems challenged a reading of the countryside as a timeless idyll; these poems speak to their contemporary reality. As Terry Eagleton notes:

> The vision of the English countryside as an Arcadian paradise of rosy-cheeked peasants was largely the creation of town dwellers. It is the myth of those for whom the country is a place to look at rather than live in. [...] Most of [the peasants] had been reduced to landless labourers by market forces and the Enclosure Acts, or driven into the satanic mills of early industrial England. There was nothing timeless or idyllic about this landscape of capitalist landowners, grinding poverty, depopulation and a decaying artisanal class.[27]

---

24 Ibid.
25 Gilbert Slater, 'A Historical Outline of Land Ownership in England' in *The Land: The Report of the Land Enquiry Committee* (London: Hodder & Stoughton, 1913), lxii–lxxxiii (lxxii).
26 Ibid., lxxvii.
27 Terry Eagleton, review of *Visions of England* by Roy Strong, *The Guardian* (1 July 2009) <http://www.guardian.co.uk/books/2011/jul/01/visions-of-england-roy-strong-review> accessed 14 July 2012.

Not simply abstract meditations on loss and death, these poems address to a greater or lesser extent the land-owning politics of their day. As the English poet Carol Rumens notes, 'Oliver Goldsmith's "The Deserted Village" is both a marvellous descriptive poem and a powerful *political essay*. Polemic comes alive when it is grounded in detail, and Goldsmith conducts his argument using an expansive array of vivid supporting material – topographies, interiors, and sharp human portraits'.[28] Moreover, in his dedication to Sir Joshua Reynolds, Goldsmith insists on the *realism* of his poem, the fact that it is rooted in an accurate depiction of contemporary events: 'To this I can scarce make any other answer than that I sincerely believe what I have written; that I have taken all possible pains, in my country excursions, for these four or five years past, to be certain of what I allege; and that all my views and enquiries have led me to believe those miseries *real*, which I here attempt to display'.[29]

Zhukovskii's 'Elegy Written in a Country Churchyard'

In an anthology dedicated to Zhukovskii's translations of English literature, A. Atarova notes, '[i]n the consciousness of readers Zhukovskii is first and foremost a translator of ancient and German poetry; however, the role of English poetry in his creative development is very significant'.[30] Indeed his most popular and influential translation was arguably of Thomas Gray's 'Elegy Written in a Country Churchyard', which the Russian writer and philosopher Vladimir Solov'ev referred to as the 'birthplace of Russian

---

28 Carol Rumens, 'Poem of the Week: "The Deserted Village" by Oliver Goldsmith', *The Guardian* (31 May 2010) <http://www.guardian.co.uk/books/booksblog/2010/may/31/poem-week-goldsmith-deserted-village> accessed 21 July 2012; my italics.
29 Ibid.
30 K. N. Atarova, 'Introduction' in V. A. Zhukovskii, *Angliiskaia poeziia v perevodakh V. A. Zhukovskogo* (Moscow: Rudomino/Raduga, 2000), 9–14 (9).

poetry'.[31] According to Solov'ev, 'Despite the foreign origins and the excess of sentimentality in certain spots, the graveyard elegy can be considered the origin of a truly human poetry in Russia'.[32] Gray's poem held a deep fascination for Zhukovskii, who returned to his translation several times in the course of his life. His first translation attempt was rejected by his mentor Karamzin for publication in his journal *Vestnik Evropy*. He revised the translation, which he successfully published, now with a dedication to his recently-deceased friend and confidant, Andrei Ivanovich Turgenev. Zhukovskii would return to the poem again toward the end of his life, completing what he considered to be a more accurate prose translation after visiting the cemetery featured in the poem, which by then contained the remains of Gray himself. The success of Zhukovskii's poetic translation, however, had the greater cultural significance, helping at the time of its initial publication to bring about the victory of the elegy (the moderns) over the ode (the ancients).

Although Zhukovskii's translation of Gray's elegy played a major role in determining the course of Russian literature, in James D. Garrison's estimation, it attenuates the political implications of Gray's poem by largely erasing the class markers and the distance between narrator/poet and the rural subject of his poem, creating in the process a 'religious elegy'. In general, Zhukovskii places greater emphasis on the spiritual themes of the poem and displays a greater affinity – even a sentimental 'merging of souls' – between the narrator of the poem and the deceased, whereas that relationship in Gray's original is rather more ambivalent, inflected as it is with class difference. Zhukovskii accomplishes this, Garrison argues, by employing a variety of techniques, such as substituting the first person singular pronoun with the collective 'we', as in the line '*we* must learn to die', and toning down class differences highlighted in Gray by the use of such descriptors as 'rustic', 'unlettered', 'uncouth', 'shapeless' and 'frail', to focus instead on the human condition. And 'where Gray creates a sense

[31] Vladimir Solov'ev, 'Rodina russkoi poezii' in *Stikhotvoreniia i shutochnye p'esy* (Moscow: Sovetskii pisatel', 1974), 118.
[32] Ibid.

of the clumsiness, even the inadequacy of the memorial, the attention in Zhukovskii is on its appropriateness'.[33] Overall, the central motif of Gray's poem – the distinctions between 'privileged and deprived' – is attenuated in the translation 'by appeal to the cosmic ideas of fate and fortune'.[34] Finally, the ambivalent ending of Gray's elegy is transformed by Zhukovskii into a 'biblical moral'.[35]

In Zhukovskii's 'Elegy' we see the emergence of a sentimental – and idealized – construction of modern Russian identity, one that mystifies the question of class in a vision of Russia as a rural community of modest, god-fearing people that stands in contrast to the materialism and individualism of the West. Another significance of his transformation of the poem is suggested by the fact that he dedicated the revised poetic translation to his dearest friend who died at the age of twenty-three. This addition reorders, one might say, the emotional thrust of the poem, lending the relationship of the narrator and the deceased a closeness, a personal connection that is not there in Gray's original. Garrison notes that Zhukovskii establishes this connection, 'in a phrase boldly added to the original – as friend of the deceased ('pochivshikh drug')', but does not trace it to Turgenev's untimely death.[36]

Beyond these explanations for Zhukovskii's accommodation of Gray's 'Elegy', there is another substantive context that illuminates Zhukovskii's project in translating and transforming the English poem. His translation conforms to the literary practices of the educated elite, reared in the beliefs and practices of freemasonry, and this context explains the attenuation of the original's political overtones and accompanying development of religious and ethical concerns. At the end of the eighteenth century and the beginning of the nineteenth, two broad-based social 'movements',

---

33   Garrison, *A Dangerous Liberty*, 133; 'skromnyi' (modest) and 'v priute' (in a refuge) are more positive and, incidentally, are somewhat reminiscent of Derzhavin's idealized Russian countryside in his poem Zhizn' Zvanskaia: 'Opriatno vse i predstavliaet Rus'' ('Everything is tidy and represents Rus''').
34   Ibid., 132.
35   Ibid., 135.
36   Ibid.

freemasonry and pietism, furthered the association of translation with progressive politics. The effects of freemasonry in Russia cannot be overestimated. 'Freemasonry did not signify a passing episode', states Florovsky, 'but rather a developmental stage in the history of modern Russian society. Toward the end of the 1770s freemasonry swept through nearly the entire educated class'.[37] The rapid spread of freemasonry throughout Russia's elite society in the late eighteenth century was accompanied by the translation of the literary works of progressive freemasons, including Oliver Goldsmith, which were widely read and translated in Russian literary circles.[38] These translations played a crucial role in the construction of a progressive intelligentsia in Russia, and many Russian freemasons of the time saw translation as service to society. One of the most influential freemasons of the late eighteenth century, Ivan P. Turgenev, translated extensively, producing translations of such influential works as John Mason's 'Treatise on Self-knowledge', Johann Arndt's 'True Christianity' and the anonymous German text 'Apology: In Defence of the Order of Freemasons'.

While the political agendas of these two movements were hardly radical, both of them involved the cultivation of mysticism, which offered a passive alternative to direct political action. As V. I. Novikov puts it, '[t]he individual was called upon to concentrate on the 'awakening of his inner christianity', not on "external affairs"'.[39] The Rosicrucian A. M. Kutuzov's translation of Edward Young's 'Complaint, or Night Thoughts' was read not as a political plan of action but rather as a spiritual primer, 'a guide for this newly awakened and sensitive generation'.[40] Nevertheless, these movements were progressive to the extent that they promoted the authority of the 'private' individual to think and act outside the confines of the Church and State. As Novikov notes, 'Masonry is an example of religiosity outside the church. On the one hand, it is a reaction to the spread of atheistic philosophy; on the other hand, it came into being because the church had lost

---

37 Georges Florovsky, *Ways of Russian Theology*; trans. R. Nichols (1979) <http://www.myriobiblos.gr/texts/english/florovsky_ways.html> accessed 2 July 2010.
38 Vatsuro and Virolainen, eds, *Zhukovskii i russkaia kul'tura*, 417 fn. 5.
39 V. I. Novikov, *Masonstvo i russkaia kul'tura* (Moscow: Iskusstvo, 1998), 27.
40 Florovsky, *Ways of Russian Theology*.

its role as a spiritual force, meekly reducing itself to service to the state'.⁴¹ Novikov goes on to claim that '[i]t was precisely in the depths of Russian freemasonry that the struggle of the individual against the despotism of the state was born'.⁴²

The political implications of the masons' work were not lost on Catherine II, who suspended the working of the lodges in 1794, although they continued to function in a clandestine fashion. The lodges were allowed officially to reopen under the more liberal Alexander I, but were suspended again in 1822, three years before the failed Decembrist Revolt. Even during the golden age of Russian masonry (1810–22), 'the lodges were under surveillance by the Special Office of the Ministry of Home Affairs'.⁴³ Among other things, freemasons translated progressive political writings by social and political activists in America such as Thomas Paine and Benjamin Franklin.

Zhukovskii was not a mason in name alone; he was deeply influenced by masonic beliefs. Among his closest friends were the Turgenev brothers, whose father, Ivan P. Turgenev, was the director of Moscow University and the leader of one of Moscow's most influential masonic lodges. Zhukovskii's affinity for masonic beliefs is suggested by repeated references to the masonic symbol of the 'star of hope' in his translations (although he made reference to the symbol only once in his original work).⁴⁴ While Zhukovskii's political views were more conservative than those of the Decembrists and for him the star of hope signalled the cult of friendship and the path to spiritual perfection, the symbol was radicalized in the works of other writers of the time, such as V. F. Raevskii, known as 'the first Decembrist'. In Raevskii's poetry, 'the metaphor of the Star of Hope also signifies freedom, but in the *Weltanschauung* of this poet [...] freedom is a fully developed philosophical and political theme of liberation, even revolution'.⁴⁵

41 Novikov, *Masonstvo i russkaia kul'tura*, 7.
42 Ibid., 21.
43 S. I. Smetanina, 'Brochure', in *Freemasonry in Russia: Early Sources from the Russian State Archives of Ancient Arts* (Moscow: IDC Publishers, undated).
44 Leighton, *The Esoteric Tradition in Russian Romantic Literature*, 40.
45 Ibid., 59.

The mysticism of Russian freemasonry fed into the pietist movement that overtook Russia under Alexander I. This led to the formation of the Russian Bible Society, which sponsored a new translation of the Slavonic Bible into contemporary Russian. By making the scriptures available to all literate people, the vernacular translation of the Bible, like freemasonry, challenged the authority of the Church and State: it placed biblical exegesis in the hands of laypeople. Freemasonry and pietism also led to the translation of many Western mystics, such as Jacob Boehme, Claude de Saint-Martin and John Mason.[46]

Pietism revolutionized Russian reading practices by empowering lay readers to interpret often heavily encoded texts on their own, outside the exegetical authority of the Church. It lent new authority to individuals, as readers, and heightened the visibility and authority of translations and translators. As with the masons, pietism's cultivation of an interior self and personal (interpretive) authority was seen as a political threat that led to the closing of the Russian Bible Society in 1826 following the failed Decembrist Revolt. As the arch-conservative Admiral Shishkov put it: 'this reading of the sacred books aims to destroy the true faith, disrupt the fatherland and produce strife and rebellion.'[47] Before closing, however, the Bible Society managed to translate and publish the first Russian vernacular Gospels in 1819, a complete Russian New Testament in 1821, and a Russian Psalter in 1822.[48] Incidentally, the Decembrist Murav'ev-Apostol would continue to translate the bible during his incarceration and exile – underscoring the idea of bible translation as an act of resistance in early nineteenth-century Russia.[49] By largely erasing the issue of class in his translation of Gray's 'Elegy', Zhukovskii presents a mystical meditation on death that applies to all humanity.

46 Florovsky, *Ways of Russian Theology*.
47 Ibid.
48 Mark Elliott, 'Translating the Russian Bible', *East–West Church and Ministry Report* 7 (Spring 1999), 7–97.
49 For more on this, see E. N. Tumanik, 'Perevod Biblii Dekabristom A. N. Murav'evym', *Gumanitarnye nauki v Sibiri* 2, 11–14 (2008).

Goldsmith's 'The Deserted Village'

While Gray's poem appears to anticipate the sharper class antagonism in England that erupted in the second half of the eighteenth century, Goldsmith's 'The Deserted Village' directly confronts the tragic effects on country life of the policy of land enclosure. 'The Deserted Village' was an especially popular work in the circle of I. P. Turgenev. Unlike Gray's elegy, it was read and translated by many of the members of the circle, and it is mentioned several times in the correspondence of Andrei Turgenev and Zhukovskii.[50] Zhukovskii produced his rather free translation of the poem in December of 1805 under the title 'Opustevsshaia derevnia'.[51] The most obvious intervention on the translator's part is in the length of the translation, which is almost thirty lines longer than the original. Other more subtle differences touch upon the politics of the poem.

Most tellingly, perhaps, the geography of the poem is altered. Goldsmith situates the poem squarely in England at a certain moment in its history:

> A time there was, ere England's griefs began
> When every rood of ground maintained its man;
> For him light labour spread her wholesome store,
> Just gave what life required, but gave no more:
> His best companions, innocence and health,
> And his best riches, ignorance of wealth.

England is not mentioned in Zhukovskii's translation and much of this stanza was omitted. Later, Zhukovskii does refer to Albion, a term not used in the original, but this obscures the specific historical moment in England's history in favour of an idealized, one could say, de-historicized, vision of England. In fact, Zhukovskii lightly 'russifies' Goldsmith's landscape by inserting *stepi* (steppes), *tundra* (tundra), and *dubravy* (oak forests). And

---

50 Turgenev, 'Pis'ma Andreia Turgeneva k Zhukovskomu', 417.
51 *Angliiskaia poeziia v perevodakh V. A. Zhukovskogo*, 75–81.

he replaces Goldsmith's 'dancing pair' with a Russian *khorovod*, a typical Slavic round dance.

In addition, Zhukovskii repeatedly tones down the politically-charged language of Goldsmith's original. Two references to tyrants – 'the tyrant's hand is seen' and 'the tyrant's power' – do not appear in his version, nor does Goldsmith's reference to the 'only master'. The effect of these choices become clear in the following stanza where Goldsmith lays blame for the destruction of the villages firmly on the shoulders of the landowners and government:

> Sweet smiling village, loveliest of the lawn,
> Thy sports are fled and all they charms withdrawn;
> Amidst thy bowers the *tyrant's hand* is seen,
> And desolation saddens all thy green:
> One only *master* grasps the whole domain,
> And half a tillage stints thy smiling plain.
>
> О родина моя, о сладость прежних лет!
> О нивы, о поля, добычи запустенья!
> О виды скорбные развалин, разрушенья!
> В пустыню обращен природы пышный сад!
> На тучных пажитях не вижу резвых стад!
> Уныдость на холмах! В окрестности молчанье![52]
>
> [O my homeland, o sweetness of years gone by!/O cornfields, o fields!/O sorrowful views of ruins and destruction!/A magnificent garden has been turned into a desert!/On the fertile pastures I see no playful flocks!/Dolefulness on the hillsides! Silence all around!]

In this passage, Zhukovskii thoroughly confuses the politics of land enclosure. The communal farmlands are described as a 'magnificent garden', thus attenuating any association with the communal lands farmed by peasants, which could hardly be described as 'magnificent'. Moreover, here and elsewhere in his translation, Zhukovskii inserts several fond mentions of sheep – 'flocks' ('stady'), a 'shepherd' ('pastukh'), and 'sheep's bells' ('ovech'ie

---

52 Ibid., 77.

zvony') – which also confuse the facts of the land enclosure policy that allowed landowners to seize peasant communal lands to use for the grazing of animals, mainly sheep. In England of the time sheep had come to symbolize the brutality of land enclosure, and Goldsmith makes no mention of them. As Slater puts it, 'Enclosure meant then, not the turning of waste lands into cultivated fields, but the conversion of the "fair fields full of folk," of Langland's phrase, into *desolate sheep walks*.'[53] In addition, Zhukovskii makes no mention of 'half a tillage', another reference to the replacement of farming with herding.

Zhukovskii does, however, include Goldsmith's reference to 'princes and lords', which becomes 'vel'mozhi i kniazi' (grandees/courtiers and princes), suggesting that the more overt references to tyranny might have been too daring for the Russian poet. A little later he includes a phrase that seems to refer to Goldsmith's verse line, 'One only master grasps the whole domain': 'Tam nyne khishchnikov vladychestvo odno' ("There is now but a single domain of plunderers'), but without some reference to 'masters', the verse loses its original class implications. Zhukovskii likewise makes no reference to 'the spoiler's hand' that destroyed the traditional way of life of the village; and he further obscures the issue of class by avoiding the word *krest'ianin* (peasant) in favour of the archaic and poetic-sounding *poselianin* and *sel'skii chelovek* (a country person). Goldsmith's 'a bold peasantry, their country's pride' is rendered by the more passive 'schast'e poselian' (the happiness of peasants).

By ignoring and attenuating the political thematics of the poem, Zhukovskii transforms Goldsmith's poem from an indictment of the 'tyrannical masters' who enclosed the lands to a first-person portrait of a young narrator 'wanderer' (*strannik, peshets uedinennyi*) who sought adventure in the world only to return to his native village to find it deserted. Goldsmith's phrase 'I still had hopes, for pride attends us still,/Around the swains to show my book-learned skill' is amplified and expanded in Zhukovskii's text: 'О гордость!.. Я мечтал, в сих хижинах забвенных,/ Слыть чудом посреди ораатев смиренных;/ За чарой, и огня, в кругу их толковать/

---

53 Slater, 'A Historical Outline of Land Ownership in England', lxix.

О том, что в долгий век мог слышать и видать.' (What pride! I had dreamed in these forgotten huts,/ To pass as a miracle among the humble orators;/With a drink and by the fire to explain/What over this long time I had heard and seen).[54]

As with his translation of Gray's 'Elegy', Zhukovskii's translation of Goldsmith's 'The Deserted Village' attenuates the politics of the original poem, especially the theme of class antagonism, by spiritualizing and de-historicizing it. Zhukovskii suggests a passive, mystical stance that tones down the simmering class resentments of the English poems. We see here, perhaps, the origins of an argument that would be made more explicitly by conservative Slavophiles in the second part of the nineteenth century, namely, that Russia never experienced the feudalism of the West and so avoided the profound class antagonisms that resulted in violence and revolution there. Kenneth Lantz paraphrases the views of one of Russia's leading Slavophiles, Konstantin Aksakov, in *The Dostoevsky Encyclopedia*: 'the Russian system of serfdom was more humane and morally superior to the feudalism of Western Europe' and the Russian people are 'essentially apolitical and, guided by Christ's statement that "my Kingdom is not of this world," they leave the management of this world to their absolute monarch.'[55]

Conclusion

This analysis of Zhukovskii's translation of two English poems that were very important in securing his reputation as a poet-translator and in introducing romantic forms and themes into Russian suggests the writer's deep ambivalence toward politics in general and to politics in poetry in particular.

---

54 *Angliiskaia poeziia v perevodakh V. A. Zhukovskogo*, 81.
55 Kenneth Lantz, *The Dostoevsky Encyclopedia* (Westport, CT: Greenwood Press, 2004), 8.

As G. M. Fridlender explains, the brutality of the French Revolution, the tyranny of Napoleon I, and a general disenchantment with enlightenment ideals 'led Zhukovskii (like Schiller) to lose his faith in the possibility of transforming individuals with a tap of a magic wand by bestowing political freedom. But having forever abandoned hope in the possibility of quick and radical transformations in his time, Zhukovskii, like Schiller, retained his faith in the possibility of transforming individuals "from the inside," by means of art'.[56]

This emphasis on transformation from the inside problematized the notion of political activism. Although a good friend of many of the Decembrists, Zhukovskii did not share their desire to introduce a 'civic poetry' into Russia that would inspire readers to political action. Not surprisingly, the metaphor that was often used by Zhukovskii's contemporaries to describe his translation practice was not one of activism, but rather of self-sacrifice. As A. N. Veselovskii put it, 'What is important for us is that Zhukovskii gave to the foreign not only everything he had, but also everything he was'.[57] The Soviet critic G. A. Gukovskii, however, interpreted Zhukovskii's turn from politics as a profound solipsism: 'Zhukovskii, having closed his eyes to the objective world, saw only his soul, his I, and this was for him the only reality'.[58] Whether a function of self-sacrifice or solipsism, Zhukovskii's focus on the life of the soul offered at best a spiritual solution to the political problems of his day.

---

56 G. M Fridlender, 'Spornye i ocherednye voprosy izucheniia Zhukovskogo' in *Zhukovskii i russkaia literatura* (Leningrad: Nauka, 1987), 5–31 (8).
57 Quoted in Zhukovskii, *Zarubezhnaia poeziia*, 10.
58 Quoted in Fridlender, 'Spornye i ocherednye voprosy izucheniia Zhukovskogo', 17.

NATALIA OLSHANSKAYA

Turgenev's Letters on Translation

By the second half of the nineteenth century, letters as an independent literary genre occupied an important place on the Russian literary scene. As in the European tradition, they not only became an important step in the development of the novelistic genre, but also acquired a growing role as political manifestos, pamphlets, proclamations, and mechanisms of literary and philosophical exchanges among Russian intellectuals.

In this respect, Turgenev's letters were not an exception. Covering more than fifty years from 1831 until his death in 1883, his surviving correspondence, including more than seven thousand published letters, reflects his views on many major political and cultural events of the nineteenth century. As a result of Turgenev's ties to many influential literary figures in Russia, France, England and Germany, his letters provide additional valuable information about little known facts concerning the cultural exchange between Russia and Western Europe, and in particular about the specific mechanisms of literary exchanges via translation.

The importance of Turgenev's correspondence was recognized already during his lifetime, when occasional, mostly unsuccessful attempts to publish several of his letters were made. Some letters appeared in print soon after his death, and in 1884 the first collection of 488 of his letters was published in Russia. This first publication seemed controversial to many of his friends and contemporaries. The editors of the volume were criticized for their selection of letters, for the breach of privacy and for inadequate editorial work.[1] Despite this criticism, it attracted several foreign

---

1   For a detailed discussion of the history of this publication and its reception see M. P. Alekseev, 'Pis'ma I. S. Turgeneva' in I. S. Turgenev, *Polnoe sobranie sochinenii i pisem*

publishers, and in 1886 was translated into German.² An attempt at collecting Turgenev's letters to French writers was undertaken several years later by Ely Halpérine-Kaminsky.³ Parts of this collection had appeared previously in several journal publications and were then translated into Russian and English. Several important studies devoted to Turgenev's correspondence with major German writers appeared in print in the first half of the twentieth century.⁴

By the middle of the twentieth century, most of the people who could have been personally affected by the publication of Turgenev's letters were dead and additional archival information was open for researchers. Most of his surviving letters appeared as part of the twenty-eight volumes of Turgenev's *Complete Works and Correspondence*.⁵ Thirteen volumes in this edition were devoted to his correspondence; they were later used by scholars who prepared annotated publications of selections from Turgenev's letters translated into English.⁶ Previously unknown letters continued to

---

v dvadtsati vos'mi tomakh. Pis'ma. Vol. 1 (Moscow and Leningrad: Nauka, 1961), 81–125.

2   I. S. Turgeniew, *Briefe. Erste Sammlung (1840–1883),* aus dem russischen übersetzt und mit biographischer Einleitung und Anmerkungen versehen von Dr. Heinrich Ruhe (Leipzig, 1886).

3   E. Halpérine-Kaminsky, *Ivan Tourguéneff d'après sa correspondence avec ses amis français* (Paris, 1901). See also *Pis'ma I. S. Turgeneva k Poline Viardo i ego frantsuzskim druziam,* izd. Gal'perinym-Kaminskim (Moscow, 1900) and *Tourguéneff and his French Circle,* ed. Ely Halpérine-Kaminsky, trans. Ethel M. Arnold (London, 1898).

4   Erich Petzet, 'Paul Heyse und Iwan Turgeniew', *Westermanns Monatshefte* (April 1924), 185–95; 'Turgeneff und Theodor Storm', *Ostdeutsche Monatshefte,* 10 (January 1923), 463–9. For a more detailed list of publications of Turgenev's letters in the first half of the twentieth century, see Iu. D. Levin, 'Noveishaia russkaia literatura o Turgeneve', *Russkaia literatura* 2 (1958), 203–4.

5   I. S. Turgenev, *Polnoe sobranie sochinenii i pisem v dvadtsati vos'mi tomakh. Pis'ma v trinadtsati tomakh* (Moscow and Leningrad: Nauka, 1961–8). All quotations from Turgenev's letters, unless otherwise stated, are from this edition with the date followed by the volume and page number. All translations are mine.

6   David Lowe was editor and translator of *Turgenev: Letters* (Ann Arbor: Ardis, 1983); A. V. Knowles was editor and translator of *Turgenev's Letters* (New York: Charles Scribner's Sons, 1983); and Barbara Beaumont was editor and translator of *Flaubert*

appear in the second half of the twentieth century,[7] although the interest in Turgenev's correspondence seems to have dwindled since 2000.[8]

Written in four languages, Russian, French, German and English, Turgenev's letters deal with arrangements and business negotiations with writers, publishers and translators, they show his efforts in promoting the translation of literary works by new or well-established writers, and they often contain advice to writers and translators about the quality of their work. Directly or indirectly his correspondence reflects attitudes towards the art of translation and the accepted criteria for evaluating translated literary work in Russia and in Western Europe. In one of his essays, which he describes as 'an autobiographical fragment', Turgenev speaks about his loyalty to Western ideas: 'I never admitted the existence of that impregnable line which some solicitous and even zealous, though ignorant, patriots are so anxious to draw between Russia and Western Europe, that Europe to which we are so closely bound by race, language and creed.'[9] Turgenev's letters are an important reminder of the writer's ceaseless efforts to cross this line and to make it less visible through promoting literary exchanges via translation. Viewed in a broad cultural context, they not only emphasize the attempts of the nineteenth-century Russian elite to promote an

---

    and Turgenev: A Friendship in Letters. The Complete Correspondence (New York: Norton, 1985).

7   See, for example, the two-volume French collection Ivan Tourguénev, *Nouvelle correspondence inédite*, introduction et notes par Alexandre Zviguilsky (Paris, 1971); and *Lettres inédites de Tourguénev à Pauline Viardot et à sa famille*, publiées et annotées par Henri Granjard et Alexandre Zviguilsky (Lausanne, 1972). For a detailed list of the publications from the 1970s, see P. R. Zaborov, 'Iz novonaidennykh pisem Turgeneva k frantsuzskim korrespondentam', in *Turgenev i ego sovremenniki* (Leningrad: Nauka, 1977), 5–24.

8   See Joe Andrew, 'Introduction: Turgenev and Russian Culture' in Joe Andrew, Derek Offord and Robert Reid, eds, *Turgenev and Russian Culture: Essays to Honour Richard Peace* (Amsterdam: Rodopi, 2008), 7–8.

9   Turgenev, 'Instead of an Introduction' in *Turgenev's Literary Reminiscences and Autobiographical Fragments*, trans. David Magarshack (London: Faber and Faber, 1957), 93–4.

all-inclusive cultural model for Russia but they also reflect a more nuanced understanding of the European response to Russian literature. Registering Turgenev's opinion of various major contemporary literary events, his letters serve as convincing evidence of close ties between literary translation and Russian efforts at cultural self-definition in the second half of the nineteenth century. These efforts were obviously important at a time when translated Russian literature was just beginning to gain popularity in Western Europe, breaking through the barriers of a general lack of interest in literature in translation. This is how Turgenev describes the attitude of the French to translated literature in a letter to a friend, the writer Mikhail Avdeev:

> Translations from foreign languages are not popular with publishers in Paris because they do not sell. Not even Dickens's novels have seen second editions (and we cannot be compared with him), meanwhile *Monsieur, Madame et Bébé* by G[ustave] Droz has seen twenty. My books have been translated, but I personally never got any money out of it, while the translator, as a special favour, occasionally received 300 or 400 francs. [...] (N. B. Even *Fumée* (*Smoke*), my most successful novel in terms of sales in Paris, did not make me any money.)[10]

Turgenev's comments make it clear that the majority of the French general public preferred popular French literature to translated novels, and publishers were disinclined to undertake the unprofitable enterprise of publishing translations. Neither the authors nor the translators were properly remunerated, and consequently undertaking a translation was either a charitable act or the leisurely occupation of untrained and often unskilful amateurs. This often impeded the quality of translations, creating a new obstacle for Russian literature on its way to the French readers. Originating in Moscow and St Petersburg salons, translations were often done by Russians whose French was inadequate. Turgenev writes to Avdeev:

---

10 18 April 1868. *Pis'ma*, 7: 130–1.

Your novels were translated by a Russian (I know Madame Chekunova), and they are probably written in this Moscow French language which the French find absolutely deplorable. Everything will have to be re-written, if it is the case, since we Russians have no idea of what purists the French are.[11]

The usual poor quality of translations from Russian into French is mentioned in Turgenev's letters on more than one occasion. According to his personal experience, both Russian and French translators were equally responsible for results of poor quality. This is how he describes the French translation of *Zapiski okhotnika* (*A Hunter's Diaries*) in his letter to his personal friend, the well known writer Sergei Aksakov:

> I have finally received the French translation of *Zapiski*, and I wish I had never seen it! This Mr Charrière has made God knows what out of me; he has added whole pages, invented things, thrown away some parts, it is unbelievable. Here is a sample of his style: for example, I write 'I fled', and he translates these two words with the following: 'I fled in a mad rush, alarmed, my hair standing on end, as if I had on my heels a whole legion of vipers commanded by a sorcerer'. And everything is like that. What a shameless Frenchman! Now thanks to him, I have been turned into a clown.[12]

Similar techniques were often practiced by German and English translators of Turgenev's works. In his letter to the Austrian poet, journalist and publicist Moritz Hartmann, Turgenev complains about a 'pathetic translation' of his novel into German, and requests Hartmann's advice on the possibility of publishing his letter of protest against this translation: 'Whole pages have been crossed out by the translator. The novel has undergone a thorough cleansing of everything that is not vulgar or obviously banal'. 'I have not had much luck with my works in Germany', he concludes.[13] He also wrote a protest to the publisher of the *Pall Mall Gazette* against the poor quality of the English translation of his novel *Dym* (*Smoke*).[14]

Meanwhile, Turgenev was well aware that no legal action could ever be brought against those who published poor translations without the writer's

11   Ibid.
12   7 August 1854. *Pis'ma*, 2: 224–5.
13   27 May 1868. *Pis'ma*, 7: 141.
14   1 December 1868. *Pis'ma*, 7: 246–7.

permission since there was no legal agreement between Russia and Germany or England about the protection of the author's rights. In 1868, he writes to the editor Julius Rodenberg: 'Unfortunately, I cannot assign to you the ownership rights since they do not exist: there is no convention between Germany and Russia, and anyone can translate anything and then publish it'.[15] And even though an agreement did exist between Russia and France, it could be, and often was, violated. 'The convention between France and Russia is so craftily written that anyone has the right to translate, abridge, or in any other way mutilate any work he chooses. Consequently, you should not even try to sue anyone, you must succumb to your Fate', writes Turgenev to the young Russian writer Adelaida Lukanina whose story 'The Hen-House Keeper' was poorly translated and then appeared in the French journal *Réforme* without her permission. He suggests that Lukanina contacts the journal and offers to translate or 'authorize' the translation of her stories, 'for any journal will prefer a translation by the author'.[16]

Translations into German and English were usually done from French, which also had an impact on the quality of the re-translated versions. It was standard practice for the German and English translations of Russian literature to appear after the French versions, and it was no secret that in most cases French translations were used as the source text, instead of the Russian original. Turgenev understood well the inevitability of this widespread practice, and in his letter to Rodenberg, who represented the editorial board of the journal *Salon* interested in publishing Turgenev's works in German, he recommends some titles with detailed references to their translations into French. He writes:

> I willingly accept the offer from the editorial board of the *Salon*, and could suggest several of my shorter works, such as 'The Jew' (*Le Juif*, which appeared in the *Revue nationale*), or 'The Brigadier' (translated in the *Journal des débates*) or 'Asia' (a longer novella, published under the title of *Annouchka* in the *Revue des deux mondes*).[17]

---

15 23 December 1868. Ibid., 255–6.
16 31 July 1880. *Pis'ma*, 12 (2): 294.
17 23 December 1868. *Pis'ma*, 7: 255–6.

In another letter, Turgenev asks the German writer Ludwig Pietsch to rework the poor German translation of *Fathers and Sons* for a publication in Riga, and to compare the existing inadequate German version to the 'impeccable' French translation on which it had been based.[18]

The omission of potentially 'boring' parts from the original and the introduction of 'exciting' new details into the target texts were practiced by many translators in their efforts to adjust translated Russian literature to the tastes of the receiving culture, or rather to the expectations of the mass readership. These efforts, disappointing as they were for the authors, were perhaps in part justifiable, since translators had to consider differences in literary traditions, in publishing practices and in literary tastes even within Western Europe. For example, William Ralston described Turgenev's sketch 'Son' (*The Dream*) as unfit for an English translation, although this story, referred to by Turgenev as 'a psychological riddle', had already appeared in France in the *Temps*.[19]

It is difficult to overestimate Turgenev's personal role in promoting Russian literature in Europe. His correspondence with the literary critic Ralston, one of the few pioneers in the translation of Russian literature into English, is a good example of his efforts. Many of the forty-four surviving letters to Ralston contain recommendations on what to translate, Turgenev's opinion on contemporary Russian writers and his praise of Ralston's activities in introducing Russian literature in England. From early on, Turgenev supported Ralston's idea to translate Ivan Krylov's fables into English. He writes:

> Your idea of translating Krylov is wonderful: he is certainly one of the most original of our writers, and the only one whose works do not lose their brilliance if placed next to Lafontaine's. He possesses a mischievous good nature and an absolutely remarkable sense of correct and honest judgment. It is Russian humour at its best.[20]

---

18 15 January 1869. Ibid., 273–4.
19 22 January 1877. Ibid., 62–3.
20 8 October 1868. Ibid., 218–19.

A year later, on receiving a copy of Krylov's fables translated by Ralston, Turgenev praised the excellent quality of the volume and suggested sending it to a friend in St Petersburg, 'so he could review it for *Vestnik Evropy*'.[21]

Turgenev applauds Ralston's intentions to spread the knowledge of Russian literature in England and then suggests that 'in addition to Gogol', the works of Count Lev Tolstoi, Ostrovskii, Pisemskii and Goncharov could be of interest since they show a new approach to understanding and creating literature'.[22] This letter is typical of Turgenev's efforts to broaden the knowledge of Europeans concerning Russian literature by spreading the word about those of his contemporaries who were, in his opinion, the most talented;[23] above all, he wrote about Tolstoi, who was then little known outside Russia.

Turgenev became instrumental in promoting Tolstoi's works in Western Europe after their first meeting in 1855. Forty-two of Turgenev's letters to Tolstoi have survived, and several of them discuss directly the translation of Tolstoi's works into European languages. One of these letters, written in very formal French during the years of the estrangement between the two writers that followed their quarrel in 1861, discusses the French translations of Tolstoi's works:

> Upon receipt of this letter, we kindly request Count L. N. Tolstoi to inform Pavel Vasilievich Zhukovskii about it, at 11 Place Pigalle, Paris. Mr Charles Rollinat has already finished 'The Raid' (*Nabeg*) and 'Three Deaths' (*Tri smerti*). His translations are being revised by I. S. Turgenev. Mr Viardot and Mr Turgenev will translate *The Cossacks* (*Kazaki*) this summer. By winter, these four novels will be published as a separate book in Paris by Hetzel.[24]

---

21 3 February 1869. Ibid., 289.
22 7 October 1866. *Pis'ma*, 6: 111–14.
23 Turgenev's efforts to make Russian literature known in France also caused some unfortunate misunderstandings. According to Turgenev, he was accused by Ivan Goncharov of passing ideas from the latter's *Oblomov* (1859) and *Obryv (The Precipice)* (1869) to French writers who then allegedly imitated Goncharov's novels, thus preventing them from being translated into French. See Turgenev's letter to P. Annenkov (12 June 1874. *Pis'ma*, 10: 250). Indeed, Goncharov not only accused Turgenev of plagiarism, but also held him responsible for passing on his ideas to Auerbach and Flaubert.
24 29 January 1875. *Pis'ma*, 11: 27.

After 1878, when Tolstoi apologized to Turgenev for his role in their years of hostilities, they renewed a friendly correspondence, and the exchange of ideas grew much more open.[25] In an 1878 letter to Tolstoi, Turgenev praises *The Cossacks*, and informs Tolstoi about the appearance of the English and the French translations expressing regret that his intention to translate this work into French had not materialized.[26] Later, Turgenev criticized the English translation by Eugene Schuyler which came out in London and New York that year, as 'wry and matter of fact'.[27] Turgenev also expresses his mistrust of the quality of the French translation by Baroness Y. I. Mengden: 'I haven't seen the French translation, but I am afraid that it will not be very good, since I know how our Russian ladies translate novels'. In a letter to Flaubert he recommends Tolstoi's *War and Peace* highly, but again doubts the ability of the female translator:

> I will soon send to you the three volumes of the novel by Count Lev Tolstoi, whom I consider to be the best contemporary writer. [...] Unfortunately the translation is by a Russian lady, and I usually do not trust these lady translators, especially when they approach writers as powerful as Tolstoi.[28]

Yet it was the quality of the work, rather than the gender of the translator, that mattered more to Turgenev, many of whose letters contain similarly harsh critical remarks about translations by men. It is also a well-known fact

---

25 Edmund Wilson comments on the striking stylistic difference between the formal letters written in French or German and the expressiveness and openness of letters written in Russian: 'We are struck by the piquant contrast between these two faces of Turgenev when we compare his letters to foreigners – rather formal, in perfect taste, always respectful to the recipient and his country – with the letters to his Russian friends'. Edmund Wilson, 'Turgenev and the Life-Giving Drop' in *Turgenev's Literary Reminiscences*, 9–59 (41).
26 1 October 1878. *Pis'ma*, 12 (1): 361–2.
27 15 November 1878. Ibid., 383.
28 15 December 1879. *Pis'ma*, 12 (2): 193. Indeed, when Turgenev later received ten copies of the French version of *War and Peace* from its translator Princess Irina Ivanovna Paskevich, he reiterated his initial opinion of its inadequate quality in a letter to Tolstoi. 29 December 1879. Ibid., 197.

that Turgenev was very active in promoting the careers of several talented young women writers and translators.

Turgenev's letters provide evidence of his role in promoting translated Russian literature in Western Europe among the influential writers, critics and publishers in his circle. He describes in a letter to Tolstoi, for example, his activities in popularizing *War and Peace* in France:

> Princess P[askevich], who translated your *War and Peace*, has finally delivered here five hundred copies, out of which I got ten. I have distributed them among the most influential writers including Taine, About and some others. I hope that they will appreciate the power and beauty of your epic. The translation does not do it justice, but it was done with love and care. With a sense of great pleasure, I have recently re-read for the fifth or sixth time this truly great work of yours. Its whole structure is far from what the French would normally appreciate or expect from their books, but in the end, the truth always wins. I hope for a steady, albeit slow conquest, if not for an immediate brilliant victory.[29]

As usual, Turgenev was active in promoting Tolstoi's work, once it arrived. One of the ten copies was sent to Anatole France, whom Turgenev had known since the 1870s. Turgenev also asks France to review Tolstoi's epic for the readers of the journal *Temps*. Other copies were sent to Alphonse Daudet, Emile Zola and, of course, to Gustave Flaubert.[30] Turgenev also wrote an 'open' letter to the editor of the French newspaper *Le XIXe siècle* suggesting that French readers could benefit from a different translation. The letter was published on 23 December 1880.[31] In another letter to Tolstoi, Turgenev again describes the translation as 'colourless' and adds: 'I delivered your *War and Peace* to all the major critics. There has not been an article

---

29 29 December 1879. Ibid., 197.
30 Flaubert, with whom Turgenev exchanged several letters on Tolstoi's novels, liked *War and Peace* and agreed that Tolstoi was a brilliant writer and a great psychologist, although he found certain chapters in the novel's third part to be repetitive and overburdened with too much philosophy: 'One can see too much of a man and of a Russian, while before it was just Nature and Humanity in front of us. At times, he reminds me of Shakespeare'. Turgenev later copied for Tolstoi excerpts from Flaubert's letter, 12 January 1880. *Pis'ma*, 12 (2): 205–6.
31 *Pis'ma*, 12(2): 523.

devoted to it yet, but four hundred copies have already been sold (out of the five hundred received)'.[32]

An enthusiastic supporter of Aleksandr Ostrovskii, Turgenev was instrumental in the appearance of the first French translation of Ostrovskii's play *Groza* (*The Storm*), as well as the first article about Ostrovskii's plays in England. In one of his letters to the Russian playwright, Turgenev characterizes the translator, French writer Emile Durand, as someone 'who is reasonably fluent in Russian'.[33] He continues:

> He does various translations, and I have recommended your plays to him, starting with *The Storm*, as it seems to be most accessible and understandable for the French. He subsequently translated it, and fairly well, I must say. We then carefully proofread it together and corrected all the mistakes. With your permission, we will definitely publish it this winter and even try to get it staged in one of the best theatres in Paris.[34]

A similar strategy was used to advertise the translation of works by lesser known writers. Occasionally, in his support of young writers, Turgenev would even volunteer to translate their works, realizing that the appearance of his name as translator was already a significant sign of the high quality of the original and could bring weight to the publication. For example, when addressing the French publisher and writer Pierre Jules Hetzel, who published almost all of Turgenev's works translated into French after 1862, Turgenev mentions one of his recent protégées Adelaida Lukanina, whose stories had appeared in the *Vestnik Evropy* (*Messenger of Europe*), and offers to translate one of them for Hetzel since 'it is only fifty pages'.[35] Turgenev first met Lukanina in Paris in 1877, subsequently helping

---

[32] 12 January 1880. *Pis'ma*, 12(2): 205–6.
[33] In a letter to Dostoevskii, Emile Durand, who had received a commission from the editor of the *Revue des deux mondes* to write a biographical and literary-critical study of famous Russian writers, is described by Turgenev as 'a well-known writer and expert on the Russian language', 'a person of highest integrity, education, and intelligence'. Turgenev requests Dostoevskii to assist Durand in gathering relevant information during his trip to Russia. (28 March 1877. *Pis'ma*, 12 (1): 129).
[34] 6 June 1874. *Pis'ma*, 10: 246.
[35] 19 December 1878. *Pis'ma*, 12(1): 406.

to further her literary career. Ten years later, she published her reminiscences of Turgenev, and also translated into French his semi-autobiographical story 'A Fire at Sea'.[36]

Another strategy Turgenev often employed was to approach better-known French experts in Russian literature with requests to translate works of promising young Russian writers. In his letter to Durand, Turgenev asks him to translate Vsevolod Garshin's story 'Night' (*Noch'*) for the *Revue politique et littéraire*. Recommending Garshin as a young writer, whose 'talent shows great promise', Turgenev offers his help in proofreading the translation: 'If you think it necessary to show me your translation before submitting it to Mr Yung, I am at your complete disposal'.[37]

Turgenev's efforts to advance the careers of talented young writers through translation often went hand in hand with his promotion of less popular national literatures. When in 1859, a minor Ukrainian writer Varvara Kartashevskaia introduced him to a group of Ukrainian intellectuals in Paris, Turgenev developed personal ties with them and expressed sincere interest in their work. He volunteered to translate into Russian a novella *Institutka* by Mar'ia Markovich, which appeared in 1860.[38] He also recommended this young Ukrainian writer to several of his friends, writers and publishers, including Hetzel who later published several translations of her stories, including 'Maroussia', which appeared in 1878.[39] At the time, Markovich's works were already gaining popularity in Ukraine under the pen name of Marko Vovchok, and, soon after, she became one of the most influential Ukrainian writers and translators of the time. Turgenev's correspondence with Markovich is represented by more than forty letters, which, in addition to personal information,

---

36   There are several English translations of the story, including one by Oscar Wilde.
37   12 August 1882. *Pis'ma*, 13(1): 318.
38   For more information on Turgenev's activity as translator, see Nicolas Zekulin, 'Turgenev as Translator', *Canadian Slavonic Papers* 50 (1–2), (2008), 155–76.
39   Hetzel sent a copy of the translated story with Turgenev's preface to it. See Turgenev's letter from Paris (19 December 1878. *Pis'ma*, 12 (1): 406).

contain his questions about and comments on the life and work of several prominent Ukrainian writers.[40]

As can be seen from the letters quoted above, many of Turgenev's letters stress the importance of faithfulness to the source text and the stylistic adequacy of the target text as criteria for evaluating translation. He also mentions translators' linguistic and cultural competencies as important factors in improving the attitude toward translated literature in Europe. His personal attempts at securing qualified translators for his own works became a significant factor in changing the accepted standards for the translation of Russian literature.

In 1869, in a letter to the Russian bibliographer Vasil'ev and at his request, Turgenev compiled a list of all the translations of his works.[41] The list included all the translations of which Turgenev was aware, irrespective of their quality and his personal opinion about them, and it is obvious that he was fortunate to have attracted some first-class translators. One of these was the French writer, literary critic and a successful translator of Nekrasov, Ostrovskii, Pisemskii and Tolstoi, Hippolyte Delaveau, who had already translated Turgenev's stories into French in the late 1850s. After spending several years in Russia, Delaveau became instrumental in introducing Russian literature to the French and Turgenev worked with him to this end. In 1856, in a letter to his friend, the Russian writer Vasilii Botkin,[42] Turgenev mentions that his story 'Faust', translated by Delaveau, appeared in the December issue of the *Revue des deux mondes* and was well received by critics.[43] A year later, Delaveau published an article on Aksakov's *Chronicle* in the *Revue des deux mondes*, for which Turgenev 'helped him

---

40   For example, see his letter to Markovich from Spasskoie, in which Turgenev characterizes Taras Shevchenko as 'a great poet' and also praises the new Ukrainian journal *The Fundamentals* (22 May 1861. *Pis'ma*, 4: 245). Turgenev's relationship with Markovich is also discussed by Leon Burnett in this volume.
41   23 June 1869. *Pis'ma*, 8: 55.
42   A separate volume of the correspondence between Botkin and Turgenev came out in the Soviet Union in 1930: N. A. Brodskii, *V. P. Botkin i I. S. Turgenev. Neizdannaia perepiska 1851–1869* (Moscow and Leningrad: Akademia, 1930).
43   25 November 1856. *Pis'ma*, 3: 45–8.

by explaining certain things'. Turgenev also praised Delaveau's knowledge of Russian in a letter to Aksakov.[44]

In later years, when he was already an established writer and well known in Western Europe, Turgenev could rely on his vast circle of friends, prominent writers and literary critics to translate his works or at least to edit the existing translations. Prosper Mérimée, who began writing about Russian literature as early as 1852 and was also one of the first translators from Russian into French, wrote a foreword to the French translation of Turgenev's *Fathers and Sons* (1863), edited the French version of *Smoke* (1868), and translated several of Turgenev's stories ('The Jew', 'Petushkov', 'The Dog', 'Phantoms'), which were published in 1869 as part of the collection *Nouvelles moscovites*.

In several letters, Turgenev comments on his generally positive experience with the translation and publication of his works in Germany, where he made the personal acquaintance of many intellectuals. Friedrich Bodenstedt, a German poet and a true expert in Russian language and culture, was responsible for several successful translations of Turgenev's stories, including 'Mumu', 'Iakov Pasynkov', 'Faust', 'A Trip to the Forest Belt' and 'First Love'. In 1864–5, he published *Erzählungen von Iwan Turgenew*, a two-volume edition of Turgenev's stories in German. In several of his letters to Bodenstedt, Turgenev praises the translator for his excellent knowledge of Russian and for his perfect style. Realizing that 'publishers have not been at all well disposed towards anything Russian', Turgenev suggests paying Bodenstedt for his work out of his own pocket, asking him to do some more translations. Turgenev reiterates his appreciation of Bodenstedt's work and the importance of being published and read in Germany.[45] In the 1860s, while in Baden-Baden, he became close to Ludwig Pietsch, a talented man-of-letters and a devoted friend, who edited many German translations of Turgenev's works, especially those by Bodenstedt.

Another positive German experience, according to Turgenev, was connected with the translations by the Austrian poet Moritz Hartmann, a man

---

44   27 December 1856. Ibid., 68.
45   25 October 1862. *Pis'ma*, 5: 65–6.

with numerous links to Russia. Hartmann translated many of Turgenev's works, including *Smoke*, 'Mumu' and 'Three Meetings', and was highly praised by Turgenev. He describes Hartmann's translation as 'graceful, beautiful, and fluid', and exclaimed of one, '[i]t is a masterpiece! You have made my work sound twenty times better'.[46]

And yet, even these generally favourable impressions of his German translators were not without an occasional disappointment. In a letter to his friend Heinrich Julian Schmidt, Turgenev mentions 'an unfortunate misunderstanding' in Claire von Glümer's translation of his 'First Love', where the old countess was changed into a young one by the translator, 'thus turning the whole story upside down. Of course, it is a minor flaw, but these flaws are still quite painful and hurtful to the poor author'.[47]

In England, in 1868, Ralston was working on the translation of *Dvorianskoe gnezdo* (*A Gentleman's Nest*). His careful approach to every single detail in the text can be traced through Turgenev's responses to Ralston's questions in several letters from 1868. Turgenev explains his use of literary allusions (Obermann, Phryne, Laïs), and the names of cultural *realia* ('triu-triu'), and he even suggests a minor change in the narrative, with regard to the original:

> May I ask you to accept one minor correction which I have introduced into *Nichée de gentilshommes*? In the scene of the last encounter of Lavretzkii and Lisa, he asks for her handkerchief. She answers: 'Take it', and drops it on his lap. I think it would be better if she allowed him to take it without saying anything. I do not have a copy of my works here, but tomorrow or the day after I'll be in Baden-Baden and shall send you this small correction, or rather omission, in Russian.[48]

Ralston suggested changing the title of the English version to *Liza*, for which he received the author's approval. 'I find the title *Liza* very appropriate, the more so that the name *Dvorianskoe gnezdo*, which is not really accurate, was chosen not by me but by my publisher'.[49] The unquestionable

---

46 27 May 1886. *Pis'ma*, 7: 141.
47 6 May 1873. *Pis'ma*, 10: 95–6.
48 19 November 1868. *Pis'ma*, 7: 246–7.
49 26 November 1868. Ibid., 250.

expertise of the translator, supported by his constant close collaboration with the author brought about very good results, and yet even Ralston's high-quality work had a hard time to find a publisher. Several years later, Turgenev wrote to Ralston: 'I very much regret that so far you have been unable to find a publisher for your translation of *Dvorianskoe gnezdo*. It would pain me to think that all your time and effort have been wasted'.[50]

A general lack of British interest in Russian literature has often been attributed to strained political relations between Britain and Russia at the time.[51] By 1886, due to a noticeable increase in the interest in Russian literature in Britain, the attitude of publishers started to change and Turgenev soon became the most frequently translated Russian writer.[52]

The nineteenth century has been referred to as the golden age of Russian translation.[53] Translation was considered by many to be equal in its creativity to original writing, and it was viewed as an important tool for perfecting a writer's style; the most prominent poets and prose writers tried their hand at translation. Taking liberties with the source text was not uncommon; it was, however, something which Turgenev criticized and argued against. Towards the second half of the nineteenth century, and

---

50   3 February 1869. Ibid., 289. For more on Ralston's translation, see Augusta L. Tove, '*Dvorianskoe gnezdo*: Pervyi angliiskii perevod', in *Turgenevskii sbornik*, vol. 2 (Moscow: Nauka, 1966), 133–43.

51   A very different reaction to translated Russian literature has been observed in America. As Gettmann notes, in the 1870s there were at least three times as many American as British translations published. *Dmitrii Roudine*, *Fathers and Sons*, and *Smoke* appeared in New York at least a decade before they came out in London. The quality of translations was also generally superior, often followed by very positive reviews in the press. See Royal A. Gettman, *Turgenev in England and America* (Urbana: University of Illinois Press, 1941).

52   On the translation and reception of Turgenev in England at the time, see May, 13–27, and Richard Freeborn, 'Turgenev' in Olive Classe, ed., *Encyclopedia of Literary Translation into English* (London: Fitzroy Dearborn, 2000), vol. 2, 1429–33.

53   See V. N. Komissarov, 'The Russian Tradition', in Mona Baker, ed., *Routledge Encyclopedia of Translation Studies* (London: Routledge, 1998), 544.

perhaps in part due to Turgenev's influence, free translations were gradually replaced by versions more faithful to the original.[54]

According to Turgenev, there was more interest in translated literature in Russia than in Western Europe, and, as a result, much more willingness on the part of Russian publishers to fund translations from French, German and English.[55] Translators and European writers were generously remunerated, especially if their works first appeared in Russian translations before the publication of the original. This practice was introduced, at Turgenev's suggestion, by Mikhail Stasiulevich, the editor of the journal *Vestnik Evropy*. Thus, prior to its publication in France, the Russian version of Zola's *La Curée* appeared in 1874 under the title *Dobycha, broshennaia sobakam* (*The Spoils Thrown to the Dogs*), with many parts censored on moral grounds. Informing Zola about the publication of *La Curée*, Turgenev mentioned that Stasiulevich hesitated to order a translation of Zola's *Conquête de Plassans* (*The Conquest of Plassans*) without an assurance that the translation would come out before the original publication in France. Turgenev also explained the financial terms suggested by the editor, according to which the author and the translator were each offered thirty roubles (105 francs) per sheet, a reasonable amount of money from Turgenev's point of view,[56] and definitely much more generous than what European publishers were willing to pay.

The translation and promotion of his works in Russia carried a very important financial incentive for Flaubert. When in 1873 Turgenev came up with the idea of publishing the translation of Flaubert's *La Tentation de Saint Antoine* (*The Temptation of Saint Anthony*) in *Vestnik Evropy*, he negotiated the price of 125 francs per sheet for its author and also stressed the importance of finding a qualified translator: 'Please let the translator be of the first rank. Flaubert's style is as if chiselled in marble. Let us

---

54   For more information on the subject, see Iurii Levin, *Russkie perevodchiki XIX veka i razvitie khudozhestvennogo perevoda* (Leningrad: Nauka, 1985); Maurice Friedberg, *Literary Translation in Russia: A Cultural History* (University Park: Pennsylvania State University Press, 1997), 36–67.
55   For example, see his previously quoted letter to Mikhail Avdeev (*Pis'ma*, 7: 130–1).
56   5 June 1874. *Pis'ma*, 10: 243.

Russians honour it'.[57] More than once, potential problems with censorship come up in Turgenev's negotiations,[58] and the plan for the Russian translation was finally abandoned, followed by the similarly unsuccessful attempts on Turgenev's part to have it translated into German.[59] Later, to make Flaubert known in Russia and also to improve Flaubert's financial situation, Turgenev translated 'Hérodias' and 'La Légende de Saint Julien l'Hospitalier'. To Flaubert's disappointment, it took Turgenev much longer to translate these stories than he initially had promised. They appeared in the *Vestnik Evropy* in the spring of 1877 with Turgenev's preface in the form of a letter to the editor. Turgenev refused payment for these translations asking for the fee to go directly to the author. Several of his letters written to Flaubert and Stasiulevich between 1876 and 1877 describe the negotiations between the author, the translator and the editor.[60]

Turgenev also arranged to have the then unknown Maupassant translated into Russian, and several of Maupassant's works appeared in leading Russian literary journals. He wrote to Maupassant: 'Your name is causing quite a stir in Russia, and they are translating everything translatable; I've brought back with me a long, very well-written complimentary article about you published by *Golos (The Voice)*'.[61] A year after the success of the Russian version of *La Maison Tellier*, Turgenev tried to convince Stasiulevich to buy Maupassant's *Une Vie* for translation and publication in *Vestnik Evropy*. Turgenev assured the editor that he had read the manuscript and stated 'it is not at all improper, unlike several of his other works', an important comment considering the censorial practices then current in Russia and Stasiulevich's previous unfortunate experiences with publishing Zola in Russian. Turgenev then added: 'I know I have earned the reputation of

---

57 19 January 1874. Ibid., 190.
58 25 January 1874 and 27 January 1874. Ibid., 192, 194.
59 21 March 1874. Ibid., 216–17.
60 For more information on these translations which became 'a bone of contention between the two writers', see Beaumont, *Flaubert and Turgenev*, 8–11.
61 26 September 1881. *Pis'ma*, 13 (1): 121. According to Knowles, the article – by G. A. Laroche – appeared in the *Novaia gazeta* (*The New Newspaper*), not in the *Voice*. Knowles, *Turgenev's Letters*, 272.

being too kind as a critic, but either I understand nothing about such matters, or Maupassant's book is really remarkable and absolutely first-class'.[62]

Turgenev's literary preferences, but also his personal biases, come through not only in his recommendations as to which works by French writers to publish but also in his choices of the works he would potentially agree to translate. For example, when approached by the Russian poet and translator Petr Veinberg with a request to translate Balzac's works for a journal of translations of the best writers outside Russia, Turgenev explains that he is not in a position to promise any translations because he has to finish his own work, but even if he had time, he would 'prefer to do a few pages of Maupassant or Rabelais, and certainly not Balzac'. He finds Balzac 'disagreeable and foreign' to his tastes.[63] At the same time, he was tireless in promoting works that could develop the taste of Russian readers and the skills of Russian writers as translators. In his letter to the Russian poet Nikolai Nekrasov, the editor of the literary journal *Sovremennik* (*The Contemporary*), where many of Turgenev's own works were published, he suggests that Nekrasov translate Robert Burns, promising to select the best of Burns for him. He quotes Burns's '*To a Mountain Daisy*' in Ivan Kozlov's translation, and comments on Burns's 'favourite metre' as 'suitable for elegiac and pensive subjects'. He assures Nekrasov that he 'will enjoy Burns and will derive immense pleasure from translating him'.[64]

In conclusion, it may be stated that the second half of the nineteenth century witnessed the emergence of a new canon of translated Russian literature in Europe, and Turgenev was instrumental in shaping it. His deep knowledge of European culture and his personal understanding of the importance of the adjustment of translations to the literary norms and to the conventional forms and themes of the receiving cultures shaped future patterns of selecting texts for translation. Crossing the gap between the elite foreign literature and the demands of the popular audiences in the receiving cultures was based on finding a balance between communicating

62 12 November 1882. *Pis'ma*, 13 (2): 99–100.
63 3 November 1882. Ibid., 76.
64 10 July 1855. *Pis'ma*, 2: 295–7.

information about foreign cultures directly and preserving the aesthetic integrity of the literary source text. A clearer concept began to emerge concerning translation and its function in communicating the foreignness of the text while adapting it to the norms of the receiving culture. The appropriation of foreign literature through translation was soon to become an important component in cultural politics both in Western Europe and in Russia.

Turgenev's letters show how over fifty years his activities were of vital importance for changing attitudes towards literary translation. His thought-provoking critical analyses of the work of European translators as well as his insistence on loyalty to the source text and on the equivalence of literary styles in the original and the translation stressed the aesthetic aspect of Russian literature. His correspondence shows how his attempts to address the legal and aesthetic aspects of translation practices contributed to raising the prestige of translators' work and the art of translation in Europe to a new level. His selectivity in recommending works for translation, his own translations and his constructive criticism of other translators' work helped to bring about a balance between free translation and a strong re-emerging tendency towards extreme literalism in Russia.

LEON BURNETT

Turgenev and the Translation of the Quixotic

In the middle of the nineteenth century, a literary fund was set up in Russia. The Literary Fund or, to give it its full title, the Society for the Assistance of Indigent Writers and Scholars (Obshchestvo dlia posobiia nuzhdaiushchimsia literatoram i uchenym) began its activities on 20 November 1859. Two months later, on 22 January 1860, an evening of literary readings took place in St Petersburg under its auspices.[1] A number of celebrated writers agreed to participate in the event: Maikov, Polonskii, Benediktov, Markevich, Nekrasov and Turgenev were all there. Turgenev, who was responsible for organizing the gathering, had prepared a lecture especially for the occasion.[2] It was entitled 'Hamlet and Don Quixote'.[3] Turgenev's reading of his paper to the assembled audience and its subsequent publication in the January issue of *The Contemporary*

---

1   In the Hall of The Passage. Dates given are New Style. For Old Style subtract twelve days.
2   Maikov read 'Prigovor', Polonskii read 'Naiad' and 'Zima', Benediktov read 'I nyne' and 'Bor'ba', Markevich read two extracts from Druzhinin's translation of *Richard III* and Nekrasov read 'Blazhen nezlobivnyi poet...' and 'Edu li noch'iu po ulitse temnoi'. Turgenev had finished writing his article on 9 January 1860. He gave a further reading of his lecture for the Literary Fund in Moscow on 6 February 1860. The other speakers were Ostrovskii, Fet, and Maikov. A third reading for the Literary Fund took place on 6 March 1860 in the Hall in St Petersburg. Ostrovskii, Pisemskii and Maikov participated. See I. S. Turgenev, *Polnoe sobranie sochinenii i pisem v dvatsati vos'mi tomakh: pis'ma v trinadtsati tomakh. Pis'ma: tom chetvertyi, 1860–1862* (Moscow and Leningrad, Nauka, 1962) [hereafter PSSP P: IV], 441–2, 447.
3   'Gamlet i Don-Kikhot' in I. S. Turgenev, *Polnoe sobranie sochinenii i pisem v dvadtsati vos'mi tomakh: sochineniia v piatnadtsati tomakh. Sochineniia: tom vos'moi, 1859–1861* (Moscow and Leningrad, Nauka, 1964) [hereafter PSSP: VIII], 169–92.

(*Sovremennik*) marked a key moment in the reception of Don Quixote in nineteenth-century Russia.

Turgenev's interest in the literary character of Don Quixote was longstanding. At certain periods in his life, it was no more than an idle diversion, but at other times it amounted almost to an obsession. In this respect, his response to the Spanish figure could itself be said to embrace the full range of what is understood by the epithet *quixotic*. If, as Turgenev asserted, there were aspects of Don Quixote to be found in his contemporaries and the type represented a phenomenon of the age in which he lived, then it may also be claimed that an essential quality of the character is to be detected in Turgenev's own involvement with the literary prototype, and especially in his wish to have *El ingenioso hidalgo Don Quijote de la Mancha* translated into his native language. Don Quixote was as much the Russian superfluous man in Mediterranean garb as Hamlet was his Northern European manifestation.

Four days before he read his essay on Hamlet and Don Quixote to the Literary Fund, Turgenev, catching up with some correspondence, wrote a belated reply to a letter which Mar'ia Aleksandrovna Markovich, a young Ukrainian writer who published under the pseudonym of Marko Vovchok, had written to him from Heidelberg the previous year.[4] In his reply, Turgenev mentioned the forthcoming event. He noted: 'In a few days we shall be having a reading in support of our Society (of which you are a member); among other things, I am reading an article entitled

---

[4] Contemporary criticism of Markovich's work prompted Dostoevskii to write his important article 'G—n –bov i vopros ob iskusstve', published in *Vremia* (*Time*) in 1861 and translated as 'Mr –bov and the Question of Art', in *Dostoevsky's Occasional Writings*; selected, translated and introduced by David Magarshack (London: Vision, 1963), 86–137. See N. E. Krutikova, 'Pis'ma M. A. Markovich (1859–1864)' in *Literaturnoe nasledstvo* t.73 kn.2 (1964), 249–302; B. B. Lobach-Zhuchenko, 'Turgenev i M. A. Markovich' in *Turgenevskii sbornik* V (1969), 374–7; and Jane Costlow's biographical essay on Marko Vovchok in Alexander Ogden and Judith E. Kalb, eds, *Russian Novelists in the Age of Tolstoy and Dostoevsky* (Detroit: Gale, 2001), reproduced online in *Literature Resources from Gale* (Gale/Cengage Learning, 2007), n.p.

"D. Quixote and Hamlet".[5] We find in this letter a piece of advice, offered by an established man of letters to a less experienced author, commending three exemplary writers. Turgenev wrote to his twenty-six-year-old correspondent: 'It is bad that you are working little, but perhaps it is also good: it means that you are gathering new impressions. Read Goethe, Homer and Shakespeare – these are the best of all. By now, I suppose you have mastered the German language.'[6]

It is, one may think, an unremarkable recommendation, but nevertheless it is worth commenting upon for two reasons. The first is that, while confirming Turgenev's high regard for Goethe and Shakespeare, we find these two authors linked with Homer rather than with Cervantes, who must have been, at the time of writing, very much in the forefront of the author's mind.[7] One possible reason for the exclusion of Cervantes from this list is attributable to Turgenev's belief that access to the work of the Castillian proto-novelist would have been denied to Markovich since the adventures of the hero, as he was to observe in his coming lecture, still awaited a 'good' translation into Russian. As he announced in public, four days later: 'A good translation of *Don Quixote* would perform a true service to the public, and universal gratitude awaits the writer who translates for us this unique creation in all its beauty'.[8]

The second point of interest is that Turgenev assumed Mar'ia Aleksandrovna had mastered the German language. This supposition was fully warranted, for his correspondent was a gifted linguist who, in the course of a successful career, would be, as one source has it, 'active as a translator of at least five languages': French, Polish, Czech, German and

5   18 January 1860. PSSP P IV: 8. All translations from the Russian are mine unless otherwise stated.
6   Ibid., 9.
7   The trio – Homer, Shakespeare, Goethe – constituted a stable point of reference for Turgenev, when he came to consider literary excellence. The same three authors are linked together a year later, in a letter that Turgenev wrote to Tolstoi from Paris, on 26 March 1861 (PSSP P IV: 217). Cervantes remained more problematic.
8   PSSP: VIII, 172.

English.⁹ This was in addition to the Russian and Ukrainian that she spoke. Marko Vovchok, born Mar'ia Aleksandrovna Vilinska on 3 January 1834,¹⁰ spent much of her early life in Orel, the region where Turgenev was born and grew up, before she met and married the Ukrainian ethnographer, A. Markovich in 1851. It was later in the same decade that she started to write tales of Ukrainian life, which appeared in her own Russian self-translation in *The Russian Herald* (*Russkii vestnik*) in 1858.¹¹ The following year, Turgenev translated and edited the Ukrainian folk tales of the woman he once referred to as 'a dark sphinx'.¹²

For Turgenev, whenever possible, preference was given to reading a literary work in the original language, rather than in translation. A little over three years earlier, in 1856, he had published in *The Contemporary* a short story, under the title 'Faust', in which Goethe's *Faust* is read by the fictional Russian narrator to the young woman that he loves. Turgenev goes to considerable lengths to make it clear that Goethe's work is read *in the original*, as the following quotation demonstrates:

> 'I shall bring you a book!' I exclaimed. (*Faust*, which I had just been reading, came into my head.)
> Vera Nikolaevna sighed softly.

9   Costlow, op. cit. Costlow notes: 'Upon her return from abroad in the late 1860s Vovchok undertook, together with her mother, the management of a translation cooperative, which produced many translations of both popular and serious works – Jules Verne's stories of adventure and travel paying the bills for a translation of Charles Darwin's *On the Origin of the Species* (1859)'.
10 22 December 1833 (O.S). She died on 10 August 1907.
11 They were published in *Russkii vestnik* XIII–XV (1858) and III (1859).
12 *Ukrainskie narodnye rasskazy* (St Petersburg: Izd. Kozhanchikova, 1859). Turgenev's translation of *Institutka* was printed in *Otechestvennye zapiski* (*Notes of the Fatherland*), I (1860). At Ventnor in the summer of 1860, Turgenev joked in a letter of 27 August that 'we called on the aid of Champollion' to understand a telegram from Markovich that had become so garbled as to be as incomprehensible as a hieroglyph (PSSP P: IV, 119). The Egyptian theme is taken up again in a letter dated 1 September, when Turgenev wrote to Markovich that she seemed to him like 'a dark sphinx around whom telegrams, equally incomprehensible, flash incessantly' (ibid., 122). Cf. also PSSP P IV: 126.

'It – it won't be George Sand?' she asked, not without shyness.
'Ah! That means you've heard of her? Well, even if it was, what's wrong in that? ...
No, I shall bring you another author. *You've not forgotten German, have you?*
'No. I haven't forgotten it.'
'She speaks it like a German,' Priimkov joined in.[13]

If true passion is to be equated with first-hand experience, then, as the passage quoted implies, this axiom is applicable not only to the human frame but to the body of the text as well.

When Turgenev's tale of frustrated passion was first published, the editor of the journal, Panaev, decided to include Strugovshchikov's Russian translation of Part One of Goethe's play in the same issue.[14] Some concern was expressed by friends of Turgenev at what they saw as a gauche juxtaposition.[15] This concern was shared by Turgenev himself, who, in a letter to

---

13   Ivan Turgenev, 'Faust: A Story in Nine Letters', in *A Lear of the Steppes etc*; trans. Constance Garnett (London: Heinemann, 1920), 151–223 (174); italics added. Compare *Rudin*, Chapter 6, in which the eponymous hero reads Goethe's *Faust* to Natalia: 'Rudin began to read Goethe's *Faust*, Hoffmann, or Bettina's letters, or Novalis, constantly stopping and explaining what seemed obscure to her. Like almost all young Russian girls she spoke German badly, but she understood it well, and Rudin was thoroughly imbued with German poetry, German romanticism and philosophy, and he drew her into these forbidden lands.' Ivan Turgenev, *Rudin*, trans. Constance Garnett (London: Heinemann, 1920), 103–4.

14   *Sovremennik*, No. 10, 1856. Turgenev's essay occupied pages 91 to 130. *Faust* was translated into Russian five times in the nineteenth century. The translators were Nikolai Kholodkovskii, Eduard Guber, Aleksandr Strugovshchikov, Afanasii Fet and Valerii Briusov. Mikhail Vronchenko, the first Russian translator of *Hamlet* (see Aleksei Semenenko's chapter in this volume), produced a partial translation. For a discussion of Strugovshchikov's approach to translation, see Iurii Levin, *Russkie perevodchiki XIX veka i razvitie khudozhestvennogo perevoda* (Leningrad: Nauka, 1985), 72–96, and Maurice Friedberg, *Literary Translation in Russia: A Cultural History* (University Park: Pennsylvania State University Press, 1997), 56–9.

15   E. Kolbasin informed Turgenev that he had told Panaev it was 'terribly clumsy' to have included his [Turgenev's] 'Faust' and Goethe's *Faust* together in the same issue of the journal. I. S. Turgenev, *Polnoe sobranie sochinenii i pisem v dvatsati vos'mi tomakh: pis'ma v trinadtsati tomakh. Pis'ma: tom tretii, 1856–1859* (Moscow and Leningrad, Nauka, 1961) [hereafter PSSP P: III], 454. Chernyshevkii had written to Nekrasov

Botkin, referred to the 'folly' of printing the two texts together.[16] Yet, when he alluded to the matter in a letter to Panaev, his response was guarded:

> I am very pleased that you like 'Faust' in its final form; may god grant that the public will like it as well. You do well to accommodate a translation of Goethe's 'Faust'; my only fear is that this colossus, even in the (probably) inadequate translation of Strugovshchikov, will crush my paltry effort; but such is the fate of the small; and one should resign oneself to it.[17]

There is more than a touch of irony in this reproach. Turgenev's self-deprecation, in referring to his 'Faust' as a paltry effort set against the image of Goethe's masterpiece as a colossus, could conceivably be construed as an exercise in modesty were it not for the almost Gogolian manner in which it is undermined by the qualification, 'even in the (probably) inadequate translation of Strugovshchikov'. Turgenev puts 'probably' in brackets to indicate that he has not read the translation. Why *should* he, the implication is, since he has access to the original. His observation, then, is based on an assumption that comes naturally to him, namely that a translation will be 'inadequate' and thus incapable of crushing anything original that he might compose.

In his ironic approval of Panaev's editorial decision, Turgenev employs the verb помещать, to accommodate: 'You do well to accommodate a translation of Goethe's "Faust"'. Although помещать, ultimately derived from the root, место, place, is a common enough verb, its employment here is indicative of Turgenev's recognition that the appearance of Strugovshchikov's translation of Goethe's *Faust* in the pages of the Russian journal would not only supplement his tale of intrigue and passion but that it was also timely in the sense that it was designed to meet an expectation of the readers

---

in Rome that 'I do not like the two "Fausts" together – not because it would be bad for the public, but rather that Turgenev will not like it.' Nekrasov, in his turn, wrote to Turgenev about it.

16 PSSP P III: 23.
17 PSSP P III: 19. In 1844, Turgenev had translated one scene from Goethe's *Faust* himself and, in 1845, had written on the egotism of Goethe's character in an article on Vronchenko's Russian translation of *Faust*.

whose appetite would be whetted for a more substantial acquaintance with the legend that served as a subtext. Goethe's dramatic composition is thus accommodated in a Russian literary context through the twofold stratagem of translation and interpretation.

To return to Markovich, we may conclude that a lack of familiarity with Homer's ancient Greek would not necessarily prove an insurmountable barrier, since she had recourse either to a 'good' translation by Gnedich, who knew ancient Greek, or to a 'creative' translation by Zhukovskii, upon which Gogol' had commented fervidly that 'This is not a translation, but rather a re-creation, a restoration, a resurrection of Homer'.[18] Homer, then, could, at a pinch, be recommended to Mar'ia Aleksandrovna to read, alongside Shakespeare and Goethe, as one of 'the best'. The Russian translator, who was to perform the task of providing a 'good' translation of *Don Quixote*, however, would not appear for a few more years, but, at least in the interim, Turgenev in his role as a cultural interpreter was eager to carry forward the project of accommodating Cervantes.

Even though, by 1860, a 'good' translation had yet to appear, Cervantes's narrative had already been converted into a Russian text on more than one occasion. We note first of all the existence of two eighteenth-century adaptations, the first by Ignatii Antonovich Teils in 1769 and the second by Nikolai Osipov in 1791, both of which were made through intermediary,

---

18   Nikolai Gogol, *Selected Passages from Correspondence with Friends*, trans. Jesse Zeldin (Nashville: Vanderbilt University Press, 1969), 33. For the original, see N. V. Gogol', *Polnoe sobranie sochinenii: tom vos'moi. Stat'i* (Leningrad: Akademiia nauk SSSR, 1952), 237. Zhukovskii wrote of his own attempt: 'The translator, not knowing Greek, attempted only to guess at Homer, having the German translations of *The Iliad* by Foss and Sohlberg in front of him. This experiment of his should not be compared, and cannot sustain comparison, with the translation by N. I. Gnedich, who translated for us Homer himself, attentive to a language natural to him. Here, so to speak, is an echo of an echo [*otgolosok otgoloska*]'. This note accompanied his translation in *Severnye tsvety na 1829 god* (*Northern Flowers for 1829*) (St Petersburg, 1828), 76–119. Zhukovskii also knew Pope's translation.

or bridging, translations.[19] *Don Quixote* entered nineteenth-century Russian literature in the trappings of a verse adaptation, which Zhukovskii brought out between 1804 and 1806.[20] In 1831, S. de Chaplette published in St Petersburg a translation heavily dependent on Zhukovskii's, which was advertised as translated from the French.[21] A noteworthy adaptation by A. N. Grech – written for children – followed, in 1846, but the standard translation at the time of Turgenev's essay (and the first from the original Spanish, rather than one relying upon an intermediary French calque), was made by K. P. Masal'skii in 1838. This literal version, however, consisted only of the first twenty-seven chapters of Cervantes's novel.[22]

In the absence of a satisfactory, and complete, Russian edition, Turgenev repeatedly stated his intention to translate *Don Quixote* himself. In a letter that he wrote to Annenkov in the summer of 1853, for example, he informed his correspondent that in the coming winter he would 'get down to a translation of D. Quixote, for which I have prepared myself extensively with constant rereading of this immortal novel.'[23] A gifted linguist, Turgenev had acquired Cervantes's work in Spanish in 1847, when he started to read it with the aid of dictionaries.[24] In the end, however, Turgenev was to content himself with his interpretative essay 'Hamlet and Don Quixote', sup-

---

19 Teils from Fillot de San Martin, and Osipov from the 1746 French version of Florian. See V. E. Bagno, 'Zhukovskii – perevodchik *Don Kikhota*', in N. A. Khramtsova, ed., *Zhukovskii i russkaia kul'tura* (Leningrad, 1987), 293–311.
20 A second edition, with minor corrections, came out in 1815. Zhukovskii worked from Florian's French translation. Later, he acquired the 1810–16 edition of Ludwig Tieck's German translation. See Bagno, op. cit.
21 See Bagno, op. cit.
22 V. E. Bagno '"Don Kikhot" Servantesa i russkaia realisticheskaia proza', in M. P. Alekseev, ed., *Epokha realizma: iz istorii mezhdunarodnykh sviazei russkoi literatury* (Leningrad, 1982), 5–67 (7–9). Masal'skii also wrote *The Don Quixote of the Nineteenth Century*. See Yakov Malkiel, 'Cervantes in Nineteenth-Century Russia', *Comparative Literature*, vol. 3 (1951), 310–29.
23 21 July 1853. PSSP P II: 172. As late as 1877, Turgenev repeated his intention to translate *Don Quixote*.
24 See Iurii D. Levin, 'Stat'ia I. S. Turgeneva "Gamlet i Don-Kikhot"', in G. V. Krasnov, ed., *N. A. Dobroliubov: Stat'i i materialy* (Gor'kii, 1965), 122–63 (127).

plemented, as critics have commented, by the incorporation of 'quixotic' attributes in the construction of his own fictional characters.[25] It was left to V. A. Karelin, to produce in 1866 the first full translation of *Don Quixote* for Russian readers, a translation made directly from the source language (but also working with the French version of Louis Viardot).[26] The date is significant, for Dostoevskii's novel, *The Idiot*, which draws heavily upon the Don Quixote prototype, began to appear in serial publication soon afterwards, in January 1868.

What is worth pointing out here is that the accommodation of Don Quixote, as a literary type, in Russia in the nineteenth century did not depend exclusively on the translation of the Spanish text. To put it another way: Cervantes may have written the original *Don Quixote* in two parts, but in Russia the central character came out in several instalments. Preceding the authoritative text of Karelin's 1866 translation, there were not only Zhukovskii's versified, Masal'skii's incomplete and Grech's juvenile versions, but also a polemical vanguard of interpretative allusions to the central character of which Turgenev's is a crucial, though not the only, contribution. The actual translation of a text into another language may be regarded as marking its definitive arrival, but before that happens – and, indeed, also after it has happened – the original is engaged in making another, parallel journey into the receiving culture.[27] Together, the twin processes of translation and interpretation assure the reception of a text in the host culture.

25 See, for example, E. Kagan-Kans, *Hamlet and Don Quixote: Turgenev's Ambivalent Vision* (The Hague: Mouton, 1975). For a discussion of Kagan-Kans, see Sander Brouwer, *Character in the Short Prose of Ivan Sergeevic Turgenev* (Amsterdam: Rodopi, 1996), 50 ff.
26 Z. I. Plavskin, 'Servantes v Rossii', in *Migel' de Servantes: Bibliografiia russkikh perevodov* (Moscow, 1959). Louis Viardot had translated *Don Quixote* into French and published an annotated edition in Paris in 1836. Turgenev would have known this work. Malkiel (op. cit., 325) refers to Karelin's translation 'into idiomatic Russian, but through the prism of an intermediate French version'.
27 Thomas Mann played upon this dynamic in his own ironic and whimsical manner, when he wrote his entertaining 'Voyage with Don Quixote' (1934), while himself making his maiden sea-crossing of the Atlantic in which he took Ludwig Tieck's four-volume translation of the Spanish novel as his reading matter.

The juxtaposition of Turgenev's short story 'Faust' and Strugovshchikov's translation of Goethe's text in the same issue of *The Contemporary* offers a compact illustration of this process.

Cervantes's character was regarded as a buffoon at the time of Turgenev's 1860 essay. As he stated at the beginning of his lecture:

> Unfortunately, we Russians have no good translation of *Don Quixote*; the majority of us have retained a vague enough memory of it; by the name 'Don Quixote' we often mean simply a fool – the word 'quixotism' [донкихотство] is for us equivalent to the word 'absurdity' – whereas in the quixotic we ought to recognize the elevated principle of self-sacrifice, only caught from the comic side.[28]

In his aim of introducing Cervantes's masterpiece to the Russian public, Turgenev saw a crucial part of his task as being that of redefining in his own language the meaning of донкихотство, the word that lay at the heart of the literary complex, in order to convey the qualities of devotion and sacrifice that he valued so highly as a liberal humanist. These were qualities that Turgenev, and Dostoevskii after him,[29] associated with the character and the deeds of Don Quixote. The word expressed a noble characteristic that could be made manifest through critical interpretation or through creative translation, but most fully, by a combination of these two means.

The interpretation of Don Quixote as a self-sacrificing idealist, disregarding the burden of practical circumstance in the name of a better future, found expression in Turgenev's account of Don Quixote, as 'a light, gay, naive, susceptible spirit, who does not enter into the depths of life, who does not embrace, but reflects all its phenomena'. The warm altruism of this southern type represented, for Turgenev, the complete antithesis to

---

28 PSSP VIII: 172. I have translated the Russian *donkikhotstvo* as 'quixotism'. English usage is fairly evenly divided between 'quixotism' and 'quixotry'.

29 During a lively and lengthy conversation on (and a reading of) Pushkin's ballad of 'The Poor Knight', which occupies much of the sixth and seventh chapters of Part Two of *The Idiot*, Aglaia mentions Don Quixote in a covert allusion to Prince Myshkin: 'The "poor knight" is the same as Don Quixote, only serious and not comic'. See F. M. Dostoevskii, *Sobranie sochinenii v piatnadsati tomakh* (Leningrad: Nauka, 1988–96) VI: 237–51 (250).

Hamlet's cold and gloomy, northern scepticism. The centrifugal force of his enthusiasm stood in contrast to the corrosive power of analysis that eventually collapsed the world in upon Shakespeare's tragic hero. Turgenev was most emphatic in his redefinition of 'quixotism' and pressed the point home in his lecture:

> Let us repeat: what does Don Quixote express in himself? First and foremost, a credo. A belief in something eternal, immutable, in truth, a truth, which, in a word, is located *outside* the individual, but which is readily granted and which demands service and sacrifices, which is accessible to constancy of service and to power of sacrifice. Don Quixote is infused with a total dedication to an ideal, for which he is prepared to be subjected to all possible privations, to sacrifice his life; his own life he values only as much as it may serve as a means to incarnate his ideal, to establish truth, justice on earth.[30]

The redefinition of the meaning of Don Quixote as a character and донкихотство as a concept was Turgenev's objective, which he originally hoped to realize in a Russian translation, but which he eventually succeeded in accommodating in an interpretative essay that still has resonance today.

What was at issue for Turgenev in his comparison of the characters of Hamlet and Don Quixote was nothing less than the conflict between, as he puts it in his essay, 'two radical, opposing characteristics of human nature'. As the Russian author's next – and most famous – novel, *Fathers and Children* (*Ottsy i deti*), published in 1862 was to imply, the reflective, sceptical Hamlet, unable to act, is reminiscent of an older generation, at its prime in the 1840s (but now morally bereft), whereas the self-sacrificing, enthusiastic Don Quixote, charging heedlessly into action, resembles the 'new' generation, either of revolutionaries or of liberal democrats, emerging in the 1860s.[31] Turgenev's age at the time of the writing of 'Hamlet and Don Quixote' was forty-one. It placed him in a good position to arbitrate between the thirty-year-old Hamlet and the fifty-year-old Don Quixote.

30 PSSP VIII: 173.
31 The difference in generations was sufficiently established by the end of the 1860s, for Pisemskii in 1869 to enshrine the 'fathers' in the title of his novel, *Liudi sorokovykh godov* (*The Men of the Forties*).

Contemporary critics immediately recognized that Turgenev was not concerned solely with the respective works created by Shakespeare and Cervantes, but in addition with what Nabokov has called 'the long shadow cast upon receptive posterity',[32] that is to say, with the interpretation of the two fundamental types that the characters represented. In undertaking to evaluate the significance of 'Hamlet' and 'Don Quixote' as 'eternal types', Turgenev was faced with the task of reassessing what had already been written about each of the two characters in order to combine the most prominent features in the form of a series of contrasts that would strike his audience as applicable to contemporary society.[33] One question to ask, then, is where was the originality in what Turgenev had to say in his speech to the Literary Fund, and what was derivative?[34]

A curious twist to a sociological study of nineteenth-century Russia is encountered in that the 'fantastic' figure of Don Quixote is more widely (and variously) evoked as an ethical example by those engaged in sustained polemical debate than the 'worldly' prince of Denmark,[35] for the former exerted little influence in political affairs, whereas the latter lived out his life at the heart of court intrigue. Belinskii, at one extreme, saw Don Quixote as embodying the worst defects of the Slavophile: stagnation, conservatism,

32   'The only matter in which Cervantes and Shakespeare are equals is the matter of influence, of spiritual irrigation – I have in view the long shadow cast upon receptive posterity of a created image which may continue to live independently from the book itself.' Vladimir Nabokov, *Lectures on Don Quixote*; ed. Fredson Bowers (London: Weidenfeld and Nicolson, 1983), 8.
33   'It seemed to us that all men belong more or less to one of these two types; that almost each one of us tends towards either a Don Quixote or a Hamlet. It is true that in our time far more have become Hamlets than Don Quixotes; but the Don Quixotes too have not disappeared' (PSSP: VIII, 172).
34   In the bypaths of historical research, one encounters some rather odd instances of the conjoining of these two characters. One such case is to be found in John Ferriar's *Essay towards a Theory of Apparitions* (London, 1813), where both Hamlet and Don Quixote are cited as exemplifying 'latent lunacy [...] an untouched field, which would afford the richest harvest to a skilful and diligent observer'. See the section in Chapter IV on 'Latent lunacy; exemplified in the character of Hamlet' (111–14).
35   See A. L. Grigor'ev, 'Don-Kikhot v russkoi literaturno-publitsisticheskoi traditsii', in *Servantes. Stat'i i materialy* (Leningrad, 1948), 13–31.

opposition to historical progress;[36] Herzen, at the other extreme, identified Don Quixote with the ill-fated outcome of the revolutionary movement of 1848.[37] Although these two interpretations stand diametrically opposed, they could be said to share a common perception of ideological bankruptcy as a defining characteristic of Cervantes's 'ridiculous' hidalgo.[38]

Pertinent, then, for Turgenev's considered response, when it finally came in 1860 – and which could be regarded as having influenced the revised ending of *Rudin* – is a remark that Herzen made in the third chapter of *From the Other Shore*, when he wrote in an ironic lament for the revolutionaries:

> What a manly, resolute expression there is upon their faces, what alacrity to translate words into action, to rush into battle, to face the enemy's bullets, to put or to be put to death! [...]
> I was sorry for them because of the sincerity of their delusions, their honest belief in what could never be, their ardent faith as pure and as unreal as the chivalry of Don Quixote.[39]

36   See Belinskii's article on Sollogub's novel, *Tarantas* (1845). This view was repeated by Pisarov in 'A Russian Don Quixote' (1862), an article directed at the Slavophile, I. V. Kireevskii. Cf. Levin, 'Stat'ia I. S. Turgeneva "Gamlet i Don-Kikhot"', 137.
37   The same association was made by the Spaniard, N. Diaz de Benjumea in two articles published in 1859 ('The Historical Significance of Cervantes' and 'Philosophical Commentaries to Don Quixote'). Benjumea was the personal secretary of the Spanish ambassador in St Petersburg from 1856 to 1861. See A. Zvigil'skii '"Gamlet i Don-Kikhot": o nekotorykh vozmozhnykh istochnikakh rechi Turgeneva', in *Turgenevskii sbornik* (Leningrad, 1969), 238–45.
38   Following Turgenev's lecture, Herzen identified the defeat of Garibaldi, Mazzini and the Italian revolutionaries with Don Quixote. See 'Ends and Beginnings: Letter to I. S. Turgenev' (1862) in *The Memoirs of Alexander Herzen*, Vol. IV (London: Chatto and Windus, 1968), 1683. See, on Herzen and Turgenev's essay, Iu. G. Oksman, *Turgenev i Gertsen v polemike o politicheskoi sushchnosti obrazov Gamleta i Don-Kikhota* (Saratov, 1958), 27–8. Cf. Chapter 1, Section 1 ('"S togo berega" Gertsena i "Gamlet i Don-Kikhot" Turgeneva') in L. M. Lotman, *Realizm russkoi literatury 60-kh godov XIX veka. (Istoki i esteticheskoe svoeobrazie)* (Leningrad: Nauka, 1974), and L. S. Radek, *Gertsen i Turgenev: literaturno-esteticheskaia polemika* (Kishinev, 1984).
39   Alexander Herzen, *From the Other Shore*; translated from the Russian by Moura Budberg and *The Russian People and Socialism*; translated from the French by Richard

There is no question but that Turgenev set out to accentuate the contradictions inherent in the figures of Hamlet and Don Quixote in his essay.[40] The opposition of irony and enthusiasm, earlier proposed by German romantic authors such as August-Wilhelm Schlegel and Heinrich Heine, supplies a key to an understanding of Turgenev's essay.[41] From these abstractions, incarnated in the two characters he discusses, Turgenev constructs a series of contrasts. 'Disinterested enthusiasm [...] contempt for direct personal advantage' is a positive characteristic that Don Quixote shares with the people, for it endows its possessor with the power of self-sacrifice. Don Quixote, the enthusiast, is, in Turgenev's words, 'a complete madman', 'restricted', and 'in no position to alter his conviction', but he displays the 'fortitude of his moral composition'. He is 'the servant of an idea'. Yet, the 'capacity for happy and honest blindness' inclines Don Quixote 'towards a half-conscious, a half-ingenuous deception, towards self-delusion – an inclination, almost always inherent in the fantasy of an enthusiast'. In all these aspects, Hamlet stands as the anti-type. He is sane, penetrating in his analysis, versatile, and, as a result of these qualities, he is 'conscious of his weakness'. It is from this 'that his irony issues, the antithesis of Don

---

Wollheim; with an introduction by Isaiah Berlin (Oxford: Oxford University Press, 1979), 56. *From the Other Shore* was first published anonymously in German as *Vom anderen Ufer* (Hamburg: Hoffman und Campe, 1850). The second, Russian, edition, *S togo berega*, was published by Herzen (under the pseudonym Iskander) in London in 1855.

40 One of the immediate critical responses to Turgenev's radical dichotomy was a counter-attempt to merge the characteristics of the two literary types. N. V. Shelgunov alluded acerbically to a hybrid type, which 'quixotizes' Hamlet. 'These Hamlets, standing with arms crossed, quixotize, giving the appearance of doing some work, of labouring for the common weal; but, in essence, not knowing to whom to adhere, whither to go, the administrative Hamlets simply do what they wish.' ('Literaturnoe chtenie v zale Passazha', in *The Russian Word*, 1860, No. 2). Turgenev, however, had anticipated this trend in his essay by noting the objection 'that reality does not deal in such sharp distinctions, that in one and the same living being both positions may take their turn, even fuse to a certain degree; but we certainly had no intention of claiming the impossibility of change and contradiction in human nature; we wished only to indicate two different attitudes of a man to his ideal' (PSSP: VIII, 173).

41 Cf. PSSP: VIII, 556–8.

Quixote's enthusiasm'. Hamlet places self-esteem above self-sacrifice. In his scepticism, he owes allegiance to no ideas but his own, and yet he is incapable either of the comical self-sacrifice for others that his counterpart exemplifies or of the melancholy sacrifice of self that he so intensely contemplates. Whereas Don Quixote exhibits all the signs of 'blindness', Hamlet is 'constantly observing himself, forever looking within himself'. Self-awareness, Turgenev points out, is a quality that Hamlet shares with 'his ironic creator, the profoundest connoisseur of the human heart', while lacking the compassion that accompanies it in Shakespeare.

The predicament of Russia had for some time been debated in terms of a fundamental opposition between Slavophile and Westernizing ideologies, and Turgenev addresses this debate indirectly, in a new key. A striking feature of this essay, which addressed the burning issues of the day, is the way in which Turgenev avoided polemical clichés. There is no reference to the 'superfluous man' or to the 'positive hero', to 'predatory' or 'meek' types, to liberals or to radicals, to repression or to revolution. Turgenev's vocabulary was neither Aesopian nor engaged. The shift in register fulfilled part of Turgenev's programme in demonstrating the value for all ages of the great archetypes of literature. Thus, he found a precedent in Hamlet and Don Quixote for the parlous state of social inertia in contemporary Russia. For Hamlet, there is 'something rotten in the state of Denmark'; for Don Quixote, the ideals of Spanish chivalry have been lost.[42] It is part of Don Quixote's lament that (in Motteux's translation):

> now, alas, sloth and effeminacy triumph over vigilance and labour; idleness over industry; vice over virtue; arrogance over valour; and the theory of arms over the practice, that true practice which only lived and flourished in those golden days, and among those professors of chivalry.[43]

---

42 Cf. Derek Offord, *Portraits of Early Russian Liberals: A Study of the Thought of T. N. Granovsky, V. P. Botkin, P. V. Annenkov, A. V. Druzhinin and K. D. Kavelin* (Cambridge: Cambridge University Press, 1985), 62–4.
43 Miguel de Servantes Saavedra, *Adventures of Don Quixote de la Mancha*; translated from the Spanish by Motteux (London and New York: Frederick Warne, n.d.), 267.

This view of the Spain of Don Quixote's day is remarkably similar to the picture of mid-nineteenth-century Russia as reflected in its literary heroes. *Sloth and effeminacy* are charges that are levelled at Goncharov's Oblomov (as elicited in his contrast with Shtol'ts), *idleness over industry* and *vice over virtue* account for Pechorin's futile presence in the world of Lermontov's ironically titled *Hero of our Time* (*Geroi nashego vremeni*) and *arrogance over valour* is a description well applied to Turgenev's own Rudin. As for the final reference to the martial art, this could be seen to carry an allusion to the activities of Insarov in the novel that Turgenev was working on while preparing his essay.[44]

In his essay, Turgenev makes one assertion which, in its taxonomic sweep, recalls Goethe's all-embracing theory of metamorphosis:

> The two powers of inertia and motion, of conservatism and progress, are the basic powers of all existence. They explain to us the growth of a flower, and they also give us the key to an understanding of the development of the mightiest nations.[45]

It is to be doubted, Goethe notwithstanding, that Turgenev was here as interested in 'the growth of a flower' as he was in 'the development of the mightiest nations'. The same might be said about the other publicists of the nineteenth century, who contributed to the cultural transposition of the hero from La Mancha to Russian soil.

After the middle of the 1860s the elegiac laments of futile egoism are drowned in the clamour of quixotic heroes who venture 'beyond the limit'. The whole complex of the centripetal-centrifugal antithesis, involving the opposition of the 'negatively attractive' and the 'positively ridiculous', between impotence (as incarnated in Hamlet) and pure love (as incarnated in Don Quixote), introduced by Turgenev in the key essay of 1860, was to have powerful repercussions. The equation, merely hinted at by Turgenev in his 1860 essay, between Don Quixote and Christ, was

---

44 Compare Dostoevskii's allusion to the exploits of Don Quixote in reference to the backwardness of Russia as a military power in the late 1870s, which is discussed at the close of the chapter.
45 PSSP: VIII, 184.

taken up in earnest by Dostoevskii, in *The Idiot*, a novel which proposes a new, psychologically developed type in its fantastic and idealistic hero, Prince Myshkin, who is introduced on the first page of the text as a passenger aboard a St Petersburg-bound train that is arriving from Western Europe.[46]

The arrival of Don Quixote, reincarnated as Prince Lev Myshkin, is the best-known instance in Russian literature of the migration – or accommodation – of Cervantes's hero. This adaptation, as a major topic in its own right, will not be discussed here,[47] but it remains to be noted that Dostoevskii had not dispensed with the Spanish classic when he finished writing *The Idiot* in 1869. Don Quixote was to resurface the following decade in a context that was dependent in an extraordinary way upon the Russian public's contemporary knowledge – or, to put it less kindly, upon its ignorance – of Cervantes's text in translation.

In September 1877, Dostoevskii published an article in *A Writer's Diary* (*Dnevnik pisatelia*), the monthly periodical that he had been producing single-handedly in order to broadcast his views on whatever matters of literary, cultural, social, political or historical significance struck his fancy. This article went by the curious title 'A Lie Is Saved by a Lie'. It contained Dostoevskii's reflections upon the Russo-Turkish war that was being fought at the time. The author's literary orientation is evident in the way that he starts off – with a reference to Don Quixote!

---

46 Dostoevskii drew his famous comparison between Prince Myshkin and Don Quixote in a letter to Sofia Ivanova, on 13 January 1868 (N.S.): 'The idea of the novel [...] is to depict a positively beautiful man. [...] of all the beautiful characters in Christian literature the most complete is Don Quixote. But he is beautiful solely because he is at the same time also ridiculous'. For the original text, see F. M. Dostoevskii, *Polnoe sobranie sochinenii v tridtsati tomakh: publitsistika i pis'ma toma XVIII–XXX. Tom dvadtsat' vos'moi, kniga vtoraia: Pis'ma 1860–1868* (Leningrad: Nauka, 1985), 251.
47 For a recent discussion of the significance of Don Quixote for Dostoevskii, see Eric J. Ziolkowski, 'Reading and Incarnation in Dostoevsky' in George Pattison and Diane O. Thompson, eds, *Dostoevsky and the Christian Tradition* (Cambridge: Cambridge University Press, 2001), 156–70.

Once upon a time Don Quixote – that very well-known knight of the doleful countenance, the noblest of all the knights the world has ever seen, the simplest in soul and one of the greatest in heart – while wandering with his faithful attendant, Sancho, in search of adventure, was suddenly struck by a puzzle that gave him cause to think for a long while.[48]

What was puzzling Cervantes's character was how it was physically possible in those 'absolutely truthful books known as the romances of chivalry', for the valiant knight on his 'glorious peregrinations' to kill unaided an entire army, sometimes amounting to a hundred thousand warriors, in one battle: '[N]o matter how he wielded his sword, a single person could not do this at once, in a few hours or so. ... How could it happen?' To answer this question, Dostoevskii quotes a long passage (in Russian), in which Don Quixote provides a rational explanation of this conundrum, by arguing that the bodies of these malignant, but magical, foes were constituted differently from those of humans (more like slugs or spiders) concluding triumphantly:

> Here the great poet and seer of the human heart perceived one of the most profound and most mysterious aspects of the human spirit. Oh, this is a great book, not the sort that are written now; only one such book is sent to humanity in several hundred years. [...] What a fine thing it would be if our young people were to become thoroughly steeped in these great works of literature.[49]

My summary has radically condensed Dostoevskii's enthusiastic account of Cervantes's work. In *A Writer's Diary*, it amounts to four pages, serving as an indirect preamble to an attack on the censuring by European politicians of Russia's role in the war against Turkey.[50] Whereas Don Quixote

---

48   Fyodor Dostoyevsky, *A Writer's Diary: Volume I, 1873–1876*; *Volume II, 1877–1881*, translated and annotated by Kenneth Lantz, with an Introductory Study by Gary Saul Morson (London: Quartet Books, 1994–95), 1127. All references are to Volume II (the pagination is continuous). For the Russian original, see F. M. Dostoevskii, *Polnoe sobranie sochinenii v tridtsati tomakh: publitsistika i pis'ma toma XVIII–XXX. Tom dvadtsat'chetvertyi: Dnevnik pisatelia* (Leningrad: Nauka, 1982).
49   Ibid., 1128.
50   On 21 July 1877, the British government had decided to declare war on Russia if Russian troops occupied Constantinople.

invented a fantasy, 'twice, thrice as fantastic as the first one, cruder and more absurd', in order to preserve his faith in 'those absolutely truthful books', the chivalric romances, Europe's politicians had spread 'absolute absurdities about Russia' in order to maintain their belief in the rightness of the Turkish cause. When we are dealing with contemporary politics, in other words, 'a lie is saved by a lie'.

In this article Dostoevskii advised Russian youth to become 'thoroughly steeped in these great works of literature', since such classics are *not written now*: 'only one such book is sent to humanity in several hundred years'. It is likely that Turgenev would have endorsed the sentiment expressed in this remark, but what is less certain is whether he would have appreciated the *double entendre* of the announcement that 'a lie is saved by a lie'.

For some sixty years, Dostoevskii's 'translation' of a paragraph from *Don Quixote* stood unexamined until a Spanish researcher, M. de Guevara, pointed out that there was no such passage in Cervantes's novel.[51] Dostoevskii had supplied his readers and posterity with an unusual example of rewriting, not a reconstruction *of* the original but a reconstruction with *no* original. The deliberate hoax (more a case of irony than a lie), perpetrated upon his readers with such assurance by Dostoevskii, was eventually uncovered by a scholar of comparative literature, who was able to cross linguistic and cultural frontiers. Presumably, if Russian youth had been as 'thoroughly steeped in' *Don Quixote* as Dostoevskii and Turgenev in their respective ways were, the deception would have been exposed much earlier. As it is, Dostoevskii's title 'A Lie Is Saved by a Lie' takes on a second meaning. Dostoevskii's 'lie', the pretence of translating Cervantes, is 'saved' by the 'lie' of his readers, the pretence of knowing the classics. In this way, the words of a more recent author writing on the subject of the fictional translation of *Don Quixote* stand vindicated: 'Historical truth [...] is not what has happened; it is what we judge to have happened'.[52]

---

51 See V. E. Bagno, 'Dostoevskii o "Don-Kikhote" Servantesa' in *Dostoevskii: materialy i issledovaniia* (Leningrad: Nauka, 1978), vol. 3, 126–35.
52 Jorge Luis Borges, 'Pierre Menard, Author of the *Quixote*', *Labyrinths: Selected Stories and Other Writings*; ed. Donald A. Yates and James E. Irby (Harmondsworth: Penguin, 1970), 62–71 (69).

KATHARINE HODGSON

Heine and Genre: Iurii Tynianov's Translations of Heine's Poetry

The only poet Iurii Tynianov ever translated was Heinrich Heine. Tynianov's engagement with Heine's work developed over a number of years, running in parallel with his work as a literary scholar and historical novelist. It resulted in the publication of three volumes of translations, one of which appeared in 1927, the other two in 1934.[1] This chapter will look at ways in which Tynianov's translations, compared with those of earlier translators, produced a Russian Heine who was both close to the original and thoroughly contemporary. It will also consider the contemporary resonance of Tynianov's translations, notwithstanding the fact that the historical target of Heine's satire was nineteenth-century Germany, a hidebound, reactionary, hierarchical society dominated by bureaucracy.

A significant proportion of the poetry Tynianov translated was drawn from Heine's satirical work, which had not been particularly well served by previous Russian translators. Not long after the first translations appeared in the 1830s, between 1848 and 1855 there was an all but complete ban on publishing Heine's work in Russia.[2] Once it became possible to publish his work again, the tsarist censorship meant that nineteenth-century

1 *Satiry*, translated and with an introduction by Iurii Tynianov (Leningrad: Academia, 1927); *Germaniia: zimniaia skazka* (Leningrad and Moscow: Gosudarstvennoe izdatel'stvo khudozhestvennoi literatury, 1933); a second edition appeared in 1934; *Stikhotvoreniia* (Leningrad: Izdatel'stvo pisatelei v Leningrade, 1934).
2 According to German Ritz, in *150 Jahre russische Heine-Übersetzung* (Bern: Peter Lang, 1981), 47, the first published Russian translations of Heine's poetry were by Fedor Tiutchev and appeared between 1827 and 1834. Other translators followed in the later 1830s and early 1840s, including Mikhail Lermontov, Afanasii Fet and Karolina Pavlova.

translators were still faced with significant obstacles if they attempted to publish translations of his political or anti-religious satires. Yet there were other reasons why Heine's satire failed to gain broad acceptance among nineteenth-century Russian readers, while his lyric poetry was widely translated and enjoyed considerable popularity. At the time, Russian translators appear to have felt more at home with a straightforward reading of Heine's lyric poetry which placed sentiment in the foreground and toned down his irony which, in an article published during the ban on Heine in 1852, had been condemned as a destructive expression of a flawed personality.[3] The uneasy response to Heine's irony meant that by the end of the nineteenth century Russian perceptions of Heine's satirical talent, according to Andrei Fedorov, were reduced to an appreciation of his witticisms, without any real sense of the serious agenda underlying his verbal play.[4] There was a widespread, and mistaken, view of Heine as a writer whose work fell into two distinct categories:

> in the consciousness of readers of Russian translations [...] there were two Heines, quite different, radically distinct from one another: one was a delicate lyric poet, who was, however, sometimes extremely ironic, and the other was a run-of-the-mill humorist, not even a satirist. But in actual fact the lyrical and emotional element, on the one hand, and, on the other hand, the satirical element, with its characteristic features of irony and parody, verging on the grotesque, do not merely coexist in Heine's work, or alternate one with the other, but are inseparably woven together.[5]

The failure to recognize the fundamental unity of Heine's poetic persona, in Fedorov's view, meant that the serious concerns of his satirical writing were obscured, if not lost altogether.[6]

What the nineteenth-century translators of Heine's poetry did amounted to moving Heine closer to his Russian readers; they were given

---

[3] Apollon Grigor'ev, 'Russkaia iziashchnaia literatura v 1852 g.', *Literaturnaia kritika* (Moscow: Khudozhestvennaia literatura, 1967), 87–98.
[4] A. V. Fedorov, 'Iurii Tynianov i ego perevody iz Geine' in *Iskusstvo perevoda i zhizn' literatury* (Leningrad: Sovetskii pisatel', 1983), 265–6.
[5] Ibid., 266.
[6] Ibid.

only a very limited opportunity to read him as a poet embodying the tensions of modernity: inner division, ambivalence and disillusion. Instead, he tended to be presented to readers in simplified form, either as a sentimental poet, the image which was promoted by the majority of his translated texts, or as a politically engaged writer, which was how the radical critics of the 1860s such as Nikolai Chernyshevskii, Nikolai Dobroliubov and Dmitrii Pisarev saw him, although few Russian translations from Heine's political poetry were available to substantiate their view of him.[7] Towards the end of the century, the Russian public was provided with a largely de-politicized Heine in toothless humorous verse written in imitation of his style and offering gentle satire of hypocritical behaviour in areas such as marriage and family life. The political significance of Heine's satire was sidelined, except in the underground revolutionary press, and at the time of the 1905 Revolution Heine's revolutionary credentials were brought to the fore once more.[8] Nevertheless, actual translations of his political satire continued to be less common in contemporary satirical journals than poems based on well-known pieces by Heine, which singled out as targets the monarchy, the bourgeoisie, the law courts, police informers and the censorship.[9] For example, his 'Zwei Grenadiere' ('Two Grenadiers') about two French soldiers after the defeat of Napoleon spawned 'Dva liberala' ('Two liberals'), 'Dva esera' ('Two Socialist Revolutionaries') and 'Dva zhandarma' ('Two gendarmes').[10] Heine's ambivalent attitude towards revolution was set aside while, as in the 1860s, Russian radicals once more promoted him as a symbol of eloquent rebellion.

In the early years of the twentieth century, while the political climate changed in ways that helped proponents of revolution to emphasize Heine's contemporary significance, it might also be argued that Russian readers were better placed than they had been in the mid-nineteenth century to

---

7   See Katharine Hodgson, 'Heine's Russian Doppelgänger: Nineteenth-Century Translations of his Poetry', *Modern Language Review*, 4 (2005), 1054–72.
8   Ia. I. Gordon, *Geine v Rossii 1870–1917 gg.* (Dushanbe: Donish, 1979), 12, 19, 35; 44–8; Ia. I. Gordon, *Geine v Rossii: XX vek* (Dushanbe: Donish, 1983), 60.
9   Ia. I. Gordon, *Geine v Rossii: XX vek*, 106–7; 120.
10 Ia. I. Gordon, *Geine v Rossii 1870–1917 gg.*, 100.

appreciate and accept the dissonance that is a prominent feature of his writing.[11] As Nigel Reeves points out, Heine's work is marked by a sense of *Zerrissenheit* (a state of inner division produced by a world that is itself fractured), of having lost the sense of wholeness that he believed to have existed in earlier times.[12] Russia had undergone rapid economic development and modernization in the late nineteenth century, and in the wake of the 1861 Emancipation of Serfs, traditional forms of agrarian society were becoming increasingly unstable, so that by the start of the twentieth century Russian readers were familiar with the disorienting effects of modernity on perceptions of their own identity and of the society in which they lived.

Furthermore, developments in Russian poetry meant that prospective translators were provided with new homegrown resources that would enable them to reproduce the particular quirks of Heine's style more effectively. As Efim Etkind points out, nineteenth-century Russian translators were scarcely equipped to deal with his poetry properly:

> German poetry of the middle of the last century [i.e. the nineteenth] had no stylistic equivalent in contemporary Russia – even Lermontov and Tiutchev, when translating Heine, transposed his poetic style into a different system, one that was much closer to classical norms. In the nineteenth century one could not have expected any really satisfactory translations of Heine.[13]

Heine's earlier Russian translators drew on a tradition of versification which offered few adequate ways of handling his metre, with its varying intervals between stressed syllables, using conventional syllabotonic metres instead. This meant that the flexible rhythms that helped to underline the

---

11 See Clara Hollosi, 'Views on Heine in Russia in the Beginning of the 20th Century' in *Heine-Jahrbuch 1978* (Hamburg: Hoffman und Campe, 1978), 174–85, for an account of how three prominent early twentieth-century Russian authors – Lev Shestov, Innokentii Annenskii and Aleksandr Blok – responded to Heine.

12 Nigel Reeves, *Heinrich Heine: Poetry and Politics* (Oxford: Oxford University Press, 1974), 28. See also Richie Robertson, *Heinrich Heine* (London: Peter Halban Publishers, 1988), 13.

13 Efim Etkind, '"Veselyi primer Geine": Geine, Tiutchev, Maiakovskii', *Tam, vnutri: o russkoi poezii XX veka* (St Petersburg: Maksima, 1995), 321.

informality of his style were replaced by formal regularity. Nineteenth-century translators also tended to 'smooth out' his poetry by neutralizing the stylistic dissonance which is a prominent feature of his work. Words drawn from clashing registers, such as the earthily colloquial and the rhetorically elevated, placed side by side, were replaced in translation by words drawn from a single, more conventionally literary register. All these constraints combined to produce a Heine characterized mainly by sentimentality; his irony was either watered down or, on occasion, clumsily exaggerated. Translations of his satirical poetry turned Heine from 'a brilliant master of language' to 'a dull versifier with a certain pretension to wit, but no traces of brilliance whatsoever'.[14]

Around the turn of the century, however, Heine's work attracted the attention of poets associated with the symbolist and acmeist movements, such as Innokentii Annenskii and Aleksandr Blok.[15] They concentrated on his lyric poetry, but, as poets with a particular concern for the nuances of style and form, were able to demonstrate the subtleties of his craftsmanship. Russian versification had, by the early twentieth century, developed more effective ways of rendering Heine's metre. Blok in particular did much to establish the *dol'nik*, often used in his own poetry, as a way of mirroring the more flexible rhythms and informal tone of Heine's work.[16] The work of Annenskii and Blok foregrounded Heine's artistry that his apparent artlessness had helped to conceal from many of their predecessors.

The Russian Heine that began to emerge after the 1917 October Revolution was in many respects different from the Heine that Russian readers had come to know during the nineteenth century. In the immediate aftermath of the Revolution translators of foreign poets with revolutionary pedigrees stood to benefit, as the new Soviet state was happy to sponsor cultural projects in tune with 'proletarian internationalism'.[17]

---

14 A. V. Fedorov, 'Iurii Tynianov i ego perevody iz Geine', 266.
15 Ia. I. Gordon, *Geine v Rossii: XX vek*, 13.
16 See James Bailey, 'Blok and Heine: An Episode from the History of Russian Dol'niki', *Slavic and East European Journal*, 1 (1969), 1–22.
17 Maurice Friedberg, *Literary Translation in Russia: A Cultural History* (University Park: Pennsylvania State University Press, 1997), 3.

Changes in political life and literary style worked together to create an atmosphere congenial to new translations. Censorship rules that had been an obstacle to publishing Heine's satires of absolutist monarchy, bureaucracy and religion, were set aside and it became possible to gain a fuller picture of Heine's satirical writing. In the early Soviet period Heine was celebrated by prominent establishment figures such as the Commissar for Enlightenment, Anatolii Lunacharskii, although Lunacharskii did in fact acknowledge Heine's ambivalence, rather than promoting him as the writer of straightforwardly revolutionary credentials that had been ascribed to him by pre-revolutionary Russian Populists and Marxists.[18] Among the earliest projects of the new publishing house, Vsemirnaia literatura (World Literature), established by Maksim Gor'kii and Lunacharskii in 1918, was a new collected works of Heine, under the editorship of Aleksandr Blok. Blok wrote in December 1918, shortly after beginning the project: 'we will supply Heine with all possible explanations and will restore everything destroyed by the censor, but we will only be able to give the Russian reader a little more than half of everything he wrote'.[19] In fact only two volumes appeared, both of which consisted of prose works. Several collections of Heine's poetry were published in the 1920s, and he remained in favour through the 1930s, providing proof of Soviet enlightened values and cultural superiority at a time when the poet's work was banned by the National Socialists in Germany.[20]

18 Anatolii Lunacharskii, 'Genrikh Geine', *Sobranie sochinenii*, 8 vols (Moscow: Khudozhestvennaia literatura, 1965), VI, 133.
19 Quoted by Ia. I. Gordon, *Geine v Rossii: XX vek*, 200.
20 During the 1920s and 1930s, the following volumes of translations of Heine's poetry, excluding those by Tynianov, were published: *Izbrannye stikhovoreniia Geine*, translated by G. Shengeli (Moscow: Gosizdat, 1924); *Disput: Izbrannaia satira*, translated and with notes by A. Deich (Moscow: Ogonek, 1928); *Lirika*, edited by Kogan (Leningrad: Gosizdat, 1928); *Izbrannye stikhotvoreniia*, deshevaia biblioteka klassikov (Moscow: Gosizdat, 1930); *Stikhotvoreniia*, edited, and with an introduction and notes by V. A. Zorgenfrei (Moscow-Leningrad: Academia, 1931); *Izbrannye proizvedeniia*, edited by A. Deich (Moscow, Leningrad: OGIZ, 1934); *Izbrannye proizvedeniia*, edited by Ia. Metallov (Moscow: Khudozhestvennaia literatura, 1935); *Atta Trol': son v letniuiu noch'* (Moscow and Leningrad: Academia, 1936); *Disput i drugie*

Tynianov published a volume of Heine's political satires in 1927, and one containing satirical and other poetry in 1934, as well as a translation of the narrative verse satire 'Deutschland: Ein Wintermärchen' ('Germany: A Winter's Tale') in 1933.[21] He was thoroughly familiar with Heine's work, having written a dissertation on Heine and Tiutchev, excerpts from which were published in the 1920s. Tynianov's translations did not meet with general enthusiasm. As a founder member of the formalist school of literary criticism and theory he was increasingly unwelcome in the Soviet literary establishment of the late 1920s and early 1930s. 'Formalism' became a label for any kind of approach to literary texts that failed to devote the required attention to their ideological content; in the field of translation, it was applied to translations that tended towards a 'literal', rather than a 'free' approach. Maurice Friedberg, in his history of Russian literary translation, suggests a number of reasons why 'literalism' came under attack: it was 'elitist', requiring the translator to demonstrate a high level of command of the foreign language; practitioners of 'literal' translation were suspected of deforming the Russian language by allowing it to be shaped excessively by the language of the original text; it was also, oddly, given the translators' concern for rendering the form and style of the original text, criticized for its alleged 'insensibility to aesthetic values'.[22] Tynianov's translations certainly show great sensitivity to the style and form of Heine's originals. Like few before him, he found convincing ways of conveying Heine's mix of colloquial and elevated language, and reproduced, or discovered equivalent ways of rendering, the play of sounds and the rhythmic flexibility that characterize Heine's verse. His translations reveal him to be a penetrating reader with an eye for fine detail.

Etkind links Tynianov's willingness to address difficulties of translation with something close to literalism and expressions that might be somewhat at odds with conventional Russian expression to the kind of

---

stikhotvoreniia, with an introduction by A. Deich (Moscow: Khudozhestvennaia literatura, 1939); *Polnoe sobranie sochinenii*, 12 vols, edited by N. Berkovskii and I. Lupoll (Moscow and Leningrad: Academia, 1935–49).
21   See note 1 above.
22   Maurice Friedberg, *Literary Translation in Russia*, 78, 83, 85.

experimentation that is typical of Russian futurist writing: 'Tynianov does not flinch before the particular properties of the German language – he forces Russian words to submit to him in line with the futurist school of word and image creation'.[23] Early twentieth-century literary experimentation found in futurist poetry by figures such as Vladimir Maiakovskii and Velimir Khlebnikov was a rich source of the kind of linguistic play and flexibility of register Tynianov needed in order to convey the style of Heine's poetry successfully. In his critical writing on Heine, Tynianov identified Heine's characteristic mixing of registers, his disruption of stylistic unity by introducing foreign words or elements of prosaic jargon.[24] The futurist idea of the 'word as such' which emphasized the aesthetic impact of aspects of the word independent of meaning seems to have informed Tynianov's approach. Newly invented words, unfamiliar words and foreign words feature prominently in his translations; words seem to be selected by virtue of sound as much as, or even more than, by meaning.

Tynianov's translation of 'Mir träumt', ich bin der liebe Gott' ('I dreamt I was the dear Lord God') illustrates the freedom with which he deploys foreign words and unconventional combinations of words so as to capture the dissonance between the speaker's dream status and his extremely casual speech. Heine's coining 'Götterfrass' to describe the oysters and Rhine wine that the dreamer miraculously causes to appear on the Berlin streets represents a distortion of the word which might be expected here, 'Götterspeise', replacing 'Speise' (food, fare) with the word 'Frass', normally used to refer to animal food; in his translation Tynianov combines the words 'sviataia' (sacred) and 'zhratva' (grub) to convey the clash of registers that might well have been too jarring to be acceptable before 1917, but was absolutely in line with the new regime's promotion of atheism and materialism. The incongruously earthly diction of Heine's dreamer is also expressed, and even enhanced, in Tynianov's comic deployment of rhyme involving foreign words. In the stanza quoted below, the original rhymes 'Gulden' (a coin

---

23   Efim Etkind, '"Veselyi primer Geine": Geine, Tiutchev, Maiakovskii', 326.
24   Iurii Tynianov, 'Tiutchev i Geine', *Poetika, Literatura, Kino* (Moscow: Nauka, 1977), 377.

used in Germany between the fourteenth and nineteenth centuries) with 'Schulden' (debts), but Tynianov selects a coin of a different denomination, to rhyme with 'deneg' (money), placing a foreign word in a prominent position that draws attention to its form, but also allows readers to guess its meaning if necessary:

> Я ем конфеты, ем пирог,
> И это всё без денег,
> Бенедиктин при этом пью,
> А долгу ни на пфенниг.
>
> [I eat sweets, I eat pie,/ And all of this without money,/ While I drink Benedictine,/ without owing a single pfennig.]

This stanza is followed by one featuring a compound rhyme, not a feature of Heine's original text, but one which captures and builds on the playfulness of the original. The dreamer complains of being bored in heaven, saying that if he were not God he would go crazy. The expression he uses for 'go crazy', 'ich könnt' des Teufels werden', has a double meaning. 'Bist du des Teufels?' is used figuratively to say 'have you taken leave of your senses', but has the literal meaning of 'are you of the devil/ do you belong to the devil?'. The Russian equivalent selected by Tynianov, 'poiti k chertu' is more straightforwardly 'to go to the devil' or 'to go to hell', and so the wordplay is transferred from its original site in lines three and four to the rhymes in lines two and four:

> Но скука мучает меня,
> Не лезет чаша ко рту,
> И если бы не был я господь,
> Так я пошел бы к черту.[25]
>
> [But boredom torments me,/ the cup won't rise to my lips,/ and if I were not the Lord,/ I would go to the devil.]

---

25 *Mastera russkogo stikhotvornogo perevoda*, ed. Efim Etkind, 2 vols (Leningrad: Sovetskii pisatel', 1968), II, 235.

The rhyme in the original stanza is formally much more conventional, rhyming 'auf Erden' (on earth) and 'werden' (become). Tynianov's rhyme 'ko rtu' / 'k chertu', with the stress on the first syllable in each case, together with the introduction of the extra consonant 'ch' in the second rhyme word, mirrors the innovative kind of approximate rhyming used by Maiakovskii. Early twentieth-century experiments may also have laid the foundations for Tynianov's resourceful handling of Heine's language.

Maiakovskii's poetry also provided Tynianov with useful models of how to render Heine's metre. Blok had already paved the way for twentieth-century translators of Heine through his use of the *dol'nik*, and Maiakovskii's work took Russian accentual verse further away from established patterns of syllabotonic metre. Etkind notes that Tynianov was closer to Maiakovskii than Blok in his handling of Heine's metre. The *dol'nik* that Blok used in his Heine translations was closely related to traditional ternary metres, with a constant anacrusis of two syllables, and a majority of intervals between ictuses of two syllables. Tynianov's translations employ an anacrusis of varying lengths, and no pattern based on traditional binary or ternary metres predominates. He is in fact closer to the type of tonic versification practised by Maiakovskii.[26] In his introduction to Heine's *Satiry* Tynianov wrote: 'To confine Heine in a small-minded way to the canons of a metrical system would be like translating Maiakovskii using iambic tetrameter, because the main feature of his verse is its intonation.'[27] The fact that Futurism and Formalism, both of which informed Tynianov's work as a translator, fell into disfavour during the later 1920s may not have been the only reason why Tynianov's translations of Heine were overshadowed by the work of other Soviet-era translators. In his translations, Heine's poetry gained a contemporary feel, rather than being presented to readers as timeless and neutral museum pieces from a different culture. The implications of translating satirical poetry in a way that might emphasize its contemporary and local relevance will be discussed further below.

---

26   Efim Etkind, '"Veselyi primer Geine": Geine, Tiutchev, Maiakovskii', 323–4.
27   Iurii Tynianov, 'Portret Geine' (introduction to *Satiry*, 1927), quoted by A. V. Fedorov, 'Iurii Tynianov i ego perevody iz Geine', 271.

Fedorov recognizes Tynianov's outstanding contribution as a translator of Heine, noting that a close affinity between translator and the author of a translated work is likely to lead to a successful outcome, and that the creative personality of a translator has its own part to play in this success. Tynianov's prolonged engagement with Heine over many years, in parallel with writing of fiction, criticism and works of literary theory, suggests that there was indeed something about Heine that made him particularly amenable.[28] In his critical writing, Tynianov responded strongly to Heine's disruption of literary convention. He saw a clear contrast between the use of adjectives in conventional romantic poetry, where they presented new aspects of an object, and in Heine's work, where emphasis was placed on the lack of connection between the adjective and the object it described: 'Heine's epithets perform no descriptive role or any role connected with reality. They are the best vehicle for playfulness'.[29] Tynianov's translations retain features essential to Heine's style, which were often edited out by earlier (and, indeed, later) translators. As a literary theorist, Tynianov saw verse as a system of interacting elements in which the interaction was closer to struggle, rather than collaboration. As a translator of Heine's poetry, therefore, he was not drawn into the 'corrective' role adopted by many of his predecessors, who toned down the stylistic dissonance and conflict of the originals, shifting towards a more conventional and more uniform register. Instead, he showed himself to be a contemporary of the futurists, for whom mockery and rejection of literary convention was a central tenet of their art. Tynianov's explorations of the role of parody in stimulating literary evolution allowed him to recognize that much of Heine's innovativeness derived from the way that his work frequently bordered on parody: 'nowhere else have we seen such a narrow boundary separating a poet's own, genuine images from parodic ones'.[30] Heine's writing, in

---

28 A. V. Fedorov, 'Iurii Tynianov i ego perevody iz Geine', 284. For an exploration of the relationship between Heine and Tynianov's work as a literary theorist, see Mikhail Iampol'skii, 'Razlichie, ili Po tu storonu predmetnosti: Estetika Geine v teorii Tynianova', *Novoe literaturnoe obozrenie*, 4 (2006), 30–53.
29 'Tiutchev i Geine', 375–6.
30 Ibid., 377.

Tynianov's view, was characterized by the poet's playful use of worn-out tropes set alongside incongruous material: 'Heine was the heir of the great era of emotional romantic lyric poetry, which had already become banal. He brought in banal, hackneyed literary material through use of a humorous concluding *pointe*. He mixed up images of conflicting feelings and objects, which had, in the work that preceded his, worked in harmony together'.[31] Heine's parodic approach was also manifested in poems that adhered to convention, but undermined it by doing so to excess. As Tynianov noted, 'an emotional atmosphere that is too elevated, overdone [perederzhannaia] plays the role of destroying illusion, which in other cases is carried out by the concluding *pointe*'.[32]

An example of this kind of hyperbolized emotion can be seen in the poem 'Im Mai' ('In May'), translated as 'V mae'. Tynianov's translation, compared with that of nineteenth-century writer and prolific Heine translator, Mikhail Mikhailov, illustrates Tynianov's innovative approach to conveying the particular qualities of the original text. 'Im Mai' turns on the painful collision between the speaker's despairing mood and the delights of spring that surround him. This is a commonplace of romantic poetry that Heine had often adopted and mocked before. The second stanza, in the original, runs as follows:

> Es blüht der Lenz. Im grünen Wald
> Der lustige Vogelgesang erschallt,
> Mädchen und Blumen, sie lächeln jungfräulich –
> O schöne Welt, du bist abscheulich![33]

> [Spring is in bloom. In the green wood/ Merry birdsong rings out,/ And girls and flowers smile in maidenly fashion –/ O beautiful world, you are horrible!]

---

31 Iurii Tynianov, 'Portret Geine' (introduction to *Satiry*, 1927), quoted by Ia. I. Gordon, *Geine v Rossii: XX vek*, 306.
32 'Tiutchev i Geine', 379.
33 'Im Mai', *Sämtliche Gedichte in zeitlicher Folge*, ed. Klaus Briegleb (Frankfurt am Main and Leipzig, 1993), 710.

The contrast between the idyllic scene and the speaker's response to it is underlined by the rhyme 'jungfräulich' (in maidenly fashion) and 'abscheulich' (horrible), as well as by the contrast in the final line. Mikhailov's translation gives us:

> Цветет весна. Опушились леса;
> В них весело птичьи звенят голоса,
> И запах цветов раздражительно-сладок.
> О мир прекрасный! Как ты мне гадок!³⁴

[Spring is in bloom. The woods are in leaf,/ In them birds' voices ring merrily,/ And the scent of flowers is annoyingly sweet./ O beautiful world! How horrible I find you!]

Tynianov's translation reads:

> Цветет весна. В зеленых лесах
> Звенит веселое птенье птах.
> Цветы и девушки, смех у них ясен –
> О мир прекрасный, ты ужасен!³⁵

[Spring is in bloom. In the green woods/ Rings the birdies' merry song./ The laughter of flowers and girls is bright –/ O beautiful world, you are horrible!]

Tynianov's version is considerably closer to the original than Mikhailov's, in its rendering both of its literal meaning and of its formal features. Mikhailov has removed mention of the 'girls' in line three, and, instead of the smiles issued by both flowers and girls (producing a curious blend of animate and inanimate), has the scent of flowers which is already tainted by the speaker's discordant mood, rather than keeping that fact concealed until the second half of the fourth line. The introduction of 'razdrazhitel'no' (annoyingly) in line three anticipates the contrast that is

---

34   M. L. Mikhailov, 'V mae', *Polnoe sobranie stikhotvorenii* (Moscow and Leningrad: Academia, 1934), 373.
35   Iurii Tynianov, 'V mae' <http://www.vekperevoda.com/1887/tynyanov.htm> accessed 20 December 2010.

emphasized in the rhyme (sladok/ gadok) that links lines three and four. Furthermore, the yoking together of adverb and adjective in line three belongs to a somewhat elevated stylistic register (reminiscent, perhaps, of Fedor Tiutchev) which is rather distant from the original, where the language used is much more straightforward. Tynianov sticks with the original register, with its assortment of clichés in the first three lines; his introduction of the colloquial 'ptakha' (bird) instead of the neutral 'ptitsa' is in keeping with the overall tone, and enables him to create an echo of the repeated consonant 'g' of 'lustige Vogelgesang' in the repeated 'pt' of 'pten'e ptakh' (birdsong) while preserving the straightforward rhyme 'lesakh' (forests) and 'ptakh'. The poem goes on to express the speaker's longing for an environment more in tune with his mood: the Underworld, where, instead of birdsong, he can hear 'Der Furien Singsang, so schrill und grell' ('the Furies' singsong, so shrill and harsh'), rendered by Mikhailov as: 'И фурий пронзительно-дикое пенье' (and the Furies' piercingly savage singing), and by Tynianov as: 'И фурий пенье – визг и вой' (and the Furies' singing – squeals and howls).[36] Mikhailov's version sticks more or less to a conventional syllabotonic metre (amphibrachic tetrameter), and, as before, combines adverb and adjective to produce an effect which is far less colloquial and abrupt than the original. Tynianov, on the other hand, is able to provide an equivalent for the use of monosyllables and their consonant repetition in 'schrill' and 'grell' in the alliterative 'vizg' and 'voi'.

Unlike 'Im Mai', which plays with and mocks literary cliché, Heine's 'Jammertal' ('Vale of tears') satirizes the unthinking and unfeeling official response to the death of a couple from cold and hunger. The poem sets up a strong contrast between the emotional and simple language used to evoke the last night of the two lovers' lives, and the heartless bureaucratic verbiage of the officials. The fourth stanza, which describes their final moments, reads as follows:

---

36 Ibid.

Heine and Genre

> Sie küssten sich viel, sie weinten noch mehr,
> Sie drückten sich seufzend die Hände,
> Sie lachten manchmal und sangen sogar,
> Und sie verstummten am Ende.[37]

> [They kissed one another many times, they wept even more,/ They pressed one another's hands, sighing,/ They laughed sometimes and even sang,/ And they fell silent in the end.]

This stanza is built around the parallel structures based on the verbs 'Sie küssten', 'Sie drückten', 'Sie lachten', 'Und sie verstummten' at the start of each line, as well as the symmetrical patterning of lines one and three. The fifth and sixth stanzas produce a rather more disjointed effect, with a predominant iambic pattern rather than the mostly two-syllable intervals between ictuses, replacing a more fluent effect with something more rigid and abrupt. This abruptness is highlighted by the more formal language, peppered with bureaucratic jargon, and in particular by the awkward transitions between several of the lines in stanzas five and six, when the officials appear to certify the deaths.

> Am Morgen kam der Kommissär,
> Und mit ihm kam ein braver
> Chirurgus, welcher konstatiert
> Den Tod der beiden Kadaver.
>
> Die strenge Wittrung, erklärte er,
> Mit Magenleere vereinigt,
> Hat beider Ableben verursacht, sie hat
> Zum mindestens solches beschleunigt.[38]

> [Next morning came the police inspector,/ And with him came a worthy/ Surgeon, who confirmed/ The death of both cadavers.// The harsh weather, he explained,/ Combined with an empty stomach,/ Had caused the decease of both, it had/ At least expedited such an outcome.]

---

37 Heinrich Heine, 'Jammertal', *Sämtliche Gedichte in zeitlicher Folge*, 811.
38 Ibid., 811–12.

Mikhailov's translation smoothes out stanza five, breaking it into two balanced halves with a prominent pause at the end of the second line, and replaces most of the bureaucratic language in stanza six with more straightforward language and a piece of homely wisdom:

> Квартальному и с ним врачу
>   Поутру было дело:
> Пришлось свидетельствовать им
>   Два свежих мертвых тела.
>
> Осенний ветер, – врач решил –
>   При пустоте в желудке,
> Простуду произвел – и смерть.
>   Ведь с ним плохие шутки![39]

[For the policeman and the doctor/ There was a job to do in the morning:/ They had to confirm/ Two fresh dead bodies.// The autumn wind, the doctor concluded,/ together with an empty stomach,/ had caused a chill – and death./ You know, such things are not to be trifled with!]

On the other hand, Tynianov's translation reflects the awkward transition between certain lines, and even accentuates it in lines two and three of stanza five, with a stuttering accumulation of the consonant 'p':

> Наутро с комиссаром пришел
> Лекарь, который, пощупав
> Пульс, на месте установил
> Отсутствие жизни у трупов.
>
> «Полый желудок, – он пояснил –
> Вместе с диетой строгой
> Здесь дали летальный исход, – верней
> Приблизили немного.[40]

---

39 M. L. Mikhailov, 'Iudol' placha', *Polnoe sobranie stikhotvorenii*, 378.
40 Iurii Tynianov, 'Iudol' placha', *Mastera russkogo stikhotvornogo perevoda*, II, 240.

[In the morning, together with the commissar, came/ The surgeon, who, having felt/ For a pulse, confirmed on the spot/ The absence of life in the corpses.// 'An empty stomach', he explained,/ 'together with a strict diet/ Here produced a lethal outcome, – or rather,/ accelerated it somewhat'.]

When referring to death, the doctor in Heine's original uses the word 'Ableben', which belongs to a very formal register, equivalent to 'demise' or 'decease' in English, rather than the more neutral 'Tod'. Where Mikhailov offers the standard *smert'* (death), Tynianov chooses a lengthier, but appropriately bureaucratic 'lethal outcome'. Mikhailov's translation cannot quite bring itself to confront the paradoxical 'death' of 'cadavers', preferring 'two fresh dead bodies', which maintains a similar, but perhaps less jarring contradiction, Tynianov's meets it head on. As a translator, Tynianov acknowledges that the deliberate awkwardness of the original has a significant role to play in constructing the meaning of the poem and conveys it with a kind of clumsiness that the norms of nineteenth-century Russian poetry would hardly have allowed. He even accentuates the awkwardness in his departure from the original in stanza five: Mikhailov correctly translates 'strenge Wittrung' with a reference to bad weather, and 'Magenleere' to an empty stomach; Tynianov's doctor speaks tautologically of the cause of death being 'an empty stomach combined with a strict diet', and so combines officious pomposity with nonsense.

Tynianov translated Heine into Russian in a way that emphasized his modernity. His work reflected contemporary style in terms of language and versification, but it also had contemporary relevance as satirical comment on present realities. The word 'komissar', quoted above, does echo the form of the original text's 'Kommissär' in 'Jammertal' very closely, and yet, for a Soviet reader of the late 1920s, would have carried specific and rather different connotations from the Civil War years. Tynianov's choice of this word is a not particularly subtle signal which brings Heine's poem out of its historical context into contemporary life: death from cold and starvation was far from uncommon in the years of revolutionary upheaval. The first readers of this translation were likely to have had their own experiences of scarce resources and unsympathetic bureaucracy. In the Soviet Union, some translators were able to use foreign texts from earlier centuries to talk about the present day in ways that would hardly have been acceptable in their own original work; Boris Pasternak's translation of *Hamlet*, the first version of which was published in 1940, would be a case in point.[41] What Pasternak did through a freer approach to translation, Tynianov did through his style, and through his choice of texts. Heine's contemporary resonance was something that Tynianov was able to capture and express through his approach to translation. Etkind sees close links between Tynianov's work as translator and his creativity as author of fiction, pointing out that he faced a similar kind of choice over his approach as author of historical fiction and as translator:

> should he transform himself into his hero and retreat into the past, stylizing his language and his thoughts so that they are determined by the laws of past times? Or, on the contrary, should he bring his hero closer to himself and his contemporaries, giving him the language of a new era, and, by so doing, gaining the reader's complete confidence? [...] Going back into another time while remaining a contemporary of his own time – that's Tynianov's principle.[42]

To a considerable extent Tynianov's selection of texts for translation was determined by what had not previously been translated into Russian. Therefore his efforts were focused on the satirical poetry. At a time when lyric poetry was viewed as a suspect manifestation of bourgeois individualism, this may be seen as a pragmatic choice, although, in the opinion of Kornei Chukovskii, Tynianov had a greater personal affinity with Heine's satirical and ironic writing, than with his lyrics.[43] Some of the texts he chose attacked faults that might easily be ascribed to a bourgeois capitalist society: 'Das Sklavenschiff' ('The Slave Ship') exposes the inhumanity of the slave trade, 'Zur Beruhigung' ('For Calming Down') mocks complacent German acceptance of absolutist rule, while 'Der Philanthrop' ('The

---

41 See Aleksei Semenenko, *Hamlet the Sign: Russian Translations of Hamlet and Literary Canon Formation*, Stockholm Studies in Russian Literature (Stockholm: Stockholm University, 2007), 94–8. See also the chapter by Semenenko in this volume.
42 Efim Etkind, '"Veselyi primer Geine": Geine, Tiutchev, Maiakovskii', 314.
43 Kornei Chukovskii, 'Pervyi roman' in *Vospominaniia o Iurii Tynianove: portrety, vstrechi*, ed. Veniamin Kaverin (Moscow: Sovetskii pisatel', 1983), 146.

Philanthropist') shows the selfish hypocrisy of the rich.[44] These were easy enough to present as an attack on everything the Soviet Union declared itself opposed to. As the 1920s gave way to the 1930s and the rise of German fascism, which selected Heine as an early candidate for book burning, the acceptability of Heine's satires in the Soviet Union was unchallengeable, as they offered irrefutable attacks against 'the militant nationalism of the German bourgeoisie, racial intolerance, obscurantism'.[45]

Many of the objects of Heine's satire, however, can also be found among the main concerns of Soviet satire in the 1920s, summarized as 'the philistine, the availability and quality of food, housing and living conditions in general, the frustrating intricacies of Soviet life (for example, occasionally mystifying Soviet jargon, pompous slogans, and the scarcity of theatre tickets), the bureaucrat and literature (how and what one should write, censorship and over-editing, talentless writers)'.[46] Tynianov's concentration on Heine's satirical poetry, as Etkind suggests, offered a reasonably risk-free way for him to use translation as a cover for criticism of Soviet realities.[47] Etkind illustrates his point with reference to Tynianov's 1927 translation of 'Die Wahlesel' ('The Election Donkeys'), in which the animals declare a wish to be ruled by just one creature rather than many – not only did this poem appear in the year that Trotskii and Zinoviev were permanently excluded from the Communist Party, but as Etkind points out, its initial version, rather than the revised one that appeared in his 1934 volume of Heine's poetry, contains phrases which, for contemporaries, were closely identified with the kind of jargon used in Communist Party meetings.[48]

44 'Das Sklavenschiff', *Sämtliche Gedichte in zeitlicher Folge*, 715, translated as 'Nevol'nichii korabl', *Mastera russkogo stikhotvornogo perevoda*, II, 237–41; 'Zur Beruhigung', *Sämtliche Gedichte*, 461, translated as 'K uspokoeniiu', *Strofy veka –2*, ed. Evgenii Vitkovskii (Moscow: Polifakt, 1998), 276–7; 'Der Philanthrop', *Sämtliche Gedichte*, 739, translated as 'Filantrop' <http://www.vekperevoda.com/1887/tynyanov.htm> accessed 25 September 2009.
45 A. V. Fedorov, 'Iurii Tynianov i ego perevody iz Geine', 267.
46 Richard E. Chapple, review of Peter Henry, ed., *Modern Soviet Satire* (London: Collet's, 1974) in *Slavic and East European Journal*, 3 (1976), 319.
47 Efim Etkind, '"Veselyi primer Geine": Geine, Tiutchev, Maiakovskii', 332.
48 Ibid.

The contemporary resonance of Tynianov's translations is a matter for speculation, but for anyone who has studied literature of the Soviet period, it is tempting to read his version of 'An einen politischen Dichter' ('To a Political Poet') as a comment on the flourishing careers of certain 'proletarian' poets. The speaker acknowledges that the political poet enjoys the enthusiastic praise of his public, but concludes with a typically Heine-esque deflationary stanza, which, in Tynianov's translation, reads:

> Раб о свободе любит петь
> Под вечер, в заведеньи.
> От этого питье вкусней,
> Живей пищеваренье.[49]

[The slave loves to sing of freedom/ Of an evening in the tavern./ This makes the food taste better/ And the digestion more lively.]

The poet's achievements are reduced to being an aid to digestion and a token of slavery, both that of his audience, and, implicitly, his own. One might also reflect on the real material benefits that were made available to ideologically reliable Soviet writers. Tynianov's translation of 'Warnung' ('Warning'), in which an anxious speaker voices his concerns to a friend who has published something unflattering about the powers that be, surely has contemporary relevance:

> Ты печатаешь такое!
> Милый друг мой, это гибель!
> Ты веди себя пристойно
> Если хочешь жить в покое.

[The things you publish!/ My dear friend, you risk disaster!/ You should behave decently/ If you want to live in peace.]

The third and final stanza demonstrates anxieties that do not seem out of place, as long as one reinterprets the reference to priests in the second line:

---

49 'K politicheskomu poetu', *Mastera russkogo stikhotvornogo perevoda*, II, 242.

Heine and Genre

Милый друг мой, я не в духе!
Все попы длинноязычны,
Долгоруки все владыки,
А народ ведь длинноухий.[50]

[My dear friend, I'm most upset!/ All priests have long tongues,/ All the rulers have long arms,/ And, of course, the people have long ears.]

The final example to be discussed is an enigmatic poem translated by Tynianov in 1934, which muses on the words overheard by the speaker as a woman, Esther Wolf, condemns an unnamed man to oblivion. In the context of the USSR in the early 1930s, the consigning of a person to oblivion seems to have plenty of potential echoes. The three concluding stanzas of Tynianov's translation run:

Да не будет он помянут,
Да в стихе изчезнет имя, –
Темный пес в могиле темной
Тлей с проклятьями моими!

Даже в утро воскресенья,
Когда звук фанфар разбудит
Мертвецов, и поплетутся
На судилище, где судят,

И когда прокричит ангел
Оглашенных, что предстанут
Пред небесными властями, –
Да не будет он помянут![51]

[He is not to be remembered,/ Not in a song, not in a book–/ Dark dog in a dark grave,/ You can rot with my curse!// Even on the day of resurrection,/ When, woken by the fanfares of the trumpets,/ trembling, the dead hordes make their way/ to the court to be judged,// And in that place the angel reads out/ Before the divine authorities/ All the names of those invited –/ He is not to be remembered!]

---

50 'Predosterezhenie', *Strofy veka 2*, 276.
51 'Da ne budet on pomianut!', *Mastera russkogo stikhotvornogo perevoda*, II, 243.

Perhaps this is a case of a covert response to the fact that by now a certain someone was being mentioned all too frequently. The speaker and her implied audience clearly know the identity of the person whose name may not be spoken, and are collectively refusing to reveal it, making the object of Esther Wolf's curse unidentifiable. Similarly, Tynianov's first readers might have shared assumptions about the unnamed person, but the text provides no clues that would give ammunition to a potential accuser, who, by making any accusation, might risk being suspected of unorthodox views. It would have been unthinkable to publish a poem which declared the General Secretary of the Soviet Communist Party unmentionable, but perfectly possible to achieve the same effect by using Heine's poem as a vehicle. Tynianov's faithful translation manages a subtle subversion that the author of the original might have appreciated.

Tynianov's translations of Heine came at a time when political change and artistic innovation made it possible to produce work which was both accurate in relation to the original text and relevant to the contemporary situation. For a few years, before the imposition of greater linguistic uniformity as socialist realist aesthetics took hold, it was possible to do justice to Heine's mixing of language from a variety of registers, including the vulgar and the bureaucratic. The futurist tradition gradually faded away in the 1930s, and, as Etkind puts it, 'Tynianov's discoveries were consigned to oblivion'.[52] The unique quality of his translations has been summed up by Etkind, who describes Tynianov's Heine as follows: 'while remaining himself – a poet of the mid- or early nineteenth century, the last of the German romantics, a writer who belonged to German, French and Jewish culture, he turned out to be a contemporary of Khlebnikov and Maiakovskii'.[53] Playfulness, identified by Tynianov as a significant feature of Heine's writing, found its expression in the artistic innovations linked with Futurism and the liberation of the word, and it enabled Tynianov to free his translations from what Blok described as the 'lumbering ten-ton liberal legend of Heine' that had come to dominate Russian views of the poet at

---

52   Efim Etkind, '"Veselyi primer Geine": Geine, Tiutchev, Maiakovskii', 326.
53   Ibid.

the end of the nineteenth century.⁵⁴ His Heine, like the historical Heine, is not a poet who can easily be enlisted to give his unwavering support to any cause. But Tynianov's Heine is equipped with contemporary language and stylistic features that make him appear to be thoroughly up to date; Etkind sees that this Heine is someone who could have been read in the 1920s and 1930s as home-grown contemporary literature: 'The modernized language lends contemporary relevance and meaning to what is being said – it's not just Heine addressing his contemporaries, but Tynianov addressing his too'.⁵⁵ Reading Tynianov's translations today shows us how brilliantly he transformed Heine's poetry into Russian, but it also gives some insight into the Soviet literary world of the late 1920s and early 1930s, in which translation was already a creative refuge but not an escape from the present.

54 Aleksandr Blok, 'Geine v Rossii: o russkikh perevodakh stikhotvorenii Geine', *Sobranie sochinenii*, 8 vols (Moscow and Leningrad: Khudozhestvennaia literatura, 1960–3), VI, 116.
55 Efim Etkind, '"Veselyi primer Geine": Geine, Tiutchev, Maiakovskii', 340.

SUSANNA WITT

Arts of Accommodation:
The First All-Union Conference of Translators, Moscow, 1936, and the Ideologization of Norms

> Если писатели – «инженеры человеческих душ», то мы – «инженеры связи», мы должны работать немедленно.¹

Introduction

Recent years have witnessed an intense interest in the culture of the Stalin period and the publication of important studies from a wide range of disciplinary and methodological angles.² One aspect of Soviet culture still largely neglected, however, is that of literary translation.³ The growing

---

1   'If writers are the "engineers of human souls", then we are the "engineers of communication", and must work hastily.' Translator Ezra Levontin on a meeting at the Translators' Section 29 October 1935 (RGALI, f. 631, op. 21, ed. khr. 8, l. 18).
2   See, for example: Sheila Fitzpatrick, ed., *Stalinism. New Directions* (London: Routledge, 2000); David Brandenberger, *National Bolshevism: Stalinist Mass Culture and the Formation of Modern Russian National Identity, 1931–1956* (Cambridge, MA: Harvard University Press, 2002); Evgeny Dobrenko and Eric Naiman, eds, *The Landscape of Stalinism: The Art and Ideology of Soviet Space* (Seattle: University of Washington Press, 2003); Karl Schlögel, *Terror und Traum: Moskau 1937* (Munich: Hanser, 2008).
3   A sign of emerging attention is Katerina Clark's recent monograph *Moscow, the Fourth Rome: Stalinism, Cosmopolitanism, and the Evolution of Soviet Culture, 1931–1941* (Cambridge, MA: Harvard University Press 2011). Highlighting the specific Soviet

significance of translations was, towards the mid-1930s, perceived and debated within the literary establishment itself. Whereas the formation of the Writers' Union and its First Congress in 1934 is an obligatory topic in any account of the period, there are no studies as yet devoted to the self-reflexion of translators and their various attempts at accommodating the turbulent processes which affected cultural life at the time. This will be the concern of the present chapter. After taking a preliminary look at the public contexts in which translation figured most prominently, I will focus on the little-known First All-Union Conference of Translators, held at the beginning of January 1936, and the clash of discourses and ideologies of translation that it featured. Crucial in many respects, the moment was a watershed in Soviet culture of the 1930s, marked by the establishment of the Committee on Arts Affairs in December 1935 (which gradually secured total state control over the cultural field), and the subsequent campaign against 'formalism in the arts' on the eve of the Great Purge.[4]

Literary translation as action crystallizes a range of problems of particular relevance within the context of Stalinist culture. At the core is the overall problem of accommodating the 'foreign' in a climate of growing suspicion and xenophobia, and of defining the 'foreign' within the framework of a discourse progressively informed by the 'friendship of the peoples' slogan. Furthermore, the procedures implied in the production and editing of translations assume specific significance in this era of 'textual

---

internationalism of the 1930s, Clark posits the incorporation of both the international (translational) and the national (Soviet) canon into the project of creating a 'world literature' à la Moscou.

[4] The conference thus delimits the first and second of the periods defined in Katerina Clark and Evgeny Dobrenko, *Soviet Culture and Power: A History in Documents, 1917–1953* (New Haven: Yale University Press, 2007), 149: 'according to the overall trajectory of cultural politics over the course of the decade it can be divided into three periods: 1932–1936, the period of reaction against the extremes of the preceding cultural revolution and also the time when Socialist Realism was instituted; 1936–1938, the time of the Great Purge and also of the campaign against "formalism" and "naturalism" in the arts; and 1938–1941, a possible third would be the post-purge phase when the country was in the shadow of the anticipated war'.

anxiety',[5] always alert to the relationship between 'the most canonical texts and any individual text generated'.[6] Taking as its point of departure material from the Soviet press, the chapter will trace the formation of Soviet translation ideology as it emerges from published and archival material relating to the 1936 conference. Special attention will be paid to the operational value and varying content of such concepts as 'literalist' and 'free' translation, and their opposition, and the role of translations in forming the 'national cultures' as an ambivalent project situated in a field of tension between the Stalinist discourse of nationalities and the latent threat of 'bourgeois nationalism'.

The Visibility of Translations: *Pravda* 1934–1936

One way of grasping the context within which problems of translation were articulated at the 1936 conference is to monitor their presence during the preceding period in *Pravda*, which, as 'the centre of the informational system'[7] by this time, was setting the coordinates of public discourse. Although the theme of translation was periodically brought up from the early 1930s in the pages of publications such as *Literaturnaia gazeta* and *Literaturnyi kritik*, representing a more internal professional discourse,[8] the focus here will be on how the topic was reflected in *Pravda*, at the top of the hierarchical system of official public culture: the ways in which translations as products and translation as process became visible in the party newspaper in the time span between the First Congress of Soviet Writers

---

5   Clark and Dobrenko, *Soviet Culture and Power*, xiii.
6   Ibid.
7   Jeffrey Brooks, *Thank You, Comrade Stalin! Soviet Public Culture from Revolution to Cold War* (Princeton: Princeton University Press, 2000), xix.
8   One period of intensified attention to problems of translation in *Literaturnaia gazeta* was in autumn 1933; the critical assessments of the articles here were discussed at the subsequent First Moscow Conference of Translators, 26 December that year.

and the Translators' Conference.⁹ The languages involved are, above all, of those nationalities which in the Russian context were designated by the hyperonym *vostochnye* ('Oriental'), that is, languages of the peoples of Caucasus and Central Asia.

It was during the Writers' Congress in August 1934, 'the first large public event in Stalinist culture',¹⁰ that the literatures of the non-Russian peoples of the Union were displayed on a large scale for the first time. *Pravda*'s coverage of the congress included numerous publications of speeches by leading figures of the Writers' Union in the national republics,¹¹ as well as reports featuring non-Russian delegates.¹² The rhetoric of these materials was largely the same: it aimed at demonstrating the great significance of the October Revolution and the new order to the respective cultures. As *Pravda* editorialized on 23 August, 'In all languages resounds the victorious song of socialism!'¹³ Maksim Gor'kii, in his speeches at the congress, emphasized the need for translations in the process of 'organizing

---

9   The same period is covered from another perspective by Elena Zemskova's chapter in the present volume.
10 Clark and Dobrenko, *Soviet Culture and Power*, 162.
11 'The literature of Ukraine' (20 August), 'The literature of Soviet Belorussia', 'The literature of Armenia' (21 August), 'Georgian literature', 'The literature of Uzbekistan', 'The Azerbaijano-Turkish literature', 'In the auls there are new songs' (about Turkmen literature) (23 August), 'The literature of a people, which was not' (about Tadzhik literature), 'In hard class struggle Tartar literature was born', 'The revolution created our literary language' (about Bashkir literature) (24 August).
12 Participants writing in languages other than Russian made up 48 per cent of the delegates at the congress (Brooks, *Thank You, Comrade Stalin!*, 277); in *Pravda*, non-Russians received 20 per cent of the articles and 12 per cent of the space (ibid.: 113). The coverage was in fact dictated by a TsK resolution of 21 August: 'To require *Pravda* and *Izvestiia* to increase their coverage of the work of the Writers' Congress, publishing reports on the national literatures and organizing space for the speeches of delegates and speakers from national literatures fully, or at least two-thirds of each report'. Andrei Artizov and Oleg Naumov, eds, *Vlast' i khudozhestvennaia intelligentsiia: dokumenty TsK RKP(b)-VKP(b); VChK-OGPU-NKVD o kul'turnoi politike 1917–1953 gg.* (Moscow: Mezhdunarodnyi fond 'Demokratiia', 1999), 229.
13 As Brooks observes, such foregrounding of national writers, 'whose status depended almost exclusively on the Soviet state rather than on their works or any national

the all-union literature as a whole',[14] and introduced the idea of a periodical anthology (*almanakh*) featuring the literature of the peoples of the USSR (which was finally to materialize in the *almanakh Druzhba narodov* of 1939, soon turned into a journal). Translation as such was not an issue at the congress.[15] The presence of translators, however, is reflected in a secret police report which registers negative attitudes among the poet-translators toward the national literatures.[16]

The single national delegate who received most attention at the congress was the Lezgin folk poet Suleiman Stal'skii of Dagestan, featured together with Maksim Gor'kii in a photograph accompanying an article about his career.[17] The reader was informed about the pre-revolutionary life of the sixty-six-year-old illiterate as a poor farmhand, whose songs 'expressed protest against mullahs and judges, against usurers and speculators', and his present existence as 'bard of the kolkhozes'. A sample of his work ('Pesnia o mulle Ramazane iz Bekemera') was included in Russian translation but with no translator indicated. In the same way, a report on Stal'skii's speech at the congress (highlighting the progress in his native country after the

 public [...] served to sanction a particularly slavish literary role' (*Thank You, Comrade Stalin!*, 113–14).

14 *Pervyi vsesoiuznyi s"ezd sovetskikh pisatelei 1934, stenograficheskii otchet*, ed. I. K. Luppol, M. M. Rozental', S. M. Tretiakov (reprint) (Moscow: Sovetskii pisatel', 1990), 680.

15 Cf. Kornei Chukovskii's remark ('Iskusstvo perevoda,' *Pravda*, 1 March 1935): 'At the Writers' Congress they (the translators) were not represented by anyone, though in the USSR it is precisely we, masters of translation, who should be accorded the greatest respect – we have such a huge political role to play in our country'.

16 As the secret source reports: 'The attention paid by the congress to the national literatures evoked unique, chauvinistically coloured moods among translators. The general tone was this: national writers are bad. It's we who actually make them into writers, sacrificing our own creativity. For this, not only do we not see any gratitude, but we encounter perpetual dissatisfaction, behind-the-scenes accusations and so on. These writers are widely published here and surrounded with esteem, chosen for central organs of the union and so forth, whereas we always take a back seat'. (Clark and Dobrenko, *Soviet Culture and Power*, 177). For more on this, see the chapter by Zemskova in this volume.

17 *Pravda*, 20 August.

revolution) carried his song dedicated to the occasion in another anonymous Russian translation.[18] Here a pattern was established, which would form the literary contributions to *Pravda* for the years to come. In 1934, prior to the congress, the paper had included only occasional 'national'[19] items in its stock of (mostly political) verse, which was produced by Russian poets like Bednyi, Gusev, Kirsanov, Surkov and other 'pravdists'. But now space was given to folk poets from the Caucasus and, above all, Central Asia, appearing in Russian translation with ideologically thoroughly calibrated material, the lion's share of which would qualify as 'Stalin panegyric'.

From April 1935, 'Oriental' material began to appear more frequently and to be systematically supplied with paratext. Most of the poems appeared under the fixed heading 'Tvorchestvo narodov SSSR', and were often accompanied by footnotes and, occasionally, by photographs. Other types of paratext were articles about different folk traditions, e.g. a report on *ashugs* (folk poets) in Azerbaijan on 19 June 1935, and one on *zhirshis* and *akyns* (folk poets) of Kazakhstan on 17 May 1936. An increasingly important role was played precisely by the latter, as shown in the following table, which indicates (1) the total number of 'Oriental' translations in *Pravda*; (2) the number of attributed translations among them; and (3) the number of translations from Kazakh.

18   *Pravda*, 23 August. Generally, Stal'skii's contributions in *Pravda* were translated by Effendi Kapiev, secretary of the Writers' Union of Dagestan (the two men can be seen visiting the paper's premises in Moscow on a photograph in *Pravda*, 22 May 1935). Other pieces of translated literature in the *Pravda* material from the congress were the poem 'Put'' na Birobidzhan' by S. Galkin, translated from Yiddish by Os. Kolychev, and 'To the First Congress of Soviet Writers' by Ianka Kupala, translated from Belorussian by Sergei Gorodetskii (24 August); *Pravda* also reports on the publication of collections of translated poetry 'in honour of the congress' – *Poety Armenii*, edited and translated by Aleksandr Gatov (10 August), and a collection of Uigur poetry from Kazakhstan, 'the first attempt at translating modern Uigur literature into Russian' (25 August).

19   The noun *natsional* and its corresponding adjective *natsional'nyi* were commonly used as referring to persons of non-Russian ethnicity; this convention reflects a situation in which Russian as the dominant ethnicity was unmarked. I will use it here as a terminological citation from the material in question.

Table 1: Translations, 1934–1936

	1934	*1935*	*1936*
'Oriental' translations	7	23	39
Translator indicated	5	13	25
From Kazakh	0	3	15

Foremost among the Kazakh bards was Dzhambul Dzhabaev, born in south-eastern Kazakhstan in 1846, whose first publication in *Pravda* was on New Year's Day, 1936.[20] Dzhambul's poem 'Pesnia ot vsei dushi', in Andrei Aldan's translation, was placed directly below the editorial 'Stakhanovskii god', promising the coming year to be a 'god polnokrovnogo sotsialisticheskogo protsvetaniia' ('a year of full-blooded socialist blossoming'), an all-too-proper designation of the year destined to be the beginning of the Great Purge. Dzhambul (commonly referred to only by his first name) became the most famous of the bards assigned propaganda roles at the time, taking part in many public events until his death in 1945. His songs were included in Soviet school anthologies and became compulsory reading also in the post-war socialist-realist canon exported to the Eastern bloc.

The case of Dzhambul was brought into Western translation scholarship by Gideon Toury as an example of 'culture planning' through pseudo-translation.[21] Toury's brief discussion, the only source for which is the memoirs of composer Dmitrii Shostakovich, presents a somewhat simplified picture of state-governed activities of planning 'from above'; I have discussed this elsewhere, and pointed out the complex intertwining of

---

20   The name is erroneously rendered here as 'Dzhimbul'.
21   Gideon Toury, 'Enhancing Cultural Changes by Means of Fictitious Translations' in Eva Hung, ed., *Translation and Cultural Change: Studies in History, Norms and Image-Projection* (Amsterdam: John Benjamins, 2005), 3–17.

motifs and incentives involved in any concrete act of translation.[22] It is true that a framework was established 'from above', which created a demand for translated texts of a certain type, but this left room for different kinds of initiatives on the part of the translators (and, occasionally, the authors), whose work was facilitated by the common use of (often anonymous) interlinear trots, *podstrochniki*. Such a demand for translations arose, for example, in connection with the festivals featuring the literature and art of the peoples of national republics (so-called *dekady*, literally 'ten days') which were organized regularly in Moscow and some other major cities from 1936 until 1941.[23]

The first Kazakh *dekada*, engaging 300 artists from the republic, was held in May 1936 and received massive coverage in *Pravda*. Poems of several *akyns* in Russian translation, reports on various forms of Kazakh folk art, literature and music, and reviews of performances were published. The event was situated in the context of the realization of socialist-realist art, foregrounding the concept of *narodnost'*. As explained in the *Pravda* editorial of 27 May ('The art of a victorious people'):

> The country requires truthful, realistic, striking works of art of a socialist orientation which are of the highest quality [...]. The path to achieving this is clear. That path is the culture of the people (*narodnost'*). Popular motifs, popular feelings, art, drawing its strength from the depths of the people, – that is what we have seen.

The same page featured a photograph of artists from the Kazakh delegation encircling Dzhambul, and a series of resolutions on awarding the participants a variety of state orders.[24]

---

22   Susanna Witt, 'Between the Lines: Totalitarianism and translation in the USSR' in Brian James Baer, ed., *Contexts, Subtexts, and Pretexts: Literary Translation in Eastern Europe and Russia* (Amsterdam: John Benjamins, 2011), 149–70.

23   For a description of the opportunities open to translators at such events, see Aleksandr Zhovtis, *Nepridumannye anekdoty: Iz sovetskogo proshlogo* (Moscow: Its-Garant, 1995), 122–3 (cited in 'Between the Lines: Totalitarianism and Translation in the USSR', 164).

24   On the occasion, Dzhambul received the Order of the Red Banner of Labour, to be followed in 1938 by the Lenin Order and in 1941 by the Stalin Prize. This practice of

Dzhambul's principal translator during the period 1936–1941, Pavel Kuznetsov, was also the man behind the very first piece of Kazakh folklore to appear in *Pravda*: on 5 October 1935 he published a song by the bard Maimbet. Displaying typical features of the genre, the song is built on the contrast between a poor, feudal, oppressed past, mirrored through the unenviable lot of a camel, and a radiant present:

> Я богат и о счастье пою:
> Самый лучший – колхозный верблюд,
> Самый быстрый – колхозный скакун,
> Самый крупный – колхозный табун,
> Самый сочный – у нас сенокос,
> Самый свежий – у нас овес.
> Юрта лучшая – это моя,
> Стал богатым в колхозе я.

> I am rich and sing of joy:
> The *kolkhoz* camel is the best,
> The *kolkhoz* racer is the fastest,
> The *kolkhoz* herd is the largest,
> Our hay harvest is the richest,
> Our oats are the freshest.
> The best *yurt* is mine,
> I have grown rich in the *kolkhoz*.

The paratextual framing included seven footnotes and a photograph of the *akyn*, seated with his *dombra* (a traditional long-necked lute) in hand. As distinct from the case of Dzhambul, there is no evidence of Maimbet's participation in any public events. According to several sources, he in fact did not exist at all, being entirely a creation of Kuznetsov's imagination.[25]

'consecration' (in Bourdieu's sense) involved several of the bards; Stal'skii, for example, received his Order of Lenin on 17 April 1936 (with *Pravda* featuring a photograph of the event).

25 Zhovtis, *Nepridumannye anekdoty*, 13–14; Evgenii Brusilovskii, 'Brusilovskii o Dzhambule', *Svoboda slova*, 26, 2007, 5–7). When a journalist working for *Kazakhstanskaia pravda*, Kuznetsov had published several poems in his paper and also released a separate volume of Maimbet's verse, but he failed to present any

The publication of Maimbet's song, however, was to resonate powerfully. Some weeks later, on 23 October 1935, *Pravda* devoted its entire front page to material related to the fifteenth anniversary of Kazakhstan: an editorial entitled 'A people reborn' and a lengthy 'Letter from the working people of Kazakhstan to comrade Stalin', signed by '626,436 shock workers from the republic'. Both pieces cited entire stanzas from the song, the editorial in fact using two. Another passage of the same song was cited in a letter to Stalin from the participants of the Kazakh *dekada*, published in *Pravda* on 1 June 1936, without mention of Maimbet's name:

> We bid farewell to you in the words of the *zhirshi*, who expressed the feelings of the whole Kazakh nation:
> 'Our dear father and friend!
> May the sun always shine above you,
> May happiness always be with you,
> Look after yourself for us,
> Live forever, our beloved!'[26]

---

evidence of Maimbet's existence when asked by the local party organization, which was preparing for the first Kazakh *dekada* in Moscow and planned to include this colourful figure in the delegation ('Brusilovskii o Dzhambule'). As the same source suggests, Dzhambul, an old *akyn* of local fame and proper appearance, may have been the solution to the problem. (The source, Evgenii Brusilovskii, a Russian composer living at the time in Alma-Ata, was presumably Shostakovich's main informant on the subject of Dzhambul; as is evident from the above-mentioned group photograph in *Pravda*, 27 May 1936, Brusilovskii was himself a participant in this *dekada*.) This version of events is essentially supported by a letter of 1939 from a group of members of the Russian section of the Writers' Union in Kazakhstan in which they express their discontent with Kuznetsov's work as an editor of the Union's journal. In this context, the writers cite Kuznetsov's 'literary trickery' (*literaturnaia afera*) with Maimbet and also point out other bards of his creation (RGALI, f. 631, op. 6, ed. khr. 521).

26 The same poem was apparently included in the publication *Stikhi i pesni narodov Vostoka o Staline*. This was reviewed by translator Adalis in *Pravda*, 11 December 1935, who cited a stanza in her piece. One more of Kuznetsov's Maimbet 'translations', a lullaby ('Pesnia nad kolybel'iu syna' ('Song for my son's cradle')), appeared in *Pravda*, 2 January 1936.

The 'Oriental' translations thus entered into the discourse of national policies, as well as that of literary politics. The moment of their appearance may be related to several factors. In practice they served to introduce a new genre in the Soviet Russian literary system, in which there had been no lyric portraits of Stalin prior to the seventeenth party congress of 1934.[27] The hymnologic representations of the leader encountered in these translations became a step in the development of the personality cult.[28] At the same time, the need for voices from national republics at the periphery should be viewed in the context of the new constitution approved 5 December 1936, the rhetoric of which promoted the idea of the USSR as a 'democracy of all the peoples'.[29] Dzhambul's poem, in Kuznetsov's translation, on the topic, 'Stalin's Great Law' ('The law according to which happiness ...') was in fact published in *Pravda* three days after the printing of the draft constitution, on 12 June, as a kind of sequel to it.[30] The voices from the periphery were supplied with a prestigious voice from abroad when in 1936 Henri Barbusse's apologetic Stalin biography was translated into Russian.[31]

27 Lazar' Fleishman, *Boris Pasternak i literaturnoe dvizhenie 1930-kh godov* (St Petersburg: Akademicheskii proekt, 2005), 389.
28 The emergence of the Oriental translations coincided with that of another genre in the literary system, the popular mass song (*massovaia pesnia*) introduced via film comedies beginning in 1934. See Hans Günther, '"Broad Is My Motherland": The Mother Archetype and Space in the Soviet Mass Song' in Evgeny Dobrenko and Eric Naiman, eds, *The Landscape of Stalinism: The Art and Ideology of Soviet Space* (Seattle: University of Washington Press, 2003), 77–95, with which they share some topoi and characteristics, differing in other respects (notably as for the role of Stalin).
29 Fleishman, *Boris Pasternak i literaturnoe dvizhenie 1930-kh godov*, 385.
30 For Kazakhstan the new constitution brought specific changes: having been an autonomous republic within the RSFSR, it was now elevated to the status of a Soviet republic.
31 Henri Barbusse, *Stalin. Chelovek cherez kotorogo raskryvaetsia novyi mir*; trans. and ed. A. I. Stetskii (Moscow: Khudozhestvennaia literature, 1936).

The Visibility of Translators: *Pravda* 1934–1936

The increasing visibility of translations in *Pravda* was not concomitant with an equal visibility of translators; as shown in the table above, a significant share of the translated material was unattributed. This fact came to interact in a specific way with another characteristic trait of these publications: the way in which claims were made for their authenticity. Basically, there were two methods of lending authority and legitimacy to the texts: detailed accounts of the circumstances of their fixation and the abundant use of footnotes to explain words referring to foreign *realia* that were retained untranslated in many of the Russian texts. An example of the first method, typically involving references to some official body, is the paratext to 'Poema o Lenine', published in *Pravda* on 15 April 1935:

> This poem has been written down from the words of the illiterate Uzbek *bakhshi* (singer) Ergash Dzhuman Bul'bulova (from the Nuratinskii region of the Uzbek Republic). The transcript was made by members of the Uzbek Academic Research Institution of Literature and Language in Tashkent.[32]

An example of the second is Dzhambul's poem 'Moia rodina', which appeared in *Pravda* on 7 May 1936 with nineteen footnotes, but with no translator indicated. Such enhancing of the 'discursive presence' of the translator,[33] yet at the same time with no individual identified as taking responsibility for these efforts to 'safeguard adequate communication with the new audience',[34] has the pragmatic effect of making visible not the translator, but the very status of the text as translation: the strategy authorizes the text as 'foreign'. The function of footnotes in these cases seems to be to *create* the context, the 'cultural embedding' of the text, whereas footnotes

---

32 A photograph of the author was included, but no translator indicated.
33 Theo Hermans, 'The Translator's Voice in Translated Narrative' in *Target* 8: (1996) 23–48 (27).
34 Ibid., 29.

usually function to decipher meaning for the target audience.³⁵ The texts abound in untranslated words which acquire an iconic quality and appear as a verbal parallel to the photographs of the authors in exotic costume, guaranteeing the authenticity of the texts.³⁶

Translations from the national languages into Russian were included in 'the performance' of public culture,³⁷ brought to bear on the cult as well as on the development of Socialist Realism. Translations *into* these languages, however, were highlighted in a completely different context. Such translations, and the corresponding translators, became visible in a form of public translation critique, which constituted one the most clear-cut expressions of 'textual anxiety' – the obsession with 'measuring the gap between the most canonical texts and any individual text generated'³⁸ – to surface in the press.

In a *Pravda* article entitled 'How Marxism was being distorted in the Crimean State Publishing House,'³⁹ the reader was informed about unsatisfactory conditions revealed during a regular party purge of the institution. A 'nest of bourgeois-nationalist elements' who had found a 'warm refuge' within the confines of the publishing house were 'editing and reviewing the most diverse books, flooding the Crimean book market with ideological rejects'. Their sins were twofold: they had neglected to translate and issue Lenin's work and Marxist classics as stipulated by party decisions ('Шеститомник Ленина на татарском языке подготовлялся четыре года, и ни одного тома не вышло'), and distortive translations of the texts were released ('При переводах часто допускаются искажения, извращающие политический смысл'). The paper provided detailed exam-

---

35 Ibid., 28.
36 The image of the peoples projected by the Oriental translations in *Pravda* displays several traits of what has been labelled 'Stalinist Orientalism', a corollary to the evolving Russocentrism of the Soviet pre-war period, expressed in the tendency to exaggerate the gap in cultural development between Russians and non-Russians, which were depicted as if 'frozen in time', Brandenberger, *National Bolshevism*, 92–3.
37 Brooks, *Thank You, Comrade Stalin!*
38 Clark and Dobrenko, *Soviet Culture and Power*, xiii.
39 26 October 1934.

ples of such distortions in the Tartar translations of texts by Lenin and Stalin. Comparison was made between the source text and a *retranslation* of the offending target text into Russian. The additional hermeneutic step (the retranslation) was not commented on.[40] In fact, the practice of withdrawing books on the grounds of the translators' faultiness sometimes led to a shortage of politically vital literature and became the subject of a Central Committee resolution directed against the activities of Glavlit (the main censorship body in the USSR).[41]

The most dramatic cases of such public translation critique appeared in the beginning of 1935 in connection with the judicial regulation of the activities of cooperative farms. During the Second All-Union Conference of Shock-workers of the Kolkhozes, held in Moscow in February, a document 'Model Statutes for Cooperative Farms' ('Primernyi ustav sel'skokhoziaistvennoi arteli') was adopted, which, according to a resolution, was to be translated into the different national languages and distributed to all cooperative farms of the Union.[42] On the basis of this model document, cooperatives were to work out, approve, and register their local statutes. The processing of the text that was implied in the procedures was referred to in *Pravda* during the following months, giving rise to headings such as 'Against the distortion of the kolkhoz statutes'

---

40 'Stalin said, for example, that "One of the fundamental tasks in the realization of the second five-year plan is to overcome the remnants of capitalism in the economy and the consciousnesses of people". In translation, this was rendered as "One of the main political tasks in the realization of the second five-year plan is to finish off or liquidate the remnants of capitalism in the people's consciousness."' *Pravda*, 26 October 1934, 3. The leadership of the publishing house was blamed for its original production in the Tartar language as well, the 'rightwing-opportunistic mistakes' of which likewise were exemplified in Russian. The purging action resulted in expulsion from the party of two leading figures of the publishing house and the secretary of its party organization.

41 Resolution of the TsK VKP(b) Orgburo 'On eliminating Glavlit's sabotaging system of withdrawing literature', 9 December 1937 (Clark and Dobrenko, *Soviet Culture and Power*, 264).

42 The text of the statutes (approved by the government and the Party's Central Committee) and the resolution were published in *Pravda*, 18 February 1935.

(19 March), 'The statutes "corrected" by the class enemy' (17 April), and 'Adopt the statutes without distortions' (23 April). In these cases, modifications had been spotted in local Russian adaptations of the text of the statutes. But translations were also attacked. In a series of resolutions issued by the Commissariat of Agriculture and the Party's agricultural department, the translations into Kalmyk, Chuvash and Karakalpak languages were condemned and the respective editions of the statutes were withdrawn. The resolutions condemning them contained the same form of public translation critique as in the case with the Crimean publishing house, displaying detailed examples of 'errors and slips': 'in the first point of the final paragraph, the word "all" has been omitted, where in the Model statute it says "make all kolkhozes prosperous"'.[43] The standardized conclusions of the resolutions decreed that 'the case with the perpetrators of the edition of the text of the Model statutes for cooperative farms into the Chuvash (etc.) language, which distorted the main propositions of the Model statutes of cooperative farms' be transferred to local governmental and party bodies for consideration.

Such harsh measures were not proposed in the sphere of literary translation, but the discourse around translation that was taking shape may be perceived here as well. During this period, *Pravda* published two articles by the foremost authority on the subject of translation, Kornei Chukovskii, one devoted to a volume of Shakespeare translations and one reviewing the problem of 'nationality' translation. In the first, significantly entitled 'Iskazhennyi Shekspir' ('Distorted Shakespeare'), published on 12 August 1934, Chukovskii demonstrated how, in a new translation of *King Lear*, 'distortion of the text is executed in eleven different ways'. The editor was blamed for failing to supply an overview of 'the social soil from which Shakespeare's works grew', and 'Shakespeare's ideology'. The second article, entitled 'Iskusstvo perevoda' ('The Art of Translation') and published

---

43 'Postanovlenie Narkomzema SSSR i Sel'skokhoziaistvennogo otdela TsK VKP(b) o tekste Primernogo ustava Sel'skokhoziaistvennoi arteli na KALMYTSKOM iazyke, izdannogo Gosudarstvennym izdatel'stvom Kalmytskoi avtonomnoi oblasti' (*Pravda*, 17 May 1935).

on 1 March 1935, focussed on the deficiencies in translations from and into the national languages, pinpointing the ideological significance of mistranslations.

The First All-Union Conference of Translators, Moscow 1936

The two distinct lines that *Pravda* foregrounded in its coverage of translation between 1934 and 1936 – the emergence of the 'nationality' translations and a politically determined translation critique – are fundamental for an understanding of the conditions under which translators were to gather at the 1936 All-Union Conference. Translation from and into the national languages was declared the main topic of the conference, and a significant proportion of the keynote speech was, as we shall see, devoted to a detailed critique in the same vein as in the *Pravda* articles, to which reference also was made explicitly.

The Translators' Section of the Writers' Union was formed on 16 October 1934, having led a previous existence within FOSP (Federation of Unions of Soviet Writers) and as a 'bureau of translated literature' within the Orgkomitet of the Writers' Union.[44] This moment of 'gaining literary citizenship'[45] was an important event concomitant with an intensified self-reflexion among translators. This period witnessed a multifaceted process of accommodation to the new cultural situation that had emerged after the 1932 party resolution on dissolving artistic organizations, the subsequent launching of Socialist Realism, and the complete inclusion of writers as actors in the 'performance' of public culture made explicit by the Writers' Congress.[46] In relation to the new artistic doctrine questions arose, for example, as to

---

44 RGALI, f. 631, op. 21, ed. khr. 14, ll. 3–4.
45 As expressed by translator Pavel Zenkevich, head of the Section, in 1935 (RGALI, f. 631, op. 21, ed. khr. 8, l. 59).
46 Brooks, *Thank You, Comrade Stalin!*, 110.

the role of translations in the codification of Socialist Realism and the formation of a Soviet canon, as well as to translators' adoption of its tenets.

Most of the topics covered at the First All-Union Conference of Translators in 1936 had already been discussed in public. Two years earlier, the First Moscow Conference of Translators (26 December 1933) had voiced many of the questions to surface in connection with the All-Union gathering: the ideological aspects of translation which demanded the ideological training of translators; the urgent need for translations from and into the languages of the USSR, and the lack of adequate competence among translators to perform this task, especially among the 'nationality cadres'; and the ubiquitous use of interlinear trots. Appalling instances of *khaltura* (poor-quality work) were reported: 'If most of our comrades are guilty of examples of strikingly bad work in the translation of Western foreign languages, then, comrades, the most mind-numbing things happen in the translations from the languages of our Union'.[47] The conference was to put an end to this 'once and for all' by initiating enhanced control and education.[48] Other questions first discussed at the 1933 meeting which reappeared later were the low level of translation critique, a projected translation journal and the predominantly negative attitudes towards translators as an 'untrustworthy' category of people, on the one hand,[49] and as an inferior type of literary worker, on the other.[50]

A preparatory meeting was held on 29 November 1935 to discuss the program of the upcoming All-Union conference, at which the organizers – the bureau of the Translators' Section, the Nationalities' Section of

---

47 RGALI, f. 631, op. 21, ed. khr. 4, l. 10 (literary functionary Pavel Pavlenko); the document is erroneously dated 1934. See also the chapter by Zemskova in this volume.
48 RGALI, f. 631, op. 21, ed. khr. 4, l. 10 and RGALI, f. 631, op. 21, ed. khr. 4, l. 15.
49 Translator Inna Zusmanovich spoke on the possibilities of travelling abroad to enhance competence in the 'live spoken language', saying: 'We are coming up against our own political backwardness. If we were politically literate, there would not be any doubts on this matter, and it would have been done long ago, but clearly there are some doubts about us', RGALI, f. 631, op. 21, ed. khr. 4, l. 31.
50 B. Illés spoke about how translators were seen as 'technical assistants in literature'. RGALI, f. 631, op. 21, ed. khr. 4, l. 5.

the Writers' Union and Goslitizdat – defined the main area of interest as translations from and into the languages of the peoples of the USSR ('our most vulnerable part').[51] The problem was stated by Pavel Zenkevich, head of the bureau, in terms that also provided a hierarchy of the material to be involved in the process:

> In our brother republics, in many of them only after the revolution, creative growth has begun and we now have a great task in translation – to produce Marx, Engels, Lenin, Stalin, and then Soviet and world literature in our own languages.
>   There is an untouched wealth of material for translation, as you can see, and it is material of great significance.
>   What is more, in many places we do not have the right cadres for this task, in terms of quality and quantity.[52]

Three principal reports were announced for the conference: one 'organizational' (to touch on the present state of translation in the USSR, the quality of translation in the respective republics and the competence of cadres), one on 'artistic questions', and one on 'everyday problems' (on the theme of 'the translator and the publishing house'). The second report was to be assigned to two speakers: the Leningrad scholar Aleksandr Smirnov[53] was to give a general talk on 'the methodology and theory of translation' and the well-known translator Mikhail Lozinskii (also from Leningrad) was to highlight problems of verse translation as a specific case in point. The choice of these two men was the most disputed matter of the preparatory meeting, for two reasons: both were strongly associated with the

---

51 For a survey of this meeting with reference to the question of the social status of translators, see the chapter by Zemskova in this volume.
52 RGALI, f. 631, op. 21, ed. khr. 8, l. 5.
53 Aleksandr Smirnov (1883–1962) was a versatile literary scholar, critic and translator. A professor at Leningrad University and a specialist on Western European literature of the Middle Ages and Renaissance, he was particularly well-known as an expert on Shakespeare: Smirnov co-edited two eight-volume *Polnoe sobranie sochinenii Shekspira* (1936–50 and 1957–60) and authored the monographs *Tvorchestvo Shekspira* (1934) and *Shekspir* (1963). For more on Smirnov see P. A. Nikolaev, ed., *Russkie pisateli 1800–1917, biograficheskii slovar'*, vol. 5 (Moscow: Nauchoe izdatel'stvo Bol'shaia entsiklopediia, 2007), 670–2.

publishing house Academia, and both were known for their translations mainly from Western European rather than 'national' languages. As poet and translator Sergei Gorodetskii argued:

> There is a whole series of questions that need to be illuminated clearly and in detail in the theoretical section of the report. From Smirnov we will have a defence of those positions I've been talking about, and disregard of anything except the practice of Academia publishers.
> As for Lozinskii, at some point in 1910–12 he, together with Gumilev, worked out a premise for the theory of translation, and Lozinskii still holds this position.[54]

Gorodetskii here alluded to a major controversy in the translation debate as it evolved in the Soviet Union, that between source-oriented and target-oriented approaches, which centred on the question of 'literalism'. The profile of the publishing house Academia, founded in Petrograd in 1921 and transferred to Moscow in 1929, was characterized by high-quality editions of translations of Western works on aesthetics and art history as well as the classics of world literature, but to some extent also translations of literature from the national republics and folkloric material, all provided with scholarly introductions and commentaries. Academia was associated with translation principles of a 'literalist' bend, of which both Lozinskii and Smirnov were exponents. Its very name was a graphic expression of its position: it was usually rendered in Latin script, which contrasted sharply with its Cyrillic context giving a pointedly 'foreign' impression,[55] and it underscored the 'academic', scientific orientation with links to Russian Formalism in literary criticism.[56]

54 RGALI, f. 631, op. 21, ed. khr. 8, l. 51.
55 See, for example, a report in *Pravda*, 11 November 1934, by Lev Kamenev, head of the publishing house: 'Rabota "Academia" za god'; cf. also the name in its Latin spelling in *Kratkaia literaturnaia entsiklopediia* vol. I (Moscow: Sovetskaia entsiklopediia, 1962). Academia ceased to exist as an independent organization in 1937 when it was incorporated into Goslitizdat. Kamenev was arrested in December 1934 following the murder of Kirov.
56 Among authors to appear with Academia were Propp, Eikhenbaum, Tynianov and Zhirmunskii. For a complete list of publications, see <http://www.knigaline.ru/razno/Academia.htm> accessed 14 September 2010.

One of the classical loci of theoretical dispute within the field of literary translation, the question of 'literalism' versus 'free translation', was at this time taking on specifically ideological overtones. During the 1920s, literalism had been a strong tendency, with well-known representatives in such translators as Evgenii Lann, Adrian Frankovskii (a member of the first advisory board of Academia) and Georgii Shengeli.[57] They did not use the term literalism, however, preferring instead to talk about 'technically exact translation', or 'the formal principle of technical precision';[58] 'literalism' (*bukvalizm*) was used as an invective by their opponents. From the 1930s, however, the trend gradually fell into official disgrace and was nearly anathematized, at least in theory and debate, until the end of the Soviet era. It was now commonly referred to as 'formalism' and opposed to 'realist translation',[59] a concept promoted by Ivan Kashkin, who first emerged as a critic of Lann's literalist Dickens translation in a 1934 discussion. Although the formalist label (originating in RAPP rhetoric) was to acquire its full repressive potential only with the launch of the anti-formalist campaign in *Pravda* on 28 January 1936, it had been used quite broadly already in spring 1933 as the antithesis of the ideal Socialist Realism now to be promoted in literature.[60]

The timing of the First All-Union Conference of Translators, held in Moscow 3–7 January 1936, was thus crucial not only with respect to the Soviet cultural climate in general, in which 'a narrowly defined, dogmatic and often backward-looking orthodoxy of Socialist Realism' was beginning

---

57 Maurice Friedberg, *Literary Translation in Russia: A Cultural History* (Pennsylvania: Pennsylvania State University Press, 1997), 87. Friedberg's assumption that the trend was 'a reaction against excesses in free translation of the prerevolutionary period' is consonant with Mikhail Gasparov's typological scheme of changes in Russian translation history, which emphasizes the literalist bias of Russian modernist translation. Mikhail L. Gasparov, 'Briusov i bukvalizm (Po neizdannym materialam k perevodu "Eneidy")' in *Masterstvo perevoda* 8, 88–128 (1971).
58 Cf. Evgenii Lann, 'Stil' rannego Dikensa i perevod "Posmertnykh zapisok Pikvikskogo kluba"' in *Literaturnyi kritik* 1, 1939, 156–71.
59 Friedberg, *Literary Translation in Russia*, 113.
60 Fleishman, *Boris Pasternak i literaturnoe dvizhenie 1930-kh godov*, 402–4.

to be imposed,[61] but also with respect to attitudes towards translation in particular. Retrospectively, the conference emerges as a key moment in the *ideologization of norms* which came to affect subsequent Soviet translation debate. It was also probably the last public event where 'foreignizing' views on translation were given weighty support.

I will dwell here on the three main speeches dealing with translation principles: the keynote address, assigned to the critic Iogann Al'tman, which was meant to provide an authoritative statement on the problems of translation in the USSR; and the speeches by Smirnov and Lozinskii respectively, in which they attempted to argue in favour of a source-oriented ('literalist', 'formalist') translation philosophy, each applying a strategy of his own.

The archival material from the conference available at present is not complete. The extant stenograph includes only Al'tman's voluminous opening address, entitled 'The cultural revolution and the tasks of literary translation' and his concluding speech.[62] Some additional material helps to reconstruct the picture of the proceedings: the main propositions (*tezisy*) of the speeches by Zenkevich ('Perevodchik i izdatel'stvo'), Smirnov ('Zadachi i sredstva khudozhestvennogo perevoda') and Lozinskii ('Iskusstvo stikhotvornogo perevoda') are preserved in the archive, as is the draft resolution of the conference (published as an appendix to this chapter).[63] A report in *Literaturnaia gazeta* on 5 January 1936 clarifies the course of events: the morning session on 4 January featured Zenkevich and Smirnov, and at the afternoon session Lozinskii's talk was followed by discussions. In its covering of the conference, the newspaper provided summaries of the main speeches and gave much space to addresses by leading figures from the national republics.[64] Later publications of conference material comprise Al'tman's talk, which was printed the same year in *Literaturnyi kritik*, Lozinskii's speech, which, as a sign of the Khrushchev Thaw, appeared in

---

61 A. Kemp-Welch, *Stalin and the Literary Intelligentsia, 1928–39* (London: Macmillan, 1991), 198.
62 RGALI, f. 631, op. 6, ed. khr. 124.
63 RGALI, f. 631, op. 21, ed. khr. 9.
64 See *Literaturnaia gazeta* 1 (5 January), 2 (10 January), 3 (15 January) 1936.

Druzhba narodov 1955, and Boris Pasternak's contribution to the discussion, which reached readers only in 1968.[65]

The conference was opened by the literary functionary Marchenko, who placed it in the context of Stalinist nationalities policy:

> What is more, it is hardly necessary to say much about the great political and cultural significance of this area of Soviet literature. In our country, which is developing a culture that is national in form and socialist in content, the significance of translation work is particularly great.[66]

These ideological implications of translation had already been codified in an article on translation ('Perevod') in the eighth volume of the *Literaturnaia entsiklopediia*, published in 1934, which was largely written by Smirnov.[67] The article begins by asserting that,

> Literary (or artistic) translation is a particular problem that extends well beyond pure literary and linguistic competence, since each translation is to one degree or another an ideological assimilation of the original.[68]

The claim is substantiated further in the article by a range of examples of ideologically motivated manipulative use of translation through history.[69] Some of these examples (e.g. a tendentious 1933 French translation

---

65   I. Al'tman, 'Kul'turnaia revoliutsiia i zadachi khudozhestvennogo perevoda', *Literaturnyi kritik* 5 (1936); M. Lozinskii, 'Iskusstvo stikhotvornogo perevoda', *Druzhba narodov* 7 (1955); B. Pasternak, 'Na pervom vsesoiuznom soveshchanii perevodchikov', *Literaturnaia Gruziia* 8 (1968) (reprinted in Boris Pasternak, *Polnoe sobranie sochinenii s prilozheniiami*, 11 vols, vol. V (Moscow: Slovo, 2004), 438–45).
66   RGALI, f. 631, op. 6, ed. khr. 124, l. 1.
67   The historical part was written by M. P. Alekseev.
68   Aleksandr Smirnov, 'Perevod' in P. Lebedev-Polianskii et al., eds, *Literaturnaia entsiklopediia*, vol. VIII (Moscow: Sovetskaia entsiklopediia, 1934), 512.
69   The topic was raised during the First Moscow Conference of Translators and it was also highlighted by Kornei Chukovskii in his 1935 article in *Pravda*: 'Fedor Sologub, for example, translating a poem by Taras Shevchenko, considered the main task to be the most accurate reproduction of the original. But the fact that Shevchenko was a revolutionary and imprisoned in Tsarist camps, while his translator was a mystic, aesthete, individual, decadent, could not fail to be reflected in the translation'.

of Sholokhov's *Podniataia tselina* (*Virgin Soil Upturned*)) are recycled in Al'tman's keynote speech, which also foregrounds the ideological significance of translation.

Iogann Al'tman (1900–55), a literary scholar and theatre critic, was apparently no authority on translation. But he had some 'national' experience (having monitored the development of theatrical life in the republics) which may have qualified him for the assignment.[70] The factual basis for the detailed translation critique displayed in his speech, which involved languages even he admitted he did not know, was provided by the Nationalities Section of the Writers' Union, the apparatus of which had carried out an extensive internal review of translations during 1935.[71] The speech may be considered an accommodation of the theme of translation to several discourses of immediate actuality: the recently established discourse of the 'friendship of the peoples' found in Stalinist nationality policies,[72] the Stakhanov discourse actualized by *Pravda*'s editorial on 1 January 1936 entitled 'Stakhanovskii god' ('The Stakhanov Year'),[73] and most important

70   Al'tman was chief editor of the paper *Sovetskoe iskusstvo* (1936–8) and editor of the journal *Teatr* (1937–41). Following the Translators' Conference he was elected member of the board of the Translators' Section in May 1936. Al'tman was called upon to perform another official function during the 1937 Pushkin celebration when he was assigned a speech on the poet's dramaturgy. In 1949 he fell victim to the 'anticosmopolitan' campaign; expelled from the Writers' Union after a denunciatory letter from Fadeev (see Clark and Dobrenko, *Soviet Culture and Power*, 469–71), he was then arrested, and released only after Stalin's death.
71   RGALI, f. 631, op. 6, ed. khr. 136, l. 5.
72   The slogan was introduced in Stalin's speech on a meeting of 'shock-workers from collective farms in Tadzhikistan and Turkmenistan' printed in *Pravda*, 5 December, 1935 (see Brandenberger, *National Bolshevism*, 43); it was quickly picked up and used with reference to translations by Adalis in her article 'Stikhi i pesni narodov vostoka o Staline', *Pravda*, 11 December 1935. Concluding the proceedings Al'tman declares, 'Russian literature is being enriched with more and more new works from the literatures of our brother republics, and the basis of this great process is the friendship between nations that comrade Stalin has spoken of'. RGALI, f. 631, op. 6, ed. khr. 124, l. 79.
73   'What else defines the Stakhanovite movement, if we want to think of it in terms of all the processes happening in our country, in terms of our tasks? It is not only

the 'wreckers discourse' of innumerable campaigns in the newspapers since the late 1920s.[74] It also included a prescriptive part, the terminology of which was to resonate in the subsequent debate on the 'Soviet school of translation' up to the end of the Soviet era'.[75]

Al'tman began his speech by declaring how 'the success of industrialization and collectivization of the land conducted under the leadership of Stalin' had lain the foundation for 'the success of the cultural revolution', involving a 'factual, not formal equality of the peoples of the USSR', and went on to exemplify the progress attained in different parts of the Union: Ukraine (where 'for centuries only some ten books have been printed in Ukrainian', but the last four years has seen the publication of 'more than a thousand titles'), Belorussia, Azerbaijan, Armenia and Uzbekistan. From the account of translations into the respective languages after 1917 emerges the picture of a Soviet translational canon: into Georgian 'the main works of Marx and Engels have been translated; the complete works of Stalin and Lenin; *Evgenii Onegin*, *Mednyi vsadnik*, Maiakovskii's works, albeit not all, Homer, Dante's *Divine Comedy*, from the originals have been translated Heine, Goethe, Balzac, Stendhal and Gor'kii'. Translations into Armenian, 'Turkic', Tartar, Tadzhik, Kirgiz and some 'small languages' added to the list of works by Gogol', Lermontov, Ostrovskii, Tolstoi, Turgenev, Chekhov, Shakespeare, Swift, Schiller, Molière, Flaubert, Barbusse and contemporary Soviet authors such as Furmanov, Sholokhov, Korneichuk, Fadeev and Tikhonov.

However, the intention of the conference, Al'tman emphasized, was not to underscore present achievements, but to discuss the major shortcomings,

---

labour, but also creative labour [...]. This labour helps the masses philosophically, generally, politically approach their tasks in a decisive way. This is what we must have in mind when we talk about literature and in parallel think about the Stakhanovite movement.' RGALI, f. 631, op. 6, ed. khr. 124, ll. 7–8.

74 On the development of the 'wreckers discourse', see Brooks, *Thank You, Comrade Stalin!*, 135–9.

75 For a (somewhat uncritical) presentation of the 'Soviet school of translation', see Lauren Leighton, *Two Worlds, One Art: Literary Translation in Russia and America* (DeKalb: Northern Illinois University Press, 1991).

which 'we have to root out from this enormously important and responsible political literary work'.⁷⁶ In view of 'the great significance of political and artistic literature' for strengthening the Soviet Union, for 'the growth of the national bonds of the masses', not only translation method but also the selection of works for translation are singled out as crucial factors:

> if good, correct, political and literary translation answers the fundamental tasks assigned to us, then bad translation does us huge damage. Good translation strengthens the Soviet Union, strengthens the international brotherhood of peoples. Bad translation or even the good translation of a harmful book strengthens chauvinism, distances the peoples of the Soviet Union from one another.⁷⁷

The passage introduces the theme of *vred* (harm) that may be caused by translations, and Al'tman devoted a significant share of his address to a detailed translation critique in the *Pravda* style as analyzed above. The criticism refers mainly to translations *into* national languages, but Russian translators were targeted too. Despite the declared 'equality of nationalities', Russian, due to its status as *lingua franca*, was regarded as the single most important language: translations into Russian make works accessible to other nationalities as well, and the possible *vred* may thus multiply.⁷⁸

The translation critique offered by Al'tman affected 'political' as well as 'artistic' translations, since, as he argues, in the republics translators often did both.⁷⁹ Translations of canonical texts into several nationality languages were scrutinized and various manipulative practices exposed. Of particular interest is the case of a Tadzhik translation of Stalin's work *Problems of Leninism*. Al'tman detected serious mistakes in the rendering of Stalin's speech on Lenin's death, juxtaposing Stalin's phrase 'Мы коммунисты, люди особого склада' ('We are communists, people of a special cast of mind') to the translation, given in Russian retranslation: 'Мы коммунисты

---

76 RGALI, f. 631, op. 6, ed. khr. 124, l. 18.
77 Ibid.
78 Ibid., l. 61.
79 Ibid., l. 18; in fact, there is no distinction: 'I think that we would do well not to separate the political meaning from the literary meaning of a translation. Let us agree that literary translation is a great political task' (Ibid. l. 23).

из особого склада и амбара' ('We are communists, people from a special storehouse and granary'), a mistranslation – if authentic – easily explained by the fact that the words *sklad* ('cast of mind') and *sklad* ('storehouse') are homonyms. Al'tman, however, commented: 'Of course, you can smell the politics here', and added:

> On no account can we take the opportunistic point of view, which still persists in some places, about the poverty of the national languages: since our language is poor, we don't have the right words for the translation, and for that reason we have to write: 'we are people from a special storehouse and granary'. References to the poverty of languages will not do at all, and no allowances will be made for this so called 'poverty', not in political or artistic literature; if politically and theoretically a book causes serious, direct political harm, and we can see this harm every day, then in the realm of artistic literature, perversions of national literature cause no less harm.[80]

The Tadzhik translator is thus assumed to have had an agenda that for manipulative purposes would *utilize* Russian preconceptions of primitivism and inferiority – an intricate twist to the orientalizing projections found in the *Pravda* translations as analysed above. Such projections, labelled 'exoticism', in fact become the target of a specific critique and are listed among the main sins for which Al'tman blames Russian translators (see below).

Accommodating the 'wreckers discourse', Al'tman's speech gradually took on features of a court proceeding, pillorying individual translators (the Tadzhik translator, for example, is mentioned by name). The established procedure was, again, to compare original texts and their translations given in Russian retranslation (which short-circuit any alternative interpretations that may have arisen among conference participants with adequate language competence). The critical vocabulary displays terms like *vreditel'skii nabor slov* ('harmful verbiage') and *gnusnoe izvrashchenie* ('vile perversion'), with *izvrashchenie* ('perversion') being the key term throughout. In order to demonstrate the 'harmful potential' of translations, Al'tman refers to the case with the repealed translations of the kolkhoz statutes, and provides additional examples of mistranslation that did not figure in the resolutions printed in *Pravda*.

80 RGALI, f. 631, op. 6, ed. khr. 124, ll. 20–1.

As for literary works, cases discussed include the translations into national languages of Shakespeare, Pushkin and socialist-realist canonical works (Serafimovich, Furmanov, Fadeev), as well as some Western contemporary works (Romain Rolland, Hans Fallada), and from Soviet national literatures into Russian. Apart from manipulative practices (mainly concerning translations into national languages), various stylistic deficiencies were commented upon, sometimes in great detail. The main problems ('*bedy*', '*opasnosti*') affecting Soviet translation, as stated by Al'tman, were specified as:

1. naturalism ('copying translation'): when, due to a low political and cultural level, 'the [national] translator imports into the language of his people unnecessary words, which could be replaced with adequate ones. This results in a lot of Russianisms, words that do not enrich the language at all'.[81] (At the same time, failure to incorporate 'internationalist', 'valuable' words such as the 'untranslatable' *bol'shevik* into a national language was seen as a nationalist distortion of 'Lenin's thesis on the purity of language');
2. formalism: when 'for the sake of rhythm, melody and sound form of the verse, content is distorted' – an evil related to the first one: 'It is not difficult to see that the naturalist and the formalist join forces in the perversion of the original';[82]
3. impressionism: when the translator is guided by inspiration, ignoring the content, an evil that 'encompasses the shortcomings of both naturalism and formalism'; and
4. exoticism, stylizing translation: when the translator 'assumes that in translating a national poet, he is obliged to provide something exotic'. Exoticism 'stresses the superficial, formal side', making the content appear as 'a specifically nationally restricted content', while stylization (*stilizatorstvo*) represents 'superficial embellishment at the expense of authentic and deep understanding of the language';

81 Ibid., l. 56.
82 Ibid., l. 67.

both 'essentially despise the national literatures' and 'stretch out a hand to the most reactionary elements, still not driven out of our literature'.[83]

The principles that should guide Soviet translation and counteract such 'diseases' Al'tman linked to the recently adopted general artistic doctrine:

> the notion of Socialist Realism is of no less relevance to translation than to the whole of Soviet literature. Socialist Realism as applied to artistic translation is opposed to naturalistic copying [...] but opposes gross tendentiousness in translation as well [...] that is the kind of tendentiousness that hinders a correct conceptualization of the work. We require creative tendencies, creative perspectives from the translator.[84]

The translation doctrine outlined here by Al'tman is as loosely defined as that of Socialist Realism, comprising vaguely synonymous, positively charged terms like 'creative' (*tvorcheskii*) and 'adequate' (*adekvatnyi*),[85] both of which had been used before and were destined to live long within Soviet translation theory. As in the case of Socialist Realism, definition is supplied by model examples. The main example to illustrate 'creative translation' is Valerii Briusov, whose range of translations was 'from *The Aeneid* to Verlaine'. Briusov, a translator 'who excellently sensed the literature of different nationalities', is credited with taking a humble position vis-à-vis the original (not aspiring to replace it) and is favourably contrasted to 'our contemporary translators, who allow themselves to process the material in such a way that we don't recognize it'.[86] Other examples of 'creative translation' provided by Al'tman are nineteenth-century classics such as Gnedich's rendering of the *Iliad* and Zhukovskii's of the *Odyssey*. Literalist translation was criticized by Al'tman, however, with a reference to Leninist aesthetic theory:

---

83 Ibid., ll. 68–9.
84 Ibid., ll. 36–7.
85 For example, 'Tvorcheskii perevod za adekvatnoe soderzhanie i formy' (*sic*) (RGALI, f. 631, op. 6, ed. khr. 124, l. 67).
86 RGALI, f. 631, op. 6, ed. khr. 124, l. 37.

Based on Lenin's theory of reflection, we require fully ideological and philological coincidence of translation with the original, richness in language, synonyms and metaphor. We require not a word-for-word translation (and certainly not an interlinear trot), but one appropriate to the original.[87]

What Socialist Realism demands of translation, Al'tman summarizes, is 'a fight against naturalism, against formalist, impressionist, exoticizing and stylizing translation'. The speech concludes with a series of suggestions aimed at 'elevating translation culture in the USSR', which were more or less reflected in the draft resolution of the conference.[88] One was that the focus should be on the question of 'rallying, increasing and stabilizing permanent cadres of translators', and another that dictionaries from and into the main languages of the Union should be produced. It was suggested that the project proposed by Maksim Gor'kii at the Writers' Congress of publishing an *Almanakh literatury narodov SSSR* in six or seven languages should be realized. Al'tman states that the question of organizing a special institute for instruction of translators into the languages of the Union should be raised, and a methodological handbook produced. Seminars, conferences and various social activities, too, should be organized to promote exchange of experience among translators. Finally, he argues that measures should be taken to enhance the authority, significance and material level of translators, including a differentiation of payment as a means to fight *khaltura*.

Since the documentation of the conference presently available does not include the discussions, we do not know how Al'tman's speech was received. Concluding the proceedings he repeated its main points; here literalism (referred to as 'inadequate, slavish, literalism') was condemned even more sharply: 'the struggle against literalism is a struggle for a higher cultural level among translators'. In this summary, reference is also made to Zenkevich's report on problems pertaining to translators' interaction with publishing houses, which pinpointed disrespectful attitudes to translators and low competence among editors; and to Smirnov's report on 'the

---

87   Ibid., l. 67.
88   See Appendix.

principles of artistic translation'. The latter was only mentioned in passing, and it was noted that the attention given to it by the audience 'testified to the high theoretical level of the conference participants'.

Smirnov's speech, 'The tasks and means of artistic translation', is not preserved in the archive. But it is evident from the detailed abstract, presented to the Translator's Section during the autumn of 1935, that it was an attempt to advance a literalist translation philosophy basically congruent with the one outlined in his part of the article on translation in the *Literary Encyclopaedia* of 1934 (cited above). In the speech, he set out to accommodate the topic of literary translation and intercultural relations within the Marxist discourse of class struggle.[89] 'Every literary translation', Smirnov stated, 'is an ideological appropriation of the original and thereby also of that historical class culture, which gave birth to this original'.[90] Class relations, he asserted, determine not only the choice of works for translation, but also translation method, which has changed accordingly over the ages. Free translation (*vol'nyi perevod*) in its two basic forms 'simplifying' (*uproshchaiushchii*) and 'improving' (*uluchshaiushchii*) was the main type of translation up to the nineteenth century, he argued, when exact translation (*tochnyi perevod*) first emerged as a 'systematic phenomenon', in connection with 'the orientation towards *nauchnost'* ('academic quality') within the rising bourgeoisie, the fast-paced development of the national languages and a range of other specific conditions'. 'Exact translation', he maintained, 'gradually grew into adequate translation'. The latter type is the only one needed 'during the present period of socialist construction, which, among other tasks, carries out the task of appropriating literary heritage'.[91] As we

---

[89] Attempts at motivating literalism from the point of view of class struggle in the 1930s were highlighted in a paper by Elena Zemskova presented at the Gasparovskie chteniia, RGGU, 11 April, 2009.

[90] RGALI, f. 631, op. 21, ed. khr. 9, l. 17.

[91] Ibid. The reason behind the dominance of 'inexact' translation during earlier periods was explicated in the encyclopaedia article: the translator, haphazardly guided by his class ideology, would underscore and amplify some elements, while weakening or even annihilating others, the result being an inevitable 'recolouring' (*perekraska*) of the work under translation.

can see, the qualifier 'adequate' is here connected to a literalist orientation, a use of the term very different from Al'tman's application of it as merely a vague marker of quality.

Adequate translation, in Smirnov's interpretation, has to convey not only the whole semantic and emotional content of the original, but also its formal properties, because 'all characteristic features of the form and style of the original are, in the end, as indicative of the ideology of the author as are the thoughts and images expressed in the work'.[92] The ideological significance ascribed to formal elements necessitates a literalist approach. But as 'absolute adequacy' is not feasible, the translator has to employ methods of compensation and sacrifice, basing his version on a stylistic analysis in order to distinguish essential from less essential traits of the work. This procedure to find the 'right key or general tonality' of the work suggests the formalist notion of *dominanta*, the dominant quality in a literary work,[93] which, however, is not mentioned by Smirnov.

The ultimate goal of adequate translation is defined by Smirnov in terms of (what we now would call) functional equivalence:

> an adequate translation takes as its aim to produce an effect on the reader that is as close as possible to that produced by the original on the readers of its nationality, culture and epoch, and to possess, at the same time, the same degree of clarity and accessibility ...

The point is developed further with the help of Goethe's metaphorical description of translation principles:

> From the two methods of translation mentioned by Goethe, of which one 'demands that the foreign author is transmitted to us in such a way that we can see him as one of us' and the other suggests to us that we should 'make a journey to the foreigner and become acquainted with his life, his mode of expression and his peculiarities', the second is undoubtedly preferable.

---

92 RGALI, f. 631, op. 21, ed. khr. 9, ll. 17–18.
93 On the *dominanta* (developed by Eikhenbaum and Tynianov), see Victor Erlich, *Russian Formalism: History – Doctrine* (The Hague: Mouton, 1965), 199.

Goethe's second method, 'to make a journey to the foreigner',[94] is advocated with a minor reservation which eventually transforms into a specific argument for literalism: the translation should be carried out in such a way that the reader, while not stopping to sense the foreignness (*inoiazychnoe proiskhozhdenie*) of the work (mainly thanks to its content), should not perceive it stylistically as a translation: the language has to be 'correct' and 'literary', although encompassing 'a certain amount of new, not entirely common phrases'. The latter may even include some 'skilfully selected' foreign idiomatic expressions, because, as Smirnov argues 'the history of literary [i.e. standard, S. W.] languages shows that sometimes such barbarisms, having slipped in through literal translation (*doslovnyi perevod*), are assimilated and enrich a national language'. Literal translation thus may contribute to the evolution of a language (a point Smirnov made also in his encyclopaedia article of two years earlier). This was in fact one of the main functions of translation, as he concluded in the speech: 'Adequate or artistically exact (*khudozhestvenno tochnyi*) translation has a threefold value: as a text of a cognitive order (in Goethe' sense), as a work of independent artistic significance, and as a means of enriching our linguistic and literary culture'.

A principal difference between Smirnov's and Al'tman's positions concerns their attitudes to 'objectivity' in translation. For Smirnov *tochnost'* may reduce the impact of ideological recolouring (*perekraska*) inevitably involved in the translation process (and given additional space in varieties of 'free' translation); for Al'tman objectivity is not to be striven for at all: the translator should not be 'objective in the worst sense'.[95]

---

94 The proposal acquires a somewhat ironic resonance in view of the fact that individual foreign trips by Soviet writers practically ceased after the First Writers' Congress in 1934 (Leonid Maksimenkov and Christopher Barnes, 'Boris Pasternak in August 1936 – An NKVD Memorandum' in *Toronto Slavic Quarterly* 6 (Fall 2003) <http://www.utoronto.ca/tsq/06/pasternak06.shtml> accessed 16 September 2010.

95 '[N]ot only political translation, but, we also see, literary translation can both politically and ideologically weaken a word, give it a different emphasis, a different orientation towards the reader, if the translator is not completely honest, or he approaches the task tendentiously. This doesn't mean, comrades, that a translator must be objective

Several of Smirnov's points are echoed in the fourth of the main speeches to be delivered during the conference, Mikhail Lozinskii's 'The Art of Verse Translation'. But Lozinskii employs another strategy to pursue his source-oriented agenda. Not only does he defend a literalist position with great passion; his argumentation is also informed by theory and concepts from the now unpopular school of Russian Formalism in literary scholarship (although in a concealed way) and, most important, he makes an effort to 'translate' his own position into an idiom compatible with Stalinist discourse.

Lozinskii ascribes translation a twofold function: aesthetic and cognitive (or educational):

> The function of translated texts is twofold: 1) aesthetic, like a literary work, and 2) educational – like monuments which acquaint us with another country, another epoch, another culture, with a way of thinking and feeling that is new to us.[96]

Historically, Lozinskii discerns two types of translation, 'reorganizational' (*perestraivaiushchii*), and 'recreative' (*vossozdaiushchii*). The first is described as domesticating, oriented towards the norms of the target culture with reference to content: 'when the content is modified to a particular mode, according to tastes [...] or because of other considerations of an ideological nature'; as well as to form: 'when instead of a form characteristic of the original, the translator substitutes his own, which seems to him better'. The latter 'reproduces with greatest possible fullness and accuracy (*tochnost'*) the form and content of the original'. Only the second type, the recreative, may be called a translation proper (although the reorganizational 'is

---

in the worst sense of the word [...] and not pursue any agenda' RGALI, f. 631, op. 6, ed. khr. 124, ll. 32–3. Smirnov's discussion of 'recolouring' is found in his encyclopaedia article (see 'Perevod'). The difference between Al'tman and Smirnov in this respect was pointed out by Elena Zemskova in her paper, referred to above.

96   This insistence on an independent role for the 'foreign' was apparently found objectionable in the 1955 publication of Lozinskii's text, where an introductory note polemicizes with the declaration, referred to as one of the 'disputable' and 'not very well thought-out' points of the talk. Mikhail Lozinskii, 'Iskusstvo stikhotvornogo perevoda', *Druzhba narodov* 7 (1955), 158–66 (159).

fully legitimate as a genre in itself, it can never replace a translation in the genuine sense, a recreative translation').

Lozinskii (like Smirnov) defines the object of a poet-translator from the point of view of functional equivalence: 'That the copy created by him should produce the same effect as the original, written in a foreign language'.[97] Since the task is ultimately unachievable and admits only of approximate solutions, the quality of a translation depends on the degree of this approximation.

The basis for Lozinskii's argumentation is the indissoluble connection between 'form' and 'content':

> Any poetic text [...] is a complex of coordinated and interdependent elements of different types, which make up something like a self-sufficient organism. Elements of content and elements of form combine to create this. Such a division of them is, of course, purely abstract, because elements of both are interdependent and in reality do not exist separately from each other. Content is realized in form; form is imbued with content.[98]

Such an insistence is very close to formalist tenets as expressed, for example, by Viktor Zhirmunskii, who stressed that 'content – emotional or cognitive – appears only through the medium of form and thus cannot be profitably discussed, indeed conceived of, apart from its artistic embodiment'.[99] Not only is the content of an artwork socially and historically conditioned, Lozinskii notes (as did Smirnov), but also its formal elements, their genesis and their meaning. Therefore it is essential to convey not only the words ('with great attention to the cultural-historical atmosphere of the original, avoiding everything that would be alien to this atmosphere'), but also the overall design (*chertezh*) of the work being translated.

For verse translation, Lozinskii argues, form is of specific significance. Although the content of foreign (*chuzhezemnykh*) verses, their imagery and flow of phrases may be rendered in prose with even greater accuracy than

---

97   Ibid., 160.
98   Ibid., 161.
99   Zhirmunskii's idea is rephrased by Erlich in *Russian Formalism: History – Doctrine*, 186.

in a verse translation, such a prose translation, Lozinskii argues, would be 'dead', because it is precisely the form that affects us emotionally: 'In order to be not dead but alive, a translation must recreate the *form* of the original, for in this form, poured into it and indivisible from it, is its *content*'.[100] Of the two elements that make up form in poetry, 'rhythm' and 'melody' (*melodiia, zvukopis'*), the former is basic: 'The inspiring strength of rhythm is broader than the boundaries of language, it is universal'. An approximate verse translation faithfully rendering the 'emotional sound' of the original may, in fact, give a closer picture of it than 'the most conscientious' prose translation. Because of its rich rhythmical resources, the Russian language, Lozinskii points out, is in a favourable position when it comes to recreating foreign poetry. As for melody (*zvukopis'*), which 'most strikingly' affects our emotionality, Lozinskii advocates an approach aimed at recreating not individual sounds, but the original's 'system of echoes and resonances' with the help of the phonetic resources of the target language.

Discussing priorities in translation, Lozinskii (again as Smirnov) implicitly evokes the formalist key notion of *dominanta*. Since it is impossible to reproduce all elements of form and content, the translator has to decide beforehand which of the elements in a work under translation are the most essential and therefore have to be reproduced at any cost. Instead of the formalists, reference is here made to Briusov, who was a literalist translator, but an ideologically acceptable (and deceased) classic: 'The choice of these elements is precisely what Valerii Briusov called the *method* of translation'.[101]

The key elements of the original may vary, Lozinskii says: sometimes it is the metaphoricity of language, sometimes the vividness of dialogue. But in verse translation there is a range of elements that *always* has to be recreated:

> Everything that characterizes the style of a work should be observed, that is to say, what is characteristic for the epoch, the country, the social group that created it, what is characteristic for the genre it belongs to, for the individual style of the author

100 Lozinskii, 'Iskusstvo stikhotvornogo perevoda', 162.
101 Ibid., 165.

(be it ideological content or a literary manner). It is very important to reproduce the structure of the original – its stanza form.[102]

Such observance of formal devices is not an end in itself, Lozinskii, emphasizes, it is a means of achieving 'the highest possible degree of aesthetic equivalence (*ravnotsennost*') to the original and expressing its cultural-historical character (*oblik*)'.

It is in the context of losses and deviations inevitably bound up with translation that Lozinskii attempts to accommodate his own position, an apotheosis of form, to a discourse evoking Stalinist rhetoric:

> There are exceptions, caused by linguistic differences, just as there are in the translation of prose. But there are also exceptions typical specifically for poetry translation. These are demanded by form. *Form is tyrannical, and it is right to be tyrannical, because without it the whole harmonic edifice of verse collapses. And it demands sacrifices.*[103]

The literalist credo is thus rephrased in societal terms associated with the dictatorship of the proletariat, a merging of discourses prepared for in Lozinskii's earlier identification of '*strofika*' with the Marxist term of '*nadstroika*'.[104]

This attempt to write 'literalism' into authoritarian discourse, however, did not prove successful: Lozinskii's theoretical position, if not his own practice,[105] was doomed almost to disappear from official debate – except as a target of critique – until the end of the Soviet era. Lozinskii's insistence on the principal value of representing the 'foreign' in its own right is diametrically opposed to the tenets of (socialist) realist translation, which increasingly informed translation debate through the rest of the Stalin period. In 1954 its main theoretician Ivan Kashkin gave the following prescriptive description of the 'best Soviet translators':

---

102   Ibid., 165.
103   Ibid., emphasis added.
104   Ibid., 162.
105   Lozinskii's own translations continued to receive favourable attention; in 1946 he was awarded the Stalin prize for his translation of Dante's *Divine Comedy*.

They try to establish for themselves what was most important in making a writer and his works significant and timely in his epoch, and they try above all to convey to our reader *all that is progressive, alive and timely in them for our time as well*, and at the same time preserve all that they were able to preserve without compromising the full, clear and faithful understanding of the idea and images of the original, *without burdening the text with unnecessary details that are typical only of the alien linguistic structure and often simply cannot be translated.*[106]

As we saw, the 'alien linguistic structure' was part of the concern for Lozinskii, as it was for other 'literalists' who were to survive into the 1950s; these included Lann and Shengeli in particular, who were both repeatedly attacked by Kashkin.[107]

Lozinskii's position may be characterized as one of functional equivalence (corresponding to his declared 'aesthetic function' of translation) combined with an effort to preserve a certain foreignness (corresponding to the 'cognitive function'), but Kashkin was to declare (in 1954) that the best Soviet translators

---

106 Ivan Kashkin, 'Voprosy perevoda' in *Dlia chitatelia sovremennika – stat'i i issledovaniia* (Moscow: Sovetskii pisatel', 1977), 427–63 (442, emphasis added). (First published in *V bratskom edinstve* (Moscow: Sovetskii pisatel', 1954).
107 Kashkin's first critique of Lann's and Krivtsova's Dickens translation at the Bureau of Translated Literature in 1934 was developed into an article in 1936 (Ivan Kashkin, 'Mister Pikvik i drugie', *Literaturnyi kritik* 5 (1936)) and sharply restated in 1952 after Lann's publication in 1939 of the intended foreword to the Pickwick translation, which outlined its principles (see Ivan Kashkin, 'Lozhnyi printsip i nepriemlemye rezultaty', in *Dlia chitatelia sovremennika – stat'i i issledovaniia* (Moscow: Sovetskii pisatel' 1977, 371–403, first published in *Inostrannye iazyki v shkole* 2 (1952); Shengeli's practice and stated principles of translation in his 1947 rendition of Byron's *Don Juan* became a target of critique in another 1952 article by Kashkin, 'Traditsiia i epigonstvo', in *Dlia chitatelia sovremennika – stat'i i issledovaniia* (Moscow: Sovetskii pisatel', 1977), 404–26, first published in *Novyi mir*, 12 (1952). At the beginning of the 1950s, Kashkin's polemic against literalism took on distinct notes from the ongoing anti-cosmopolitan campaign; predominant here is the theme of the literalists' alleged disrespect for the Russian language and their submission to the 'foreign' (see, for example, Ivan Kashkin, 'O iazyke perevoda', *Literaturnaia gazeta*, 1 December 1951).

manage to produce versions of writers (be it Shakespeare, Dickens, Navoi, Nizami, Burns, Omar Khayyam, or Dzhambul) that do not lose their stylistic and individual peculiarities, yet *read in Russian translation as though the author had written this word in Russian*, naturally and with great mastery, freely employing all of its imaginative effects.[108]

While Lozinskii and Smirnov articulated thoughts gravitating towards Goethe's and Schleiermacher's romantic principles of 'taking the reader abroad', socialist-realist translation has been linked to eighteenth-century Russian neoclassical doctrine.[109] Here faithfulness to the norms of the target culture is primary; that is, in the case of the Soviet norms of Socialist Realism, a focus on the 'typical traits' of a work to be translated (as viewed from the translator's more advanced and privileged position).[110] The kind of 'free translation' promulgated by Kashkin opened up a space for manipulation, legitimating, for example, minor censorship of foreign literary texts.[111]

At the 1936 conference, 'free' translation was given support also in Boris Pasternak's contribution, apparently delivered as an improvised speech during the discussion. Pasternak argued in favour of free translations, not however in ideological but in purely literary terms. In an account of his work with the Georgian classic Vazha Pshavela and the search for an accurate Russian metrical form he anticipates such notions as the semantics of metre and rhyme.[112] In retrospect, Pasternak's repeatedly declared preference for free translation may look like an accommodation of the emerging official translation doctrine, but at the same time it offered him a certain artistic

---

108 Emphasis added. Cf. Smirnov's warning in *Literaturnaia entsiklopedia*: 'However, it would be very dangerous to promote the thesis that the translator should try to find the literal expression of the author's thoughts as they would have been expressed, had the author been writing in the language of the translator, in his time and his social environment.' 'Perevod', 528.
109 Friedberg, *Literary Translation in Russia*, 113.
110 For later Soviet critique of some of Kashkin's points, see Friedberg, *Literary Translation in Russia*, 105.
111 Ibid., 16, 105.
112 On Pasternak's translation of Pshavela, see Zemskova in this volume.

latitude during periods when his original work was not published.¹¹³ In his Shakespeare and Goethe translations Pasternak made effective use of the 'intended liberty' (*namerennaia svoboda*) to which he refers in his preface to the *Hamlet* translation of 1940.¹¹⁴

Concluding Remarks

The 1936 conference of translators resulted in a crystallization of policy about various aspects of translation. On a practical level it led to organizational changes in the work of the Translators' Section which arguably promoted the demanded professionalization of 'the cadres'. A variety of committees was set up and began working: an academic committee (led by Kashkin), an editorial committee, a committee for popularization (*massovaia kommissiia*), a material-legal committee, an international committee, and a committee for the training and evaluation of cadres.¹¹⁵ In the process of evaluating prospective members of the section, reference was incidentally made to criteria established during the conference: however diffuse and contradictory these may appear they could obviously serve as a canonical basis for the procedure.¹¹⁶ The problems concerning translation into

---

113 Friedberg, *Literary Translation in Russia*, 16.
114 See Susanna Witt, 'Perevod kak mimikriia: *Gamlet* Pasternaka', *Swedish Contributions to the Thirteenth International Congress of Slavists, Ljubljana, 15–21 August*, ed. Birgitta Englund Dimitrova and Alexander Pereswetoff-Morath (Lund: Lund University, 2003), 145–56, and Witt, 'Between the Lines'.
115 RGALI, f. 631, op. 21, ed. khr. 12.
116 For example V. Toper's 1936 evaluation of E. Greiner-Gekk: 'I must make this comment: this translation came out in 1929, therefore, comrade Greiner-Gekk worked on it in 1929, and perhaps in 1928. The directives for translators at that time, as we all know, were very different from those that were announced and enforced by the First Congress of Translators. Therefore I am not going to pick holes in those parts of the translation which, in my opinion, do not conform to what we conventionally refer to as an adequate translation.' (RGALI, f. 631, op. 21, ed. khr. 17, l. 25).

and from languages of the national republics, addressed by Al'tman at the conference, were to resurface regularly within the Writers' Union during the following decade as the organization had to relate to the continued flourishing of translations of the *Pravda* type discussed above. Recurrent cries for education were accompanied by condemnations of the 'temporary' practice of *podstrochnik* translation.[117]

As for translation ideology, the plea for a literalist orientation of translation principles ultimately proved ineffective. Neither Smirnov's Marxist motivation for 'artistically exact translation', nor Lozinskii's attempt at writing his position into an authoritarian discourse was successful. On the contrary, in the annual account of the Nationalities' Section of the Writers' Union (one of the organizers of the conference) given in 1936 both speakers were denounced:

> However, it must be said that the reports by Lozinskii and Professor Smirnov contained the sins of extreme abstraction and formalism, which was noted in the abstracts which they put forward. The mistakes made by these delegates were subject to harsh criticism both from the speakers taking part in the debates: Romm, Vol'pe and others, and from the main speaker, comrade Al'tman, in his concluding remarks.[118]

The question as to why literalism was not an option at the time may be linked to the Stalinist doctrine of national cultural policy. Al'tman stressed the role of translators in the literary process of the USSR precisely in these terms: 'the formation of a new socialist literature, multilingual yet unified in its socialist content and its ideological structure'.[119] The formula 'national in form, socialist in content' postulates that there is no organic relation between 'form' and 'content', and that, furthermore, 'form' can have no meaning of its own.

The overall significance of Al'tman's speech, which as a theoretical-methodological statement was quite unclear and inconsistent, lies in its official establishment of a terminology that was to inform subsequent

---

117 For more on the problems of *podstrochnik* translation, see 'Between the Lines'.
118 RGALI, f. 631, op. 6, ed. khr. 136, l. 1.
119 Ibid., 124, l. 7.

Arts of Accommodation

translation critique and especially the promotion of 'realist translation'.[120] It was thus an important contribution to the ideologization of norms that was to peak in the early 1950s. In the short term, the applicability of the formalist label in the notorious campaign of spring 1936, combined with the accommodation of the theme of translation to the 'wreckers discourse', was ominous for the already ambiguous status of translators.

Appendix: The draft resolution of the 1936 All-Union Conference of Translators[121]

Проект резолюции 1-ого Всесоюзного совещания переводчиков

1. Первое Всесоюзное Совещание Переводчиков отмечает, что после Съезда Писателей произошел известный сдвиг в деле взаимного обогащения братских литератур народов СССР. Однако, размах культурной революции предъявляет переводческому делу все более высокие требования.
2. В области теории перевода имеют место всевозможные формалистские и эстетские теории и до настоящего времени нет достаточно разработанной, научно-обоснованной марксистко-ленинской теории перевода. Бюро Секции критиков надо организовать разработку основных вопросов художественного

---

120 See, for example, Kashkin's use of the terms 'formalist', 'naturalist', and 'impressionist' in 'Voprosy perevoda', 430–31. Significantly, the 1936 edition of Kornei Chukovskii's classical book *Iskusstvo perevoda* is provided with an editorial preface that declares 'It is particularly valuable that our book is sharply opposed to formalist tendencies in our translation practice'. Quoted in Kornei Chukovskii, *Vysokoe iskusstvo: o printsipakh khudozhestvennogo perevoda* (Moscow: Iskusstvo, 1964), 354.
121 RGALI, f. 631, op. 21, ed. khr. 9, ll. 1–2 (1935). As a result of lacunae in the documentation, it is not clear whether the resolution was adopted in this form, or subjected to changes. No publication of this document has been discovered as yet.

перевода и освещения этих вопорсов в литературной периодической печати.

3. Для подготовки высоко-квалифицированных переводчиков поставить перед Правительством вопросы: а/ об организации Всесоюзного Инс-та переводчиков на языки народов СССР по основным языковым группам и б/ специальных курсов в нацреспубликах и областях.

4. Для планомерной работы в области перевода классиков мировой литературы на языки отсталых в прошлом народов, по примеру Комитета нового алфавита организовать научно-исследовательское учреждение для практической помощи переводчикам малых народов по вопросам подбора первоочередных произведений мировой и русской литературы и проведения соответствующей текстологической работы.

5. Для работы над классиками мировой литературы в нацреспубликах совещание рекомендует издательствам создавать объединенные бригады из переводчиков обоих языков.

6. Отмечая чрезвычайно низкое качество подстрочников и вопиющие факты искажений и отсебятины, при переводе с нацязыков на русский предложить издательствам повысить требование к качеству подстрочников и в целях привлечения высоко-квалифицированных кадров одновременно максимально увеличить гонорар за подстрочники.

7. Просить Правление ССП поставить вопрос перед директивными органами о крайней необходимости создания толковых словарей с языков народов и на языки народов СССР.

8. Просить Академию наук организовать работу по изучению и разработке поэтики народов СССР.

9. Органозовать при ССП Кабинет нацлитературы, который должен стать научно-исследовательской базой ССП и Гослитиздата.

10. Поставить вопрос о необходимости повышения гонораров переводчикам художественной литературы и просить издательства национальных республик повысить гонорар за переводы

Arts of Accommodation

классиков мировой и русской литературы до уровня авторского гонорара.

11 Просить ССП СССР и ССП Нацреспублик заслушать отчеты издательств о системе оплаты труда переводчиков и наметить конкретно меры по улучшению условий труда и быта переводчиков.

12 Поставить вопрос о создании всесоюзного бюллетеня переводчиков для обмена опытом и разработки теорий художественного перевода.

Draft Resolution of the First All-Union Conference of Translators

1 The First All-Union Conference of Translators notes that after the Writers' Congress there was an acknowledged development in the mutual enrichment of our brother literatures of the nationalities of the USSR. However, the scale of the cultural revolution presents the sphere of translation with greater and greater demands.

2 In the area of translation theory, all manner of formalist and aestheticist theories can be found, and at present there is not a sufficiently developed scientific theory of translation based on Marxist-Leninism. The Bureau of the Section of Critics should undertake to work out the fundamental questions of literary translation and discuss them in the periodical press.

3 In order to train highly qualified translators, the following questions should be raised before the government: a) about the organization of the All-Union Institute of Translators into the basic linguistic groups of the languages of the nationalities of the USSR, and b) about special courses in the national republics and regions.

4 In order to achieve the planned work in the sphere of the translation of the classics of world literature into the languages of nationalities previously lagging behind, following the example of the Committee for the new alphabet, to organize a scientific-research institution to give practical help to translators from the minority nationalities

with selecting the more important texts for translation from world and Russian literature, and to carry out corresponding textual work.

5 For work on the classics of world literature in the national republics the conference recommends that publishing houses create united brigades of the translators of both languages.

6 Noting the extremely low quality of interlinear translations and the howling examples of perversions and 'individual interpretation' in translation from the national languages into Russian, suggest to publishing houses that they raise their demands in terms of the quality of their interlinear trots and, with the aim of attracting highly qualified cadres, at the same time they increase the payment offered for interlinear trots by as much as possible.

7 Ask the Board of the Writers' Union to put to its directing organs the question of the urgent need to create dictionaries into and out of the languages of the nationalities of the USSR.

8 Request that the Academy of Sciences organize the work of studying and developing the poetics of the nationalities of the USSR.

9 To organize an Office of National Literature at the Writers' Union, which would become the scientific-research base for the Writers' Union and Goslitizdat.

10 To raise the question of the necessity of increasing payment to translators for literary translation, and to request that publishing houses in the national republics increase the rates for the translation of world classics and Russian literature, so that they reach the level of authors' rates.

11 Request that the Writers' Union of the USSR and the Writers' Union of the national republics pay attention to the reports of publishing houses about the system of payment for translation work and take definite measures to improve the working conditions and everyday circumstances of translators.

12 To raise the question of creating an all-Union bulletin for translators to facilitate the exchange of experience and to develop the theory of literary translation.

ELENA ZEMSKOVA

Translators in the Soviet Writers' Union: Pasternak's Translations from Georgian Poets and the Literary Process of the Mid-1930s

This chapter is about people who became Soviet translators in the 1930s. It is a well-known fact that many of those members of the literary intelligentsia who stayed in Russia throughout the 1920s turned to translation as the only possible way to make a living. Up to the late 1950s, many already famous poets and intellectuals (e.g. Anna Akhmatova, Georgii Shengeli and, until their arrests in the mid-1930s, Osip Mandel'shtam, Boris Iarkho and Gustav Shpet), as well as younger figures, who had not yet seen their works published (e.g. Mariia Petrovykh or Arsenii Tarkovskii), engaged mainly in translations, very often from the languages of the Soviet Republics or Eastern languages, mostly using Russian interlinear glosses. For many of them, translation became the only route to socialization in the strict hierarchy of a totalitarian society.

The majority of research into the history of translated literature in Russia has dealt with the principles and methods of translation, comparative analyses of the original and translated texts, as well as examining how original works by a given author have found reflection in the style of his translations. This chapter takes the approach established in the late 1920s by Boris Eikhenbaum, one of the founders of Russian Formalism, who declared that the role of literature in the society of that time had changed so profoundly that 'the question *how to write* has been if not replaced with, then at any rate complicated by, another one – *how to be a writer*'.[1] In this

---

1 B. M. Eikhenbaum, 'Literaturnyi byt'' in B. M. Eikhenbaum, *O literature* (Moscow: Sovetskii pisatel'', 1987), 428–36 (429).

work, Eikhenbaum introduced the notion of 'literary everyday life', and paid attention to the social conditions in which literary activity happened, rather than to poetic manner and stylistic devices. His article aimed neither to analyse the translations done in the 1930s nor to examine the principles for translation of the time. Similarly in this chapter, I shall examine what it meant *to be a translator* at that time; this is all the more interesting during this period because, for many translators, 'escape into translation' became the only possible answer to the question of *how to be a writer*.

A comprehensive social analysis of translators' work in the USSR can be made only after identifying and systematizing numerous historical sources, which are mostly unpublished documents both of personal and institutional character, in particular documents from the Union of Soviet Writers, from translation editorial offices of state publishing houses, and other such institutions.

This chapter aims at a preliminary description of some essential aspects of how 'the translation guild' functioned in the middle of the 1930s – at the time of the emergence of the so-called 'Soviet school of translation'. It focuses on the translations of Georgian verse by Boris Pasternak, the publication of which became an important milestone in the history of Soviet literature of the 1930s. The research examines specifically the perception of these translations by various members of the contemporary literary establishment.

Discussions of Pasternak's Translations of Georgian Verse in Literary Criticism and Official Discourse, 1934–1936

In 1934, after his trip with a delegation of writers to Georgia, Pasternak translated a number of works by Georgian poets, in particular the epic *The Snake-Eater* (*Zmeeed*) by the nineteenth-century Georgian classic author Vazha Pshavela and several lyric poems by contemporary Georgian lyricists Titsian Tabidze, Paolo Iashvili, Valerian Gaprindashvili, Kolau Nadiradze and others.² In 1935 the translations, which had earlier appeared in journals, were published as a separate volume under the title *Boris Pasternak. Georgian Lyricists*.³ Beside the epic by Pshavela, the collection mainly comprised lyrics by poets who were close to the association *Blue Horns* of the 1920s, and which were rather marginal to the then topical issues of Soviet reality. Typical of the time, however, was the inclusion in the volume of the translations of two odes to Stalin by Iashvili and Nikolo Mitsishvili.

Lazar' Fleishman points out that these translations were Pasternak's first attempt to fit in with official literature, and that, under pressure of circumstances, he had to make 'an obvious artistic trade-off'.⁴ He clarifies that Pasternak 'had to translate texts he would never have chosen of his own accord, but which he couldn't refuse' because of his bonds of friendship with the Georgian poets. The period 1934–1936 was for Pasternak a time of engagement in public literary life. In his keynote speech at the First Congress of Soviet Writers, held in Moscow in August 1934, Nikolai Bukharin ranked Pasternak first among the figures of contemporary poetry.⁵ Bukharin's patronage, and the collaboration with the Georgian delegation, allowed Pasternak to become part of the Soviet literary establishment for a short time. That period was brief, however, and took place during the few years when writers still had some opportunity to express independent opinions. When in February 1936 the so-called 'discussion of formalism' was launched, which rapidly turned into a campaign against any kind of pluralism in the arts, Pasternak refused to support the official point of view. Already then, and even more so after Bukharin's arrest, Pasternak began to

---

2   On the poetics of Pasternak's translations in the context of Russian-Georgian cross-cultural relations see: Harsha Ram, 'Towards a Crosscultural Poetics of the Contact Zone: Romantic, Modernist and Soviet Intertextualities in Boris Pasternak's translations of Titsian Tabidze' in *Comparative Literature* 59/1 (Winter 2007), 63–89.
3   Boris Pasternak, *Gruzinskie liriki* (Moscow: Sovetskii pisatel', 1935).
4   Lazar' Fleishman, *Boris Pasternak i literaturnoe dvizhenie 1930-kh godov* (St Petersburg: Akademicheskii proekt, 2005), 187–9.
5   *Pervyi vsesoiuznyi s"ezd sovetskikh pisatelei 1934, stenograficheskii otchet*, ed. I. K. Luppol, M. M. Rozental', S. M. Tretiakov (Moscow: Sovetskii pisatel' 1990) [Reprint of 1934 edition], 494–5.

be persecuted in the press. Even though he escaped arrest during the Great Terror, Pasternak was eventually forced out of literary life.

This chapter will focus on the short span of time between the First Congress of Soviet Writers and the First All-Union Conference of Translators held in January 1936.[6] The issue to be examined here is not Pasternak's position regarding literature, nor the attitude towards him of the press and those in power in the literary world, which varied significantly, nor his own reaction to 'the symptoms of *worshipping* him in the Soviet press',[7] which has been comprehensively studied and convincingly presented by Fleishman. This chapter is concerned with the reception of Pasternak's Georgian translations by individuals in the literary sphere during this period, and most importantly, by those within the translation guild. Using a variety of sources, I shall demonstrate how the image of Pasternak as a translator was constructed, and in what way that image affected the conception of the translator's task and work in Soviet literature.

The sources used in this study fall into two clear groups. The first group encompasses texts published 1934–6. First of all, these are texts of speeches given at the First Congress of Soviet Writers, which were edited and published in 1934 as a separate volume of verbatim reports. Besides these, the image of Pasternak the translator was also created through critical articles published in the newspaper *Literaturnaia gazeta*, and the journals *Znamia* and *Krasnaia nov'*, as well as through the detailed reports of the Conference of 1936 (published in *Literaturnaia gazeta*). All these texts can be regarded as belonging to the official discourse of the epoch. They enable us to trace the formation of public, official views of Pasternak's work as a translator. All the texts were censored so as not to diverge from the 'official line'. As such, they also partially reflect the evolution of that 'official line' regarding translation activity *per se*. The second group of sources contains uncensored evidence, which will be characterized later.

---

6 On the First All-Union Conference of Translators, see the chapter by Susanna Witt in this volume.
7 Fleishman, *Boris Pasternak i literaturnoe dvizhenie 1930-kh godov*, 361.

The Georgian theme was among the most important ones discussed at the First Congress of Soviet Writers. As Fleishman points out,

> in the propaganda campaign launched by officials to accompany the Congress, Georgian literature was persistently underlined as *universally important*. M. Torshelidze gave a paper on the literature of the Georgian SSR, which was not limited to the post-revolutionary Soviet period, but, as Stalin insisted, went back to ancient times. The paper, according to one of the delegates, *literally created a big stir*.[8]

At a meeting with the Georgian delegation at the Congress, Pasternak and his colleague from Leningrad, Nikolai Tikhonov, read out their translations of Georgian poetry. Almost all the members of the delegation evaluated the translations as a breakthrough in the process of introducing Georgian poetry to the Russian reader. It was particularly stressed that these translators were very talented authors, whose own work was marked by an original poetic voice. In this respect, Bukharin's high praise for Pasternak's poetry in his speech at the Congress was of great importance. All the speakers, including Iashvili and Tabidze who had been translated by Pasternak, called the two translators 'talented masters'.

Mikhail Iavakishvili pointed out that, as a rule, Russian translators did not learn Georgian, and so the quality of their translations tended to be very poor. This problem, however, did not affect the translations by Pasternak and Tikhonov:

> The literature of the peoples of our Soviet Union, including that of Georgia, loses its stylistic appeal [in translation] more than usual. This has to do with the fact that not a single Russian author has, nor ever has had, any command of the Georgian language, whereas it used to be and continues to be studied by many Europeans. Due to the absence of curiosity on the part of our Northern brothers, we have nothing to do but translate each other and make auto translations. But our Russian is not perfect enough, so the results are very unsatisfactory. All this is mostly true for prose. Our poetry has received more fortunate treatment in the translations by such highly talented masters as Pasternak and Tikhonov.
> *(Remark from audience: Right!)*[9]

---

8 Ibid., 264–5.
9 *Pervyi vsesoiuznyi s"ezd*, 147.

The remark from the audience here is significant: the verbatim report has only a few such remarks. In every case they stress the audience's support for the speaker, most often being a record of 'applause'. No critical remarks, of course, were registered in the report.

Paradoxically, the prose writer Sergei Tretiakov, who had argued for the necessity of studying the languages of the nationalities of the USSR, evaluated Pasternak's and Tikhonov's translations made from interlinear glosses highly:

> Won't we, professionals, be able to learn [national languages]? That opens up a path of true communication for us. Recently, we met the Georgian poets here, and Pasternak and Tikhonov read out their translations. For the first time, we saw great poetry and we were petrified – what strength! Yet Pasternak and Tikhonov broke through the fence between us without even resorting to a frontal attack. They just bypassed it without any knowledge of Georgian. Imagine what great results we could expect if people learnt this language![10]

Notably, the representatives of other national republics either did not mention Russian translations at all or criticized the translators. For instance, Rafili, the delegate from Azerbaijan, stated:

> We have a lot of poets and Russian writers who have been translated into Turkic. Our poetry, however, the verse of Soviet Azerbaijan, has been translated into Russian and other languages poorly.
> For the Georgians, comrades Pasternak and Tikhonov have done a lot. They have considerably raised the prestige of Georgian poetry, and rightly so, for Georgia has wonderful poets. [...] Translation should be strengthened. It should be arranged that Tikhonov and Pasternak translate not only Tabidze, but also [...] other poets of the Soviet Caucasus.[11]

Thus, Pasternak and Tikhonov were, from the very beginning, considered as role models for translators in the official discourse; this had to do with their reputations as the best Russian poets (and this was ultimately true for

10   Ibid., 345.
11   Ibid., 529.

Pasternak). It was their poetic artistry that excused their lack of knowledge of the source language.

The first negative opinion of Pasternak's Georgian translations appeared in *Literaturnaia gazeta* in spring 1935, in a review of Vazha Pshavela's *The Snake-Eater*.[12] While praising highly the Georgian masterpiece, the anonymous reviewer pointed out that Pasternak's translation utterly failed to convey the specific nature of the Georgian verse or to embrace fully its stylistic features. An objection to such criticism that detracted from Pasternak's status as a model for translators was raised almost at once by the then influential critic Dmitrii Mirskii in a press review of 1934, where he called 'the true discovery of the poetry of our brother Soviet nations' the most important event of the poetical life in the entire year, while calling the work by Pasternak and Tikhonov 'a most valuable contribution to our common poetical heritage'.[13]

Kornelii Zelinskii, the editor of Pasternak's volume *Georgian Lyricists*, was the first literary critic to speak out on the subject in his public lecture, 'The Construction of the History of Soviet Literature', which was later published in the journal *Literaturnii kritik*. He was the only critic who observed that, in Pasternak's case, 'the poetry of the translator clearly eclipses the poetry translated' and that national features of the Georgian verse get obliterated in the Russian translation. At the same time, Zelinskii rated Pasternak's translations as 'excellent in terms of their artistic quality'.[14]

This attempt to present Pasternak's translations as less significant was again fiercely opposed by Mirskii, who responded to Zelinskii in his article 'Pasternak and Georgian poets', published in *Literaturnaia gazeta*: 'There is an opinion [...] that Pasternak, while translating Georgian poets, deprives them of their individuality and replaces it with that of his own, that he so to speak, "pasternakizes" [опастерначивает] them. [...] Opinions of this sort can only be based on a superficial reading of Pasternak's translations'.[15] In

---

12 B. N., 'Pshavela i Pasternak', *Literaturnaia gazeta* 18 (1935), 4.
13 Dmitrii Mirskii, 'Stikhi 1934 goda. Stat'ia pervaia', *Literaturnaia gazeta* 21 (1935), 4.
14 Kornelii Zelinskii, 'Voprosy postroeniia istorii sovetskoi literatury', *Literaturnii kritik* 2 (1935), 8–9.
15 Dmitrii Mirskii, 'Pasternak i gruzinskie poety', *Literaturnaia gazeta* 59 (1935), 2.

order to prove that Pasternak preserves the original voice and poetic manner of each Georgian poet, Mirskii compares the translations by Pasternak and Tikhonov and arrives at the conclusion that both poets convey in a similar way the distinct poetic style of Leonidze, so that he cannot be confused with any other Georgian poet. Using all the tools and techniques of poetic language, Mirskii asserts, Pasternak manages to convey the poetic system of each and every poet translated: 'Pasternak writes in Russian as a poet, that is, not as a slave of the language but as its master'. At the same time, he argues, Pasternak's translations demonstrate his individual poetic talent:

> That, of course, is not to say that we do not feel Pasternak too and do not hear him all the way. A translator who is also a major and original poet is bound to have his hand seen in every translation he does, in his very poetic manner, the very layout of the tissue of verse.

Mirskii believed that Pasternak, with his poetic artistry, helped create new poets: 'the Russian Leonidze', 'the Russian Tabidze'. He explained that Pasternak's lexical repertoire 'gives them a rich vocabulary that is so characteristic of the Georgian language and that leaves far behind the language of Russian poetry before Futurism'.

While trying to distinguish between Pasternak's more successful translations and those less satisfactory, Mirskii speaks about the degree of 'congeniality' of Pasternak to this or that Georgian poet, that is, the similarity of their poetic worlds. For instance, Pasternak, more than Tikhonov, is congenial to Leonidze, but Tabidze is the closest to him. As Pasternak is not so close to Vazha Pshavela, the classic poet of the nineteenth century, so his translation of *The Snake-Eater* has many more 'blank spots and poetic liberties'. Mirskii's view was echoed by the critic Anatolii Tarasenkov in an article published in the journal *Znamia*.[16] Tarasenkov opens with the paradoxical statement that Pasternak's translations from the European languages that he knew well, 'despite being elaborate, do not go beyond the standard of any competent job done properly. The individuality and artistic

---

16 Aleksandr Tarasenkov, 'O gruzinskikh perevodakh Pasternaka', *Znamia* 9 (1935), 201–9.

specificity of the big poet almost disappear altogether'. Yet, he continues, Pasternak, without knowing Georgian, produced real poetic masterpieces by 'creatively discovering the country, the poetry and history of which are glorified in the excellent verses he translated'.

Tarasenkov fiercely criticized the artistic level of translations from languages of the other Soviet Republics into Russian, illustrating his point with translations by A. Rom and others:

> Until recently, the poetry of our brother Republics did not enjoy any significant popularity. The reason for this seemingly enigmatic fact is, undoubtedly, a poor job on the part of the translators. Their gloomy verses are hack jobs; their pale epithets are clichés and often artistically incompetent [...] although our major journals have now started publishing competent, elaborate translations by D. Brodskii, M. Tarlovskii and B. Brik. Even those comrades, however, who take poetic translation seriously, still often slip into bad taste, clichés, and gloomy rhetoric.[17]

Tarasenkov engages in a polemic with the opinion, apparently widespread in 'quasi-literary circles,' that the popularity of the Georgian poets is to be credited mainly to Pasternak's poetic fame. Tarasenkov's arguments are in essence close to Mirskii's views:

> Pasternak has undoubtedly put a lot of his artistic ego into his Georgian translations. But that did not interfere with the original voices of P. Iashvili and T. Tabidze; on the contrary, it resulted in the artistic uniqueness that is obligatory for any work of art. We learnt and felt Georgian poetry through Pasternak, but with a degree of objectivity that did not impede us from grasping its own individual character. The sweet sugar doesn't prevent us from feeling the slightly bitter taste of the tea. That is how Pasternak's individuality is dissolved in the Georgian poetic material, which, as a result, has become sweeter, tastier, if you wish, but which has not lost its own smell and flavour.[18]

Similar arguments for the advantage of Pasternak's translations were expressed by Viktor Goltsev in his article published in early 1936 in the

---

17 Ibid., 204.
18 Ibid., 208.

journal *Krasnaia nov'*.[19] He also argued for the ideological importance of the translations:

> The volume *Georgian Lyricists* is indeed an event in literature, its cultural and political significance is enormous. Only after the proletarian revolution could this book appear. It testifies to the true friendship between writers from the Soviet Republics, which has been brought about by the Lenin-Stalin national policy of the Party.[20]

Like Tarasenkov, Goltsev considers it quite possible to use word-for-word translations of the original texts to produce a translation; he refers to the authority of Vasilii Zhukovskii, who rendered Homer's *Odyssey* into Russian using German interlinear glosses:

> Of course, a literary translation is far from being perfect if one uses interlinear, word-by-word rendering, even if it is provided with the Latin or Russian transcription of the Georgian text and comments that help the Russian poet to grasp the metre and rhythm of the Georgian verse. And yet Zhukovskii still translated Homer's *Odyssey* without knowing the language of the Hellenes, and using German word-by-word rendering![21]

Goltsev holds it 'by default, hopeless to try to imitate Georgian syllabic verse with the Russian', and considers the precision of the translation as less important than its ability to convey the individual poetic manner of the author translated:

> After all, almost every poetic translation is either an artistic interpretation of the original or an attempt to replicate it; the latter, however, is often made to the detriment of artistic qualities. Demanding total accuracy in a translation leads to missing the most essential thing [...] it stems from a failure to understand what is the most essential in literary translation. [...] It is much more important for a translator to seize the 'spirit' of the original, reach its core essence, grasp the author's rhythmical trot rather than produce streamlined, rhymed word-by-word renderings.[22]

19 Viktor Goltsev, 'Poety Gruzii i Boris Pasternak', *Krasnaia nov'* 1 (1936), 228–37.
20 Ibid., 228.
21 Ibid., 230.
22 Ibid., 234.

Arguments put forward by these critics made a considerable contribution to the reception of Pasternak's translations in the official discourse as a model for introducing the literature of a Soviet Republic to the Russian-speaking reader. This idea was firmly established at the First Conference of Translators (January 1936), when Pasternak was elected member of the presidium of the Conference. In the speech published the next day in *Literaturnaia gazeta*, Gaprindashvili, the Georgian representative at the conference, once again rebutted the criticisms made by some unnamed opponents:

> there is a myth that Pasternak and Tikhonov have reinvented the Georgian poets rather than translated them – somebody even created the words 'pasternakize' and 'tikhonovize' [*opasternachit'* and *otikhonovit'*]. I claim that these words were invented by people who do not have any idea of the Georgian language.
>
> Pasternak ultimately manifests his high artistry in these translations. They read like original works. But this is not at all to say that his translations have nothing to do with the original texts. In many cases, when I compare the Georgian text with its reflection in Pasternak's translation, I discover how close the two are.[23]

To summarize the basic features attributed in the official discourse to the translator's role model, in this case personified by Pasternak, the following observations can be made. First of all, the task of successfully creating the idea of a 'family of peoples', as well as of representing a national literature at the USSR level, required more than just a translator; a famous poet was needed. His name, and not the names of the authors he translated, was printed on the book's cover. What was required of a translation from the language of a national literature differed a lot from the requirements imposed on translations of foreign classic authors, since in the latter case critics could refer to the original, which they trusted much more that the translation. There is only one reference to the original in the articles on Pasternak's Georgian translations, and the role of original was played by a word-for-word Russian rendition. This means that all the maxims about

---

23 'Perevod – dvoinik originala. Rech' t. Gaprindashvili', *Literaturnaia gazeta* 3 (566) (1936), 4.

successful translations from the national languages, which were not known by critics or translators, were formed without any reference to original texts. From the critics' point of view, a model translation was not supposed to be an invention or a fabrication. Not only should it be close to the original in terms of word choice and stylistics, but it also had to convey the 'spirit' of the original, its inner poetic form. Such a translation could only be produced by a genuine poet who had mastered 'poetic artistry'. It was to be the fruit of a poetic insight into the source culture, and its creative interpretation. Ideas of this kind can be found quite often in the history of European translation and mainly stem from the culture of the German romantics, who viewed translation as a representation of the poetic spirit of the original and the genius of the author.[24] In Russia, they can be traced back to Belinskii,[25] who became the highest authority in Soviet literary criticism, in particular for translation criticism.

Meanwhile, in the context of the Soviet culture of the 1930s, any opinion expressed by official literary critics was sure to acquire a prescriptive meaning. Statements by critics were, in a way, guidance coming from the 'official party line' to all translators engaged in the ideologically important work of translating literature from the vernacular languages of the Soviet republics. Taken as such a guideline, criticism of Pasternak's Georgian translations appears to have been rather ambiguous. Faithfulness to the original could turn out to be the wrong approach, but so could digression from it in an attempt to produce a creative interpretation, if the translator had not mastered 'poetic artistry' well enough. Both approaches could be viewed as incorrect treatment of the source text. The problem of using interlinear glosses did not receive a definitive solution either. A true 'master' did not

---

24   See Andreas Poltermann, 'Die Erfindung des Originals. Zur Geschichte der Übersetzungskonzeptionen in Deutschland im 18. Jahrhundert' in *Die literarische Übersetzung: Fallstudien zu ihrer Kulturgeschichte* (Berlin: Hrsg. von Brigitte Schulze (= Göttinger Beiträge zur internationalen Übersetzungsforschung. Bd. 1.), 1987), 14–52.

25   See Iurii Levin, 'Ob istoricheskoi evoliutsii printsipov perevoda (iz istorii perevodcheskoi mysli v Rossii)' in M. P. Alekseeva, ed., *Mezdunarodnye sviazi russkoi literatury. Sbornik statei* (Moscow and Leningrad: Nauka, 1963), 4–63.

have to know the source language, whereas the lack of such knowledge often became grounds for criticizing other (ordinary) translators.

'Second-Rate Writers': Pasternak's Georgian Translations and the Soviet Translator's Social Status

A careful reading of the censored sources mentioned above enables one to see the ambiguous attitude towards Pasternak's translations in the literary community. I have already referred to the critical article published in *Literaturnaia gazeta* and the review by Zelinskii. Vague hints of the opinions of some 'opponents' can be found in many of the comments cited. Below I will reconstruct these 'contrary opinions' within the translators' community itself.

For historians, classified documents of state security agencies often turn out to be the most useful source of knowledge about public attitudes in totalitarian states. In the case of Russia, a report from the NKVD Secret Political Department, entitled 'Writers' attitudes towards the recent writers' congress and the new administration of the Soviet Writers' Union', written in September 1934, clearly indicates a certain 'area of discontent' with the official Party line for translations from the Soviet languages. The report registers the discontent of the translators of poetry from languages of the Soviet republics:

> The general tone was as follows: national writers are bad. In fact, we actually make them into writers, sacrificing our own creativity. For this, not only do we not see any gratitude, we are facing constant discontent, behind-the-scenes accusations and the like. Here these writers are extensively published, honoured, get elected to the central organs of the Union and so forth, while we are always being given a back seat.[26]

---

26 A. Artisov, O. Naumov, eds, *Vlast' i khudozhestvennaia intelligentsiia. Dokumenty ZK RKP(b) – VKP(b), VChK – OGPU – NKVD o kulturnoi politike. 1917–1953 gg*

The quoted opinion contains some elements which are utterly in conflict with the official discourse: translators of the vernacular authors not only introduce their own style into their renditions; they also make, out of worthless texts, something that could pass for literature. The example below is directly related to Pasternak and the situation around his translations as discussed at the Conference:

> Gatov was furious with the Armenians, who in their letters admired his translations, but fell silent at the Congress because they became envious of the Georgians, who had been translated by Pasternak; now they are whispering behind his back that his (Gatov's) book is bad. Having mentioned that Tikhonov and Pasternak were not going to engage in translation again and were finding their commitment burdensome, he concluded that he was not going to translate either, at least, not until 'they come and beg'.
>
> Gusev also said that, having worked with the Uzbeks, he clearly saw the worthlessness of their works, their insincerity, and the rottenness of their literary community, where everyone hates everybody and rats everybody out, and that he would not translate anything again.
>
> N. Ushakov said with bitterness that the nationals demanded translations but on their part did not want to translate anybody, while acting 'as if they are in a conquered country'. He would finish the translations he had taken but after that he 'would starve but write his own texts'.[27]

This document registered the attitudes of translators present at the First Congress of the Writers' Union. Apparently, for them, as well as for many other participants of the Congress, what was officially said from the podium was rather indirectly related to reality. It is known that reports such as the above, based on the testimony of informants, tend to exaggerate the level of discontent; in this case, however, the objectivity is corroborated by a variety of other sources, in particular unpublished materials related to the work of the Translation Section of the Soviet Writers' Union.

(Moscow: Mezdunarodnyi fond 'Demokratiia', 2002), 248–9. An English translation of part of the document can be found in K. Clark and E. Dobrenko, eds, *Soviet Culture and Power: A History in Documents, 1917–1953* (New Haven: Yale University Press, 2007), 177–8.

27   Ibid., 249.

Chronologically, the first relevant document is the verbatim transcript of the Moscow Translators' Conference held in December 1933 by the Bureau of Translated Literature at the *Orgkomitet* of the Writers' Union.[28] As we can understand from the transcript, the main aim of the Bureau was to make sure that translators would be able to join the future Writers' Union on equal terms with other authors – poets, prose writers, and critics. Petr Pavlenko, representing the *Orgkomitet*, admitted that translators

> were in extremely poor material conditions [...]. The translators' organization is spiritless, dispersed, and very passive. Translators do not know what they are going to do tomorrow, they do not feel secure about their literary future [...] our task is to reverse this mood and create such conditions that translators feel they are literary staff members, important literary workers.[29]

During the Conference, speakers made many suggestions for the work of the Section, including the organization of Evenings of Translated Poetry, as well as seminars and workshops for translators, work with publishing houses and discussion of the quality of translations at its meetings.

A discussion of translation reviews had been published in *Literaturnaia gazeta* on 23 October 1933. This editorial, entitled 'Higher Quality Literary Translation' (Выше качество художественного перевода) argued that translation was creative work, and was just as artistic as the work of any writer.[30] On the other hand, that issue of the newspaper contained a number of articles fiercely criticizing the quality of translations being produced. The stenograph of the December Moscow Translators' Conference shows that the conference organizers wanted to show that the quality of translations would improve dramatically if most of the translators were admitted to the Writers' Union on equal terms with others. The Bureau of Translated Literature was supposed to prepare a report for the forthcoming first Writers' Union Conference on this subject, but this intention was not realized; there was no separate report on translation problems given at the

---

28 RGALI, f. 631, op. 21, ed. khr. 4, 5.
29 RGALI. f. 631, op. 21, ed. khr. 4. ll. 7–8.
30 *Literaturnaia gazeta* 49 (1933), 1.

Conference, and the speakers at the Conference rarely mentioned translations or translators. The statistical data of the Conference Credentials Commission did not include translation as a separate category of literary activity (unlike poetry, prose, dramaturgy, criticism and even children's literature, which presented an additional opportunity for socialization for those members of the intelligentsia who could not find employment anywhere else).[31] On one of the last working days of the conference, K. Chukovskii,[32] who, though at the time representing children's writers, was also engaged in translation, talked briefly about the problems faced by translators; his comments only emphasized the absence of a separate translation 'corporation' at the Conference.

Unlike the edited official report of the Writers' Congress, the unpublished and uncensored verbatim records of the meetings of the Translation Section have preserved more than just prepared speeches. All the discussions in the Section, however, were still made in public and did not contain, unlike the NKVD Report, opinions uttered in private discussions. Nevertheless, they register a much greater number of spontaneous and emotional remarks and replies than any censored source. These records enable us to find evidence of the attitudes among translators towards the critics' opinions, in particular with regard to Pasternak.

In this respect, the most interesting transcript is that of the Translation Section meeting held on 29 October 1935, at which the agenda for the forthcoming All-Union Translators' Conference was discussed.[33] The participants' opinions of the positions of critics are particularly interesting, as are the discussions of the translator's status in the Writers' Union. One of the points for discussion was the report to be made by Pavel Zenkevich, the head of the Section, entitled *Translators and Publishing Houses*, which, as he phrased it in bureaucratic jargon, 'concerned everyday issues'. In his report, he planned to

---

31 *Pervyi vsesoiuznyi s"ezd*, 697.
32 Ibid., 565–7.
33 For a complete description of the preparation meeting, see Susanna Witt in this volume.

touch upon, probably for the first time, the status of the translator in our country, the issues of his everyday life, his financial situation and legal status. The time has come to reconsider the 'normal' contract that exists among publishing houses. It's time to make sure that translators have equal rights with other members of the Writers' Union family, if the former are now to be considered family members.[34]

The content of his would-be report provoked rather emotional and pointed critical remarks. First of all, the participants were upset with the stand the literary critics had taken with regard to their work. Critics' work had been the special subject of the Second Plenary Session of the Board of Directors of the Soviet Writers' Union held in Moscow in early March 1935. During the Session and the 'discussion of criticism' which ensued in the press, it had been repeatedly stressed that critics' reviews could not be neutral or panegyric; rather, they should contain more tart and unmasking criticism, which should prevail regardless of the author's personality and merits.[35] It seems that translators had in some cases become 'easy meat' for critics who were trying to keep up with this general line.

Dissatisfaction with the criticism of literary translation was expressed by N. Volpina at this meeting: she suggested that a separate report should be compiled on this issue. Ezra Levontin's remark, that translators were commonly seen as second-rate writers, was taken up by many speakers after him:

> As for the issue of everyday life [...] both translators of prose and translators of poetry are treated as second-rate writers. We should confront that. For instance, Selivanovskii in his article about the Russian translation of 'Eshabib' states that this translation is an 'event in Russian poetry'. So, one can write such things in a newspaper, but apparently one can also trample on us as *second-rate writers*.[36]

---

34 RGALI, f. 631, op. 21, ed. khr. 8. l. 7.
35 *Vtoroi plenum pravleniia Soiuza sovetskikh pisatelei SSSR. Mart 1935 g. Stenograficheskii otchet* (Moscow: Goslitizdat, 1935); M. Shaginian, 'Zametki o kritike' in *Pravda*, 22 February 1935; 'K itogam diskussii o kritike', *Literaturnaia gazeta*, 6 March 1935. Also see: K. M. Polivanov, 'Politicheskii aspekt biografii Pasternaka (na materiale noveishikh dokumentov)', *Novoe literaturnoe obozrenie* 20 (1996), 102–3.
36 RGALI, f. 631, op. 21, ed. khr. 8. l. 20. My emphasis.

The most extensive comment during the discussion came from the translator Aleksandr Romm, who was criticized in Tarasenkov's article referred to above, as well as in other publications. According to Romm, literary critics did not see anything positive in translators' work in principle, and did not recognize or contribute to their success, unlike the success of writers:

> just as we can be sure that the opinion of society about any Soviet writer who is prominent enough and respected by readers and publishers will be confirmed or, rather, created by Soviet critics, we can also firmly say that no translator, however great and influential he might be, has been supported, let alone approved of and promoted, by the critics [...]. Once, when Anna Radlova was reading her translations of Shakespeare, and I don't really understand why it was her they supported and praised, well anyway, it was the only case when the critics praised somebody.[37]

Against this background, the critics' very positive attitude towards Pasternak's Georgian translations was viewed by Romm as unfair, since it differed sharply from that towards translators who did not have reputations as original authors:

> The newspaper that was condemning me contained an article entitled 'Pasternak's Georgian Translations'. On no occasion did I ever say to anyone that I place myself on a par with Pasternak, who is one of the greatest poets of our time, but let me assure you that the issue here is not just about the greatness of Pasternak; it has to do with the fact that he, who was not a translator before, has all of a sudden produced a book of translations.
> It's true that that article was to some extent bowing and scraping to the Georgian poets, but still, its every line was stressing that Pasternak was to be given credit, so much so that Georgian poets such as Tabidze and Iashvili were left in the shadows.[38]

Further on in his speech, Romm described very clearly the social position in which some authors found themselves, not having the reputation of 'prose writers' or 'poets' and not being able to publish their original works. For them, translation became the only way to make a living and the only

37 Ibid., l. 25.
38 Ibid., l. 26.

form of socialization within the Soviet literary hierarchy. Romm describes the humiliating, inferior status of translators compared with other members of the 'literary guild'. In his opinion, the Translation Section and its activities were ignored by everyone whose reputation was more than 'just a translator':

> Somebody mentioned here that we are treated like second-rate writers. If that were the case, it could have been tolerated. We are treated like second-rate translators, and the first-rate translators despise us. Our Section member, translator Osip Kolychev, who submitted a feuilleton to *Pravda* about today's meeting, hasn't come. Where are the people whose translations have been filling up our magazines and newspapers? Where are Svetlov, Golodnyi, Pasternak, whose work, though sometimes better than ours, is at times worse than what we do?[39]

Romm blames the critics, who never praise the translators' works, for the shortage of translators and translation's lack of appeal for the young:

> This is a disaster, which makes people groan because there are not enough people [...]. We have idealized five or six occupations to such an extent – pilot, engineer, writer and polar scientist – that literally all young Soviet people who are worth anything rush into them, so we don't recruit into translation; this is despite the fact that the situation with learning foreign languages isn't that bad.
> People are learning foreign languages, and in the old grammar schools education was worse, not better compared with what people get in contemporary schools. Yet people don't want to become translators because of the sense of social inferiority which accompanies a translator from birth, through his life, and to his miserable death, and prevents people from wanting to become translators. People do it against their will.[40]

According to a speech by P. Karaban, the feeling experienced by translators of being 'second-rate' stemmed from the way that material benefits were distributed among the members of the Writers' Union, with translators being excluded from the system:

---

39   Ibid., l. 27.
40   Ibid., l. 28.

> On the everyday life question, I will only say one thing – what is horrible is not that we are second-rate writers, as comrade Romm put it, but that we are second-rate translators. Let me illustrate: the Group Committee receives a note from the Union saying 'Comrades who wish to become members of the Litfond are kindly requested to file an application'. Comrades kindly file them, but out of the 50 applicants only 5 get accepted; as for the other 45, there is the mysterious phrase 'refrain from admission'. What is this? This has nothing to do with literature. Our representative working on everyday issues should take note of it, or we will find ourselves deprived of our rights, dependants.[41]

Karaban makes reference here to the legal and material aspects of social status: according to the Constitution of the RSFSR of 1918, which was still in force at the time: the 'deprived of our rights' were citizens limited in their rights due to their social origin or occupation, while the status of 'dependants', given to children and the unemployed, virtually excluded its bearers from welfare mechanisms.[42]

At the end of the session, Pavel Zenkevich, as the Chairman and reporter on 'everyday issues', expressed his view on the matter, dismissing the talk about being 'deprived' and giving examples of those translators who had 'achieved literary citizenship':

> A lot has been said about criticism. Aleksandr Ilych [Romm] very humorously talked about various things, and the atmosphere grew merry, but I was extremely upset and wasn't at all satisfied with his speech and with the speech by Nadezhda Davydovna [Volpina]. Why do we portray ourselves as though we translators are miserable and 'second-rate' people? Why all that defeatism?
>
> Nadezhda Davydovna was right to say that nobody wants to write about us or people write the wrong things. Translation criticism is unsatisfactory alright, but lessons should be also learnt, and now that the doors of the Writers' Union have been opened to translators, granting them literary citizenship, the rest is up to us. That is not to say we should act as if we were geniuses, but I object to this line as humiliating translators. Our job is not that unworthy.[43]

---

41 Ibid., l. 48.
42 Sheila Fitzpatrick, *Everyday Stalinism: Ordinary Life in Extraordinary Times. Soviet Russia in the 1930s* (Oxford: Oxford University Press, 1999).
43 RGALI, f. 631, op. 21. ed. khr. 8, l. 56.

It becomes clear from the remark by Zenkevich that the speech made by Romm, as the most emotional and pointed one, had stirred genuine interest among the listeners and gained their support. Romm's remark crystallized the dissatisfaction among translators with the 'positive role model' for the Soviet translator promoted by the critics, in particular in the case of Pasternak. As viewed by many participants of the discussion, the bar for success in translation had been raised so high that it was impossible to reach.

The optimistic tone of Zenkevich's remarks could be explained by his being Head of the Section. Romm had spoken of the low appeal of the Translation Section for those members of the Union who, though actually translators, at the same time had the opportunity to be classed as poets or prose writers. As Romm put it, and other speakers agreed with him, the bureaucratic resources of the Section were too limited to assert a translator's status within the Union. In reply to his colleagues, however, Zenkevich spoke mainly as a bureaucrat from literature, dwelling on the failures and successes in the Bureau. In this context, the very fact of acknowledging the status of the translator as a writer was viewed as a serious bureaucratic achievement, as was the existence of a separate Translation Section, which, its head thought, could, through purely bureaucratic means, elevate the status of its members. Zenkevich did not argue with his colleagues on a matter of principle, but invited them instead to view the situation as the interim result of work that was far from finished. To judge by the resolution prepared by Zenkevich and other organizers of the Union Conference, they did hope to establish a better material status for translators.[44] In the report that Zenkevich delivered at the Writers' Union Conference he made pointed remarks, although his criticism was directed at publishing houses rather than at the Writers' Union:

---

44   One of the points of the resolution project was: 'Bring up for discussion the question of higher fees for belles-lettres translations and request publishing houses in national republics to raise the fees for translations of world and Russian classics to the level of authors' royalties. Request the Soviet Writers' Union and the Writers' Unions of the national republics to hear reports by publishing houses on payment systems and to plan specific arrangements to improve translators' working conditions'. RGALI, f. 631, op. 21. ed. khr. 9, l.1. See the appendix to Susanna Witt's chapter in this volume.

The unsatisfactory material and housing conditions of translators affects the quality of translations and doesn't allow for the right growth of our personnel. Publishing houses should radically change their attitude towards translators. Translators, equal members of the Writers' Union, need an individual approach, just like writers creating original pieces of literature. Translators' works should be treated according to their artistic qualities, their value and skillfulness. As well as the number of printed sheets, the level of difficulty of a translation should be taken into account. To confront dilettantism, hackwork and a utilitarian approach, we should create favourable working conditions for those translators who have been doing well. The rights given to the translator by Soviet laws should not be infringed.[45]

Pasternak's name and the issue of the evaluation of his Georgian translations resurfaced during the preliminary discussion of the Conference agenda, this time in the context of 'creative questions', as opposed to everyday ones.[46] For the purposes of this chapter, of special importance is the extensive speech on the mechanism of a translator's work made by Sergei Gorodetskii, a prominent poet of the 1910s, who in the 1930s committed himself exclusively to translation and libretti.

Like the rest of the Section members, Gorodetskii supported the statement that was put forward by *Literaturnaia gazeta* in 1933 about translation being a creative process. He argued that

> a vital question is that of creativity. Of course, I can't imagine non-creative translation; nothing will come out of it without creative inspiration. Sometimes, you are sitting all day and have fifty lines done by the end of it, another day it's only four. This process is very much the same as when you're creating something yourself. It is co-creation.

Gorodetskii's statement links 'creative' issues to 'everyday-life' ones and to the issue of low remuneration and tight deadlines, which, in his view, are impossible to meet because of the creative nature of the work. He does not, however, associate the creative aspect of translation with the necessity to express in the translation an individual translator's style. Unlike the critics' comments on Pasternak's and Tikhonov's works referred to earlier,

45 RGALI, f. 631, op. 21, ed. khr. 9, l. 15.
46 This aspect of the Conference is reviewed in detail in the chapter in this volume by Susanna Witt.

Gorodetskii considers it unacceptable on the part of a translator to commit such a serious divergence from the original text, calling it a 'fantasy':

> As for the limits on fantasy, this question must be discussed seriously. Our poet comrades, for instance, pull this off – they use all the rhymes they've ever come up with, create four images for each line. Tikhonov and Pasternak are excellent poets, but what have they done with the Georgians? Their translations have nothing in common with the Georgian language.

In the stenograph, this is followed by a dialogue consisting of two remarks, such as are often registered in initial transcripts of the meetings, but virtually never appear in the officially published reports:

> ROMM: Have you written about this?
> GORODETSKII: I have, but it's been a year and my article still has not been published.[47]

It is not clear whether or not Gorodetskii himself would have brought up the subject of his unpublished article if he had not been asked about it by Romm.

At the moment, we are unable to see in what way the questions discussed during the preliminary meeting were posed at the All-Union Translators' Conference, since the materials are not fully available.[48] The report by Zenkevich referred to above is available in two versions – a typewritten copy of the main points of the report, which is held in the archive of the Writers' Union, and the official report published in *Literaturnaia gazeta*, which is in fact a brief summary of the actual talk and differs from the typewritten copy significantly as far as its main theme is concerned. The newspaper account focuses mainly on the part of the talk in which the speaker set out the facts, and Zenkevich is presented as having been much more severe in his 'self-criticism' – one of the main rhetorical methods in the public speeches of the time – than the archived typewritten report suggests:

---

47 RGALI, f. 631, op. 21, ed. khr. 9, ll. 52–3.
48 See also Susanna Witt's chapter in this volume.

In his talk, Comrade Zenkevich describes the situation with translators, their relations with the publishing houses and severely criticizes the work of the Translation Section at the Soviet Writers' Union [...]. Most of the translations produced are usually of mediocre quality, or even lower. Besides these, however, stand out a number of great successes by certain comrades.[49]

The fact that Zenkevich spoke of the translators' dissatisfaction with their own status and financial situation is barely mentioned in the published article. Other published materials relating to the conference do not touch upon this question at all.

The question of Pasternak's importance as a 'model translator' was also addressed. As already mentioned, Pasternak was invited to the Presidium of the Conference, which was an acknowledgement of his merit as a translator; he was given the floor to make his speech,[50] and his translations were highly praised by the members of the Georgian delegation. We have available only one stenograph of the main speech, made by the critic Iogann Al'tman, and the follow-up discussion which contains remarks from the audience as well. This record registers not only the official point of view about Pasternak, but also the voices of the discontented. An edited version of Al'tman's speech was also published in the report by *Literaturnaia gazeta*, where it was, of course, stripped of all spontaneous remarks.[51] Below is the excerpt of the verbatim transcript in which Al'tman argues about Briusov as a translator:

> AL'TMAN: Briusov took a very modest stand, unlike our translators, who think they have the right to work with the material in such a way that we can't recognize it afterwards.
> REMARK FROM THE AUDIENCE: 'to pasternakize' [опастерначивать].

---

49 'Perevodchik i izdatel'stvo. Doklad t. Zenkevicha', *Literaturnaia gazeta* 3 (5 January 1936), 1.
50 For more details, see Fleishman, *Boris Pasternak i literaturnoe dvizhenie 1930-kh godov*. See also the chapter by Susanna Witt in this volume.
51 Iogann Al'tman, 'Kul'turnaia revolutsiia i zadachi khudozhestvennogo perevoda', *Literaturnaia gazeta* 2 (1936), 2.

AL'TMAN: Take Gorodetskii – he has a very long last name, so we can't quite use the same term for him, though maybe we can say 'to gorodize' [огораживать]. Anyway, we often can't recognize the original.[52]

In this case, we can attribute the remark from the audience: the author of that remark was clearly Sergei Gorodetskii, and the speaker spontaneously replies to him, treating his name in the same way that Pasternak's was used to create the neologism 'to pasternakize'. Later on, Al'tman comes back to Gorodetskii's interjection:

> I should say, however, that we have many wonderful examples of translation, we have many good translations into Russian. The luckiest are our Georgian and Armenian comrades. Recently, I read Charents's poem 'The curly-haired boy' translated by Pasternak. Pasternak as a translator has his own very distinct style. Comrade Gorodetskii is wrong in his remark. It could be clearly seen while analysing 'The curly-haired boy'. I read the original poem and saw that the translation is accurate. The translation is congenial to the original, the translation is quite good.[53]

This small dialogue within the main ideological report at the Translators' Conference points again to the importance attached to the 'positive example' of Pasternak in the official discourse on translation. The speaker had to digress twice from the prepared text and clarify his position by stressing that he considered Pasternak's translations not only talented but accurate as well.

Concluding Remarks

In the 1930s, literary translation in the USSR was established as an independent intellectual profession, a process that was closely connected with the ideologization and bureaucratization of literary life and the creation of

---

52   'Pervaia vsesoiuznaia konferentsiia perevodchikov. Stenogramma doklada I. Al'tmana', RGALI, f. 631. op. 6, ed. khr. 124, l. 37.
53   Ibid., l. 67.

the Writers' Union. It was motivated by the need to manage the projects of producing translations from the national languages of the Soviet republics, and of translating world classics so as to furnish the new proletarian class with 'all the treasures of world literature'. The social status of translators was constructed through the bureaucratic activity of the Writers' Union and through publishing houses. The bureaucratic machine allowed some intellectuals to find legitimacy as translators within the narrow confines of the Soviet social system.

Translation was constructed as an activity that only experts could carry out, that required some training and qualifications. At the same time, it was conceptualized as a creative activity. These two criteria led to some ambiguity about the nature of the profession, and a 'real artist' was always praised and valued more highly than just a professional translator. For some writers and translators this situation, combined with the impossibility of publishing their original works and the uncertainty of their position in the literary world, led to discontent and dissatisfaction, which is visible in the unpublished transcripts of meetings and conferences and some other sources.

Not all the remarks made by translators of the 1930s referred to in this chapter directly concern Pasternak and his translations. It is more that the very name of Pasternak or, rather, its derivative 'to pasternakize', represents the attitude towards the official line on the translator's work and his social and literary status. The name of Pasternak as a translator of Georgian poetry resurfacing in unofficial spontaneous remarks by members of the Translation Section marks a certain area of discontent, where the latter expressed their emotions. These separate remarks are a symptom, demonstrating how utterly dissatisfied translators were with their social status and the situation in their professional milieu.

As demonstrated by Fleishman in his book, Pasternak, no less than others, suffered from the uncertain status of translators in Soviet culture.[54] Although in the 1930s he was for a short time recognized, Pasternak was forced completely into translation by the end of the decade and could

---

54   See Fleishman, *Boris Pasternak i literaturnoe dvizhenie 1930-kh godov*, Chapters 10–11.

not publish his original works, just like many of his former writer colleagues. Thus, Pasternak, who translated not only from national languages of the Soviet republics but was the author of famous Russian renditions of Goethe and Shakespeare, for a long time remained a 'Soviet translator' – a writer deprived of the opportunity to express himself directly in his original writing.

ALEKSEI SEMENENKO

Identity, Canon and Translation: *Hamlets* by Polevoi and Pasternak

The translation of canonical texts seems thus far to have escaped academic scrutiny: seen as marginal and probably irrelevant, little has been written on it as a separate theoretical problem. Nevertheless, the question of canon translation actualizes the opposition of target-culture oriented and source-culture oriented approaches to translation, which in turn raises the question of the relation of the translation to its original. Does translation replace the original or just create an 'image' of it? Can the translation be 'better' than the original? Can we compare these two texts at all?

It is hard to find any translation analysis that would not involve the comparison of the target text with the source text: the connection between them seems to be the most natural point of departure of any evaluation of a translation. But even at this point it appears that all translations are different in the way they relate to their originals. It seems that we first have to distinguish between two large groups of texts: artistic and non-artistic (it should be noted that this opposition is rather schematic and presents the extremes of the contrasting poles; in reality, the boundary separating non-artistic and artistic texts from one another is not static but dynamic and recipient-specific). In the case of non-artistic texts, the adequacy and correctness of the translation are vital. If the instructions for, say, a TV set are poorly translated, I will probably not be able to operate my TV set; if I misunderstand a legal act or a warning sign on the road because they are wrongly translated, I can easily get in trouble. The reason is obvious: the primary function of this type of texts is to *convey* information in the best way possible. The interpretive possibilities of these texts should be minimal in order to decrease the entropy of the communicative act. In such texts, the content of the message can easily be separated from the plane of expression, and there is always a variety of ways to express the content of a message for better understanding. In semiotic terms, the primary function of non-artistic texts is *indexical*, i.e. they always refer to some extratextual reality.

With artistic texts, however, the situation is quite different: as Iurii Lotman stated in his seminal work, the artistic text, paradoxically, not only conveys but also *generates* information.[1] The creative function of the text is the direct result of the asymmetry of the communicative act, in which the codes of the sender and the recipient are not identical but rather overlapping. Translation is thus a creative act because it is based on an asymmetrical relationship (the combination of mutual untranslatability and conventional translatability) and involves the constant need for *choice*, thus enhancing the interpretive possibilities of the translator. As opposed to the indexical function of non-artistic texts, the primary function of artistic texts is *symbolic*; that is, an artistic text does not directly refer to any extratextual reality but rather to itself and/or other texts. But its most crucial feature is a virtual fusion of the content with the mode of expression: 'Under the complex operations of meaning-generation language is inseparable from the contents it expresses.'[2]

All this makes the relation of the translation to its source text less straightforward than in non-artistic texts. The translation of a literary text is always context- and culture-specific and to a great extent depends on the network of relations between the readers, writers and texts of the target culture. In a more general view, culture itself may be presented as a collective memory consisting of texts. As Lotman puts it,

> The sum of the contexts in which a given text acquires interpretation and which are in a way incorporated in it may be termed the text's memory. This meaning-space created by the text around itself enters into relationship with the cultural memory (tradition) already formed in the consciousness of the audience. As a result the text acquires semiotic life.[3]

---

[1] Yuri M. Lotman, *Universe of the Mind: A Semiotic Theory of Culture*, trans. Ann Shukman (London: Tauris, 1990), 11–19.
[2] Ibid., 15.
[3] Ibid., 18.

It is, then, no wonder that any new element of culture, be it a translation or an original text, is inevitably perceived against the background of all the other texts that are preserved in the collective memory. A textbook example of how the collective memory shapes the perception of the text is Laura Bohannan's article 'Shakespeare in the Bush',[4] where she tested the thesis of universal intelligibility of 'the greater tragedies' by retelling *Hamlet* to the elders of an African tribe. The result of her retelling was that the Shakespearean play was consistently adapted to the norms of the target culture and completely 'Africanized'. Bohannan's attempts to orient her audience to the source text were considered 'wrong' and were corrected according to the recipients' expectations. This case is of course the most emblematic example of an 'aggressive' accommodation of a foreign element in culture, but it well illustrates the transformations that are inevitable in the transfer of any text and also emphasizes the role of translators in the process of cultural accommodation.

The situation is much more complex when the object of the translation is a canonical text, i.e. a well-established classic in one or several cultures. Nevertheless, even in the field of literary translation, the most common practice of a reviewer or a critic is to compare a translator's work with the source text and indicate 'right' and 'wrong' renditions of the original. As I intend to show, this seemingly natural approach does not take into account the actual process of reception and adaptation of a foreign text to the national culture, and demonizes the original as the source of imaginary truth. In the case of translations of *Hamlet*, the concept of the original brings up several important questions: first of all, is there just one original text? As we know, there are at least three main versions, the First 'Bad' Quarto (1603), the Second Quarto (1604–5) and the First Folio (1623), not counting numerous subsequent editions. The choice of one of them or a certain combination of them is also one of the constituents of the translator's strategy. Second, what was the donor culture? It is wrong

---

4   Laura Bohannan, 'Shakespeare in the Bush' in James Spradley and David W. McCurdy, eds, *Conformity and Conflict: Readings in Cultural Anthropology* (New York: Longman, 1997), 34–43.

to assume that it was only English: in the eighteenth century, the French Neoclassical renditions greatly influenced the process of the reception of Shakespeare's texts in Russia; at the beginning of the nineteenth century, the romantic paradigm, and especially Goethe's interpretation of Hamlet the character and August Schlegel's 1798 translation of *Hamlet*, were crucial for the reception of Shakespeare in Russia and in most of Europe. Third, *Hamlet* as a multimodal text (literary and theatrical) presupposes intersemiotic translation, i.e. from one semiotic mode to another (e.g., literature, theatre, or film), which creates even more possibilities for interpretation than the translation from one language to another.

In the analysis of the translation of canonical works, all these questions have to be taken into account. In my recent work on the Russian canon of *Hamlet*, I came to the conclusion that the canon could be considered dual.[5] There were simultaneously two canonical texts, both in the nineteenth and twentieth centuries, which coexisted more or less 'peacefully' owing to the fact that they occupied different mediums: one in literature, another in the theatre. The two canonical translations in each period were also in opposition to each other: a written text that is stable and tends to be 'accurate' (according to the norms of the period) compared with a performance-oriented text that is multimodal, fluid and dynamic, and therefore offers greater latitude to the creative power of the translator and/or director. Taking the example of the two most successful Russian translations in two centuries, this chapter will demonstrate that the translator's personality often plays a pivotal role in the success of the translation of a canonical text.

---

5   Aleksei Semenenko, *Hamlet the Sign: Russian Translations of Hamlet and Literary Canon Formation* (Stockholm: Almqvist & Wiksell International, 2007).

Nikolai Polevoi (1796–1846)

The first Russian translation of *Hamlet* from the English original was made by Mikhail Vronchenko in 1828, but it was not until 1837 that one could talk about the adaptation of the Shakespearean classic to Russian culture. The well-known journalist and playwright Nikolai Polevoi was a true adept of the romantic school and frequently expounded his views on literature and translation in his journal *Moskovskii telegraf* (*Moscow Telegraph*, est. 1825), one of the most popular and influential periodicals of the time.

Polevoi's advocacy of Romanticism in opposition to Neoclassicism followed the German pattern: the characteristics of Romanticism are that it shows the creative uniqueness of the human soul and that it is formed afresh not only by every nation, but also by each great writer. Romanticism is multiform and universal, for it takes the form of the time, spirit and place of the nation in which this or that romantic poet is born; it rejects all the classical norms and conventions, mixes genres and its creative power is identified with the human spirit itself.[6]

In one of his reviews, Polevoi gives a definition of the perfect translation:

> Translation must be a faithful copy of the essence, external forms and smallest details of the original. Only where the original is absolutely untranslatable should the translator use the closest possible paraphrase (imitation); in other cases he goes step by step with the Author, the most important thing being to show the soul, colour and nuances of the foreign work. This is the perfect translation![7]

At the same time, Polevoi rejects adaptations and paraphrase, characterizing this type of translation as follows:

---

[6] Ksenofont and Nikolai Polevoi, *Literaturnaia kritika: Stat'i i retsenzii 1825–1842* (Leningrad: Khudozhestvennaia literatura, 1990), 124–6.

[7] Nikolai Polevoi, 'Russkaia literatura: *Makbet*', *Moskovskii telegraf* 27 (1830), 79–82 (79).

without following exactly every word and detail of the original, the translator keeps to the sense and speaks on his own. Unfortunately, like body and soul, the sense and the forms of expression are often closely linked. The original will be seen, of course, but as a phantasmagoria, a pencil drawing of a painting.[8]

In 1834, the *Moscow Telegraph* was banned by the authorities, and Polevoi, as a 'politically unreliable' person, was forbidden to continue his editorial practice. This was a real setback for him, for journalism and literary activity were his greatest aspiration. To continue working, he was forced to cooperate with Faddei Bulgarin and Nikolai Grech, journalists with a 'reactionary' reputation, after which he was not only held in contempt by the authorities but also scorned by his former colleagues and friends.

This was the situation in 1837 when Polevoi started translating Shakespeare, and the choice of *Hamlet* appears to have been obvious. For Polevoi, the translation of *Hamlet* was not only a literary act but also an instrument of self-reflection. He based his translation on the Russian theatrical tradition, used traditional rhetoric and even referred to some Russian classics. He freely edited his 'dramatic performance', deleting several scenes and characters he considered unimportant and shortening some soliloquies, while at the same time russifying the text and eliminating foreign specifics. In modern terms, it was a translation very much oriented toward adaptation of the original to render it adequate to the norms of the target system. Moreover, the romantic interpretation of Hamlet as a weak person, suffering from lack of will, was reflected in the translation and complemented by Polevoi's own contribution: for example, the epithet *nichtozhnyi*, meaning 'worthless', 'contemptible', 'vain', 'naught' etc., became something of a leitmotif of the tragedy, especially in Hamlet's discourse:

О женщины! ничтожество вам имя!
[Frailty, thy name is woman!, I.2];

Какое я ничтожное созданье!
[What a rogue and pleasant slave am I, I.2];

---

8   Ibid., 80.

Identity, Canon and Translation

> Ничтожный я, презренный человек
> [dull and muddy-mettled rascal, peak, I.2];

> Мне жизнь моя ничтожна
> [I do not set my life at a pin's fee, I.4]

The most famous words of this translation do not exist in the original. In his conversation with the Queen, Hamlet says:

> Когда и старость падает так страшно,
> Что ж юности осталось? *Страшно,*
> *За человека страшно мне!*[9]

> ['I fear, I fear for the man!']

> [Rebellious hell, / If thou canst mutine in a matron's bones, / To flaming youth let virtue be as wax/ And melt in her own fire; 3.4]

Other examples also emphasize Polevoi's contempt for mankind:

> Что от людей ждать! Какая-нибудь мерзость!
> [Marry, this is miching mallecho; it means mischief; 3.2]

> Ты погубила веру в душу человека!

> [Translates as 'You have destroyed belief in the human soul'; there is no such phrase in the original 'closet' scene, 3.4]

The connotations of humiliation and existential fear introduced into Hamlet's discourse appear to correspond to Polevoi's view of his own situation. The translator arguably identified himself with the Prince of Denmark; to some extent, he recreated *Hamlet* on his own terms, through his own experience, as a text about himself. As we are going to see later, the practice of using *Hamlet* as a 'mirror' is one of the hallmarks of 'Hamletism'.

Polevoi's *Hamlet* was a tremendous success. After the first night in Moscow on 22 January 1837, the actor Pavel Mochalov (1800–48) became

---

9   My italics.

one of the most popular tragedians in Russia, just as the play became a classic of the Russian theatre. It would not be an exaggeration to state that the appropriation of *Hamlet* by Russian culture was to a large extent due to Polevoi.

Two seminal articles were to appear in 1838 – 'Mochalov as Hamlet' and 'Hamlet, Prince of Denmark', both written by Vissarion Belinskii, the distinguished nineteenth-century Russian critic whose influence on the literary process of his time was paramount. In the first article Belinskii described the play and gave his understanding of it, and also the performance, praising Mochalov's skill. The second essay was dedicated to Polevoi's translation. In the first article,[10] Belinskii described Hamlet's character in a traditionally romantic way and was probably the first critic in Russia to formulate the essence of Hamletism and its universal applicability: 'everyone is Hamlet'. In this spirit, the words which Polevoi introduced into his translation ('I fear for the man!') were not rejected by Belinskii but considered congenial to the original text of the tragedy. These words, wrote Belinskii, express the state of mind of a man who penetrates into himself and analyses his every feeling.[11] Thus, reflecting and irresolute, Hamlet acquired a permanent residence permit in Russian culture.

The main function of Polevoi's translation was to adapt Shakespeare to the Russian literary/theatrical system. The transplantation of the Bard into Russian soil was effected with the help of two strategies. The first involved the simplification and transformation of Shakespeare's language and style, with consistent russification of the text. Polevoi aimed at an adequate 'nationalization' of the English play so that it corresponded to the recipient culture, and for 1837 it was no doubt a successful adaptation.

The second strategy applied by Polevoi involved the attention to the scenic aspect of the text, following, but at the same time renovating, the Russian stage tradition. It is important to mention that the romantic aesthetics in the theatre introduced a new standard of acting. If the neoclassical

---

[10] Vissarion Belinskii, *Polnoe sobranie sochinenii v 13 tomakh*, vol. II (Moscow: Akademiia nauk SSSR, 1953), 237.
[11] Ibid., 432.

tradition was a tradition of theatrical *declamation*, the new aesthetics established two new manners of speech: *singing*[12] and *speaking*, respectively. If the former manner turned acting into an elocutive procedure, the latter did not accept declamation in principle. However, the *speaking* manner was far from everyday speech, but was rather an expressive combination of different registers of emotional speech. Polevoi wrote in his memoirs that the *singing* trend was almost universal in the beginning of the nineteenth century, and he was very much opposed to it.[13] Polevoi's text obviously takes account of spoken delivery, and his intention was amply fulfilled by Mochalov, whose energy and expression were corroborated by many reviewers, Belinskii the first among them.

Finally, we can note that Polevoi's early declarations on the correctness of translation, quoted above, were neglected in his own *Hamlet* translation. Generally speaking, this neglect can be seen as evidence of the discrepancy between actual translational process and its metalevel: that is, the norms and conventions most translators proclaim are often idealized and are seldom applied in practice.

The reception of Polevoi's translation is as interesting as the text itself. The first comments, most of which were performance reviews, were very approving. The 'beautiful poetic translation', as Belinskii called it,[14] was in general positively evaluated. In the above-mentioned article, 'Hamlet, Prince of Denmark', Belinskii stated that though Polevoi had cut and changed the original text in accordance with the laws of theatre, the appearance of such a translation was a very important event for the general public. Comparing Polevoi's rendition with Vronchenko's, he preferred the former, and praised its language for being natural and vivid.[15] In Belinskii's terminology, a 'poetic' translation is the translator's interpretation of the original,

---

12 The Russian word *penie* can be translated as *singing* or *chanting*, but one must distinguish between actual singing and the theatrical manner of declaiming the text in a certain melodic way.
13 Mikhail Panov, *Istoriia russkogo literaturnogo proiznosheniia XVIII–XX vv.* (Moscow: Nauka, 1990), 247–50.
14 Belinskii, *Sobranie sochinenii*, vol. II, 429.
15 Ibid., 429, 432–4.

an adaptation, whereas the 'artistic' translation is almost an exact copy which seeks to replace the original.[16] In his view Polevoi's translation is not the best one possible, but it is definitely better than Vronchenko's version.

Many other critics stated that Polevoi had successfully adapted the English classic to the Russian stage, though they were united in their criticism of Polevoi's 'unfaithfulness' to the original. The situation got much worse at the end of the 1830s, when Polevoi's reputation was decidedly ruined. In 1840 Andrei Kroneberg published an article entitled '*Hamlet*, corrected by Mr. Polevoi', accusing Polevoi of numerous distortions of the original. At the same time, Belinskii radically changed his attitude to Polevoi, considering him a reactionary journalist like Bulgarin and Grech. There were hardly any positive reviews until the writer's death in 1846, especially after Kroneberg's new translation of *Hamlet* in 1844 which almost unanimously was considered to be more 'accurate'. All the criticism notwithstanding, Polevoi's position in Russian culture and especially the theatre canon was unshakeable until the Soviet period.[17]

Boris Pasternak (1890–1960)

A number of scholarly works have been written on Boris Pasternak's *Hamlet* and I therefore limit myself to some pivotal points of Pasternak's translation and its place in the history of the Russian canon of *Hamlet*. Pasternak's translation of *Hamlet* first appeared in 1940 in the journal *Molodaia gvardiia*,[18] after Mikhail Lozinskii's (1933) and Anna Radlova's translations (1937).

---

16   Ibid., 427.
17   Between 1837 and 1897 alone there were 262 performances of *Hamlet* in Polevoi's translation (see E. G. Kholodov, *Istoriia russkogo dramaticheskogo teatra v semi tomakh* (Moscow: Iskusstvo, 1977–1987); and Semenenko, *Hamlet the Sign*, 88–9).
18   The first attempt to translate *Hamlet* dates back to 1924, but as Pasternak writes in a letter to Ol'ga Freidenberg (2 November 1924), he had barely begun it at that time.

First of all, let us recall two main principles of Pasternak's translation:

1. Pasternak explicitly opposed the literalist or equivalence-oriented translation and argued that the translation must be produced by an author who has experienced the impact of the original before the actual act of translating.[19] He also emphasized the importance of the liveliness and naturalness of language: 'A translation must produce an impression of life, not of "literariness" (*slovesnost*)'.[20]
2. Accordingly, he focuses on producing a modern and scenic text in translation. Here are his famous remarks in the preface to the journal edition of Hamlet:

> Instead of translating words and metaphors I turned to the translation of thoughts and scenes. The work should be judged as an original Russian dramatic work because apart from its accuracy, equilinearity with the original, etc., it contains more of that intentional liberty without which there can be no approach to great things.[21]

It must be noted that Pasternak's self-description is quite accurate: his translation does sound like a modern Russian dramatic work, and bears the distinct influence of his poetics. The translation is written in a vivid expressive manner and is characterized by an eclectic combination of contemporary idioms, russicisms (including archaisms), and also technical terminology (argotisms). These features attracted major criticism in the 1940s and led to another, no less important feature.

Pasternak's translation of *Hamlet* has appeared in about twelve editions altogether.[22] The first book edition was 'corrected' on the insistence

---

19 Boris Pasternak, 'Zametki perevodchika', *Znamia* 1/2 (1944), 165–8 (165).
20 Boris Pasternak, *Polnoe sobranie sochinenii: s prilozheniiami: v odinnadtsati tomakh*, vol. V (Moscow: Slovo, 2003–5), 72.
21 Ibid., 43–4, translated in Christopher Barnes, *Boris Pasternak: A Literary Biography*, vol. II (Cambridge: Cambridge University Press, 1998), 70. First sentence in the citation is translated by me.
22 Evgenii Pasternak, 'K istorii perevoda *Gamleta*' in Vitalii Poplavskii, ed., *'Gamlet' Borisa Pasternaka: versii i varianty perevoda shekspirovskoi tragedii* (Moscow: Letnii sad, 2002), 5–11 (10).

of Nemirovich-Danchenko and the actors, and was published in 1941 by *Goslitizdat*. The publishing house also demanded that the text be corrected; in the unpublished preface to the translation, Pasternak explained the corrections as due to 'the pressure of necessity' and asked readers 'with understanding and taste' to turn to the 1940 journal variant.[23] This was by no means the last correction of the text. In the next edition published by *Detgiz* in 1942, the text underwent more changes. The editor, Mikhail Morozov, a well-known Soviet Shakespeare scholar, became a 'private critic' (and censor) of Pasternak's Shakespeare. On the one hand, he helped Pasternak with publishing, as if legitimizing his work, but on the other, his approach was the complete antithesis to Pasternak's: he urged the writer to keep to almost literal 'accuracy', the concept most alien to Pasternak.[24]

All the published editions of his *Hamlet* – 1940, 1941, 1942, 1947, 1949, two editions in 1951, 1953, 1956, and even the posthumous edition of 1968[25] – differ from one another. Pasternak was also asked to alter the translation in 1954 for Grigorii Kozintsev's production of *Hamlet*. Pasternak was very sensitive about the corrections, but usually obeyed because he did not have much choice.[26] But it would be all too easy to claim that all the variants after 1940 are 'distorted' and not authentic. First of all, multiple variants of the same work are a characteristic feature of Pasternak's poetics,[27]

---

23   Evgenii Pasternak, *Boris Pasternak: materialy dlia biografii* (Moscow: Sovetskii pisatel', 1989), 544.
24   See Boris Pasternak, 'K perevodam shekspirovskikh dram' in *Masterstvo perevoda* 6 (1970), 341–63, and Barnes, *Boris Pasternak*, vol. II, 191–2. In a letter to Grigorii Kozintsev dated 20 October 1953, Pasternak wrote that during the periods of total intimidation (*zapugannost'*) he was forced to make the translations almost literal because the editors needed someone to blame, in case something happened (Pasternak, *Sobranie sochinenii*, vol. IX, 754). The same explanation is given in Pasternak's letter to Ariadna Efron (see below).
25   The last edition of 1968 was published posthumously by Evgenii Pasternak and is much closer to the edition of 1941.
26   Pasternak, 'K perevodam', 342, and Evgenii Pasternak, *Boris Pasternak: materialy*, 542–3.
27   Mikhail Lotman, *Mandel'shtam i Pasternak (popytka kontrastivnoi poetiki)* (Tallinn: Aleksandra, 1996), 91.

Identity, Canon and Translation

and it is hard to believe that all alterations in the text were only 'mechanical'. In 1953, before sending the translation to Kozintsev, Pasternak wrote to the director saying that, after so many years and continual corrections, he himself did not know which version to pick.[28] For example, if we compare the 'to be or not to be' soliloquy translation in two variants (the 1940 version and the one that was used in Kozintsev's production of 1954 and his film of 1964, as one of the most widely known), the difference becomes clear:

The 1940 version

Быть иль не быть, вот в чем вопрос. Достойно ль
Души терпеть уколы и щелчки
Обидчицы судьбы, иль лучше встретить
С оружьем море бед и положить
Конец волненьям?
[...]
А то кто снес бы униженья века,
Гонителя насилья, спесь глупца,
Любовь без разделенья, волокиту,
Ругателей приказных и пинки
Нестоящих, лягающих достойных,
Когда так просто сводит все концы
Удар кинжала?
[...]
Так всех нас в трусов превращает мысль
Так блекнет цвет решимости природной
При тусклом свете бледного ума,
И замыслы с размахом и почином
На всем ходу сворачивают вбок,
Лишаясь званья действий.

---

28 Pasternak writes in his letter of 25 October 1951 to Ariadna Efron that revisions can be turned to his advantage and that the revised text will ultimately last for thirty or fifty years. This perspicacious remark proves that Pasternak did realize that he was creating a canonical text. Pasternak, *Sobranie sochinenii*, vol. IX, 642.

The 1964 version

Быть иль не быть, вот в чем вопрос. Достойно ль
Смиряться под ударами судьбы
Иль надо оказать сопротивленье,
И в смертной схватке с целым морем бед
Покончить с ними?
[...]
А то кто снес бы ложное величье
Правителей, невежество вельмож,
Всеобщее притворство, невозможность
Излить себя, несчастную любовь
И призрачность заслуг в глазах ничтожеств.
Когда так просто сводит все концы
Удар кинжала?
[...]
Так малодушничает наша мысль
И вянет, как цветок, решимость наша
В бесплодье умственного тупика.
Так погибают замыслы с размахом,
Вначале обещавшие успех,
От долгих отлагательств.

Original text

To be, or not to be: that is the question:
Whether 'tis nobler in the mind to suffer
The slings and arrows of outrageous fortune,
Or to take arms against a sea of troubles,
And by opposing end them?
[...]
For who would bear the whips and scorns of time,
The oppressor's wrong, the proud man's contumely,
The pangs of despised love, the law's delay,
The insolence of office and the spurns
That patient merit of the unworthy takes,
When he himself might his quietus make
With a bare bodkin?
[...]

> Thus conscience does make cowards of us all;
> And thus the native hue of resolution
> Is sicklied o'er with the pale cast of thought,
> And enterprises of great pith and moment
> With this regard their currents turn awry,
> And lose the name of action.

In the 1964 version, the tendency to make the verse 'smoother' and the translation less literal (cf. 'терпеть уколы и щелчки обидчицы судьбы' vs. 'смиряться под ударами судьбы') is obvious. One may also notice the elimination of 'russicisms' (*prikaznye, pochin*) and much freer rendition. The second variant sounds much more like a separate poem written by Pasternak and is less dependent on the dictate of the original (the last five lines are especially illustrative).

The most conspicuous feature of the translation, however, has to do with Pasternak's interpretation of *Hamlet* the play and Hamlet the character. The pressure that Pasternak experienced for twenty years found reflection in the text of his translation. In the late 1930s and 1940s, Pasternak was actively translating, not least because translations became for him almost the only means of making a living.[29] The reason he turned to translating *Hamlet* was not purely economical, however. As the poet confessed in a letter to his father, the translation of *Hamlet* really saved him 'from many things,' and he 'would have gone insane' without it.[30] In other words, Pasternak himself had a strong personal interest in the translation of the Shakespearean classic.

---

29   In the Soviet period this situation was experienced by many prominent poets and writers, such as Anna Akhmatova, Marina Tsvetaeva, and Mikhail Zoshchenko (see, for example, Maurice Friedberg, *Literary Translation in Russia: A Cultural History* (University Park: Pennsylvania State University Press, 1997), 193–4). During a certain period Pasternak even claimed that translations hindered him from his own creative work. For example, in his letter to Morozov of 30 September 1947 Pasternak wrote, 'I am a translator not by good fortune but through misprision, and if conditions were better I ought not to be translating at all' (translated in Barnes vol. II, 249).
30   Evgenii Pasternak, *Boris Pasternak: materialy*, 543.

As Markov notes,[31] five lines of the 'to be or not to be' soliloquy in Pasternak's translation of 1947 and 1951 have nothing in common with the original but a lot to do with Pasternak's situation:

А то кто снес бы *ложное величье*
Правителей, невежество вельмож,
Всеобщее притворство, *невозможность*
Излить себя, несчастную любовь
И призрачность заслуг в глазах ничтожеств.

The emphasized phrases translate as 'the false grandeur of the rulers', 'common hypocrisy', and 'the impossibility of expressing oneself': these are the words not of the Danish prince but of Pasternak himself, or rather of Pasternak disguised as Hamlet. Another obvious reference to the translator's situation is found in Hamlet's words 'Смотрите же, с какой грязью вы меня смешали!' / 'Why, look you now, how unworthy a thing you make of me!'[32]

In the history of the Russian Shakespeare, as we have seen, this was not the first time Hamlet the play was made into a 'lyrical confession camouflaged as a translation',[33] and Hamlet the character into the translator's alter ego.[34] A comparison of Pasternak's situation with that of Polevoi suggests itself: both writers were in disgrace with the authorities and both found in Hamlet a means of expressing themselves; both focused on the theatrical performance and contemporary Russian language, and both were criticized for doing so. These parallels do not seem to be forced if we

---

31 Vladimir Markov, 'An Unnoticed Aspect of Pasternak's Translations', *Slavic Review* 3 (1961), 503–8 (505–6).
32 On the association of Pasternak with Hamlet see Aleksandr Gladkov, 'Zima v Chistopole', *Literaturnoe obozrenie* 4 (1978), 103–11 and Barnes, vol. II, 166, 373.
33 Ibid., 506.
34 On this topic see also Anna Kay France, 'Boris Pasternak's Interpretation of Hamlet', *Russian Literature Triquarterly* 7 (1973), 201–26; Susanna Witt, 'Perevod kak mimikriia: Gamlet Pasternaka', *Swedish Contributions to the Thirteenth International Congress of Slavists, Ljubljana, 15–21 August 2003* (Lund), 145–56; and Aleksei Semenenko, '"Gamletovskii kontekst" Borisa Pasternaka', *Scando-Slavica* 51 (2005), 31–48.

remember T. S. Eliot's 1920 essay 'Hamlet and His Problems', describing the appropriative stance writers and critics have taken toward Hamlet. Identifying oneself with Hamlet, argued Eliot, and/or projecting one's own personality onto the prince of Denmark has been especially tempting to 'the most dangerous type of critic':

> the critic with a mind which is naturally of the creative order, but which through some weakness in creative power exercises itself in criticism instead. These minds often find in Hamlet a vicarious existence for their own artistic realisation. Such a mind had Goethe, who made of Hamlet a Werther; and such had Coleridge, who made of Hamlet a Coleridge[35]

It is difficult to share Eliot's point of view; on the contrary, what we see here is a spectacular testimony to the power of the canonical text to make *Hamlet* so special among other classics.

We have finally come to the most crucial feature of the translation – Pasternak's interpretation of the play in the context of his Hamletism. As is widely known, Pasternak's *Hamlet* is closely linked with the novel *Doktor Zhivago*, which he commenced around 1945, and the poet's historiosophy and neo-Christian philosophy. The most evident connection is the poem 'Gamlet' in the collection of Zhivago's poetry where Christ's words are repeated almost literally: 'Если только можно, Авва Отче, / Чашу эту мимо пронеси'.[36] The theme of Hamlet as Christ in Pasternak's translation has been discussed in many papers, and the author himself unequivocally points out this analogy, especially when he equates the 'to be or not to be' soliloquy with the Gethsemane prayer.[37] Thus Pasternak

---

35 T. S. Eliot, *The Sacred Wood: Essays on Poetry and Criticism* (London: Methuen, 1950), 95.
36 See also Evgenii Pasternak, *Boris Pasternak: materialy*, 587–8 and Boris Pasternak, *Sobranie sochinenii*, vol. IX, 473.
37 Boris Pasternak, *Sobranie sochinenii*, vol. V, 76. Pasternak was not the first to use this interpretation; Gordon Craig in his production also saw Hamlet as a Christ-like figure (Laurence Senelick, '"Thus Conscience Doth Make Cowards of us All": New Documentation on the Okhlopkov *Hamlet*' in Irena R. Makaryk and Joseph G. Price, eds, *Shakespeare in the Worlds of Communism and Socialism* (Toronto:

presents Hamlet as a messianic hero, 'a judge of his time and a servant of a more remote time',[38] and the main motifs of the play become duty and self-sacrifice. Apart from these two motifs, Pasternak also emphasizes the motif of 'judge of his time'. This motif in a messianic context appears to be prevalent in Pasternak's oeuvre: it embraces a body of poems written between 1918 and 1959,[39] Pasternak's translations (such as Shakespeare's *Hamlet* and Sonnet 66, Calderón's *Príncipe constante*, von Kleist's *Prinz Friedrich von Homburg*), and finally the novel *Doktor Zhivago*, an epic about the fate of the intelligentsia at the turn of epochs. This neo-mythological theme can be generally described as a plot in which the hero (usually a poet) sacrifices himself for the sake of the approaching epoch – his death makes it possible for the new age to come, and his sacrifice turns out to be one of the mechanisms of history. This theme – together with the image of the poet as a mediator of history – gradually becomes more and more personal, and the hero becomes Pasternak's alter ego.[40]

The reception of Pasternak's *Hamlet* in the Soviet period was in many ways predetermined by the situation of the official control that has already been mentioned. The main 'supervisor', Mikhail Morozov, in one of his

---

University of Toronto Press, 1982), 136–56 (136). As Stanislavskii writes, for Craig, 'Hamlet was the best of men, who passed like Christ across the earth and became the victim of a cleansing sacrifice' (quoted in Eleanor Rowe, *Hamlet: A Window on Russia* (New York: New York University Press, 1976), 120). See also J. Douglas Clayton, 'The Hamlets of Turgenev and Pasternak: On the Role of Poetic Myth in Literature', *Germano-Slavica* 6 (1978), 455–61 (460); France, 'Boris Pasternak's Interpretation of Hamlet', 202; and Nils Åke Nilsson, 'Life as Ecstasy and Sacrifice: Two Poems by Boris Pasternak', *Scando-Slavica* 5 (1959), 180–98 (193).

38 Boris Pasternak, *Sobranie sochinenii*, vol. V, 75.
39 See Semenenko, 'Gamletovskii kontekst'.
40 There is another interesting connection in Pasternak's oeuvre. Zhivago, Hamlet, and the author himself are united by the connotation of *intelligentnost'*: Pasternak had the reputation of a 'poet-*intelligent*' (see, for example, Valerii Briusov, 'Vchera, segodnia i zavtra russkoi poezii' in *Sobranie sochinenii v semi tomakh*, vol. VI (Moscow: Khudozhestvennaia literatura, 1973), 493–532 (518)); as a typical Russian *intelligent*, Zhivago was identified with the author, as was Hamlet; finally, Pasternak's Hamlet, especially after Smoktunovskii's performance in Kozintsev's film, was perceived as a Russian *intelligent* as well.

first reviews,[41] praised Pasternak's creativity and the liveliness of the new translation, though reproaching the translator for a number of 'unclear' and 'non-transparent' places in his translation. In his 1944 essay Morozov also wrote that thanks to Pasternak *Hamlet* had become 'the property of Russian literature' to a much greater extent than it was before.[42] Many critics and translators, as could be expected, compared the translations by Lozinskii and Pasternak as two opposing models of translation: the 'poetic' Pasternak translation vs. the 'academic'/'bookish' Lozinskii version.[43] Indeed, these texts seem to be the perfect antagonists: Lozinskii attempted to recreate the 300-year-old English classic, Pasternak tried to create a modern Russian play; Lozinskii oriented himself toward the literary tradition, Pasternak – toward the theatrical; Lozinskii advocated academic accuracy, Pasternak – 'intentional liberty'. Finally, Lozinskii continued the tradition of the philological (or educational) translation of *Hamlet*; Pasternak made Hamlet his alter ego, and the play – a part of a large neo-mythological theme in his own oeuvre. In general, most of the critics of the Soviet period were unanimous in the opinion that Pasternak's personality is apparent in the text of the translation: the poet was blamed – or, alternatively, praised – so many times for the 'pasternakishness' of his *Hamlet* that it has finally become a cliché.

It is noteworthy that in the post-Soviet period Pasternak's translation has received even more negative criticism, probably because official control – which had admitted Pasternak, although half-willingly, to the Soviet Shakespeare canon – ceased to exist. The monograph by Nadezhda Nikiforovskaia can be seen as the quintessence of anti-Pasternak criticism.[44] In her analysis of his 'terrible' and 'vulgar' translation of *Hamlet*, Nikiforovskaia condemns Pasternak for numerous cases of 'distortion of the meaning', 'illiteracy', 'absurdities', 'vulgarisms', 'bureaucratese', etc.

---

41 Mikhail Morozov, *Izbrannoe* (Moscow: Iskusstvo, 1979), 145–6.
42 Ibid., 383.
43 See, for example, Ivan Chekalov, 'Perevody *Gamleta* M. Lozinskim, A. Radlovoi i B. Pasternakom v otsenke sovetskoi kritiki 30-kh godov', *Shekspirovskie chteniia 1990* (Moscow: Nauka, 1991), 177–200.
44 Nadezhda Nikiforovskaia, *Shekspir Borisa Pasternaka* (St Petersburg: BAN, 1999).

The critique is accompanied by the opinions of some renowned Soviet Shakespeare scholars, critics, actors and directors. Pasternak's version is compared to some imagined 'correct' version – which is a heavy interlinear translation – and thus denounced as 'wrong'.

The new period of *Hamlet* translation is at its apogee right now, and Pasternak, as the embodiment of the canon of the twentieth century, is chosen by a majority of new translators as the main antagonist with whom they contend.[45] None the less, even to date, the hegemony of Pasternak in the theatre and in print has not been contested, which proves the validity of the Pasternak legacy and reveals one of the essential mechanisms of canonization: competition with the existing canonized text(s).

The Asymmetrical Dialogue

The history of *Hamlet* translation in Russia seems to contradict the widespread belief that 'good' translations should be 'transparent' and 'accurate' and good translators – totally 'invisible'. In reality, as we have seen, the very act of translation presupposes the asymmetric relationship that actualizes the creative function of the text, making such terms as 'adequacy', 'equivalence' and 'accuracy' highly relative and context-specific. It is evident that both *Hamlets* by Polevoi and Pasternak proved to be vital by virtue of the translators' contribution to the text and to the target culture. The interpretive power of the translator in a given cultural context appears to be one of the most crucial factors in the process of adaptation of a foreign text to the national culture.

The translator of an artistic text turns out to be not an impartial transmitter of some static 'sense' from one language to another but, on the contrary, a co-creator who facilitates the text's perpetuation through time in a different culture. Similarly, in the analysis of literary translations it

---

45 Semenenko, *Hamlet the Sign*, 102–21.

is important to focus not on the ideal (and conventionally constructed) correlation between the source and target text but on translators' strategies, cultural contexts and the actual reception process in diachronic and synchronic perspective.[46]

On a general note, practically any example of successful literary translation provides evidence of the fact that translation is a process of intercultural dialogue, and not of an imaginary 'replacement' or almost identical 'recreation' of the original. In order for translation to be identical with its original, the cultures must be identical as well, which is of course impossible and contradicts the very purpose of communication, be it between individuals or cultures. As Lotman notes, 'A text that is absolutely comprehensible is at the same time a text that is absolutely useless',[47] which means that only difference between individuals, languages, cultures – in other words, between different semiotic spheres – can create meaning. Therefore, a creative translation, which provides the dialogue between cultures and brings about changes in the domestic system, has much greater potential to prevail in the collective memory than its 'accuracy-oriented' counterpart.

---

46   Aleksei Semenenko, '"No Text is an Island": Translating *Hamlet* in Twenty-First Century Russia' in Brian James Baer, ed., *Contexts, Subtexts, and Pretexts: Literary Translation in Eastern Europe and Russia* (Amsterdam: John Benjamins, 2011), 249–63.
47   Lotman, *Universe of the Mind*, 80.

PHILIP ROSS BULLOCK

Not One of Us?
The Paradoxes of Translating Oscar Wilde in the Soviet Union[1]

In 1928, as Joseph Stalin launched his policies of collectivization, industrialization and cultural revolution, Soviet readers were offered a brief and unexpected opportunity to read a work by an author who had enjoyed enormous popularity before the October Revolution of 1917, but whose reputation had waned during the course of the 1920s. A. I. Deich's preface to his retranslation of *The Ballad of Reading Gaol* (his first attempt had been published in 1910) is prescient in its examination of the discourses that would shape Oscar Wilde's potentially awkward reputation in Soviet Russia. Here, the central paradox rested on the assumption that Wilde, as both an adversary and victim of the hypocrisy of late-Victorian England, could be read through the prism of the Soviet Union's own antibourgeois ideology:

> The English bourgeoisie, primly hypocritical, sanctimoniously servile or coldly cruel, was simply waiting for the opportunity to be rid of a member of society who stood head and shoulders above it, whose brilliant paradoxes often sounded like a slap in the face of its age-old traditions.[2]

---

[1] I should like to thank Stefano Evangelista and Polly Jones for their invaluable advice and criticism during the composition of this essay, and Julian Graffy for help in obtaining a number of sources.

[2] A. Deich, 'S.33', in Oskar Uail'd, *Ballada ridingskoi tiur'my*; trans. A. Deich (Moscow: Ogonek, 1928), 3–8 (5). For the earlier translation see *Ballada ridingskoi tiur'my*, trans. A. Deich (Kiev: Gong, 1910). Deich's account of his translations can be found in his *Den' nyneshnii i den' minuvshii: Literaturnye vpechatleniia i vstrechi* (Moscow: Sovetskii pistatel', 1969), 242–318.

Yet for all that Wilde could be interpreted as an exemplary victim of a reviled ideology, the fact remained that his works themselves were hardly fit material for Soviet readers: 'Of course, he is in no way "our" writer. The proletariat has nothing to learn from his philosophy, which was so significant for the remarkable short-sightedness of bourgeois society'.[3] After the death of Stalin in 1953, however, Wilde was to be comprehensively 'rehabilitated' and even canonized as a classic of world literature in Russian translation. How, then, did Wilde come to be 'one of us' for Soviet readers and critics? How did this arch-aesthete survive in a culture dominated by the moral and ethical codes of Socialist Realism? How was his abiding individualism reconciled with the collective ideal? And how, in turn, did the incorporation of Wilde into the approved and accepted canon of foreign literature facilitate a partial rediscovery of Russia's own occluded heritage of artistic Modernism?

Although much of the Soviet reception of Wilde was based on promoting an image of him as a victim of British – and more specifically *English* – bourgeois hypocrisy (from the outset, the question of Wilde's Irishness seems to have figured little in his Russian reception),[4] Wilde had been thoroughly domesticized in Russia before the October Revolution (playing a role not unlike that of Byron in Russian Romanticism). Lev Tolstoi, for instance, had singled him out for particular censure in *What is Art?* (1898), where he figures predominantly as a disciple of Nietzsche:

> the wrong attitude towards art has long been manifest in our society, but lately, with its prophet Nietzsche and his followers, as well as the decadents and English

---

3 Deich, 'S.33', 3–4.
4 As Stefano Evangelista notes, 'it was only very rarely that early European commentators noted Wilde's Irish identity as a possible reason for his critique of English institutions. [...] We have had to wait until the late twentieth century and the advent of postcolonial criticism for [the] image of a frankly Irish Wilde to reach the wider European public'. See 'Introduction: Oscar Wilde: European by Sympathy', in Stefano Evangelista, ed., *The European Reception of Oscar Wilde*, The Reception of British and Irish Authors in Europe, vol. 18 (London: Continuum, 2010), 1–19 (11). More generally, see Jerusha MacCormack, ed., *Wilde the Irishman* (New Haven: Yale University Press, 1998).

aesthetes identical with them, it has been expressing itself with particular insolence. Decadents and aesthetes like Oscar Wilde choose as the theme of their works the denial of morality and the praise of depravity.[5]

Rather like Max Nordau, who had discussed Wilde – and his relationship to Nietzsche – in his infamous tract, *Entartung* (which was, incidentally, widely known in Russia at the time),[6] Tolstoi saw Wilde as a symbol of all that was to be deplored about modernity. Others, however, willingly embraced the decadent Wilde, both on his own terms and as a way of distancing themselves from the values of the immediate literary past.[7] For some, Wilde offered a powerful example of how life and art could be fused into a single act of aesthetic self-fashioning (or, to give it its Russian name, *zhiznetvorchestvo*).[8] Alongside interest in Wilde's aestheticized persona ran another strain in his early Russian reception, that of voluntary suffering and poetic martyrdom. Whether in romantic notions of the poet as prophet (expressed most famously by Aleksandr Pushkin),[9] or in

---

5 Leo Tolstoy, *What is Art?*, trans. Richard Pevear and Larissa Volokhonsky (London: Penguin, 1995) 143–4.
6 *Entartung* was translated into Russian as *Vyrozhdenie*, ed. R. I. Semintkovskii (St Petersburg: Pavlenkov, 1894).
7 On Tolstoi's formative role in shaping – positively and negatively – aspects of early Russian Modernism, see Olga Matich, *Erotic Utopia: The Decadent Imagination in Russia's Fin de Siècle* (Madison: University of Wisconsin Press, 2005).
8 Betsy F. Moeller-Sally, 'Oscar Wilde and the Culture of Russian Modernism', *Slavic and East European Journal* 34/4 (1990), 459–72. More generally, see Irina Paperno and Joan Delaney Grossman, eds, *Creating Life: The Aesthetic Utopia of Russian Modernism* (Stanford: Stanford University Press, 1994), where *zhiznetvorchestvo* is explicitly described as the set of 'attitudes and forms of behavior of which Oscar Wilde became a symbol' (2).
9 See, for instance, Pamela Davidson, 'The Moral Dimension of the Prophetic Ideal: Pushkin and his Readers', *Slavic Review* 61/3 (2002), 490–518; 'The Validation of the Writer's Prophetic Status in the Russian Literary Tradition: From Pushkin and Iazykov through Gogol to Dostoevsky', *Russian Review* 62/4 (2003), 508–36; and 'Between Derzhavin and Pushkin: The Development of the Image of the Poet as a Prophet in the Verse of Zhukovsky, Glinka, and Kiukhelbeker', in Catherine O'Neill, Nicole Boudreau and Sarah Krive, eds, *Poetics. Self. Place. Essays in Honor of Anna Lisa Crone* (Bloomington: Slavica, 2007), 182–214.

symbolist responses to the ideas of Dostoevskii and Nietzsche, Russian literary culture had been profoundly shaped by ideas of artistic suffering and self-sacrifice, the Christological overtones of which mapped closely onto the myth of Wilde himself (not for nothing did *The Ballad of Reading Gaol* and *De profundis* become his most widely translated and discussed works).[10] Although Mikhail Kuzmin – the closest candidate for the soubriquet of the 'Russian Wilde' – explicitly rejected this interpretation of both the literary vocation and the fate of the modern homosexual,[11] Wilde's exemplary agony was to remain a prominent theme in his Russian reception (even if the judicial and moral reasons for it were rarely alluded to during the Soviet period).

If the ideas of Russia's early modernists reveal organic connections with the legacy of European Romanticism, then the avant-garde proper seized on Wilde as a symbol of Russia's own social, political and artistic transformation around the time of the October Revolution. The work that most clearly reveals this change of tone is *Salome*. Although the play itself had been available in a number of translations since 1904,[12] attempts to stage it foundered on the opposition of the ecclesiastical censorship. In 1908, a planned production at Vera Komissarzhevskaia's theatre in St Petersburg was closed before its official opening on 29 October (although a dress-rehearsal the day before did take place).[13] Aleksandr Tairov's production at Moscow's Chamber Theatre in October 1917 (complete with cubist designs by Aleksandra Ekster) constituted, therefore, a twin rejec-

10   Evgenii Bershtein, '"Next to Christ": Oscar Wilde in Russian Modernism', in Evangelista, ed., *The European Reception of Oscar Wilde*, 285–300 (esp. 289–96). See also Evgenii Bershtein, 'The Russian Myth of Oscar Wilde', in Laura Engelstein and Stephanie Sandler, eds, *Self and Story in Russian History* (Ithaca and London: Cornell University Press, 2000), 168–88.
11   Bershtein, '"Next to Christ": Oscar Wilde in Russian Modernism', 296–300.
12   *Salomeia*, trans. V. and L. Andruson, ed. K. D. Bal'mont (Moscow: Grif, 1904). A number of other translations quickly followed, including one by Konstantin Bal'mont himself, with illustrations by Aubrey Beardsley. See *Salomeia*, trans. K. D. Bal'mont and E. A. Andreeva (St Petersburg: Panteon, 1908).
13   William Tydeman and Steven Price, *Wilde: Salome* (Cambridge: Cambridge University Press, 1996), 58–66.

tion of the strictures of the past; if *Salome* had challenged the prudery and conservatism of the British establishment (it was officially banned by the Lord Chamberlain until 1931), it had equally been the victim of tsarist obfuscation and obscurantism.[14] The flourishing of artistic innovation in the immediate post-revolutionary era recast Wilde as a leading member of European Modernism (a process begun with Max Reinhardt's productions of *Salome* in Berlin in 1902 and 1903, and consolidated in Richard Strauss's operatic version of the play in 1905), and even incorporated him into the avant-garde itself (a process that can also be traced back to Vsevolod Meierkhol'd's 1915 film version of *The Picture of Dorian Gray*). To English readers and audiences, used to Wilde as the author of late-Victorian society comedies and purveyor of incessant witticisms, paradoxes and *bons mots*, such a transformation would have seemed remarkable, although it was wholly in keeping with Wilde's European reception more generally.[15]

Studies of Wilde in the context of turn-of-the-century Russian Modernism and the early-Soviet avant-garde have generally positioned him as a fully fledged representative of European high culture. But, as Rachel Polonsky suggests, Wilde's 'aesthetic aristocratism' could also be read as a form of 'aesthetic democratism', and his reception in early twentieth-century Russia was as much the product of a growing popular taste for modern European writing as of the recondite practices of the symbolists.[16] Although scholars have tended to favour translations made by Russian modernist writers such as Valerii Briusov or Kostantin Bal'mont which were published in the small-circulation journals of the Silver Age (*Vesy* was a particularly important venue in this respect, as was the publishing house *Skorpion*),[17] a thorough bibliographical study of Wilde's first Russian translations also

14 Ibid., 66–77.
15 See Evangelista, ed., *The European Reception of Oscar Wilde*.
16 Rachel Polonsky, *English Literature and the Russian Aesthetic Renaissance* (Cambridge: Cambridge University Press, 1998), especially Chapter 7, 'How Important it is to be Serious: Oscar Wilde's Popularity', 152–69 (quotation on 155).
17 See, for instance: *Ballada Redingskoi tiur'my*, trans. K. D. Bal'mont (Moscow: Skorpion, 1904); 'De profundis', trans. E. Andreeva, *Vesy*, 3 (1905), 1–42; *Florentinskaia tragediia*, trans. M. Likiardopulo and A. Kursinskii, *Vesy*, 1 (1907), 17–38.

reveals that he was widely disseminated in popular journals for a broader audience.[18] Amongst the very first publications of Wilde in Russia are translations of his stories 'The Happy Prince' and 'The Devoted Friend' in *Detskii otdykh* in 1898,[19] and 'The Birthday of the Infanta' followed in *Iunyi chitatel'* in 1903.[20] A number of works – including 'The Decay of Lying', 'The Artist as Critic', 'The Nightingale and the Rose' and *The Picture of Dorian Gray* – appeared in *Novyi zhurnal literatury, iskusstva i nauki* between 1899 and 1905.[21] And any comparison of the two multi-volume editions of Wilde's works available in Russia before 1917 needs to take into account not just the quality of the translations, but also the intended readership of these volumes.[22] The first of these, despite the poor quality of its translations, was published in print-runs of between three and five thousand volumes each,[23] and the second – containing translations by Russia's leading modernists – 'was published by the popular journal *Niva*, a byword for mass readership'.[24] From the very outset, Wilde was positioned within Russian culture as a popular writer, a factor that would be pre-eminent in his Soviet reception.

Such pre-revolutionary attitudes to Wilde – whether as victim of the English social system, as dandy whose greatest work of art was his

---

18   Iu. A. Roznatovskaia, *Oskar Uail'd v Rossii: bibliograficheskii ukazatel'*, *1892–2000* (Moscow: Rudomino, 2000).
19   'Schastlivyi prints', *Detskii otdykh*, 9 (1898): 89–100, and 'Predannyi drug', *Detskii otdykh*, 11 (1898), 75–88.
20   'Den' rozhdeniia infanty', trans. O. F. Sherstobitova, *Iunyi chitatel'*, 15 September 1903, 89–108.
21   'Upadok lzhi', trans. O. M. Solov'eva, *Novyi zhurnal literatury, iskusstva i nauki* 4 (1899), 40–7, 5 (1899), 155–66; 'Iskusstvo kritiki', trans. O. M. Solov'eva, *Novyi zhurnal literatury, iskusstva i nauki* 5 (1901), 439–57, and 6 (1901), 554–74; 'Solovei i roza', trans. Z. T., *Novyi zhurnal literatury, iskusstva i nauki* 3 (1903), 218–21; *Portret Doriana Greia*, trans. A. T., *Novyi zhurnal literatury, iskusstva i nauki* 7 (1905), 1–16, 8 (1905), 17–32, 9 (1905), 33–48 and 10 (1905), 49–80.
22   *Polnoe sobranie sochinenii*, 8 vols (Moscow: Sablin, 1905–9); *Polnoe sobranie sochinenii*, ed. Kornei Chukovskii, 4 vols (St Petersburg: A. F. Marks, 1912).
23   Polonsky, *English Literature and the Russian Aesthetic Renaissance*, 161.
24   Ibid., 164.

own life, as archetypal figure of the poet as martyr, as innovative modernist and precursor of the avant-garde, or as astute and successful populist and entertainer – continued to inform Soviet perceptions of him as an artist, and shaped both what was translated and how it was presented to the Soviet reader. A significant contribution to the Soviet interpretation of Wilde's place within British aestheticism came in the form of Dmitrii Mirskii's book on the British intelligentsia (published first in Moscow in 1934, and in English translation the following year). Here, Mirskii sought to explain why Britain lacked a separate class of independently minded intellectuals committed to social and political reform. The nearest that Britain came to developing its own intelligentsia on the Russian model were those artists and critics who set themselves against the philistinism of nineteenth-century bourgeois society:

> the only group which did at that time exhibit some signs of intellectual independence was that of works in literature and the arts. It is possible, even at this early period, to distinguish the intelligentsia type among writers, journalists and artists. Thus we can have no doubt about there being intelligentsia traits in Carlyle, in Ruskin, or in the pre-Raphaelite movement. But nevertheless there was no independent bohemian class in Britain till the 'eighties and 'nineties, and those individual examples of the type of people who achieve 'independent thinking' made no difference to the general picture of the complete absorption of the class of educated people in the one class of the bourgeoisie.[25]

Mirskii's interpretation of aestheticism as a tradition arguably cognate with the Russian intelligentsia was based on the idea that a free-thinking, separatist ideology could potentially have served as a source of anti-bourgeois, anti-imperial resistance within British society. Moreover, because of Wilde's indebtedness to figures such as William Morris and John Ruskin, his aestheticism could even be reinterpreted as a form of socialism (although Soviet discussion of his essay, 'The Soul of Man under Socialism', was always rather problematic and sketchy, precisely because its appeal to socialism as the guarantor of a heightened sense of individualism failed to accord with

---

25   Dmitri Mirsky, *The Intelligentsia of Great Britain*; trans. Alec Brown (London: Victor Gollancz, 1935), 11–12.

Marxist-Leninist principles).[26] Mirskii linked Wilde's own downfall with the general failure of aestheticism to transform itself into a fully fledged British version of the Russian intelligentsia. In a gesture redolent of Russia's own Silver Age, he elevated Wilde from a self-fashioning decadent to the status of a social – and even political – martyr:

> British decadentism as a living thing was cut rudely short by the trial and fall of Oscar Wilde. Wilde's crash and imprisonment carried him from cheap posing and snobbism to real human tragedy in his sole surviving work – *The Ballad of Reading Gaol*.[27]

By depicting Wilde as a tragic hero, Mirskii was appealing to a pre-existing pattern of reception, and in doing so, helped to establish a way of incorporating him into Soviet ideology (that Vladimir Maiakovskii had subtitled the first section of his long poem, *Pro eto*, 'The Ballad of Reading Gaol' provides a further organic connection between the Silver Age and the Soviet period).[28] Wilde and his writings were not so much anti-Soviet as insufficiently politically engaged; this insufficiency could be explained, historicized and contextualized, and thereby rendered potentially acceptable.

A further – and arguably *contradictory* – strategy in the domesticization and accommodation of Wilde within the Soviet context was the evisceration of all meaning from his language. Anyone who has ever taught English in Russian educational establishments, or talked with educated Russians about their reading of English-language authors, will have been struck by a very different canon from the one usually read and taught in the West.

---

26 The essay does not appear to have been included in Soviet-era publications until 1990. See Oskar Uail'd, 'Dusha cheloveka pri sotsialisme', trans. O. M. Kirichenko, *Chelovek: Obraz i sushchnost' (gumanitarnye aspekty)* 1 (1990), 227–67.
27 Mirsky, *The Intelligentsia of Great Britain*, 96.
28 The fusion of life and art represented by Wilde finds further reference in a letter from Maiakovskii to his lover, Lili Brik, on 19 January 1923. The two were then undergoing a period of separation, and Maiakovskii referred to his temporary confinement at home as 'Reading Gaol' and signed himself 'Oscar Wilde' (as well as 'The Prisoner of Chillon', after Byron's poem of the same name). See *Love is at the Heart of Everything: Correspondence between Vladimir Mayakovsky and Lili Brik, 1915–1930*, ed. Bengt Jangfeldt, trans. Julian Graffy (Edinburgh: Polygon, 1986), 114–15.

Not One of Us?

Certain writers – John Galsworthy, Somerset Maugham, O'Henry, Jack London, Theodor Dreiser – were promoted throughout Soviet schools, colleges and universities as models of English style (alongside discussion of the social aspects of their works). Wilde played a particularly prominent role in this process, and as early as 1940 (even before the wartime alliance that so helped to promote Anglo-Soviet cultural relations),[29] a volume of adapted versions of four of his tales was published as the first in a series of books entitled (in English) 'Learn to Read'. Designed to help learners to read works of English literature in the original, it contained no biographical or critical details about the author or his works.[30] If Mirskii's account had advanced an interpretation of Wilde and his writings in terms that were potentially acceptable to Soviet ideas on the historical role of the educated classes, then this aid to language learning repudiated content and context altogether in favour of a deliberately superficial emphasis on style above all else. Wilde's surface brilliance and ostensible repudiation of content (at least in his pre-trial works) were, ironically enough, the partial pledges of his subsequent survival. Publications such as this one were to become a persistent feature of Soviet pedagogical practice, and recall Borges's claim that 'in verse or in prose Wilde's syntax is always very simple. Of the many

---

29 In 1942, on the pages of *Internatsional'naia literatura*, one critic had even suggested that 'the most talented representatives of English aestheticism and symbolism, such as Oscar Wilde, for example, turned to Russian literature in the search for a way out of the dead end of decadence'. See A. A. Elistratova, 'Russkie klassiki v Anglii', *Internatsional'naia literatura*, 11 (1942), 119–25 (120), cited in Roznatovskaia, *Oskar Uail'd v Rossii*, 171. Wilde's reception in Russia was in part facilitated by his acquaintance with figures of the nineteenth-century radical emigration such as Kropotkin (described in *De profundis* as having 'a soul of that beautiful white Christ which seems coming out of Russia') and Stepniak-Kravchinskii. Wilde's 'Russian' play, *Vera, or the Nihilists* (inspired by Vera Zasulich's attempt on the life of the governor of St Petersburg in 1878) was consistently omitted from Russian and Soviet publications, and discussion of it was generally cursory.
30 G. V. Khanna, D. A. Eshe and I. R. Gal'perin, eds, *Chetyre skazki po Oskaru Uail'du* (Moscow: Mezhdunarodnaia kniga, 1940).

British writers, none is so accessible to foreigners.'[31] As one of the writers most frequently available in both the original and in translation, Wilde constitutes an interesting case study by combining contrasting modes of reading and reception.

If Wilde's slender reputation in the 1940s had been contingent on political events and was ultimately marginal in the context of the overall literary scene, then a more complete rehabilitation took place from 1956 onwards. Evidence that an author was to be accorded greater official favour usually came in the form of a positive article in a leading journal or newspaper (similarly, a critical notice would indicate that translations and scholarly works were unlikely to be forthcoming). In the autumn of 1956, a brief account of Wilde's life and works appeared in *Sovetskaia kul'tura*, the official organ of the Soviet Ministry of Culture, written by Aleksandr Deich (the translator of *The Ballad of Reading Goal* discussed at the beginning of this chapter). Deich's article sketches in outline all of the features that would characterize Soviet writing about Wilde for the next two decades or so. Readily admitting that Wilde is 'an aesthete, a decadent, imbued with reactionary and romantic opinions about life and art', he interprets Wilde's aestheticism and decadence as a protest against late nineteenth-century British society, and presents his trial as the retribution of that society without mentioning the homosexual scandal that provoked it. Finally, Deich redeems Wilde's literary legacy itself: 'Rejecting all that is reactionary, anti-realistic in Wilde's aesthetic views, we can take from his legacy those works of great talent which continue to summon up in us corresponding feelings of humanity and nobility and stir us with the inextinguishable light of true poetry.'[32]

According to a longstanding Russian misapprehension going as far back as the late nineteenth century, Wilde was widely believed to have been born in 1856 (rather than the correct year of 1854), and Deich's article

---

31 Jorge Luis Borges, 'About Oscar Wilde', in *Other Inquisitions, 1937–1952* (Austin: University of Texas Press, 1964), 79–81 (79).
32 Aleksandr Deich, 'Oskar Uail'd: K 100-letiiu so dnia rozhdeniia', *Sovetskaia kul'tura*, 13 October 1956, 4.

perpetuates the error in spectacularly public fashion. Even the Moscow Arts Theatre was not immune; on 2 November, it dedicated the 515th performance of its long-running production of *An Ideal Husband* to its author on the occasion of the hundredth anniversary of his birth.[33] Wilde himself would surely have appreciated the irony of this situation, as he had deliberately lied about his age during his trials in order to make himself seem two years younger than he in fact was. But 1956 was also the year of Khrushchev's 'secret speech' at the Twentieth Party Congress that inaugurated a period of increasing liberalization in all spheres of Soviet life.[34] Although not as striking as, say, the encounter with Picasso,[35] the music of the Second Viennese School or contemporary European modernist composers,[36] or even literary figures such as the previously scorned Proust and Kafka, or the more modern Camus and Sartre, or Faulkner, Hemingway and Salinger,[37] the rehabilitation of Wilde in fact reveals much about limits and possibilities of cosmopolitan literary taste in the Soviet Union. In particular, where many instances of Soviet interest in modern European art from the late nineteenth century onwards were restricted to the sphere of the cultural intelligentsia (whether through official publications with limited print runs or through unofficial networks of underground publication and

33 'Stoletie so dnia rozhdeniia Oskara Uail'da', *Sovetskaia kul'tura*, 3 November 1956, 4.
34 Momentous as 1956 was, it had in fact been presaged by events in the preceding three years or so. In terms of literary cosmopolitanism, a decisive moment was the launch of *Inostrannaia literatura* as the successor journal to *Internatsional'naia literatura*, which had run from 1933 to 1942, but was closed in early 1943, around the time of the dissolution of the Comintern. On *Internatsional'naia literatura*, see Nailia Safiullina, 'Window to the West: From the Collection of Readers' Letters to the Journal *Internatsional'naia literatura*', *Slavonica*, 15/2 (2009), 128–61.
35 Eleonory Gilburd, 'Picasso in Thaw Culture', *Cahiers du monde russe* 47/1–2 (2006), 65–108.
36 Peter J. Schmelz, *Such Freedom, if only Musical: Unofficial Soviet Music During the Thaw* (Oxford: Oxford University Press, 2009).
37 Raisa Orlova and Lev Kopelev, *My zhili v Moskve* (Ann Arbor: Ardis, 1988), 117–41; Jekaterina Young, 'Dovlatov's Reception of Salinger', *Forum for Modern Language Studies* 36/4 (2000), 412–25; and Carl Proffer, ed. and trans., *Soviet Criticism of American Literature in the Sixties: An Anthology* (Ann Arbor: Ardis, 1972).

dissemination), Wilde was published in surprisingly extensive quantities and made available to the broad spectrum of Soviet Russian readers in ways that made him — or at least a version of him — a figure of official approval.

In keeping with the previous Stalinist approach to incorporating Wilde into the Soviet canon, 1956 saw the publication of several of his tales in the original English.[38] Issued by the Ministry of Enlightenment, this volume is indicative of a decision taken at the very highest level to incorporate Wilde within the school curriculum, and demonstrates the canonicity his stories in particular were to enjoy from now on. The introduction to this edition is especially revealing for the way in which it sets the tone for Wilde's reception during much of the rest of the Soviet period:

> His tales are distinguished by their simplicity of form, their colourfulness and precision of language, and their wit. Although they are rather static in terms of content (they contain little action), they are nevertheless easy and interesting to read thanks to the writer's great skill. Moreover, elements of fantasy are so closely bound up with reality that they can often be read as a satire on the bourgeois society of Wilde's own time.[39]

The tendency to read elements of fantasy as coded social commentary is consolidated in the didactic exercises that follow each story; that such works would have been read and discussed in class merely reinforces the sense that young readers were being encouraged to draw an edifying moral conclusion. Yet, in the reference to Wilde as 'a brilliant stylist' who places 'form above content',[40] there is also a frank acknowledgement that one of his greatest achievements is in the realm of style above all else. Writing about his plays, the author of the introduction observes that 'these comedies, stripped of action and characterization, are written in a wonderful language, full of

---

38   Oskar Uail'd, *The Happy Prince and Other Tales/Schastlivyi prints i drugie rasskazy dlia chteniia na angliiskom iazyke v 8-m klasse srednei shkoly* (Moscow: Gosudarstvennoe uchebno-pedagogicheskoe izdatel'stvo ministerstva prosveshcheniia RSFSR, 1956).
39   S. K. Folomkina, 'Oskar Uail'd (1856–1900)', in Uail'd, *The Happy Prince and Other Tales/Schastlivyi prints i drugie rasskazy*, 4–6 (5).
40   Ibid., 6.

wit, effective aphorisms and paradoxes'.[41] Ironically, then, the superficiality of Wilde's style – the very feature that might have prevented, or at least hindered, his reception and translation in Soviet Russia – meant that his works came to be seen as exemplary models for the teaching and learning of English as a foreign language, something that remained a dominant feature of Wilde reception throughout the Soviet era and continues even to this day.

The ground was now set for a more complete reconsideration of Wilde's work in the Soviet Union. Accordingly, 1960 witnessed two major publications that long enjoyed critical dominance in Russian Wildeana: a two-volume selected works;[42] and a volume of his plays.[43] Most of the necessary critical work in shaping Wilde's reputation was done by Aleksandr Anikst. A leading figure in the Soviet-era study of foreign literature in the post-Stalin period, he edited and published on a wide variety of English-language authors, including Defoe, Dickens, Dreiser, O'Henry, Shakespeare, Shaw and Thackeray, as well as editing books on the theory and history of drama, and a ten-volume edition of Goethe. In addition to the two prefaces he provided for the two Wilde publications of 1960,[44] Anikst had previously included a section on Wilde in his important survey of English literature, which appeared in the same year as Khrushchev's secret speech.[45] In his introduction to the main two-volume edition of Wilde's selected works, Anikst constantly stresses that Wilde is an author formed by the crisis of bourgeois, capitalist society. He then goes on to summarize Wilde's views on art (largely because they are so frankly stated that they cannot be effectively ignored or refuted), but then argues that Wilde's works themselves frequently contradict these views (thus effecting a useful

---

41 Ibid., 5.
42 Oskar Uail'd, *Izbrannye proizvedeniia*, 2 vols (Moscow: Khudozhestvennaia literatura, 1960).
43 Oskar Uail'd, *P'esy* (Moscow: Iskusstvo, 1960).
44 Aleksandr Anikst, 'Oskar Uail'd (1856–1900)', in Uail'd, *Izbrannye proizvedeniia*, I, 5–26; 'Oskar Uai'ld i ego dramaturgiia', in Uail'd, *P'esy*, 5–19.
45 A. Anikst, *Istoriia angliiskoi literatury* (Moscow: Gosudarstvennoe uchebno-pedagogicheskoe izdatel'stvo ministerstva prosveshcheniia RSFSR, 1956), 377–83.

separation between the artist and his works that would also serve to occlude any discussion of Wilde's sexuality). Basing his argument on the stories in particular (as would many Soviet critics), Anikst offers his own version of a pseudo-Wildean paradox: 'Wilde the theoretician declared the freedom of art from morality, but in his stories, Wilde the artist foists upon us a certain morality'.[46]

Anikst also uses Wilde's invocation of beauty to reclaim him as a romantic idealist, whose tragedy lay principally in his inability to realize the logic of his own conclusions; like many commentators, Anikst sees the essay 'The Soul of Man under Socialism' as an indication both of Wilde's idealism and of his concomitant failure to seek beauty in social action. Similarly, Anikst uses Wilde's imprisonment to argue that in his final works (*De profundis, The Ballad of Reading Gaol*), Wilde was at last moving to an art based on sympathy and suffering; like the hero of a socialist realist novel, the post-prison Wilde embraces suffering and even martyrdom in the service of a higher goal. Furthermore, Wilde's early death allows a good deal of room for speculation about the directions in which his work may have developed. Anikst's introduction to the 1960 volume of Wilde's plays covers much of the same ground. In particular, the plays are seen, for all their triviality, as conveyors of social debate:

> The attentive reader will notice that during their relaxed conversations, the characters in Wilde's plays touch on a very wide array of questions. Social life and politics, morals and moral principles, question of the family and of marriage – they discuss all of this, sometimes with a playfulness that seems excessive. But it is precisely this lightness with which they approach everything that expresses Wilde's particular position in respect of bourgeois society.[47]

The 'attentive reader' of this passage will also notice that Anikst refers to 'readers' of Wilde's plays, and not 'viewers', since Wilde's reappearance on the Soviet stage was as delicate a task as the republication of his works. The Moscow Arts Theatre had first staged its popular long-running production

---

46 Anikst, 'Oskar Uail'd (1856–1900)', 13.
47 Anikst, 'Oskar Uail'd i ego dramaturgiia', 18.

of *An Ideal Husband* in 1946, but other plays came only later. An enduring production of *Lady Windermere's Fan* at Moscow's Malyi Theatre opened in 1959, and a tour by the Old Vic brought *The Importance of Being Earnest* to Soviet audiences in 1961 (offering Soviet audiences the chance to brush up on their comprehension of spoken English).

Ultimately, though, the most significant figure in the successful incorporation of Wilde within the Soviet canon of permitted foreign writers was Kornei Chukovskii, editor of the 1960 two-volume edition of Wilde's selected works. Not only had he edited the most complete pre-revolutionary edition of Wilde's works,[48] he had also edited three volumes of his stories in Gor'kii's *World Literature* series in the early 1920s, evidence that, initially at least, Wilde was deemed suitable for the new Soviet mass reader.[49] His translation of *The Happy Prince*, originally included in the 1912 edition of Wilde's works, was extensively reprinted from the 1960s onwards, and his various articles constituted an accessible – and officially approved – introduction for new readers unsure as to how best to interpret Wilde for themselves. As a leading example of Soviet Russia's non-party intelligentsia, loved by all as the nation's finest children's writer, Chukovskii stood for a broader understanding of what was acceptable within the Soviet canon after the all-or-nothing, with-us-or-against-us culture of the Stalin era; Wilde, like Chukovskii, could be accommodated and assimilated as a kind of 'fellow-traveller' within the more generous literary culture of the 'thaw'. Furthermore, Chukovskii enjoyed a direct link to Wilde himself, having met Wilde's friend and executor, Robert Ross, whilst in London in 1916; according to Chukovskii, Ross presented him with a page from the original

---

48 Significantly, Deich was involved in this project as translator of 'The Truth of Masks' and 'London Models' (he had also published a translation of 'The Sphinx' in Kiev in 1912). Deich's memoir of his collaboration with Chukovskii ('Pervoe znakomstvo') can be found in his *Den' nyneshnii i den' minuvshii*, 257–60, reproduced in K. I. Lozovskaia, Z. S. Papernyi and E. Ts. Chukovskaia, eds, *Vospominaniia o Kornee Chukovskom* (Moscow: Sovetskii pisatel', 1977), 53–5.
49 Oskar Uail'd, *Kentervill'skoe prividenie i drugie skazki* (Petrograd: Vsemirnaia literatura, 1919); *Schastlivyi prints i drugie skazki* (Petrograd: Vsemirnaia literatura, 1920); *Granatovyi dom* (Petrograd: Vsemirnaia literatura, 1922).

manuscript of *The Ballad of Reading Gaol*.⁵⁰ A less sentimental anecdote was reported by Vladimir Nabokov in *Speak, Memory*. Here, Nabokov claimed to give details of a trip made to London in 1916 by members of the Russian press, who were received in some style by the British establishment:

> There had been an official banquet presided over by Sir Edward Grey, and a funny interview with George V whom Chukovski, the *enfant terrible* of the group, insisted on asking if he liked the works of Oscar Wilde – 'dze ooarks of OOald.' The king, who was baffled by his interrogator's accent and who, anyway, had never been a voracious reader, neatly countered by inquiring how his guests liked the London fog (later Chukovski used to cite this triumphantly as an example of British cant – tabooing a writer because of his morals).⁵¹

Chukovskii was familiar with Nabokov's account, although he took issue with its tone and accuracy:

> Quoting his father, Vladimir Dmitrievich Nabokov, the novelist writes in his memoirs that when I was at Buckingham Palace I asked King George V a question about Oscar Wilde. Rubbish! The King delivered a speech from a prepared text, as did Vladimir Dmitrievich. Talking to the King was out of the question. It's just a story. He is trying to discredit his father.⁵²

Although many of these details would naturally remain unknown to Soviet readers, Chukovskii was nonetheless a living link both to Wilde himself,

---

50   K. I. Chukovskii, *Oskar Uail'd* (St Petersburg: Raduga, 1922), cited according to 'Oskar Uail'd', in *Sobranie sochinenii*, 15 vols (Moscow: Terra-Knizhnyi klub, 2001–9), III (2001), 373–414 (373).
51   Vladimir Nabokov, *Speak Memory: An Autobiography Revisited* (London: Penguin, 2000), 196.
52   Kornei Chukovsky, *Diary, 1901–1969*; ed. Victor Erlich, trans. Michael Henry Heim (New Haven and London: Yale University Press, 2005), 452–3. As Polonsky notes (*English Literature and the Russian Aesthetic Renaissance*, 161), this incident closely reprises Bal'mont's experience of visiting Oxford: 'Balmont asks a gentleman at an academic gathering in 1897 what he thinks of Wilde. The gentleman pretends not to have heard, and asks Balmont whether he is enjoying England. When the question is put again, Balmont is cut dead with the retort, "We have many fine writers in England"'.

and to his earlier reception in late-Imperial and even early-Soviet Russia. If the cultural politics of the thaw demanded a repudiation of the Stalin era and a concomitant rehabilitation of the periods directly preceding it, then both Chukovskii and Wilde could play an important role in the process of reasserting an apparent sense of continuity between the early twentieth century and the Khrushchev era itself.

Chukovskii's principal contribution to the domesticization of Wilde took the form of a major essay he published in 1960.[53] This was, in fact, based on pieces written much earlier,[54] evidence that his complex and decidedly equivocal interpretation was clearly a genuinely felt attitude, rather than merely a reflection of official literary culture. The approach to Wilde's personality and art that Chukovskii was to elaborate over the course of the next fifty years or so is already present in outline in his 1912 study, which concluded with the following striking paragraph:

> We Russians somehow carelessly and out of boredom passed Wilde by, when he appeared before us as an aesthete, as an apostle of pleasure. But when we heard from him this hymn of the happiness of suffering, we cried out: he is ours, we have discovered his heart, and Oscar Wilde has long since been our own Russian writer.[55]

---

53 Kornei Chukovskii, 'Oskar Uail'd', in *Liudi i knigi*, 2nd edn (Moscow: Gosudarstvennoe izdatel'stvo khudozhestvennoi literatury, 1960), 625–70, republished (with minor revisions) in *Sobranie sochinenii*, 6 vols (Moscow: Khudozhestvennaia literatura, 1965–9), III (1966), 666–725. The main changes in the 1966 edition of the essay relate to amplifications made possible by the recent publication of Wilde's letters (and a number of intervening studies). See Rupert Hart-Davis, *The Letters of Oscar Wilde* (London: Hart-Davis, 1962). Of course, this was exactly the kind of material that could be made available to Soviet readers only because of the selective intervention of a figure such as Chukovskii himself.

54 In chronological order: 'Oskar Uail'd: Etiud', *Niva*, 49 (1911), 910–14; 'Oskar Uail'd (1854–1900): Etiud', in Oskar Uail'd, *Polnoe sobranie sochinenii*, I, i–xxxiii; 'Oskar Uail'd', in *Litsa i maski* (St Petersburg: Shipovnik, 1914), 7–55; and *Oskar Uail'd* (see fn. 49). Because of the possible confusion over editions involved here, subsequent references to Chukovskii's 1922 and 1960 versions of this essay (for publication details, see fns 49 and 51 respectively) will be given with the year of publication in square brackets.

55 Chukovskii, 'Oskar Uail'd (1854–1900): Etiud', xxiii.

From the outset, then, Chukovskii was interested in promoting not just a translated version of Wilde, but a thoroughly domesticated one as well. The means of this domesticization were, however, to change in keeping with broader cultural and ideological trends. In the 1922 version of the essay, Chukovskii revisits symbolist interest in Wilde as a figure of martyrdom that was so characteristic of his conclusion one decade earlier, yet suggests that the redemptive potential of this role was vitiated by the fact that Wilde's aphoristic style and love of paradoxes was little more than a trite and superficial technique: 'A widely accepted thought is taken and almost mechanically turned on its head. Of course, a banality remains a banality, but it gives the impression of a paradox'.[56] For Chukovskii, even the 'wise and humble suffering' of Wilde's prison narratives was 'just as much a pose as all the rest.'[57] Yet by 1960, the emphasis had changed still further. In the wake of the publication of his earlier essay, Gor'kii had written to Chukovskii, agreeing that Wilde's use of paradox was formulaic, but proposing a more positive interpretation of this literary device:

> You are indisputably right when you say that Wilde's paradoxes are 'inside-out commonplaces', but do you not suppose that beyond this striving to turn all 'commonplaces' inside out there is a more or less conscious desire to spite 'Mistress Grundy' and to shake English Puritanism? It seems to me that such phenomena as Wilde and Bernard Shaw are too unexpected for England at the end of the nineteenth century, and at the same time are completely natural. English hypocrisy is the best organized form of hypocrisy, and I would suggest that paradox in the field of morality is a very fitting weapon in the fight against Puritanism.[58]

Wilde's aestheticism was always going to be impossible to gainsay, but here again, it is historicized and explained away. Chukovskii's defence of Wilde would appear all the more incontrovertible because of his appeal to no less an authority than Gor'kii (just as Gor'kii's allusion to the more properly socialist Shaw could potentially incorporate Wilde within the fold of politically engaged writers).

---

56   Chukovskii, 'Oskar Uail'd' [1922], 387.
57   Ibid., 409.
58   Cited in Chukovskii, 'Oskar Uail'd' [1960], 641.

But Chukovskii's boldest manoeuvre was to reject the dominant historicist reading of Wilde altogether, replacing it with 'another' (*drugoi*) Wilde explicitly fashioned as such by the processes of reception and translation. Towards the end of the 1922 version of his essay, Chukovskii contemplated Wilde's enormous popularity: 'Is it not strange that this salon aesthete became, within a few years of his death, one of the most democratic, plebeian writers?'[59] Moreover, this popularity guaranteed him an audience well beyond the confines of his homeland:

> Those features of his creative personality which seem to us so original, could not appeal to the English to the same extent, for whom he was an imitator. They often felt him to be a vulgarizer of their sages and poets. Wilde's success in Russia can in part be explained by the fact that Russian readers knew neither Keats, nor Swinburne, nor the Pre-Raphaelites, nor Ruskin, nor Walter Pater, nor Symonds, nor other inspirers of that *renaissance*, whose brilliant epigone was Oscar Wilde.[60]

Chukovskii takes a charge traditionally made against Wilde – that of his derivativeness – and transforms it into his claim to greatness. Moreover, it is only in translation that this greatness becomes truly apparent:

> They [the writers mentioned above] could not write for everybody, for the vast international crowd, they wrote only for a narrow circle of connoisseurs. But he appealed to all, to all humanity, and – alone of his generation – became a world writer.[61]

Chukovskii's approach was arguably conditioned by his involvement with Gor'kii's *Vsemirnaia biblioteka* enterprise at this time. Yet by 1960, his argument had become even more emphatic and wide-ranging:

> He is no less well-known and loved in Romania than in Italy; no less in France than in Mexico. New books about him and his life and works continue to appear to this day, particularly in America and England. His plays are always on the stage. [...] It is no wonder that the entire system of Oscar Wilde's decadent aesthetics has remained

---

59 Chukovskii, 'Oskar Uail'd' [1922], 413.
60 Ibid., 414.
61 Ibid.

alien to his polyglot readers. It does not interest them at all. They do not even notice it. It is *another* Wilde that is dear to them, one going against his credo, one rejecting the very nihilistic decadent ideas that he so often braved.[62]

It was, then, the process of reading – and reading in translation – that was central to producing a Soviet Wilde. Prefaces, essays and encyclopaedia entries could – and did – play their part, but they would always be faced with Wilde's anti-realist, decadent aestheticism and the individualist tenor of his tenuous socialist beliefs. Reading, however, displaced the problems of dealing with the historical context onto a more flexible and regenerative pattern of reception. Furthermore, by emphasizing the role of the reader in shaping the literary canon, Chukovskii was defending the importance of popular taste at a time when the relationship between artists, audiences, critics and the Party was itself being extensively re-evaluated.

After the surge of interest in Wilde during the Thaw, Wilde's Soviet reception endured a period of stability and even stagnation: English-language readers continued to be issued,[63] and the preface to a 1976 edition of Wilde and Kipling is remarkable only for its conventionality, testament perhaps to the burden of canonization in the Brezhnev years (although the volume did include some of the first publications of Wilde's poetry for a long time);[64] issued as part of the 'Library of World Literature' series in a comparatively large print-run of 303,000, it was the kind of volume that sat on the shelves of readers as testament to their broad cultural level and proof of the Soviet Union's status as 'the most well-read nation' ('samyi

---

62   Chukovskii, 'Oskar Uail'd' [1960], 660.
63   Oscar Wilde, *The Happy Prince and Other Tales*/Oskar Uail'd, *Schastlivyi prints i drugie skazki: kniga dlia chteniia na angliiskom iazyke dlia IX klassa srednei shkoly*, 2nd edn (Moscow: Prosveshchenie, 1969).
64   D. Urnov, 'Pod"em i padenie talanta', in Oskar Uail'd, *Stikhotvoreniia. Portret Doriana Greia. Tiuremnaia Ispoved'*/Rediard Kipling, *Stikhotvoreniia. Rasskazy* (Moscow: Khudozhestvennaia literatura, 1976). For a comparative study of Kipling, see Katharine Hodgson, 'The Poetry of Rudyard Kipling in Soviet Russia', *Modern Language Review* 93/4 (1998), 1058–71.

chitaiushchii narod').⁶⁵ A 1972 translation of the stories contained another preface by Anikst designed to present an acceptable account of Wilde's reputation and legacy.⁶⁶ This particular essay is revealing for the way in which Wilde's aestheticism is explicitly traced back to Ruskin's critique of nineteenth-century capitalism: 'Ruskin preached that for a complete spiritual life it was necessary to revive people's aesthetic basis, to make the need for beauty an everyday part of people's lives'.⁶⁷ Thus, Wilde's radical individualism is tamed by association with Ruskin's more emphatically moral vision, although Anikst is forced to concede that Wilde ultimately lacks political engagement: 'Good humour alone is not enough. Good should be the real result of a just regime, founded on social equality, the lack of oppression and true freedom'.⁶⁸ Just what the young readers for whom this edition was intended made of this attempt to shape their reading of Wilde is difficult to assess – as indeed are the private experiences of Soviet readers more generally.⁶⁹ Yet such writings retain considerable programmatic interest for scholars interested in the changing fortunes of Soviet literature in general and the reception of Wilde in particular, since they demonstrate the ways in which censorship was not merely a negative process designed to remove dangerous elements from the public sphere, but functioned as it were 'positively', directing readers towards politically acceptable interpretations of the works available to them. In the case of translation, this process was particularly acute, since decisions about material to be translated and about information to be made available to a non-specialist audience were dependent on a small group of trained scholars. Restrictive – and restricted – principles of selection, translation and edit-

---

65 Stephen Lovell, *The Russian Reading Revolution: Print Culture in the Soviet and Post-Soviet Eras* (Basingstoke: Macmillan; New York: St Martin's Press, 2000), especially Chapter 3, 'The Arrival of the New Reader: The Post-Stalin Period', 45–71.
66 Aleksandr Anikst, 'O skazkakh Oskara Uail'da', in Oskar Uail'd, *Mal'chik-zvezda* (Moscow: Detskaia literatura, 1972), 106–11.
67 Ibid., 107.
68 Ibid., 111.
69 Anikst himself admits that 'perhaps our examination of Wilde's stories has become too serious and should not have descended into such deliberations?' (Ibid., 111).

ing (at least in comparison with the multi-volume editions of canonical Russian writers, typically furnished with variant texts, non-literary works, letters, diaries and extensive commentaries) meant that the presentation of foreign authors was an altogether more partial affair than that of native writers, and that readers would have had a correspondingly narrower range of competing interpretations to draw on.

Yet this seemingly predictable account of publication and criticism in a strictly regimented one-party state is far from being the whole truth, and, just as the history of Wilde's Soviet-era translations illustrates the restrictive forces at work in the dissemination of literary knowledge, so too does it reveal unexpected instances of resistance and re-evaluation (prefigured, perhaps, by Chukovskii's emphasis on the importance of the reader in the processes of reception and canon-formation). As early as 1956, an edition of a selection of Wilde's stories included the following significant admission: 'Wilde's works, and particularly his aesthetic views, were a great influence on decadent literature in all countries, including Russian decadents at the end of the nineteenth century'.[70] Included here as a negative appraisal of Wilde's influence (and one, moreover, that Chukovskii, keen to assert Wilde's interest in the concrete and the everyday, had repeatedly questioned),[71] such comments may nonetheless have elicited the interest of the curious reader – however unintentionally. Wilde's Soviet reception came to be accompanied by a parallel and related process, the slow and

70 Folomkina, 'Oskar Uail'd (1856–1900)', 6.
71 Already in 1922, he had asserted: 'Eternity and infinity were not for Oscar Wilde. [...] In vain did the Russian symbolists, who appeared at the start of the twentieth century, consider him their own. Symbolism was alien and hostile to him' (cited in 'Oskar Uail'd' [1922], 400). By 1960, this interpretation had become yet more categorically materialist: 'It is well known that at the start of the twentieth century, the Russian symbolists, who appreciated Oscar Wilde for his detachment from the reality and actuality of life, claimed him for their own and placed him alongside Maeterlinck, Przybyszewski, Huysmans and Gabriel d'Annunzio. All of this was a great delusion, since it is hard to imagine a more vehement enemy of Symbolism. He was never seduced by mysticism and metaphysics. He admitted no abstract notions in art. "Form and colour speak to us of form and colour – and of nothing else", he claimed on more than one occasion' (cited in 'Oskar Uail'd' [1960], 656).

tentative rediscovery of Russia's own literature of the turn of the century. The more works by and about Russia's modernists were published, the more Wilde's impact upon the history of Russian literature was revealed; conversely, as more was written about Wilde, it seemed more necessary to deal with the legacy of Russia's own late Imperial and early Soviet culture. Tairov's production of *Salome* would be recalled extensively in thaw-era studies and memoirs,[72] as would Meierkhol'd's film version of *Dorian Gray*.[73] In both cases, this rediscovery could be justified by the fact that both directors sympathized with the Soviet regime. A 1964 edition of Kommisarzhevskaia's letters and other documents, however, revealed much unfamiliar material about pre-revolutionary cultural life in St Petersburg, including – *en passant* – the prohibition of *Salome* in 1908.[74] Although the 1960 edition of Wilde's selected works generally favoured modern versions by Soviet translators, the 1960 volume of his plays did include Briusov's version of *The Duchess of Padua*, and Bal'mont and Andreeva's version of *Salome*. Much as critics may have wished to impose a moral or even redemptive interpretation on Wilde's works, discussion of his historical significance during these earlier phases in his Russian reception began to raise difficult questions of aestheticism and Modernism. Moreover, because the study of foreign languages and literatures was less easily supervised by non-specialists, scholarship in these fields became a way of exploring ambiguous elements within Russian culture itself.

Over a number of decades, then, literary scholars slowly laid the foundations for a more nuanced interpretation of Wilde, although this specialist work would do little to challenge broader popular perceptions. The first Soviet dissertations on Wilde were written in the early 1970s and deal

---

72 Iu. Golovashenko, *Rezhisserskoe iskusstvo Tairova* (Moscow: Iskusstvo, 1970), 11–12, 26–8, 187–8.
73 B. S. Likhakhev, 'Materialy k istorii kino v Rossii (1914–1916)', in *Iz istorii kino: materialy i dokumenty*, 3 (Moscow: Izdatel'stvo Akademii nauk SSSR, 1960), 37–103 (78–9).
74 Vera Fedorovna Komissarzhevskaia, *Pis'ma aktrisy, vospominaniia o nei, materialy* (Leningrad and Moscow: Iskusstvo, 1964), especially A. Zheliabuzhskii, 'Poslednie gody', 274–94 (280–85 on *Salome*).

with aspects of his dramatic technique, prose style, use of language and aesthetic views.[75] But the most significant widening of the critical perspective was Tat'iana Pavlova's 1986 dissertation dealing with Wilde's impact on Russia's own turn-of-the-century authors.[76] Indicative of the effects that Gorbachev's *glasnost'* and *perestroika* were to have on the literary world in the second half of the 1980s, Pavlova's work constitutes an important stage in the rediscovery of Russia's own cosmopolitan literary heritage. These developments in scholarship were accompanied by a change of policy in terms of translation and publishing. 1986 – the year of Pavlova's dissertation – also saw the appearance of a new edition of Wilde's selected works – by far the most important single Wilde publication since 1960.[77] Although still penned within the framework inherited from Anikst (Wilde as a victim of capitalist society, as an opponent of bourgeois hypocrisy, as a closet moralist despite the amoral surface of this works), its preface is far more attentive to Wilde's place in late nineteenth-century decadence than had previously been admitted. In addition to Ruskin, considerable attention

75   I. F. Taits, *Nekotorye osobennosti dramaturgicheskogo metoda O. Uail'da* (Moscow, 1971); S. A. Kolesnik, *Proza O. Uail'da* (Moscow, 1972); T. A. Boborykina, *Dramaturgiia O. Uail'da (K probleme ideino-khudozhestvennogo svoeobraziia estetizma O. Uail'da)* (Leningrad, 1981); L. M. Obazova, *Svoeobrazie estetiki angliiskogo dekadansa 90-kh godov* (Moscow, 1982); T. A. Porfir'eva, *Osobennosti poetiki O. Uail'da (Novelly, roman, skazki)* (Moscow, 1983). See also Iu. Ia. Kissel, *Okkazional'noe ispol'zovanie frazeologicheskikh edinits v proizvedeniiakh B. Shou i O. Uail'da* (Voronezh, 1975).

76   T. V. Pavlova, *Oskar Uail'd v Rossii (konets XIX–nachalo XX veka)* (Leningrad, 1986). An accessible summary is T. V. Pavlova, 'Oskar Uail'd v russkoi literature (konets XIX–nachalo XX v.)', in Iurii Levin (ed.), *Na rubezhe XIX i XX vekov: iz istorii mezhdunarodnykh sviazei russkoi literatury. Sbornik nauchnykh trudov* (Leningrad: Nauka, 1991), 77–128.

77   A. Zverev, 'Portret Oskara Uail'da', in Oskar Uail'd, *Izbrannoe* (Moscow: Khudozhestvennaia literatura, 1986), 3–20. Other selections of Wilde's works published in the very end of the Soviet era reprised many of the points made in this 1986 edition. See, for instance, *Izbrannoe* (Moscow: Pravda, 1989), with an introduction ('Roman zhizni Oskara Uail'da') by S. Belza (5–26); *Izbrannoe* (Moscow: Prosveshchenie, 1990), with an afterword by D. Poddubnyi and B. Kolesnikov ('Oskar Uail'd'), 360–77. Half a million copies of this latter edition were published, by far the largest print run for a volume of Wilde in the Soviet Union.

is devoted to the profound significance of Walter Pater (in what may possibly be one of the first serious and sustained references to Pater in Soviet criticism).[78] References to Baudelaire, Keats and Rossetti widen the range of reference yet further,[79] although the author is still keen to disavow the evident influence on Wilde of Huysmans's *A Rebours*: 'Dozens of times people have tried – and in the West people are still trying – to portray Wilde as a decadent, as almost the prototype of Huysmans's hero. It is hard to be more unfair on the author.'[80] How meaningful such references actually were remains uncertain; there had been, for instance, no edition of Pater in Russia since translations of his *Imaginary Portraits* in 1908 and 1916, and *The Renaissance* in 1912.[81] Moreover, the process of rediscovering and republishing Russia's own 'decadent' writers was only just beginning. Nonetheless, it is striking that the rehabilitation of Russia's own Silver Age was in part begun in the prefaces to mass-circulation editions of the more widely read and more carefully canonized Wilde.

Yet important elements of Wilde's life and personality remained unmentionable during much of the Soviet period, in official texts at least. In 1922, Chukovskii had devoted the third chapter of his short study to a discussion of how Wilde's sexuality was connected to his literary style. Subtitled 'modo vir, modo femina', it is thoroughly indebted to the kind of pseudo-psychological notions of homosexuality as pathology that were so widespread around the turn of the century. Noting that Wilde was 'an ideal reflection' of the theories of Otto Weininger (whose *Geschlecht und Charakter* of 1903 was translated a number of times into Russian in the early twentieth century),[82] Chukovskii described Wilde as having 'a poor

78 Zverev, '*Portret* Oskara Uail'da', 5–6.
79 Ibid., 10.
80 Ibid., 7.
81 See Philip Ross Bullock, 'The Cruel Art of Beauty: Walter Pater and the Uncanny Aestheticism of Isaak Babel's *Red Cavalry*', *Modern Language Review*, 104/2 (2009), 499–529, and Polonsky, *English Literature and the Russian Aesthetic Renaissance*, 170–87.
82 Laura Engelstein, *The Keys to Happiness: Sex and the Search for Modernity in Fin-de-Siècle Russia* (Ithaca: Cornell University Press, 1992), 301–2 (fn. 9). See too Evgenii

woman's soul, imprisoned in a man's body',[83] and traced his love of surface brilliance, tendency to imitation and eagerness to please to a feminized psychopathology. Unsurprisingly, this chapter – along with frequent passing references to Wilde's 'feminine' persona – was completely excised in the 1960s revisions of the essay. Chukovskii effected a complete and explicit separation of Wilde the man from his literary legacy. By claiming that 'Wilde's works turned out to be stronger than Wilde himself',[84] Chukovskii was implicitly promoting the Wilde of Soviet translation and criticism over any historically informed reality. Indeed, translation itself could actively serve to promote a more acceptable version of Wilde than either biography or literary history, as demonstrated by Chukovskii's version of *The Happy Prince*. In the English original, the swallow is masculine, and there is a tender, even erotic, tinge to his relationship with the statue of the prince (whom he kisses before he dies). This poses a particular problem for the translator, since in Russian, 'swallow' is a feminine noun, 'lastochka'. Chukovskii retains the feminine gender, turning the platonically homoerotic relationship between the bird and the statue into a more conventionally heterosexual one.[85] Moreover, this act of separation also denied the kind of fusion of life and art that was so central both

---

Bershtein, 'Tragediia pola: dve zametki o russkom veiningerianstve', *Novoe literaturnoe obozrenie*, 65 (2004), 208–28. Here (on 209), Bershtein cites a newspaper article by Chukovskii from January 1909, where Chukovskii is recorded as noting the universal presence of Weininger, shortly after the appearance of the first complete Russian translation of *Geschlecht und Charakter* the previous year.

83 Chukovskii, 'Oskar Uail'd' [1922], 382.
84 Chukovskii, 'Oskar Uail'd' [1960], 662.
85 This is a feature of other translations of *The Happy Prince*. As Rita Severi writes of the first Italian translation (by F. Bianco in 1904): 'Bianco perfectly understood the bond of friendship between the prince and the little swallow in Wilde's original: most contemporary versions of the tale render the English bird "swallow" as the feminine "rondine", but Bianco opted for the masculine diminutive "rondinino", thereby underlining the strong Platonic relationship between the two male characters, the prince and his helper'. See Rita Severi, '"Astonishing in my Italian": Oscar Wilde's First Italian Editions 1890–1952', in Evangelista, ed., *The European Reception of Oscar Wilde*, 108–23 (113).

to Wilde's own life in general, and to his Russian modernist reception in particular. Elsewhere, a variety of euphemisms was employed to describe Wilde's relationship with Alfred Douglas: in 1928, Deich, writing before the recriminalization of male homosexuality in the Soviet Union in 1933, had suggested that 'Oscar Wilde's friendship with Alfred Douglas seemed unnatural and depraved'.[86] A later writer suggested that their 'passionate friendship would become the pretext for the filthiest of insinuations'.[87] A 1908 edition of the 'Priest and the Acolyte' (not, in fact, by Wilde at all, but by Jack Bloxam, editor of the journal in which the story first appeared in 1894), was confined by Glavlit to a *spetskhran* in 1949 on account of its quasi-pornographic homosexual content.[88] Some Soviet-era discussions of the trials hinted at an unspecified form of 'immorality',[89] yet even here Wilde's fall was not due to his (unmentioned) sexuality or even to the accusations of the Marquis of Queensbury, but was the result of his persecution by a philistine mob. As late as 1990, discussion of Wilde as victim effaced any discussion of his sexuality:

> Of course, the issue had nothing to do with Queensbury and his rude, egoistical son Alfred, but with the great mass of Victorians, with their failure to understand the radiant, deep, human art of Wilde, with their embittered view of anything that contradicted the words and image of their teacher Calvin.[90]

The fact that this statement comes from a school edition explains some of the concern to avoid mention of Wilde's sexuality. The absences and evasions that characterize Soviet discussion of Wilde's sexuality are understandable, given both Soviet moral codes in general and Wilde's crucial role in

---

86 Deich, 'S.33', 5.
87 Zverev, 'Portret Oskara Uail'da', 15.
88 The decision was reiterated in 1951, although the book was returned to general circulation in 1958. See A. V. Blium, 'Index librorum prohibitorum zarubezhnykh pisatelei (v perevodakh na russkii iazyk 1917–1991 gg.)', *Novoe literaturnoe obozrenie* 92 (2008), 125–39 (135). The edition in question was *Tsar' zhizni* (Moscow: Ikar, 1908).
89 Anikst, *Istoriia angliiskoi literatury*, 378.
90 Poddubnyi and Kolesnikov, 'Oskar Uail'd', 364.

the school curriculum in particular. By contrast, Sokolianskii's biography of the same year – a work aimed at university students and postgraduates – does at last refer to Douglas as Wilde's 'intimate friend'.[91] Published in Kiev and Odessa, and therefore challenging the predominant view of Wilde from the late-Soviet periphery, this detailed and dispassionate 1990 work was, remarkably enough, the first book-length biography of Wilde published in the Soviet Union. Only towards the very end of the twentieth century would major Western biographies by Jacques de Langlade, Richard Ellman and Peter Ackroyd appear in Russian translation (the first of these in the standard Soviet and subsequently Russian series, *Zhizni zamechatel'nykh liudei*);[92] that Langlade and Ackroyd's works were published with the support of the French Ministry of Culture and the British Council respectively demonstrates how a distinctly Soviet view of Wilde came to be challenged by translated works written originally for a quite different audience. Before this, Russian readers relied on the selective interpretations included in officially sanctioned prefaces and on their intuitive grasp of the texts made available in translation (the extent to which illicit knowledge of Wilde's sexuality circulated unofficially remains the subject for another kind of study).[93]

---

[91] M. G. Sokolianksii, *Oskar Uail'd: Ocherk tvorchestva* (Kiev, Odessa: Lybin', 1990), 9.

[92] Zhak de Langlad, *Oskar Uail'd, ili Pravda masok*; trans. V. I. Grigor'ev (Moscow: Molodaia gvardiia; Palimpsest, 1999); Richard Ellman, *Oskar Uail'd: Biografiia*; trans. L. Motylev (Moscow: Nezavisimaia gazeta, 2000); and Piter Akroid, *Zaveshchanie Oskara Uail'da*; trans. L. Motylev (Moscow: B.S.G.-PRESS, 2000).

[93] Further evidence of the discomfort caused by discussion of Wilde's homosexuality comes in the form of Soviet reactions to the showing of Ken Hughes's *The Trials of Oscar Wilde* (1960) at the 1961 Moscow Film Festival. Writing in *Sight and Sound*, David Robinson noted: 'The social impact was perhaps more curious [than that of a showing of *Saturday Night and Sunday Morning*]. Of course critics complained that "other socially more important aspects of the famous writer's life could have been taken to provide a fuller and pithier image of his moral make-up" (G. Kapralov). Still, the effect of bringing into open discussion a subject that had been practically ignored since Stalin re-introduced the repressive measures against homosexuals which had been abandoned in 1917, was significant. The film may have been a minor Wolfenden for the U.S.S.R.' 'Moscow', *Sight and Sound* 30/4 (1961), 171–2 (171).

In the Soviet Union, however, it was above all the 'democratic' and 'plebeian' Wilde who would survive and even prosper. Just as the verse of that other unlikely figure, Kipling, would be valued precisely because it was 'unashamedly popular, simple, and accessible',[94] so too did Wilde – for all his aestheticism, amorality, individualism and disdain for realism – come to be a widely appreciated poet in a culture where the dominant Western distinction between popular and elitist art was denied, and writers (and indeed all artists) were instead encouraged and required to produce works of art for a broadly conceived mass readership. Yet where Kipling posed problems of how to render adequately – if at all – 'a certain perceived "vulgarity" in his energetic use of colloquial speech',[95] Wilde could more readily be put into the kind of correct, literate Russian taught in schools. Even in translation, style – not substance – was his marker. This process of translating and accommodating Wilde in the Soviet Union was, moreover, modelled on his own successful and determined appeal to a wide audience,[96] the very aspect of his work and personality that had been so potentially problematic for subsequent generations of British modernist writers and critics.[97] Soviet commentators seized on this popularizing gesture as the very feature of Wilde's literary persona that ultimately prevailed over his unacceptable aesthetics, yet once more it was accompanied by the kind of de-historicizing, universalizing approach so typical of his Russian reception. Where Wilde's own career as a writer was profoundly shaped by the concerns of the market, in the Soviet Union, the elevation of clarity, accessibility and popularity to the status of artistic virtues meant that his legacy to Russian readers could be freed from the imputation of any sort of mercantile opportunism, and be interpreted instead as an exemplary, if paradoxical, form of social engagement. Moreover, in a culture where the

---

94 Hodgson, 'The Poetry of Rudyard Kipling in Soviet Russia', 1062.
95 Ibid.
96 Regenia Gagnier, *Idylls of the Marketplace: Oscar Wilde and the Victorian Public* (Stanford: Stanford University Press, 1986).
97 For a wide-ranging survey of twentieth-century British responses to Wilde, see: Joseph Bristow, 'Picturing His Exact Decadence: The British Reception of Oscar Wilde', in Evangelista, ed., *The European Reception of Oscar Wilde*, 20–50.

party line was continually changing, works with apparently little definable content stood a paradoxical chance of survival precisely because they were unlikely ever to contradict the current state of political correctness, and therefore ran little risk of being branded objectionable, tendentious or erroneous. Although studies of Soviet literature may have emphasized Socialist Realism's trinity of 'party-mindedness', 'nationality' and 'ideology' as central to the literary process, appeal and accessibility were equally as important, as were the demands and tastes of a varied readership. Never a straightforwardly top-down process, cultural politics in the Soviet Union was based on a complex and evolving negotiation between the interdependent fields of official ideology and popular taste. That Wilde, European Modernism's most astute and fashionable advocate, should have become such a felicitous figure in this process is not the least of the paradoxes concerning his translation and accommodation in the Soviet Union.

EMILY LYGO

Free Verse and Soviet Poetry in the Post-Stalin Period

During the cultural Thaw after the death of Stalin, the Soviet authorities began to permit more publication of poetry in translation, and in so doing they enabled readers to catch up with developments in Western poetry which had not been accessible to them in the preceding decades. For the most part, the establishment – the Party operatives who controlled literary policy – remained conservative and resistant to avant-garde, abstract and free form in the arts,[1] but the tendency of progressive Western poets to use non-classical verse form meant that Soviet translators had to explore the potential for free verse in Russian. In large-scale publications intended for a wide audience, non-classical poetry was accompanied by wary commentary, but within more specialist poetry circles, the translation of Western avant-garde poetry became a subject for considerable discussion. Liberal members of the intelligentsia put forward their view that 'non-classical' poetry could be translated effectively only if translators took existing Russian works in free verse as models. In this way, they argued for the recovery of poets who had been 'forgotten' during the Stalin period because their work did not conform to the methodology of Socialist Realism. With the recovery of this past arose questions of the meaning and significance of free verse, and of why it had been taken up so little by Soviet poets. Altogether, this was a period in which the translation of Western poetry raised important questions about the history and development of Russian poetry.

During the early revolutionary period, the translation of foreign, especially Western works took an important, even central role in literary life: Gor'kii's project to have world classics translated into Russian and

---

[1] Khrushchev's outrage at the exhibition of non-figurative art in the Manezh and the Bulldozer exhibition is the most famous evidence of this tendency.

made available for the common man or woman was set in motion with the establishment of the publishing house 'Vsemirnaia literatura', and from 1918 to 1924 its publications offered a wide selection of world literature to readers. Censorship was applied to works in translation as much as to original Russian, which meant that the publication of authors and works was skewed by political considerations; nevertheless, there were attempts to provide Soviet readers with information about and translations of literary developments in the West. In the field of Western poetry, notable publications include the anthology of English poetry compiled by D. S. Mirskii but published as the work of Gutner after Mirskii's arrest in 1937, which provided a good selection of developments in English poetry in the early years of the twentieth century,[2] and the 1939 anthology of American poetry *Poety Ameriki* which brought many contemporary American poets to the Russian readership, including Robert Frost, H. D. and William Carlos Williams.[3] With reasonable access to European and World literature, writers in the USSR were working in at least some kind of dialogue with Western literature and the prevailing movement of European Modernism.

After the Great Patriotic War, Russian poetry became cut off from both the traditions and developments of modernist and more generally experimental poetry. In terms of Russian poetry, the modernists (with the significant exception of Maiakovskii) were anathematized by the Soviet establishment. In the terror of the late 1930s, quite a number of these figures had been arrested, and in the late Stalin period the futurists and OBERIU were no longer published: their work disappeared from official history and criticism of Soviet literature. In terms of Western poetry, the anticosmopolitanism and isolationism of the late Stalin period meant that the general reading public in the USSR had virtually no contact with Western literature. The separation of the totalitarian USSR from the democratic West by the 'iron curtain' was reflected in the literary world by the closure,

2 *Antologiia novoi angliiskoi poezii: vstupitel'naia stat'ia i komentarii M. Gutnera* (Leningrad: Khudozhestvennaia literatura, 1937).
3 Mikhail Zenkevich and Ivan Kashkin, eds, *Poety Ameriki: XX vek* (Moscow: Khudozhestvennaia literatura, 1939).

in 1943, of the journal *Internatsional'naia literatura*. Even members of the Writers' Union were not given access to contemporary Western literature, which was acquired by libraries but shut up in special, closed collections. All this is not to say, of course, that all knowledge of modernist poetry disappeared from Soviet society. Many intellectuals preserved books and memories of the Russian modernists, so that the understanding of this tradition never disappeared entirely, it was simply erased from official discourse. Similarly, Western Modernism published before the war survived in personal libraries. During the 1940s, however, there was a hiatus in the reception of Western poetry in the USSR which meant that Russian poetry lost contact with the developing experimental poetic traditions in the West. While Western poets continued the experiments of the modernist period and in particular developed their use of free verse, poetry in the USSR stagnated in the form of Stalinist Socialist Realism.

By the post-war period, Socialist Realism had developed into a narrow and predictable methodology for writing poetry. Poems had to be simple, formal and regular, with no complexity or experiment in unusual metres, unexpected rhymes or complicated stanza forms. To deviate from this was deemed to be a preoccupation with form for form's sake (*formalizm*). This was seen as a trivialization of and distraction from literature's main purpose in communicating a politically relevant message to readers. Since poetic form had no positive political contribution to make to a literary work, its over-emphasis was deemed to be politically incorrect. It is fair to say that the influence of the modernist period had been completely erased from published Soviet poetry. This situation did not change until the Khrushchev Thaw.

During the Khrushchev Thaw the authorities significantly broadened the range of literature that could be published in the USSR, and the translation of foreign and especially Western literature was a key element of this development. Maurice Friedberg notes that as early as December 1953, the journal *Sovetskaia kul'tura* gave indications that foreign literature and culture were due to return to the USSR.[4] Sergei Zav'ialov surmises that it must have been the following year, in 1954, that the decision was taken to relaunch the journal *Internatsional'naia literatura*. This was renamed *Inostrannaia literatura*: the first issue was published in January 1955 and opened with a selection of Walt Whitman's poetry. It is significant that such a central figure of American poetry should have been chosen for this opening number, for America occupied a particular place in the world rediscovered by Soviets during the Thaw. In 1955, the journal *Amerika* was also established, and that same year the musical *Porgy and Bess* was staged in Leningrad.[5] In the 1960s, Hemingway achieved great popularity and cult status, influencing a whole generation not only in literary style, but also lifestyle, ethics and conduct.[6]

For Soviet poetry, the Thaw meant a return to the publication of experimental poetry such as had not been seen in print for decades. As early as 1953, Moscow gave instructions that Soviet poetry needed to modernize and develop to keep up with other genres of Soviet literature. This led to far-reaching changes to the sponsorship and publication of poetry in the USSR.[7] Instructions to introduce new themes and forms to Soviet poetry were passed down first by the Party to the Writers' Union, and then by the Union to writers. At the Second Congress of Writers held in 1954, the poet Lugovskoi called for a greater variety of themes and for more experiment in form to be introduced into Soviet poetry, referring specifically to foreign poets such as the Turkish poet Nazim Hikmet and the Chilean Pablo Neruda as models:

> The task of Soviet poetry is to educate our people morally and aesthetically. But, along our path, stereotype, coldness, 'uncontentious' ideas, and the lacklustre cliché

4   Maurice Friedberg, *A Decade of Euphoria: Western Literature in Post-Stalin Russia, 1954–64* (Bloomington: Indiana University Press, 1977), 6.
5   Aleksandr Genis and Petr Vail', *60-e: mir sovetskogo cheloveka* (Ann Arbor: Ardis, 1988).
6   Ibid., 64–73.
7   I have described this in the chapter 'The Post-Stalin Thaw 1953–64' of my *Leningrad Poetry 1953–75: The Thaw Generation* (Oxford: Peter Lang, 2010), 13–82.

that's repeated a thousand times stand in our way, like black shadows. Yet poetry is flight. Maiakovskii said that 'all poetry is a journey into the unknown!'
Our editorial boards encourage and nurture general, uncontentious ideas and clichéd methods. Every cliché, created with the best intentions, hopelessly extinguishes the fire of a poem. Let our Soviet poetry be seeking, be bold, be searching! Let no one be afraid of novelty, unusual content, unusual form. We can move forward *only if we take risks*. We want to develop the great expressiveness of Soviet poetry, such as we find in Maiakovskii's poetry, and also in our great comrades-in-arms, such as Nazim Hikmet and Pablo Neruda.[8]

At the conference of young writers held in Leningrad in April 1956, the excesses of Stalinist Socialist Realism were criticized, and promises were given that foreign authors would soon begin appearing in the Soviet press. In his opening address to the conference, A. L. Dymshits (1910–75) made reference to a list of foreign authors that had been drawn up and approved for publication in the coming years. He had not seen the list at that point, so could not give any details.[9]

Inostrannaia literatura was largely responsible for publishing the writers on that list over the coming years, and consistently published a wide range of foreign authors, including many poets. Zav'ialov has analysed the modernist poets featured in the journal and identified five principal groups to which they belong. These groups were: 1) Poets who became classics of Modernism between the wars or died early and were soon canonized; 2) foreign communists from Western countries; 3) foreign 'leftists' who sympathized with the USSR; 4) modernists from Socialist countries; 5) poets from capitalist countries. The range of poets published was truly wide and impressive, including extracts from the radical Allen Ginsberg's 'Howl' (1961) and the highly conservative modernist T. S. Eliot (1970).[10] Other

---

8 *Vtoroi vsesoiuznyi s"ezd sovetskikh pisatelei 15–26 dekabria 1954 goda. Stenograficheskii otchet* (Moscow: Sovetskii pisatel', 1956), 132.
9 'Piataia oblastnaia konferentsiia molodykh pisatelei, 1-oe zasedanie. 14 aprelia 1956' TsGALI St Petersburg: f. 371; op. 1; d. 298.
10 Sergey Zav'ialov, '"Poeziia – vsegda ne to, vsegda drugoe": perevody modernistskoi poezii v SSSR v 1950–1980-e gody', *Novoe literaturnoe obozrenie* 92 (2008) <http://magazines.russ.ru/ nlo/2008/92/za10.html> accessed 27 October 2009.

publications of Western poetry included an extensive anthology of English poetry of the first half of the twentieth century (1967), and one of modern American poetry (1975). The works of individual poets were also published separately in book or booklet form, especially from the 1970s on.[11]

The corpus of Western modernist poetry was, of course, only one half of the body of work that had disappeared from publication during the Stalin period: many of the Russian Silver Age poets had suffered the same fate, and the question of their rehabilitation was also now raised. Many writers of the 1910s and 1920s were in fact rehabilitated during the 1950s and 1960s, but fewer were actually republished and returned to the official canon. A situation developed in which the names of writers were sometimes restored to literary discourse, but their works were still scarcely available. The Silver Age poets who had been selectively republished during the Thaw included Akhmatova, Pasternak, Tsvetaeva and Khlebnikov, and in the 1970s works by Mandel'shtam also appeared, though all were subject to considerable censorship. But the list of missing poets was still huge, and included a large proportion of the more experimental writers of the modernist period, including Mikhail Kuzmin, Konstantin Vaginov, Nikolai Oleinikov,[12] Aleksandr Vvedenskii, David Burliuk, and Aleksei Kruchenykh. Most of these would not be published again until the *glasnost'* period.

It is significant that the Silver Age poets who were not republished tended to be the more experimental figures: it points to the persistence of anxieties over the literary sin of *formalizm*. Even though much lip-service was paid to the reintroduction of varied form into Soviet poetry, really only a handful of poets published work in non-classical form, for example Voznesenskii, Rozhdestvenskii and Vinokurov in Moscow and Viktor Sosnora in Leningrad. By and large, Soviet poetry continued to use predominantly 'classical' metres, regular stanza forms and alternating

---

11 For example the booklets of poems by Robert Frost in 1968, Léopold Senghor in 1969, Yiannis Ritsos in 1973, Carl Sandberg and Paul Celan in 1975.
12 Clearly there were hopes that some of these poets would reappear during the Thaw. In the Leningrad *Den' poezii* of 1964, I. Bakhterev and A. Razumovskii published the essay 'O Nikolae Oleinikove' which introduced this figure of the OBERIU and expressed the hope that his work would soon be republished.

rhyme schemes,[13] while excessive experimentation continued to carry the stigma of western-style decadence. This stigma was found across the Arts and included resistance to non-figurative art and sculpture and to more experimental music as well.

As Zav'ialov has pointed out, the association of formal experimentation with bourgeois decadence created a problem for Soviet publishers, editors and critics. In the West, experimentation in art and literature carried associations of progressive and even left-wing ideals, so it is not surprising that many Western poets sympathetic to the USSR wrote free or experimental verse. It was desirable politically that such works be published in the USSR, of course, but editors were apparently uneasy about how to present to their Soviet readership these works that could be construed as 'formalist' and that contravened the methodology of Socialist Realism. This was especially the case for editors of publications with a large print run intended for a non-specialist audience. While the relatively few readers of the specialist magazine *Inostrannaia literatura* could probably be presented with free verse and be trusted to understand it 'correctly', the readers of general anthologies of Western poetry apparently needed instruction in how to understand the kinds of experimentation that they were to encounter in the collection.

One example of the kind of introduction to free verse supplied by editors is found in the anthology *Sovremennaia amerikanskaia poeziia*, published in 1975, which included a wealth of poets writing in free verse. In his introduction A. Zverev (1939–2003, a leading scholar of American literature) considers the American experience of this form through the figure of Whitman and his legacy. He begins with Whitman, since his reputation as a 'revolutionary' had been well established by the criticism of Chukovskii among others:

> Whitman's greatest discovery was the free verse in modern form that he introduced to world poetry: it is without any parallelism of literary constructions, as one finds in folklore, and without hidden syllabic rhythms or the logical organization of stressed

---

13 The norms of poetry published in Leningrad during this period are described in Lygo, *Leningrad Poetry 1953–75*. See 134–55.

syllables on the principles of accentual verse. Whitman's free verse appeared as a truly innovative poetic system, born above all from the decisive break its creator made with the canonical understanding of the poetic quality of one or another aspect of life, by his determination to introduce into poetry as wide as possible a range of everyday things.[14]

Zverev underlines Whitman's credentials as a revolutionary when he links his poetic style to the task of representing his era of change and upheaval in American society. Without this 'artistic revolution', he asserts, Whitman would not have been able to express the world around him in his poetry. For later poets, however, the connection between free verse and subject is seen as not so organic or natural. Carl Sandberg's poetry is criticized for blindly following Whitman's example, and neglecting the order and form necessary in free verse:

> Sandberg's experience shows the inadequacy of blindly following Whitman. It shows the danger of being too preoccupied with free verse, that it is possible to be so anxious to use this verse system as much as possible to grasp and record the most varied aspects of everyday life, that you forget that free verse is not without form, that, on the contrary, it demands a very strict structure, a solid structure, that can carry the weight of the whole edifice of the poem.[15]

This comment about Sandberg makes it clear that free verse cannot be considered a verse form equally as valid as 'classical' verse: while it can be successful, it may also lead to the erosion of poetry's distinctiveness as a literary form. Zverev argues that American poetry suffers when free verse is so close to prose that it cannot be distinguished from it. When the desire of poets to capture reality in their free verse has, at times, led them only to reproduce this reality, without transforming it into art, he considers that the value of the work as art has been lost:

---

14   A. Zverev, 'Tridtsat' let amerikanskoi poezii' in *Sovremennaia amerikanskaia literatura: Antologiia* (Moscow: Progress, 1975), 5–34 (9–10).
15   Ibid., 12.

The shifting nature of the boundary that separates a work of art from a simple copy of reality in all its chaos and disorder, the absence of a definite boundary between artistic reality and the surrounding world, these are the dangers that free verse holds.

The rather ill-defined category of 'artistic reality' serves as the basis for an objection to free and experimental verse that is viewed as inimical to the idea of true poetry. In fact, Zverev goes on to elaborate that poets who simply reproduced the outward signs of mass culture not only failed in their attempts to write effective free verse, but also to draw attention to the failings of mass culture: the insufficient didacticism seems to lie at the heart of his rejection of them, and his warning words seem to be as much directed towards would-be poets as readers of American poetry:

> The unchecked spread of this kind of free verse, in which everything is reduced to the chaotic piling up of newspaper stories, jargon words and 'intellectual' clichés creates too great a risk. It turns out that not only poetic form comes under threat – the very meaning of poetic work does as well.

Value and meaning in poetry is connected to the degree of 'freedom' of its form, with excessive freedom suggesting lower value.

In his attempt to draw attention to the right type of free verse, Zverev discusses the distinction he sees between William Carlos Williams and e. e. cummings. For Zverev, Williams is the central figure of twentieth-century American poetry because his career follows the trajectory of the wider development of his country's poetry and because his work is deemed to have moved beyond formal experimentation to the expression of what is loosely termed 'living reality'. Williams himself, Zverev argues, always found this 'living reality' more interesting and richer than ideas; he rejected the kind of purely linguistic, deeply aesthetic and limited experimentation that, according to Zverev, absorbed Cummings. By tracing a lineage from Williams back to Whitman, he asserts that the tradition of free verse has been successful in American poetry, but there have been many cul-de-sacs and wrong turns along the way.

Free verse was presented in Zverev's introduction as having proved successful for some foreign writers, but unsuccessful for others, and as bearing a rather complicated relationship to context and subject that meant it was not always an appropriate form to adopt. Through such introductions to anthologies and publications of such poets, editors guided their readers in their understanding and appreciation of poetic novelty and experimentation, seeking, as was customary in so much of Soviet culture, to provide them with the correct interpretation of what was perceived as a largely Western phenomenon.

Although this publication from 1975 shows that attitudes towards free verse remained circumspect, within more specialist circles the Thaw witnessed significant exploration of the use of 'non-classical' verse forms in translation. There were still conservative and nationalist translators and critics who questioned whether or not free verse could, in fact, be translated into Russian satisfactorily. Some such translators, usually working from line-by-line translations (*podstrochniki*), changed the form from free verse to a strict, 'classical' metre. Yet others, and especially European-orientated figures of the intelligentsia who were engaged in translating such poems, saw that these works presented a particular opportunity to recover the Russian modernist tradition. Members of the older generation were aware that free and experimental verse was not a uniquely Western phenomenon and that, during the early years of the twentieth century, many significant Russian poets had used such forms but had been anathematized by the late Stalin period. They saw the task of translating Western experimental verse into Russian as an opportunity to draw attention to these 'forgotten' Russian writers, arguing that Soviet translators would not be able to produce fine, authentic translations without an appreciation of the equivalent corpus of work in Russian. The figures arguing for this recovery of Russian modernist verse were mostly distinguished, senior members of the literary intelligentsia who sought to introduce their younger counterparts to a literary heritage that had been denied them for the past two decades. In the context of specialist debates, events and publications, they made the case that free verse was a legitimate and serious form of poetry, and sought to recover the beginnings of a Russian free verse tradition at the beginning of the twentieth century which had been interrupted by the Stalin period.

There are several instances which illustrate this strategy of using the translation of foreign free verse as a vehicle for the rehabilitation of Russian Silver Age poetry. In the translation seminars she ran for students from 1954 into the 1980s, El'ga Linetskaia put such ideas into practice and introduced her students to poets who had been expunged from the canon of Russian literature; in his seminal work *Poeziia i perevod*,[16] Efim Etkind argued for the place of free verse in modern Russian poetry and poetry translations; and arguments about free verse translation and its relation to the Russian tradition were put forward by several leading translators and literary scholars during a round table discussion of the problems of translating poetry which was published in 1972.

El'ga Linetskaia was one of several important figures who taught literature and translation to young people, mostly students, in Leningrad from the 1950s. She received this position in the early Thaw; along with others of her generation such as Anna Akhmatova, Lidiia Ginzburg, and Dmitrii Maksimov, she became an important teacher and interlocutor for the young generation during the Thaw and the late Soviet period.[17] She argued that translators of foreign poetry needed to know Russian poetry, and used her seminars to pass on to her students the literary culture that she had known in her youth. The unusual friendships between the older and younger generations in Leningrad during this time played a key role in the transmission of cultural knowledge and values that had been sidelined and censored during the Stalin period.[18]

Records of Linetskaia's seminars and of the exciting encounters with forbidden poetry that took place in them exist only in memoirs: fortunately, these were collected and published by one of her former students, Mikhail Iasnov, in 1999.[19] Several accounts of her seminars refer to her theory that translations of poetry can only be successful if they draw on the tradition of the language of translation, and describe how she put this theory into practice:

---

16 Efim Etkind, *Poeziia i perevod* (Leningrad: Sovetskii pisatel', 1963).
17 See Elena Kumpan, 'Nashi stariki' in *Istoriia Leningradskoi nepodtsenzurnoi poezii* (St Petersburg: Dean, 2000), 29–38.
18 I have written about this in the first chapter of *Leningrad Poetry 1953–75*.
19 Mikhail Iasnov, ed., *El'ga L'vovna Linetskaia. Materialy k biografii: iz literaturnogo naslediia* (St Petersburg: Symposium, 1999).

> El'ga L'vovna rightly believed that translated poetry should draw on the source of Russian poetry; otherwise it would not have any life in it; for this reason, at her seminars there were always discussions of Russian poetry and poets – from Derzhavin to the present day. In those days, a lot of poets from the beginning of the century had still not recovered from being forcibly 'forgotten', and at her seminar many of us heard for the first time the names Mandel'shtam, Gumilev, Kuzmin, Parnok, Vaginov and others. All classes began with the recital of Russian poem, like prayers. Sometimes we chose the poems, sometimes El'ga L'vovna herself. Everybody read one poem. Sometimes El'ga L'vovna would ask us to guess the author. And since we always had to read a Russian poet in preparation for the seminar, we lived constantly in an atmosphere of Russian poetry and never lost the feeling of our native soil, our native traditions.[20]

Leonid Tsyv'ian has described the same readings of Russian poetry, remembering that Linetskaia introduced him to both Khodasevich and Vaginov;[21] and Elena Baevskaia, too, associates Linetskaia with 'unpublishable' or little-known literature that she made available to her students: Khodasevich, Nabokov and Kuzmin.[22]

Linetskaia's translation seminars were one of many literary groups across Leningrad and also in other cities in which members of the older generation shared the quest to pass on their literary culture and knowledge to students and young people. In many informal relationships between older translators and poets and young students of poetry and translation – including the famous friendships between Joseph Brodsky and Anna Akhmatova, Aleksandr Kushner and Lidiia Ginzburg – this culture and knowledge was also passed on; such relationships developed in academia as well, through meetings such as Dmitrii Maksimov's Blok seminars and the guidance and supervision of graduate students by Maksimov and Iurii Lotman.[23]

---

20 Maia Kviatkovskaia, 'O seminare El'gi L'vovny Linetskoi' in *El'ga L'vovna Linetskaia*, 139–42 (139–40).
21 Leonid Tsyv'ian, 'Takikh liudei bol'she net' in *El'ga L'vovna Linetskaia*, 146–8 (147).
22 Elena Baevskaia, 'Ob El'ge L'vovna Linetskoi' in *El'ga L'vovna Linetskaia*, 158–63 (159).
23 'Iz perepiski D. E. Maksimova s Iu. M. Lotmanom i Z. G. Mints', *Zvezda* 12 (2004), 110–44 (117).

Translation was a distinctive forum for these important literary relationships because the methodology of translation gave rise to not only a grass-roots and informal literary culture in which 'forgotten' authors were rediscovered, but also to a public debate about the importance of the Russian modernist tradition for translators of foreign poetry. Etkind's *Poeziia i perevod* was a landmark publication that made an important statement about the connection between the art of translation and the knowledge and understanding of Russian poetry, and furthered arguments for the recovery of the Russian Silver Age.

Etkind's book addresses various aspects of the translation of poetry; one chapter is devoted to free verse. This first sets out Etkind's argument as to why free verse is a valid and effective form for modern poetry: before he even approaches the question of its translation into Russian, he asserts the unique power that this form brings to a poem. He argues that the traditional division between poetry and prose may have been defined in terms of metre, rhyme and other elements of poetic form, but that modern poetry is defined by the intimacy of its tone, the intensity of its expression and its concentration of ideas:

> Poetic language is freed from singsong loftiness, from declaratory pathos, – its highest artistic quality becomes the living, and totally natural conversational intonation of an intimate exchange; the significance of the poetic subject is not increased by any external means. The poetic line [...] takes on such a powerful poetic expressiveness, that there is no need for external signs to show that it is different from prose.[24]

This establishment of the integrity of the form is crucial to Etkind's defence of it: he goes on to argue that Russian translators fail to translate free verse adequately into Russian because they do not appreciate its subtleties or special qualities. He is particularly critical of the way that many translators fail to capture the intonational organization of a poem, falling back instead on the use of compensatory additions to give the poem some structure. Such

---

24 Etkind, *Poeziia i perevod*, 321.

strategies include extraneous use of elaborate metaphors, the complication of the original and even the use of a 'classical' metre.²⁵

Etkind addresses the argument he claims some translators put forward in defence of their translations: that they render free verse in a strict form because Russian has no tradition of free verse and to do otherwise would be unsuccessful. At the heart of his refutation of this argument is the figure of Blok — a powerful authority whose reputation had survived the Stalin period to some degree, but whose work attracted renewed interest and acclaim during the Khrushchev Thaw. Etkind cites Blok's own works written in free verse, pointing to the existence of a tradition and model in Russian poetry, and argues that this free verse tradition which began with Blok was developed during the early decades of the twentieth century by Khlebnikov among others. Although Khlebnikov had been published during the Stalin period, his style of poetry had become unacceptable for poets and Etkind now suggests that translators return to this tradition to cope with the challenges presented to them by foreign free verse. He also draws attention to Blok's positive reviews of free verse translations made by Valerii Briusov, demonstrating that translation using free verse was an existing tradition in Russian which, again, had been broken by the Stalin years.

Etkind illustrates how translations of free verse which introduce strict form in the Russian version produce inadequate results by comparing Russian translations of free verse by the Turkish poet Nazim Hikmet and the Chilean Pablo Neruda, both of whom, as socialists and sympathizers with the Soviet cause, were widely translated in the USSR. In both cases, one translator has used strict form in Russian and the other has stayed closer to the original and produced a version in free verse; in both cases Etkind argues that the free verse translation is far superior. The imposition of metre on free verse, he argues, inevitably destroys the simplicity and distinctive effect of the original. To illustrate just how far this destroys the essence of the original, Etkind rewrites the opening stanza of Maiakovskii's *Oblaka*

---

25 Ibid., 322.

v shtanakh ('Cloud in Trousers') in iambic pentameter.[26] By deforming this canonical work by the most hallowed of all Soviet poets, he shows the kind of corruption introduced into foreign works when they are badly translated. The example also reinforces his argument that not all Russian poetry is written in strict form, and that the work of Maiakovskii provides a good example of the kind of free and experimental verse form required to translate Hikmet, Neruda and others.

The discussion of free verse and the problems it presents translators with is shown to have implications for the USSR's modern poets too: Etkind makes it clear that he believes the development of free verse is a modern, advanced stage in the development of poetry as an art. This analysis chimes with the official line at this point: that Soviet poetry had to develop and improve its level. When Etkind defines free verse in terms of its shift of emphasis from the formal features to the simplicity of individual words used precisely and without excess ornamentation, he seems to be pointing to the direction he believes Soviet poetry, too, might take:

> The work of many of the best poets of the twentieth century is based on an attempt to restore the value of the simple word, which is unadorned and not elevated by any means – not by the singsong quality of the line, nor the pathos of declaration. The poetry of Paul Eluard is like this, and of Bertold Brecht, Nazim Hikmet, Yiannis Ritsos, Pablo Neruda, Vítězslav Nezval, Langston Hughes – to name only those who are our closest contemporaries.[27]

In his analysis, the most important thing to understand about modern free verse written by foreign poets is that the careful choice of words – unhindered by considerations of metre and rhyme – is ultimately a more genuine form of expression than any other type of poetry. This creates a strong link between free verse and sincerity, one of the key concepts of the Thaw period introduced by writers such as Pomerantsev in 1954 and closely associated with the new *molodaia literatura* that had blossomed under Khrushchev's more liberal regime:

---

26   Ibid., 333.
27   Ibid., 325.

> A poet working on the translation of the newest poetic forms of a foreign poetry cannot fail to start thinking about the aesthetic meaning of these unusual, yet meaningful forms, even if they seem to him unusual in the poetry of his own tongue. Perhaps these forms are not better than the traditional ones he is used to. But they are different, and therefore able to convey to the reader a different poetic content. We must not forget the artistic meaning of free verse that was born of the twentieth century: in this poetic system, that has no pretensions, no violent emotion, no exaggeration, with all its modulations and shades, we hear a natural human voice: a voice that is not beholden to any external formal rules, and is therefore completely individual and genuine. Free verse is the contemporary form of a lyrical confession.[28]

Etkind here appeals to the spirit of the Thaw, invoking its enthusiasm for a more lyrical, individual voice in poetry, greater sincerity in literature and an unvarnished picture of reality, to make the case for the Soviet acceptance of foreign experiments in free verse, the rehabilitation of Russia's own modernist tradition and its incorporation into the range of forms acceptable for Soviet poetry.

Etkind's *Poeziia i perevod* appeared in 1963, just after what was arguably the height of the Thaw in 1962. His chapter on free verse was, in effect, a public polemic about the significance of free verse for the USSR at this point. While it is, of course, virtually impossible to assess the impact of Etkind's publication, it is clear that the problem he raised of how to translate Western poetry – especially more experimental poetry – was not resolved or forgotten. In the decade after the publication of Etkind's work, there were many more translations of foreign poets in free verse, but the significance of this form and its relationship to Soviet poetry remained difficult questions for Soviet translators. In 1972, the journal *Inostrannaia literatura* published a long article entitled 'Poeziia i perevod' ('Poetry and translation'), which comprised statements by a number of leading translators summarizing their contributions made to a round table discussion of this subject. Among the participants were Efim Etkind himself, the scholar Mikhail Gasparov, and the poets Semen Lipkin and Boris Slutskii.[29] From the discussion it is clear that the case for free verse and its significance was still the subject of

---

28 Ibid., 343–4.
29 'Poeziia i perevod', *Inostrannaia literatura* 2 (1972), 189–223.

argument, and that translators were still having to justify to a conservative establishment its use in both translations and original poetry in Russian.

E. Gal'perina's contribution to the discussion was devoted to the problem of free verse; specifically she addressed the subject of 'Variety within free verse and the possibilities for its translation'. She began by reminding the discussants that many progressive poets in the West who wrote on socialist themes and were sympathizers of the USSR used free verse in their work, obliging Soviet translators to find effective ways of translating the form:

> Happily we no longer face the dilemma of 'snotty, but on our side' or 'talented, but not one of us'. It is possible to draw freely from wide-ranging, varied progressive poetry from many countries. But it is very often written in free verse, and therefore it is natural that at the centre of our attention is the problem of translating free verse.[30]

The fact that she raises this question of how to translate free verse indicates that this was still a much-debated and unresolved question in 1972. This impression is reinforced by the inordinate amount of attention paid specifically to free verse in the discussion of poetry translation more broadly.

There was wide acknowledgement that free verse posed a particular challenge to Russian translators, largely because of its infrequent use in Soviet poetry, and this meant that the discussion of translation technique again led to reflections upon the Russian poetic tradition and the history of free verse therein. Kirill Koval'dzhi argued that, because free verse had been used relatively little in the Russian tradition, its translation posed a particular problem. As with many others, he sidestepped the issue of why this was so, attributing the phenomenon to various factors:

> In Russian poetry a variety of reasons has meant that there has not been an objective need to develop free verse, therefore it is still not widely developed here and, since it is not sufficiently developed, it poses so many problems for translators.[31]

In the arguments of some others, however, there was more of an acknowledgement that the tradition of free verse in Russia had not been allowed

30   Ibid., 212.
31   Ibid., 198.

to develop as it might have, but that it now needed to be recognized and used by translators to inform their work. V. Ivanov made a strong case for translators returning to the Russian free verse tradition, especially that of the Silver Age:

> When we talk about free verse it is important to underline that there is a Russian tradition of free verse, which we've managed to forget or not notice. Fet's free verse poems are famous. At the beginning of the century, apart from individual poems by Blok, Khlebnikov ('Zverinets' and others), Gumilev, Mandel'shtam and apart from other experiments in free verse there were also whole books in vers libre. In a recently published book containing the letters of the Russian diplomat and music specialist G. V Chicherin about Mozart, he talks about the contemporary dissonance in music created by Kuzmin for the words of his 'Alexandrian Songs'. But the contemporary, wonderful form of this cycle is free verse, constructed on the basis of syntactic parallelism of lines, the principles of which V. M. Zhirmunskii was working out back in the 1920s in his work on the composition of lyric poems. We must turn to this, our tradition, and master it – this will be the key to the success of future translations, which must create free verse using the means available in Russian verse.[32]

The specific references in this argument underline that in the 1920s there was still an active interest in free verse in the USSR and that there is much that can be recovered and used in the development of adequate translations in free verse. The specific detail continues Etkind's earlier polemic, again identifying specific authors and works relevant for translators working with free verse.

Vil' Ganiev also proposed that in order to make successful translations of free verse into Russian, translators would have to uncover the potential for free verse specific to the Russian language, and that this work had not yet been done. He criticized the fact that translations in free verse often sounded like literal, line-by-line versions (*podstrochniki*) rather than polished translations, as though the poet had 'retold' rather than 'recreated' the poems. His contribution, entitled 'Continuing the search', asserted that there was much work to be done by translators if they were to reach

---

32 Ibid., 204.

higher standards and produce adequate translations of poets such as Hikmet working in free verse.[33]

Vladimir Ognev argued that for the successful translation of free verse in Russia, translators need to be aware of the different currents within their own tradition. He suggested that at different points in history there has been more or less readiness to translate certain authors. Thus, before Blok began to use the *dol'nik*, modern Russian poetry was not ready to produce good translations of Heine. Lermontov's and Tiutchev's irregular rhythms were needed to disrupt the too smooth, 'sing-song' style in poetry so that harsher-sounding poets could be translated well into Russian. In terms of modern authors, he suggests that in order to translate Neruda, Hikmet, Ritsos and Różewicz, Russian translators will need to know not only Maiakovskii and the free verse used by Briusov and Chukovskii in translations of Verhaeren and Whitman, but also the work of contemporary poets Tikhonov, Sel'vinskii and Slutskii.[34] By highlighting the history of foreign influence on Russian poetry that was brought about through translations, he refuted the idea that Russian poetry had a path of development separate from Western European and American literature. His conception of translation methodology as a combination of innovations in Russian poetry and influences from translations embraced the idea that the relationship between Russian poetry and translation was one of mutual influence and dependency.

Other contributors, too, argued not only that Russian translators must look to their own poetry to learn how to translate free verse, and concomitantly that this requires the recovery of poets who have been neglected during much of the Soviet period, but also that the translation of free verse stimulates the further development of Russian poetry. Lev Ozerov argues that in the nineteenth and twentieth centuries translators have had to search for new forms in order to cope with the task of translation, and that this has been useful for Russian poetry as well as for translation:

33 Ibid., 219–20.
34 Ibid., 196.

> For translations of poets like Lorca and Tuwim, Pablo Neruda and Nicolás Guillén, new forms of expression had to be found. Of course, these turned out to be in Russian verse, or rather, in Russian speech, but they had to be found. And these very attempts to find them brought unquestionable benefit to our poetry – not only to translations, but to original works as well.[35]

Like Etkind's *Poeziia i perevod*, Ozerov's contribution to this debate proposed not only that translation of free verse should draw upon strengths of the Russian tradition which had often been neglected, but also that the process of translation – a dialogue with other traditions – should bring new ideas to and refresh modern Soviet poetry, specifically introducing free verse into Russian poetry. This far-reaching argument was largely beyond the pale until the very end of the Soviet period (and, arguably, conservatism remained dominant in Russian poetry well after 1991 as well), but it demonstrates that theorists and critics used translation not only as an argument for the recovery of the Silver Age, but also to try to alter the norms of Soviet poetry.

This chapter has shown that, in the context of a conservative establishment and continuing censorship, the openness to the West in vogue during the Thaw created a moment when a sudden influx of Western poetry and the challenge to translate it threw open questions about Russian poetry. As in other periods of Russian literary history, translation again became a focal point for questions about the development of Russian poetry. These questions looked both backwards and forwards: on the one hand reconsidering the shape of the canon of Russian poetry, and on the other addressing questions of how formal norms of Soviet poetry should further develop.

---

35   Ibid., 211.

Select Bibliography

The select bibliography contains works related to the study of translation as accommodation, as defined in this volume, and attempts to establish the field for this approach to the subject. It includes works on the cultural significance and reception of translation but excludes many linguistic and methodological studies. The main focus is on English and Russian publications, but some works of importance in other languages also appear.

Adamantova, Eva (1991), 'L'art de traduire selon Maximillian Volochine: la fidélité et la créativité – *Le cygne* de S. Mallarmé', *Meta*, 36:2–3, 461–70
Adams, Robert M. (1973), *Proteus: His Lies, His Truth: Discussions of Literary Translation*, New York: Norton
Aiwei, Shi (2004), 'Accommodation in Translation', *Translation Journal*, 8:3
Alekseev, M. P. (1964), 'William Ralston and Russian Writers of the Later Nineteenth Century', *Oxford Slavonic Papers*, 11, 82–93
—— (1994), *Vil'iam Rol'ston – propagandist russkoi literatury i fol'klora: s prilozheniem pisem Rol'stona k russkim korrespondentam*, St Petersburg: Nauka
——, ed. (1963/1994), *Mezhdunarodnye sviazi russkoi literatury: Sbornik statei*, Moscow and Leningrad: Nauka
Alexeeva, Irina, ed. (2004), *Vvedenie v perevodovedenie*, St Petersburg: St Petersburg State University
Alvarez, Román & Carmen-Africa Vidal, eds (1996), *Translation, Power, Subversion*, Clevedon: Multilingual Matters
Amos, Flora Ross (1920/73), *Early Theories of Translation*, New York: Octagon
Andrews, Edna & Elena Maksimova (2009), *Russian Translation: Theory and Practice*, London: Routledge
Anschel, Eugene, ed. (1974), *The American Image of Russia, 1775–1917*, New York: Ungar
Apter, Emily (2005), *The Translation Zone: A New Comparative Literature*, Princeton: Princeton University Press
Apter, Ronnie (1984), *Digging for Treasure: Translation after Pound*, New York: Peter Lang
Arnold, Matthew (1861/1978), *On Translating Homer*, London: AMS Press

Baer, Brian James (2011), 'Oppositional Effects: (Mis)translating Empire in Modern Russian Literature' in Dimitris Asimakoulas & Margaret Rogers, eds, *Translation and Opposition*, Clevedon: Multilingual Matters, 93–110

——, ed. (2011), *Contexts, Subtexts, and Pretexts: Literary Translation in Eastern Europe and Russia*, Amsterdam: John Benjamins

Bailey, James (1969), 'Blok and Heine: An Episode from the History of Russian Dol'niki', *Slavic and East European Journal*, 13:1

Baker, Mona (2006), *Translation and Conflict: A Narrative Account*, London: Routledge

—— (2010), *Critical Readings in Translation Studies*, Abingdon: Routledge

—— & Gabriela Saldanha (2008), *Routledge Encyclopedia of Translation Studies*, 2nd edn, London: Routledge

Balcerzan, Edward (1978), 'Perevod kak tvorchestvo', *Babel*, 24:3–4, 124–6

Barnstone, William (1993), *The Poetics of Translation: History, Theory, Practice*, New Haven: Yale University Press

Bassnett, Susan (1980/2002), *Translation Studies*, 3rd edn, London: Routledge

—— (1993), *Comparative Literature: A Critical Introduction*, Oxford: Blackwell

——, ed. (1997), *Translating Literature*, Cambridge: Brewer

—— & André Lefevere (1998), *Constructing Cultures: Essays on Literary Translation*, Clevedon: Multilingual Matters

—— & André Lefevere, eds (1990), *Translation, History and Culture*, London: Pinter

—— & Harish Trivedi, eds (1999), *Post-Colonial Translation: Theory and Practice*, London: Routledge

Bates, E. S. (1943), *Intertraffic: Studies in Translation*, London: Jonathan Cape

Beasley, Rebecca & Philip Ross Bullock, eds (2011), *Translating Russia, 1890–1935* [Special issue of *Translation and Literature* 20:3]

Beaujour, Elizabeth Klosty (1989), *Alien Tongues: Bilingual Russian Writers of the 'First' Emigration*, Ithaca: Cornell University Press

Belitt, Ben (1978), *Adam's Dream: A Preface to Translation*, New York: Grove Press

Bell, R. (1991), *Translation and Translating: Theory and Practice*, London: Longman

Benjamin, Andrew (1989), *Translation and the Nature of Philosophy: A New Theory of Words*, London: Routledge

Benjamin, Walter (1923/1955), 'Die Aufgabe des Übersetzers' in Walter Benjamin, *Baudelaire: Tableaux parisiens*, Heidelberg [reprinted (1955) in *Schriften*, ed. Theodor Adorno et al., 1, 40–54, Frankfurt: Suhrkamp; trans. Harry Zohn (1992), as 'The Task of the Translator' in Rainer Schulte & John Biguenet, *Theories of Translation*, 71–82]

Berkov, P. N. (1935), 'Rannie russkie perevodchiki Goratsiia', *Izvestiia AN SSSR. Otdelenie obschestvennykh nauk*, 10, 1039–56

Berman, Antoine (1984), *L'Epreuve de l'étranger: Culture et traduction dans l'Allemagne romantique*, Paris: Gallimard [trans. S. Heyvaert (1992), as *The Experience of the Foreign: Culture and Translation in Romantic Germany*, Albany: State University of New York Press]
—— (1985/99), *Traduction et la lettre ou l'auberge du lointain*, Paris: Seuil
—— (1995), *Pour une critique des traductions: John Donne*, Paris: Gallimard [trans. & ed. Françoise Massardier-Kenney (2009), as *Toward a Translation Criticism: John Donne*, Kent, OH: Kent State University Press]
—— (2008), *L'âge de la traduction: 'La tâche du traducteur' de Walter Benjamin, un commentaire*, Saint-Denis: Presses universitaires de Vincennes
Bernofsky, Susan (2005), *Foreign Words: Translator-Authors in the Age of Goethe*, Detroit: Wayne State University Press
Bershtein, Evgenii (2000), 'The Russian Myth of Oscar Wilde' in Laura Engelstein & Stephanie Sandler, eds, *Self and Story in Russian History*, Ithaca: Cornell University Press, 168–88
Bhabha, Homi (1994), *The Location of Culture*, London: Routledge
Biguenet, John & Rainer Schulte, eds (1989), *The Craft of Translation*, Chicago: University of Chicago Press
Blium, A. V. (2008), 'Index librorum prohibitorum zarubezhnykh pisatelei (v perevodakh na russkii iazyk 1917–1991 gg.)', *Novoe literaturnoe obozrenie*, 92, 125–39
Bly, Robert (1983), *The Eight Stages of Translation*, Boston: Rowan Tree
Boase-Beier, Jean & Michael Holman, eds (1999), *The Practices of Literary Translation: Constraints and Creativity*, Manchester: St Jerome
Boéri, Julie & Carol Maier (2010), *Translation/Interpreting and Social Activism*, Manchester: St Jerome
Bohannan, Laura (1997), 'Shakespeare in the Bush' in James Spradley & David W. McCurdy, eds, *Conformity and Conflict: Readings in Cultural Anthropology*, New York: Longman
Bolt, Ranjit (2010), *The Art of Translation*, London: Oberon
Bowker, Lynne, Dorothy Kenny & Jennifer Pearson, eds (1998 onwards), *Bibliography of Translation Studies*, Manchester: St Jerome
Brandenberger, David (2002), *National Bolshevism: Stalinist Mass Culture and the Formation of Modern Russian National Identity, 1931–1956*, Cambridge, MA: Harvard University Press
Brodzki, Bella (2007), *Can these Bones Live? Translation, Survival, and Cultural Memory*, Stanford: Stanford University Press
Brown, M. H. (1994), *The Reception of Spanish American Fiction in West Germany 1981–91*, Tübingen: Niemeyer

Budick, S. & W. Iser, eds (1996), *The Translatability of Cultures: Figurations of the Space Between*, Stanford: Stanford University Press

Bullock, Philip Ross (2009), 'The Cruel Art of Beauty: Walter Pater and the Uncanny Aestheticism of Isaak Babel's *Red Cavalry*', *Modern Language Review*, 104:2, 499–529

Burke, Peter & R. Po-chia Hsia, eds (2007), *Cultural Translation in Early Modern Europe*, Cambridge: Cambridge University Press

Burnett, Leon (1996), 'Neither Nomos nor Polis: Locating the Translator', *Translation and Literature*, 5, 149–66

—— (2000), 'Dostoevsky's "New Word": A Short and Curious Note on Language Acquisition', *New Comparison*, 29, 81–6

—— (2003), 'Languages (Un)twinned: The Dynamic of Differentiation in Mandelstam and Radnóti', *Translation and Literature*, 12:2, 205–30 [includes appendix: 'About Translation, by Miklós Radnóti', trans. Anita Klujber & Leon Burnett, 227–30]

—— (2003), 'On First Looking into Zhukovskii's Homer: Gogol and Cultural Assimilation', *Essays in Poetics*, 28, 12–35

——, ed. (1997), *Word in Time: Poetry, Narrative, Translation. Essays for Arthur Terry on the Occasion of his 70th Birthday*, Colchester: University of Essex

Bushmanova, Natalya I., ed. (1997), *Russian Translation Studies*, Copenhagen: University of Copenhagen

Chekalov, Ivan (1991), 'Perevody *Gamleta* M. Lozinskim, A. Radlovoi i B. Pasternakom v otsenke sovetskoi kritiki 30-kh godov' in *Shekspirovskie chteniia 1990*, Moscow: Nauka, 177–200

Chesterman, Andrew (1997), *Memes of Translation: The Spread of Ideas in Translation Theory*, Amsterdam: John Benjamins

——, ed. (1989), *Readings in Translation Theory*, Helsinki: Finn Lectura

Cheyfitz, Eric (1991), *The Poetics of Imperialism: Translation and Colonization from The Tempest to Tarzan*, Oxford: Oxford University Press

Chukovskii, Kornei (1964), *Vysokoe iskusstvo: o printsipakh khudozhestvennogo perevoda*, Moscow: Iskusstvo

—— (1984), *The Art of Translation: Kornei Chukovsky's 'A High Art'*, trans. & ed. Lauren Leighton, Knoxville: University of Tennessee Press

Chukovskii, Kornei & Andrei Fedorov (1930), *Iskusstvo perevoda*, Leningrad: Academia

Clark, K. & E. Dobrenko, eds (2007), *Soviet Culture and Power: A History in Documents, 1917–1953*, New Haven: Yale University Press

Classe, Olive, ed. (2000), *Encyclopedia of Literary Translation into English*, 2 vols, London: Fitzroy Dearborn

Clayton, J. Douglas (1978), 'The Hamlets of Turgenev and Pasternak: On the Role of Poetic Myth in Literature', *Germano-Slavica*, 6, 455–61

―― (1983), 'The Theory and Practice of Poetic Translation in Pushkin and Nabokov', *Canadian Slavic Papers*, 25:1, 90–100
Cronin, Michael (1996), *Translating Ireland: Translation, Languages, Cultures* Cork: Cork University Press
―― (2000), *Across the Lines: Travel, Language, Translation*, Cork: Cork University Press
―― (2003), *Translation and Globalization*, London: Routledge
Delabastita, Dirk & Lieven D'hulst, eds (1993), *European Shakespeares: Translating Shakespeare in the Romantic Age*, Amsterdam: John Benjamins
Delisle, Jean & Judith Woodsworth, eds (1995), *Translators through History*, Amsterdam: John Benjamins
Deriugin, A. A. (1995), 'Soderzhanie perevodcheskogo priema *sklonenie na nashi (russkie) nravy*', *Izvestiia RAN. Seriia literatury i iazyka*, 54:5, 61–4
Derrida, Jacques (1982), *The Ear of the Other: Otobiography, Transference, Translation*, trans. Peggy Kamuf, Lincoln: University of Nebraska Press
―― (1985), 'Des tours de Babel' in Joseph F. Graham, ed., *Difference in Translation*, Ithaca: Cornell University Press, 209–48 [trans. Joseph F. Graham in same volume, 165–207]
―― (1998), *Monolingualism of the Other; or the Prosthesis of Origin*, trans. Patrick Mensah, Stanford: Stanford University Press
Dingwaney, Anuradha & Carol Maier, eds (1995), *Between Languages and Cultures: Translation and Cross-Cultural Texts*, Pittsburgh: University of Pittsburgh
During, Simon (2007), *Cultural Studies Reader*, 3rd edn, London: Routledge
Easthope, Antony (1991), *Literary into Cultural Studies*, London: Routledge
Eco, Umberto (2001), *Experiences in Translation*, trans. Alastair McEwen, Toronto: University of Toronto Press
―― (2003), *Mouse or Rat? Translation as Negotiation*, London: Phoenix
Egunov, A. N. (1964), *Gomer v russkikh perevodakh XVIII–XIX vekov*, Moscow and Leningrad
Emerson, Caryl (1983), 'Translating Bakhtin: Does his Theory of Discourse Contain a Theory of Translation?', *University of Ottawa Quarterly*, 53:1, 23–33
Etkind, Efim (1963), *Poeziia i perevod*, Leningrad: Sovetskii pisatel'
Evangelista, Stefano, ed. (2010), *The European Reception of Oscar Wilde*, London: Continuum
Even-Zohar, Itamar (1990), 'Polysystems Studies', *Poetics Today*, 11:1
Fabricius-Hansen, Cathrine & Johannes Ostbo, eds (2000), *Übertragung, Annäherung, Angleichung: sieben Beiträge zu Theorie und Praxis des Übersetzens*, Frankfurt am Main: Peter Lang

Fawcett, Peter (1997), *Translation and Language: Linguistic Approaches Explained*, Manchester: St Jerome
Fedorov, A. V. (1953/1958), *Vvedenie v teoriiu perevoda*, 2nd rev. edn, Moscow: Literature in Foreign Languages [3rd edn (1968), published as *Osnovy obshchei teorii perevoda*, Moscow: Vysshaia shkola]
—— (1983), *Iskusstvo perevoda i zhizn' literatury*, Leningrad: Sovetskii pisatel'
—— (2006), *O khudozhestvennom perevode: Raboty 1920–1940-kh godov*, St Petersburg: Philological Faculty of St Petersburg University
Feleppa, R. (1988), *Convention, Translation, and Understanding: Philosophical Problems in the Comparative Study of Culture*, Albany: State University of New York Press
Fleishman, Lazar' (2005), *Boris Pasternak i literaturnoe dvizhenie 1930-kh godov*, St Petersburg: Akademicheskii proekt
Flotow, Luise von (1997), *Translation and Gender: Translating in the 'Era of Feminism'*, Manchester: St Jerome
France, Anna Kay (1973), 'Boris Pasternak's Interpretation of Hamlet', *Russian Literature Triquarterly*, 7, 201–26
France, Peter, ed. (2000), *The Oxford Guide to Literature in English Translation*, Oxford: Oxford University Press
—— & Kenneth Haynes, eds (2006), *The Oxford History of Literary Translation in English 4: 1790–1900*, Oxford: Oxford University Press
Frawley, William, ed. (1984), *Translation: Literary, Linguistic and Philosophical Perspectives*, Newark and London: Associated University Presses
Friedberg, Maurice (1977), *A Decade of Euphoria: Western Literature in Post-Stalin Russia, 1954–64*, Bloomington: Indiana University Press
—— (1997), *Literary Translation in Russia: A Cultural History*, University Park: Pennsylvania State University Press
Gachechiladze, G. R. (1970), *Vvedenie v teoriyu khudozhestvennogo perevoda*, Tbilisi: Izdatel'stvo TGU
—— (1972), *Khudozhestvennyi perevod i literaturnye vzaimosviazi*, Moscow: Sovietskii Pisatel'
Gambier, Yves & Luc van Doorslaer (2011), *Handbook of Translation Studies 1*, Amsterdam: John Benjamins
—— & Luc van Doorslaer, eds (2009), *The Metalanguage of Translation*, Amsterdam: John Benjamins
Ganiev, V. Kh. et al., eds (1973), *Khudozhestvennyi perevod: vzaimodeistvie i vzaimoobogashchenie literatur*, Erevan: Izd. Erevanskogo universiteta
García Yebra, V. (1982), *Teoría y práctica de la traducción*, Madrid: Gredos
Garrison, James D. (2009), *A Dangerous Liberty: Translating Gray's Elegy*, Newark: University of Delaware Press

Gasparov, Mikhail L., ed. (2001), *O russkoi poezii*, St Petersburg: Azbuka
Genis, Aleksandr & Petr Vail' (1988), *60-e: mir sovetskogo cheloveka*, Ann Arbor: Ardis
Gentzler, Edwin (1993/2001), *Contemporary Translation Theories*, 2nd rev. edn, Clevedon: Multilingual Matters
Gettman, Royal A. (1941), *Turgenev in England and America*, Urbana: University of Illinois Press
Giblett, Rodney (1987), 'Translating "the other": Nabokov and theories of translation', *Babel*, 33:3, 157–60
Gillespie, Stuart & John Hopkins, eds (2005), *The Oxford History of Literary Translation in English Volume 3: 1660–1790*, Oxford: Oxford University Press
Girivenko, Andrei N., ed. (2002), *Iz istorii russkogo khudozhestvennogo perevoda pervoi poloviny XIX veka: Epokha romantizma*, Moscow: Nauka
Gordon, Ia. I. (1979), *Geine v Rossii 1870–1917 gg.*, Dushanbe: Donish
—— (1983), *Geine v Rossii: XX vek*, Dushanbe: Donish
Goscilo, Helena (1990), 'Introduction: A Nation in Search of its Authors' in Helena Goscilo & Byron Lyndsey, eds, *Glasnost: An Anthology of Russian Literature under Gorbachov*, Ann Arbor: Ardis, xv–xlv
Graham, Joseph F., ed. (1985), *Difference in Translation*, Ithaca: Cornell University Press
Grayson, Jane (1977), *Nabokov Translated*, Oxford: Oxford University Press
Grossman, Joan Delaney (1973), *Edgar Allan Poe in Russia: A Study in Legend and Literary Influence*, Würzburg: Jal-Verlag
Guenthner, F. & M. Guenthner-Reutter, eds (1978), *Meaning and Translation: Philosophical and Linguistic Approaches*, London: Duckworth
Gutt, Ernst-August (1991/2000), *Translation and Relevance: Cognition and Context*, 2nd edn, Manchester: St Jerome
Hardwick, Lorna (2000), *Translating Words, Translating Cultures*, London: Duckworth
Hatim, Basil & Ian Mason (1990), *Discourse and the Translator*, London: Longman
—— & Ian Mason (1997), *The Translator as Communicator*, London: Routledge
Hermans, Theo (1996), 'The Translator's Voice in Translated Narrative', *Target*, 8:1, 23–48
—— (1999), *Translation in Systems: Descriptive and Systemic Approaches Explained*, Manchester: St Jerome
—— (2007), *The Conference of the Tongues*, Manchester: St Jerome
——, ed. (1985), *The Manipulation of Literature: Studies in Literary Translation*, London: Croom Helm
——, ed. (2006), *Translating Others*, 2 vols, Manchester: St Jerome
Heylen, Romy (1993), *Translation, Poetics and the Stage: Six French Hamlets*, London: Routledge

Hodgson, Katharine (2005), 'Heine's Russian Doppelgänger: Nineteenth-Century Translations of his Poetry', *Modern Language Review*, 4, 1054-72

Hofstadter, Douglas R. (1997), *Le Ton beau de Marot: In Praise of the Music of Language*, New York: Basic Books

Holmes, James S. (1988), *Translated! Papers on Literary Translation and Translation Studies*, 2nd edn, Amsterdam: Rodopi

——, ed. (1970), *The Nature of Translation: Essays on the Theory and Practice of Literary Translation*, The Hague: Mouton

—— & R. C. Holub (1984), *Reception Theory: A Critical Introduction*, London: Methuen

——, José Lambert & Raymond van den Broeck, eds (1978), *Literature and Translation*, Leuven: Academic

Homel, David & Sherry Simon, eds (1988), *Mapping Literature: The Art and Politics of Translation*, Montreal: Véhicle Press

Honig, Edwin, ed. (1985), *The Poet's Other Voice: Conversations on Literary Translation*, Amherst: University of Massachusetts Press

Hung, Eva, ed. (2005), *Translation and Cultural Change: Studies in History, Norms and Image-Projection*, Amsterdam: John Benjamins

—— & Judy Wakabayashi, eds (2005), *Asian Translation Traditions*, Manchester, St Jerome

Iasnov, Mikhail, ed. (1999), *El'ga L'vovna Linetskaia: Materialy k biografii. Iz literaturnogo naslediia*, St Petersburg: Symposium

Iser, Wolfgang (1995), 'On Translatability: Variables of Interpretation', *The European English Messenger*, 4:1, 30-8

Ivbulis, Viktors, ed. (2002), *Language, Literature and Translation Manipulations*, Riga: University of Latvia

Jachia, Paolo (1992), 'Il problema della traduzione in Michail Bachtin', *Koiné*, 1-2, 129-36

Jauss, Hans Robert (1982), *Toward an Aesthetic of Reception*, trans. from the German by Timothy Bahti, Brighton: Harvester Press

Jin, Di (2003), *Literary Translation: Quest for Artistic Integrity*, Manchester: St Jerome

Kahn, Andrew (2000), '*Le Fils naturel* et la réforme de la comédie russe' in *Etudes sur Le Fils naturel et les Entretiens sur le Fils naturel de Diderot*, ed. Nicholas Cronk, Oxford: Voltaire Foundation, 159-70

Károly, Kristina & Ágota Fóris, eds (2005), *New Trends in Translation Studies: In Honour of Kinga Klaudy*, Budapest: Akadémiai Kiadó

Kashkin, Ivan (1977), *Dlia chitatelia sovremennika: stat'i i issledovaniia*, Moscow: Sovetskii pisatel'

Kazakova, Tamara A. (2006), *Khudozhestvennyi perevod: teoriia i praktika*, St Petersburg: In"iazizdat

Kelly, Louis G. (1979), *The True Interpreter: A History of Translation Theory and Practice in the West*, Oxford: Blackwell

Kemppanen, Hannu, Marja Jänis & Alexandra Belikova, eds (2012), *Domestication and Foreignization in Translation Studies*, Berlin: Frank & Timme

Khairoulline, Vladimir (2010), *Perevod i freimy*, Moscow: Librocom

Kittel, Harald, ed. (1988), *Die literarische Übersetzung: Stand und Perspektiven ihrer Erforschung*, Berlin: Erich Schmidt

—— & Armin Paul Frank, eds (1991), *Interculturality and the Historical Study of Literary Translations*, Berlin: Erich Schmidt

—— et al., eds (2004), *Übersetzung – Translation – Traduction: An International Encyclopedia of Translation Studies*, Berlin: de Gruyter

Koller, Werner (1979/1992), *Einführung in die Übersetzungswissenschaft*, 4th rev. edn, Heidelberg: Quelle & Meyer

Komissarov, V. N. (1990), *Teoriia perevoda*, Moscow: Vysshaia shkola

—— (1998), 'The Russian Tradition' in Mona Baker, ed. *Routledge Encyclopedia of Translation Studies*, London: Routledge

Korsak, Mary Phil (1992), *At the Start: Genesis Made New: A New Translation of the Hebrew Text*, London: Doubleday

Kuhiwczak, Piotr & Karin Littau, eds (2007), *A Companion to Translation Studies*, Clevedon: Multilingual Matters

Kujamäki, Pekka et al., eds (2011), *Beyond Borders: Translations Moving Languages, Literatures and Cultures*, Berlin: Frank & Timme

Kuzio, Anna (2010), *Gender, Culture and Ideology in Translation*, Saarbrücken: LAP Lambert

Larose, Robert (1989), *Théories contemporaines de la traduction*, 2nd edn, Quebec: Presses de l'Université du Québec

Lecercle, Jean-Jacques (1990), *The Violence of Language*, London: Routledge

Lefevere, André (1975), *Translating Poetry: Seven Strategies and a Blueprint*, Assen: Van Gorcum

—— (1982), 'Mother Courage's Cucumbers: Text, System and Refraction in a Theory of Literature', *Modern Language Studies*, 12:4, 3–20

—— (1986), 'Why the Real Heine Can't Stand up in/to Translation: Rewriting as the Way to Literary Influence', *New Comparison*, 1, 83–92

—— (1992), *Translating Literature: Practice and Theory in a Comparative Literature Context*, New York: Modern Language Association of America

—— (1992), *Translation, Rewriting, and the Manipulation of Literary Fame*, London: Routledge

——, ed. (1992), *Translation/History/Culture: A Sourcebook*, London: Routledge
Leighton, Lauren (1991), *Two Worlds, One Art: Literary Translation in Russia and America*, DeKalb: Northern Illinois University Press
Leppihalme, Ritva (1997), *Culture Bumps: An Empirical Approach to the Translation of Allusions*, Clevedon: Multilingual Matters
Leuven-Zwart, Kitty M. van (1989), 'Translation and Original: Similarities and Dissimilarities, I', *Target*, 1, 151–82
—— (1990), 'Translation and Original: Similarities and Dissimilarities, II', *Target*, 2, 69–96
—— & Ton Naaijkens, eds (1991), *Translation Studies: The State of the Art*, Amsterdam: Rodopi
Levin, Iurii (1985), *Russkie perevodchiki XIX veka i razvitie khudozhestvennogo perevoda*, Leningrad: Nauka
—— (1988), *Shekspir i russkaia literatura XIX veka*, Leningrad: Nauka
——, ed. (1991), *Na rubezhe XIX i XX vekov: iz istorii mezhdunarodnykh sviazei russkoi literatury. Sbornik nauchnykh trudov*, Leningrad: Nauka
——, ed. (1995), *Istoriia russkoi perevodnoi khudozhestvennoi literatury. Drevniaia Rus': XVIII vek. Tom I: Proza. Tom II. Dramaturgiia. Poeziia.*, St Petersburg: Russian Academy of Sciences Institute of Russian Literature
—— & Andrei Fedorov (1960), *Russkie pisateli o perevode*, Leningrad: Russkii pisatel'
Levine, Suzanne Jill (1991), *The Subversive Scribe: Translating Latin American Fiction*, St Paul, MN: Graywolf Press
Levý, Jiri (1963), *Umění překladu*, Prague: Československý spisovatel [trans. W. Schamschula (1969), as *Die Literarische Übersetzung: Theorie einer Kunstgattung* Frankfurt: Athenäum]
—— (2011), *The Art of Translation*, trans. Patrick Corness, Amsterdam: John Benjamins
Lianeri, Alexandra & Vanda Zajko, eds (2008), *Translation and the Classic: Identity as Change in the History of Culture*, Oxford: Oxford University Press
Lotman, Iurii M. (2000), 'Ocherki po istorii russkoi kul'tury XVIII–nachala XIX veka', *Iz istorii russkoi kul'tury*, IV, Moscow: Iazyki russkoi kul'tury
Lotman, Yuri M. (1990), *Universe of the Mind: A Semiotic Theory of Culture*, trans. Ann Shukman, London: Tauris
Louth, Charlie (1998), *Hölderlin and the Dynamics of Translation*, Oxford: Legenda
Lowell, Robert (1961), *Imitations*, New York: Farrar, Straus & Giroux
Luppol, I. K., M. M. Rozental' & S. M. Tretiakov, eds (1934/1990), *Pervyi vsesoiuznyi s"ezd sovetskikh pisatelei 1934, stenograficheskii otchet*, Moscow: Sovetskii pisatel'
Lygo, Emily (2010), *Leningrad Poetry 1953–1975: The Thaw Generation*, Oxford: Peter Lang

Makaryk, Irena R. & Joseph G. Price, eds (1982), *Shakespeare in the Worlds of Communism and Socialism*, Toronto: University of Toronto Press
Markov, Vladimir (1961), 'An Unnoticed Aspect of Pasternak's Translations', *Slavic Review*, 3, 503–8
Masterstvo perevoda (1955–1990), 1–13, Moscow: Sovetskii pisatel'
Matejka, Ladislav & Krystyna Pomorska, eds (1971), *Readings in Russian Poetics: Formalist and Structuralist Views*, Cambridge, MA: MIT Press
May, Rachel (1994), *The Translator in the Text: On Reading Russian Literature in English*, Evanston, IL: Northwestern University Press
McLean, Hugh (1963), 'The Adventures of an English Comedy in Eighteenth-Century Russia: Dodsley's *Toy Shop* and Lukin's *Ščepitil'nik*' in *American Contributions to the Fifth International Congress of Slavists, Sofia, September 1963*, The Hague: Mouton, 201–12
Meyer, Priscilla (2008), *How the Russians Read the French: Lermontov, Dostoevsky, Tolstoy*, Madison: University of Wisconsin Press
Milton, John & Paul Bandia, eds (2009), *Agents of Translation*, Amsterdam: John Benjamins
Moeller-Sally, Betsy F. (1990), 'Oscar Wilde and the Culture of Russian Modernism', *Slavic and East European Journal*, 34:4, 459–72
Moracci, Giovanna (1996), 'Gallomania, società e morale nella commedia russa fra il XVIII e XIX secolo', *Ricerche slavistiche*, 43, 381–416
Mounin, Georges (1955/1994), *Les Belles infidèles*, 2nd edn, Lille: Presses Universitaires de Lille
—— (1963), *Les problèmes théoriques de la traduction*, Paris: Gallimard
Mueller-Vollmer, Kurt & Michael Irmscher, eds (1998), *Translating Literatures, Translating Cultures: New Vistas and Approaches in Literary Studies*, Stanford: Stanford University Press
Munday, Jeremy (2001/2012), *Introducing Translation Studies: Theories and Applications*, 3rd edn, Abingdon: Routledge
Nabokov, Vladimir (1941/1981), 'The Art of Translation' in *Lectures on Russian Literature*, New York: Harcourt, 315–21
Nägele, Rainer (1997), *Echoes of Translation: Reading between Texts*, Baltimore: Johns Hopkins University Press
Neubert, Albert & G. M. Shreeve (1993), *Translation as Text*, Kent, OH: Kent State University Press
Newmark, Peter (1981), *Approaches to Translation*, Oxford: Pergamon
Nida, Eugene A. (1964), *Toward a Science of Translating, with Special Reference to Principles and Procedures Involved in Bible Translation*, Leiden: Brill

Nida, Eugene A. & Charles R. Taber (1969), *The Theory and Practice of Translation*, Leiden: Brill
Nikiforovskaia, Nadezhda (1999), *Shekspir Borisa Pasternaka*, St Petersburg: BAN
Niranjana, Tejaswini (1992), *Siting Translation: History, Post-Structuralism, and the Colonial Context*, Berkeley: University of California Press
Nord, Christiane (1997), *Translating as a Purposeful Activity: Functionalist Approaches Explained*, Manchester: St Jerome
O'Sullivan, Carol, ed. (2008), *Translation and Negotiation*, Portsmouth: University of Portsmouth
O'Sullivan, Emer (2005), *Comparative Children's Literature*, Abingdon: Routledge
Palumbo, Giuseppe (2009), *Key Terms in Translation Studies*, London: Continuum
Papadima, Liviu, David Damrosch & Theo D'haen, eds (2011), *The Canonical Debate Today: Crossing Disciplinary and Cultural Boundaries*, Amsterdam: Rodopi
Parks, Tim (2007), *Translating Style: A Literary Approach to Translation – A Translation Approach to Literature*, Manchester: St Jerome
Pasternak, Boris (1944), 'Zametki perevodchika', *Znamia*, 1/2, 165–8
Paz, Octavio (1971), *Traducción: Literatura y Literalidad*, Barcelona: Tusquets [trans. Irene del Corral (1992), as 'Translation: Literature and Letters' in Rainer Schulte & John Biguenet, eds, *Theories of Translation*, 152–62]
Pinsent, Pat, ed. (2006), *No Child Is an Island: The Case for Children's Literature in Translation*, Lichfield: Pied Piper
Pokorn, Nike K. (2005), *Challenging the Traditional Axioms: Translation into a Non-Mother Tongue*, Amsterdam: John Benjamins
Polevoi, Nikolai (1830), 'Russkaia literatura: *Makbet*', *Moskovskii telegraf*, 27, 79–82
Polonsky, Rachel (1998), *English Literature and the Russian Aesthetic Renaissance*, Cambridge: Cambridge University Press
Poplavskii, Vitalii, ed. (2002), *'Gamlet' Borisa Pasternaka: versii i varianty perevoda shekspirovskoi tragedii*, Moscow: Letnii sad
Pound, Ezra (1954), *Literary Essays*, ed. T. S. Eliot, London: Faber & Faber
Proffer, Carl, ed. & trans. (1972), *Soviet Criticism of American Literature in the Sixties: An Anthology*, Ann Arbor: Ardis
Pushkin, Aleksandr (1837), 'O Mil'tone i perevode "Poteriannogo raia" Shatobrianom', *Sovremennik*, 6
—— (1964/1975), *Eugene Onegin: A Novel in Verse*, translated from the Russian with a commentary by Vladimir Nabokov in four volumes, rev. edn, London: Routledge & Kegan Paul
Pym, Anthony (1992), *Translation and Text Transfer: An Essay on the Principles of Intercultural Communication*, Frankfurt: Peter Lang
—— (1998), *Method in Translation History*, Manchester: St Jerome

—— (2010), *Exploring Translation Theories*, Abingdon: Routledge
Qvale, Per (2003), *From St Jerome to Hypertext: Translation in Theory and Practice*, trans. Norman R. Spencer, Manchester: St Jerome
Radice, William & Barbara Reynolds, eds (1987), *The Translator's Art: Essays in Honour of Betty Radice*, Harmondsworth: Penguin
Radó, György (1975), 'Indirect translation', *Babel*, 21:2, 51–9
Raffel, Burton (1971), *The Forked Tongue: A Study of the Translation Process*, The Hague: Mouton
—— (1988), *The Art of Translating Poetry*, University Park: Pennsylvania State University Press
Ram, Harsha (2007), 'Towards a Crosscultural Poetics of the Contact Zone: Romantic, Modernist and Soviet Intertextualities in Boris Pasternak's translations of T'itsian T'abidze', *Comparative Literature*, 59:1, 63–89
Rao, J. Prabhakara & Jean Peeters, eds (2010), *Socio-Cultural Approaches to Translation: Indian and European Perspectives*, New Delhi: Excel India
Reid, Robert (1986), 'The Critical Uses of Translation (Lermontov's *A Hero of our Time*)', *Essays in Poetics*, 11:2, 55–90
Reiss, Katharina (1971), *Möglichkeiten und Grenzen der Übersetzungskritik: Kategorien und Kriterien für einer sachgerechte Beurteilung von Übersetzungen*, Munich: Hueber [trans. Erroll F. Rhodes (2000), as *Translation Criticism: The Potentials and Limitations: Categories and Criteria for Translation Quality Assessment*, Manchester: St Jerome]
—— & Hans J. Vermeer (1984), *Grundlegung einer allgemeinen Translationstheorie* Tübingen: Max Niemeyer
Retsker, Ia. I. (1974), *Teoriia perevoda i perevodcheskaia praktika*, Moscow: Mezhdunarodnye otnosheniia
Ricoeur, Paul (2006), *On Translation*, trans. Eileen Brennan, London: Routledge
Robinson, Douglas (1991), *The Translator's Turn*, Baltimore: Johns Hopkins University Press
—— (1997), *Translation and Empire: Postcolonial Theories Explained*, Manchester: St Jerome
—— (2011), *Translation and the Problem of Sway*, Amsterdam: John Benjamins
——, ed. (1997/2002), *Western Translation Theory from Herodotus to Nietzsche*, 2nd edn, Manchester: St Jerome
Rose, Marilyn Gaddis (1997), *Translation and Literary Criticism: Translation as Analysis*, Manchester: St Jerome
Rowe, Eleanor (1976), *Hamlet: A Window on Russia*, New York: New York University Press

Roznatovskaia, Iu. A. (2000), *Oskar Uail'd v Rossii: bibliograficheskii ukazatel', 1892–2000*, Moscow: Rudomino

Ryl'skii, Maksim (1986), *Iskusstvo perevoda: stat'i, zametki, pis'ma*, Moscow: Sovietskii pisatel'

Ryou, Kyongjoo (2006), 'Aiming at the Target: Problems of Assimilation and Identity in Literary Translation' in Juliane House, María del Rosario Martín Ruano & Nicole Baumgarten, eds, *Translation and the Construction of Identity*, Seoul: International Association of Translation and International Studies, 96–108

Safiullina, Nailia (2009), 'Window to the West: from the Collection of Readers' Letters to the Journal *Internatsional'naia literatura*', *Slavonica*, 15:2, 128–61

Said, Edward (1978), *Orientalism*, London: Penguin

Salevsky, Heidemarie & Ina Müller, eds (2010), *Die russische Kultur und ihre Vermittlung*, Frankfurt: Peter Lang

Saussure, F. de (1916/83), *Cours de linguistique générale*, Paris: Éditions Payot [trans. R. Harris (1983), as *Course in General Linguistics*, London: Duckworth]

Savory, Theodore (1957/1969), *The Art of Translation*, London: Jonathan Cape

Schäffner, Christina, ed. (1999), *Translation and Norms*, Clevedon: Multilingual Matters

—— & H. Kelly-Holmes, eds (1995), *Cultural Functions of Translation*, Clevedon: Multilingual Matters

Schnaiderman, Boris (1994), 'Púchkin, tradutor de Gonzaga', *TradTerm*, 1, 67–71

Schulte, Rainer & John Biguenet, eds (1992), *Theories of Translation: An Anthology of Essays from Dryden to Derrida*, Chicago: University of Chicago Press

Scott, Clive (2012), *Literary Translation and the Rediscovery of Reading*, Cambridge: Cambridge University Press

Sdobnikov, Vadim V. & Olga V. Petrova, eds (2006), *Teoriia perevoda*, Moscow: AST / Vostok-Zapad

Semenenko, Aleksei (2005), '"Gamletovskii kontekst" Borisa Pasternaka', *Scando-Slavica*, 51, 31–48

—— (2007), *Hamlet the Sign: Russian Translations of Hamlet and Literary Canon Formation*, Stockholm: Almqvist & Wiksell International

Shuttleworth, Mark & Moira Cowie, eds (1997), *Dictionary of Translation Studies*, Manchester: St Jerome

Shveitser, Aleksandr D. (1988), *Teoriia perevoda: status, problemy, aspekty*, Moscow: Nauka

Simon, Sherry (1996), *Gender in Translation: Cultural Identity and the Politics of Transmission*, London: Routledge

Simpson, P. (1993), *Language, Ideology and Point of View*, London: Routledge

Snell-Hornby, Mary (1988/1995), *Translation Studies: An Integrated Approach*, rev. edn, Amsterdam: John Benjamins
—— (2006), *The Turns of Translation Studies*, Amsterdam: John Benjamins
——, Z. Jettmarová & K. Kaindl, eds (1997), *Translation as Intercultural Communication*, Amsterdam: John Benjamins
——, Franz Pöchhacker & Klaus Kaindl, eds (1994), *Translation Studies: An Interdiscipline*, Amsterdam: John Benjamins
Sorvali, Irma (1996), *Translation Studies in a New Perspective*, Frankfurt, Peter Lang
St André, J., ed. (2010), *Thinking through Translation with Metaphors*, Manchester: St Jerome
Steiner, George (1975/1998), *After Babel: Aspects of Language and Translation*, 3rd edn, Oxford: Oxford University Press
——, ed. (1966), *The Penguin Book of Modern Verse Translation*, Harmondsworth: Penguin
Steiner, T. R. (1975), *English Translation Theory: 1650–1800*, Assen: Van Gorcum
Stockhurst, Stefanie, ed. (2010), *Cultural Transfer through Translation: The Circulation of Enlightened Thought in Europe by Means of Translation*, Amsterdam: Rodopi
Stoliarov, M. (1939), 'Iskusstvo perevoda khudozhestvennoi prozy', *Literaturnyi kritik*, 5–6, 242–54
Störig, Hans-Joachim, ed. (1963), *Das Problem des Übersetzens*, Darmstadt: Wissenschaftliche Buchgesellschaft
Sullivan, J. P. (1964), *Ezra Pound and Sextus Propertius: A Study in Creative Translation*, Austin: University of Texas Press
Szegedy-Maszák, Mihály (2003), 'Canon, Translation, and Literary History', *Across Languages and Cultures*, 4:1, 5–18
Thelen, Marcel & Barbara Lewandowska-Tomasczyk, eds (2010), *Meaning in Translation*, Frankfurt am Main: Peter Lang
Tomlinson, Charles, ed. (1980), *The Oxford Book of Verse in English Translation*, Oxford: Oxford University Press
Toper, Pavel Maximovich & Vil' Ganiev, eds (1992), *Literatura i perevod: problemy teorii*, Moscow: Litera
Torop, Peeter (1995), *Total'nyi perevod*, Tartu: Tartu University Press
Tosi, Alessandra (2006), *Waiting for Pushkin: Russian Fiction in the Reign of Alexander I (1801–1825)*, Amsterdam: Rodopi
Toury, Gideon (1980), *In Search of a Theory of Translation*, Tel Aviv: Porter Institute
—— (1995), *Descriptive Translation Studies and Beyond*, Amsterdam: John Benjamins
Trivedi, Harish (1995), *Colonial Transactions: English Literature and India*, Manchester: Manchester University Press

Turkevich, Ludmilla B. (1950), *Cervantes in Russia*, Princeton: Princeton University Press
Tymoczko, Maria (1999), *Translation in a Postcolonial Context: Early Irish Literature in English Translation*, Manchester: St Jerome
—— (2010), *Translation, Resistance, Activism*, Amherst: University of Massachusetts Press
—— & Edwin Gentzler, eds (2002), *Translation and Power*, Amherst: University of Massachussetts Press
Tytler, Alexander Fraser [Lord Woodhouselee] (1790/1978), *Essay on the Principles of Translation*, ed. J. F. Huntsman, Amsterdam: John Benjamins
Tyulenev, Sergey (2010), 'Modernization as Translation: Eighteenth-Century Russia' in Ton Naaijkens, ed., *Event or Incident: On the Role of Translations in the Dynamics of Cultural Exchange*, Bern: Peter Lang, 15–28
—— (2011), *Applying Luhmann to Translation Studies: Translation in Society*, Abingdon: Routledge
——, ed. (2004), *Teoriia perevoda*, Moscow: Gardariki
Vaseva, I. (1980), *Teoriia i praktika perevoda*, Sofia: Nauka i isskustvo
Venuti, Lawrence (1995/2008), *The Translator's Invisibility: A History of Translation*, 2nd edn, London: Routledge
—— (1998), *The Scandals of Translation: Towards an Ethics of Difference*, London: Routledge
——, ed. (1992), *Rethinking Translation: Discourse, Subjectivity, Ideology*, London: Routledge
——, ed. (2000/2012), *The Translation Studies Reader*, 3rd edn, Abingdon: Routledge
Vinay, J.-P. & J. Darbelnet (1958/1977), *Stylistique comparée du français et de l'anglais: Methode de traduction*, Paris: Didier [trans. & ed. J. C. Sager & M.-J. Hamel (1995), as *Comparative Stylistics of French and English: A Methodology for Translation*, Amsterdam: John Benjamins]
Warren, Rosanna, ed. (1989), *The Art of Translation: Voices from the Field*, Boston: Northeastern University Press
Weissbort, Daniel, ed. (1989), *Translating Poetry: The Double Labyrinth*, London: Macmillan
—— & A. Eysteinsson (2006), *Translation: Theory and Practice*, Oxford: Oxford University Press
Welsh, David J. (1966), *Russian Comedy 1765–1823*, The Hague: Mouton
Will, Frederic (1993), *Translation, Theory and Practice: Reassembling the Tower*, Lampeter: Edwin Mellen

Witt, Susanna (2003), 'Perevod kak mimikriia: Gamlet Pasternaka', *Swedish Contributions to the Thirteenth International Congress of Slavists, Ljubljana, 15–21 August 2003*, Lund, 145–56

Wolf, Michaela et al., eds (2010), *The Power of the Pen: Translation and Censorship in Nineteenth-Century Europe*, Vienna: Lit Verlag

Wolff, Tatiana, ed. (1971), *Pushkin on Literature*, London: Methuen

Yifeng, Sun (2003), 'Translating Cultural Differences', *Perspectives*, 11:1, 25–36

Young, Jekaterina (2000), 'Dovlatov's Reception of Salinger', *Forum for Modern Language Studies*, 36:4, 412–25

Zaborov, Piotr (1985), 'Le théâtre de Diderot en Russie au XVIIIe siècle' in Anne-Marie Chouillet, ed., *Colloque international Diderot (1713–1784)*, Paris: Aux amateurs de livres, 493–501

Zekulin, Nicolas (2008), 'Turgenev as Translator' *Canadian Slavonic Papers*, 50:1–2, 155–76

Zhang Longxi (1992), *The Tao and the Logos: Literary Hermeneutics, East and West*, Durham: Duke University Press

—— (2005), *Allegoresis: Reading Canonical Literature East and West*, Ithaca: Cornell University Press

Zhukovskii, V. A. (1985), *Zarubezhnaia poeziia v perevodakh V. A. Zhukovskogo v dvukh tomakh*, Moscow: Raduga

—— (2000), *Angliiskaia poeziia v perevodakh V. A. Zhukovskogo: sbornik*, sostavl. K. N. Atarovoi & A. A. Gugnina, Moscow: Izd. Rudomino/ OAO Izd. Raduga

Zlateva, Palma, ed. (1993), *Translation as Social Action: Russian and Bulgarian Perspectives*, London: Routledge

Zuber, Ortun, ed. (1980), *Language of Theatre: Problems in the Translation and Transposition of Drama*, Oxford: Pergamon

Zuber, Roger (1968/1995), *Les 'Belles Infidèles' et la formation du goût classique*, rev. edn, Paris: Albin Michel

Index

academia 21, 159–60
Acmeism 20, 121
adaptation 2, 3, 7, 23, 37, 38, 41, 53, 103, 104, 113, 155, 215, 217–22, 232
adekvatnost' see adequacy
adequacy 89, 102, 167–72, 179n.116, 213, 218, 220, 232, 277, 278, 282–3
aestheticism 241–4, 252, 254–5, 257, 263
Akhmatova, Anna 22, 185, 227n.29, 270, 275, 276
Aksakov, Konstantin 74
Aksakov, Sergei 81, 89–90
akyn (bard) 146, 148, 149, 150n.25
Alexander I 69, 70
Alexander II 56, 57
Al'tman, Iogann 161, 163–73, 180, 208–9
America 25, 26, 69, 92n.51, 253, 268, 270, 272
  American literature 23, 283
  American poetry 28, 266, 268, 272, 273
  American Revolution 61
Amerika 269
Anikst, Aleksandr 247–8, 255, 258
Annenskii, Innokentii 20n.54, 120n.11, 121
anti-cosmopolitanism 23, 163n.70, 177n.107, 266
assimilation 1, 3, 4–5, 11, 162
Auden, W. H. 28
Avant-garde 238, 239, 241, 265
Azerbaijan 146, 164, 190

Bal'mont, Konstantin 18, 20, 23, 238n.12, 239, 250n.52, 257
Balzac, Honoré de 16, 95, 164

bard 145, 147, 149, 150n.25
  see also folk poet
Baudelaire, Charles 18, 19, 259
Belinskii, Vissarion 15, 56n.2, 108, 196, 220, 221–2
belles infidèles 15
Bible, translation of 59, 70
Blok, Aleksandr 19, 120n.11, 121–2, 126, 138, 276, 278, 282–3
Bodenstedt, Friedrich 90
Bolshevism 24
Botkin, Vasilii 89, 101–2
Brezhnev era 254
Briusov, Valerii 18–19, 101n.14, 168, 175, 208, 239, 257, 278, 283
Brodsky, Joseph 27, 28, 276
Bürger, Gottfried 12
Bukharin, Nikolai 187, 189
bukvalizm see literalism
Bulgarin, Faddei 218, 222
Burns, Robert 95, 178
Byron, George Gordon, *Baron* 12n.28, 15, 17, 61, 177n.107, 236, 242n.28

canon 5, 24, 126, 222, 229, 242, 254, 269–70, 275, 284
  canonical, translation as 18, 95, 216, 222, 225n.28
  canonical texts, translation of 213, 215–16
  canonicity 8, 232, 236, 246, 256
  Soviet canon 23, 28, 142n.3, 143, 147, 153, 157, 164–7, 179, 231, 246, 249, 259
Carlyle, Thomas 10–11, 16, 241

Catherine II ('the Great') 5, 10, 32–4, 42n.38, 50n.64, 59, 69
Caucasus 144, 146, 190
censorship 55, 119, 135
  in eighteenth-century Russia 59
  in nineteenth-century Russia 57, 60, 94, 117
  in Soviet period 23, 24, 26, 28, 122, 154, 178, 255, 266, 270, 284
  in twentieth-century Russia 29, 238
Central Asia 144, 146
Cervantes Saavedra, Miguel de 16, 99
  Don Quixote (character) 98–9, 105–15
  Don Quixote (novel) 98, 99, 103–6, 115
  quixotic as epithet 98, 104–7, 112
  see also Dostoevskii, Fedor; and Don Quixote
  see also Turgenev, Ivan Sergeevich; 'Gamlet i Don-Kikhot' ('Hamlet and Don Quixote')
Chateaubriand, François-René de 15, 62
Chénier, André 61–2
Chernyshevskii, Nikolai 101n.15, 119
Chukovskii, Kornei 134, 145n.15, 155, 162n.69, 181n.120, 200, 249–56, 259–60, 271, 283
Comédie Française 36, 42
creativity 11, 14, 92, 134, 145n.16, 197, 206, 231
cultural revolution 142n.4, 161, 164, 183, 235
cummings, e. e. 273

Dagestan 145, 146n.18
  see also Caucasus
Dante Alighieri 10, 164, 176n.105
Decadence 17, 19, 243n.29, 244, 258, 271
Decembrists 57, 61, 69, 70, 75
Deich, Aleksandr 235, 244, 249, 261
Delaveau, Hippolyte 89–90

Destouches, Philippe Néricault 42–7, 51
Detgiz 224
Detskii otdykh 240
Diderot, Denis 39
dol'nik 121, 126, 283
dominanta 171, 175
doslovnyi perevod see literal translation
Dostoevskii, Fedor 16–18, 87n.33, 98n.4, 238
  and Don Quixote 106, 113–15
  Idiot 105, 106n.29, 113
Douglas, Alfred, *Lord* 261–2
Druzhba narodov 145, 162
Du Bos, Jean-Baptiste 37, 40
Dzhabaev, Dzhambul 147

Eikhenbaum, Boris 185–6
Eliot, T. S. 229, 269
émigré writers 25
England 11, 40, 64, 71, 73, 77, 82, 83–4, 87, 91, 235, 250n.52, 252, 253
  English translation 81, 82, 83, 85, 88n.36, 241
equivalence 96, 106, 120, 123, 125, 130, 133, 171, 174, 176–7, 223, 232
Etkind, Efim 120, 123, 126, 134–9, 275, 277–84
exoticism 166–7

faithfulness 58, 89, 93, 138, 175, 177, 178, 196, 217, 222
First All-Union Conference of Translators 142, 156–81, 181–4, 188
First Congress of Soviet Writers 143, 146n.18, 187, 188–9
Flaubert, Gustave 84n.23, 85, 86, 93–4, 164
folk poet 146
  see also bard
folklore 149, 159, 271

Index

Fonvizin, Denis 34, 51, 52, 60
formalism 24, 28, 123, 126, 142, 160, 167,
    180, 187, 267, 270
    see also Russian Formalism
formalizm see formalism
France 10, 15, 18, 32, 38, 40, 42, 45n.48,
    62, 77, 82, 83, 84n.23, 86, 93, 253
    French literature 15, 16, 61, 62, 80
    French translation 15n.39, 50n.64,
        60, 81, 82, 83, 84, 85, 87, 90,
        104n.20, 162
France, Anatole 86
free translation 12, 24, 25, 26, 58, 59, 71,
    93, 96, 123, 134, 143, 160, 170, 178,
    227
freemasonry 57, 59, 67–9, 70
Friedberg, Maurice 1–2, 23, 27, 123, 267
Futurism 126, 138, 192

Gaprindashvili, Valerian 186, 195
Garshin, Vsevolod 88
Gautier, Théophile 16
Georgia (Georgian SSR) 186, 189, 190
    Georgian language 164, 189, 192,
        195, 207
    Georgian literature 144n.11, 189
    see also Boris Pasternak, *Georgian Lyricists*
Germany 12, 77, 81, 82, 90, 117, 122, 125
    German translation 83, 90, 103n.18
Gertsen, Aleksandr *see* Herzen,
    Alexander
Ginsberg, Allen 269
Ginzburg, Lidiia 275–6
glasnost' 28, 258, 270
Glavlit 154, 261
Gnedich, Nikolai 13–14, 103, 168
Goethe, Johann Wolfgang von 12–13n.12,
    32, 99, 103, 112, 164, 171–2, 178,
    179, 211, 216, 229, 247
    Faust 100–3, 106

Gogol', Nikolai 10, 15, 56n.2, 84, 103, 164
Goldsmith, Oliver 68
    'The Deserted Village' 63–5, 71–4
Goltsev, Viktor 193–4
Goncharov, Ivan 84, 112
Gor'kii, Maksim 21, 122, 144–5, 164, 169,
    249, 252–3, 265
Gorodetskii, Sergei 159, 206–9
Goslitizdat 158, 159n.55, 184, 224
Gottsched, Johann Christoph 37–9
Gray, Thomas 66
    'Elegy, written in a Country
        Churchyard' 11, 13n.30, 63–7, 70
Gumilev, Nikolai 20–1, 159, 276, 282

Hartmann, Moritz 81, 90–1
Heine, Heinrich 110, 117–39, 164, 283
Hemingway, Ernest 26–7, 245, 268
Herzen, Alexander 108–10
Hikmet, Nazim 268–9, 278–9, 283
Homer 12–14, 32, 99, 103, 164
    Iliad 13, 103n.30, 168
    Odyssey 12–13, 58, 168, 194
Horace 59–60
Huysmans, Joris-Karl 256n.71, 259

Iashvili, Paolo 186–7, 189, 193, 202
impressionism 167
Inostrannaia literatura 245n.34, 268, 269,
    271, 280
intelligentsia 68, 185, 200, 230, 241, 242,
    245, 249, 265, 274
internationalism 121, 143n.3
Internatsional'naia literatura 243n.29,
    245n.34, 267, 268
Iunyi chitatel' 240

Johnson, Samuel 14

Kafka, Franz 27, 245
Karelin, V. A. 105

Kashkin, Ivan 160, 176–9, 181n.20
Kazakhstan 146n.18, 147, 150n.25, 151n.30
  dekada 148, 150
  see also Central Asia
khaltura 157, 169
Khlebnikov, Velimir 124, 138, 270, 278, 282
Khrushchev 25, 245, 247, 251, 265n.1
  see also Thaw
Kipling, Rudyard 254, 263
Kiukhel'beker, Vil'gelm 61
Kozintsev, Grigorii 224, 225, 230n.40
Krasnaia nov' 188, 194
Krylov, Ivan 83–4
Kuzmin, Mikhail 238, 270, 276, 282
Kuznetsov, Pavel 149–51

Lann, Evgenii 160, 177
Lefevere, André 3, 6, 7
Lenin, Vladimir 152, 153, 154, 158, 164, 165, 167, 169, 194
  Order of Lenin 148–9n.24
Leningrad 158, 189, 268, 269, 270, 275, 276
Lermontov, Mikhail 10, 117n.2, 120, 164
Linetskaia, El'ga 275–6
literal translation 24, 25, 104, 123, 172, 224n.24, 227, 282
literalism 25, 67, 96, 123, 159, 160–1, 167, 169–73, 175–7, 180, 223
literalist translation, *see* literalism
literary translation 1–3, 5, 9–29, 80, 96, 123, 141–2, 155, 160–1, 183–4, 194, 199, 201, 209, 215, 232–3
literature of the non-Russian republics 144, 159, 163n.72
  see also Boris Pasternak, *Georgian Lyricists*
Literaturnaia gazeta 13, 143, 161, 188, 191, 195, 197, 199, 206, 207, 208
Literaturnyi kritik 191

London, Jack 25, 243
Lotman, Iurii 4, 53, 214, 233, 276
Lozinskii, Mikhail 158–9, 161–2, 173–80, 222, 231
Lukanina, Adelaida 82, 87
Lukin, Vladimir 31, 34–41, 48–9, 53–4
  Mot, liuboviiu ispravlennoi 34–5, 41–53
Lunacharskii, Anatolii 122

Maiakovskii, Vladimir 124, 126, 138, 164, 242, 266, 269, 278–9, 283
Maimbet 149–50
Maksimov, Dmitrii 275–6
Mandel'shtam, Osip 7–8, 20–2, 185, 270, 276, 282
Markovich, Mar'ia *see* Vovchok, Marko
Marx, Karl 153, 158, 164
Marxist-Leninism 183, 242
masonry *see* freemasonry
Maupassant, Guy de 94–5
Meierkhol'd, Vsevolod 239, 257
Merezhkovskii, Dmitrii 18
Mérimée, Prosper 90
Mikhailov, Mikhail 128–33
Milton, John 15
Mirskii, Dmitrii 191–3, 241–3, 266
Mochalov, Pavel 219–21
Modernism 236, 239, 257, 266, 267, 269
Molodaia gvardiia 222
Morozov, Mikhail 224, 230–1
Moscow 10, 16, 80, 81, 148, 150n.25, 154, 159, 160, 187, 201, 219, 238, 245, 248, 249, 262n.93, 268, 270
Moscow University 56, 69
Moskovskii telegraf (*Moscow Telegraph*) 62, 217
Murav'ev-Apostol 70

Nabokov, Vladimir 25, 108, 250, 276
narodnost' 48n.56, 148

national languages 22, 153, 153–6, 159,
    165–6, 167, 170, 180, 183, 184, 185,
    190, 193, 196, 197, 210, 211
naturalism 144, 167, 169
Nekrasov, Nikolai 89, 95, 97, 101–2n.15
Nemirovich-Danchenko, Vladimir
    223–4
Neruda, Pablo 26, 268–9, 278–9, 283–4
Nietzsche, Friedrich 236–7, 238
Niva 240
Nordau, Max 19n.50, 237
Novyi zhurnal literatury, iskusstva i nauki
    240

OBERIU 266, 270n.12
October Revolution 21, 121, 144, 235,
    236, 238
Ognev, Vladimir 283
Orient 12, 144, 146–7, 151, 153n.36, 166
oriental translations 146, 151, 153n.36
original and translation
  closeness of translation to original
    20, 123, 138, 162n.69, 207–9,
    217–18
  relation of translation to original 19,
    23, 38–9, 58, 100–2, 117, 213–15,
    221–2, 233, 278
  translation evaluated in comparison
    with original 3, 12, 14n.33, 22,
    67, 71–2, 74, 123–33, 166–79, 185,
    194–7, 219–21, 260
  translation regarded as equal to
    original 11, 31, 33, 56, 83, 91–3, 96,
    218, 223
Ostrovskii, Aleksandr 84, 87, 89, 97n.2,
    164
Ozerov, Lev 283–4

Panaev, Ivan 101–2
Paris 16, 36, 39, 40, 61, 62, 80, 84, 87, 88,
    99n.7, 105n.26

parody 118, 127
Pasternak, Boris 22–4, 134, 162, 178–9,
    270
  Dr Zhivago 229–30
  Hamlet translation 222–32
  and translation of Georgian poetry
    186–211
Pater, Walter 253, 259
Paul (Grand Duke) 34, 35
perestroika 28, 258
Peter I ('the Great') 32, 59
pietism 70
Pietsch, Ludwig 83, 90
podstrochnik 148, 180, 274, 282
Poe, Edgar Allan 17–20
Polevoi, Nikolai 228
  Hamlet translation 217–22, 232
Poroshin, Semen 34, 43–4, 50n.66
post-Stalin era 27, 247, 265–84
Pravda 143–51, 152–6, 159n.55, 160,
    162n.69, 163, 165, 166, 180, 203
Pshavela, Vazha 178, 186–7, 191–2
Puskhin, Aleksandr 9–11, 12n.28, 13–15,
    16–17, 20n.55, 25, 56–7, 61–2,
    106n.29, 167, 237

Radishchev, Aleksandr 60–1
Raevskii, V. F. 69
Ralston, William 83–4, 91–2
RAPP 160
ravnotsennost' see equivalence
Realism 16, 17, 18, 65, 263
reception 2, 3, 5, 105, 215, 233, 251
  in eighteenth-century Russia 53
  in nineteenth-century Russia 14, 16,
    18, 26, 98, 216, 221
  of Pasternak's translations 188–97,
    230–2
  of Russian authors 25
  of Wilde 236–47, 253–7, 260–1, 263
Riccoboni, Luigi 40, 45

Romanticism 63, 217, 238
  German 12, 101
  Russian 12, 236
Romm, Aleksandr 180, 202–5, 207
Ruskin, John 241, 253, 255, 258
Russian Formalism 159, 173, 185
  see also dominanta

Sand, George 16, 101
Sandberg, Carl 272
satire 117, 118, 119, 122, 123, 135, 246
Schiller, Friedrich von 12n.12, 16, 57, 61, 75, 164
Schlegel, August-Wilhelm 110, 216
Scott, Walter, Sir 15, 17, 57
serfdom 60, 74
Shakespeare, William 16–17, 22, 86n.30, 99, 103, 155, 158n.53, 164, 167, 177–8, 179, 202, 211, 216, 247
  Hamlet 22n.62, 101n.14, 106–12, 134, 179, 215–33
  King Lear 22n.62, 155
  Macbeth 22n.62, 57–8
Shelley, Percy Bysshe 19–20, 23n.63
Shengeli, Georgii 160, 177, 185
Silver Age 19, 239, 242, 259, 270, 274, 277, 282, 284
Skorpion 239
Slavophile 5, 16, 74, 108, 109n.36, 111
Smirnov, Aleksandr 158–62, 169–75, 178, 180
Socialist Realism 23, 24, 27, 142n.4, 153, 156–7, 160, 168–9, 178, 236, 264–5, 267, 269, 271
Society for the Translation of Foreign Books 10, 59
source text 3, 6, 22n.60, 82, 89, 92, 96, 154, 196, 213, 215, 233
Sovetskaia kul'tura 244, 267
Sovremennik 15, 95, 98
sphinx 100, 249n.48

St Petersburg 16, 34, 62, 80, 84, 97, 119n.37, 113, 238, 243n.29, 257
  see also Leningrad
Stal'skii, Suleiman 145–6, 148–9n.24
Stalin 26, 150, 151, 154, 158, 163n.72, 165, 187, 189, 194, 235, 236, 262n.93
Stalin period 24, 25, 28, 249, 251, 265, 266, 270, 274, 275, 278
Stalin prize 148n.24, 176n.105
Stasiulevich, Mikhail 93, 94
State Publishing House (*GIZ*) 21
Strugovshchikov, Aleksandr 101–2, 106
Sumarokov, Aleksandr 31n.1, 35–6
Symbolism 17, 243n.29, 256n.71
  French Symbolism 19
  Russian Symbolism 19, 20

Tabidze, Titsian 186, 189, 190, 192–3, 202
Tadzhik 144n.11, 164, 165, 166
  see also national languages
Tarasenkov, Anatolii 192–4, 202
target text 3, 83, 89, 154, 213, 214, 233
Tartar 144n.11, 154n.40, 164
  see also national languages
Teplov, Grigorii 50
Thaw 26–8, 162, 249, 251, 254, 257, 265, 267–8, 270, 274, 275, 278–80, 284
theatre 5, 216
  in Catharine's Russia 34, 35n.15, 36, 37, 39, 40, 43n.42, 44n.46, 46, 47, 48, 51, 52n.71, 53
  in nineteenth century 87, 220, 221, 222
  in twentieth century 232, 238, 245, 248, 249
Tikhonov, Nikolai 164, 189–92, 195, 198, 206–7, 283
Tiutchev, Fedor 117n.2, 120, 123, 130, 283
Tolstoi, Lev 26, 89, 164, 236–7
  The Cossacks 84–5
  War and Peace 85–6

translation
  in eighteenth-century Russia 1–2,
    9–10, 31–54, 59–61, 63, 67–8,
    103–4
  in nineteenth-century Russia 1–2,
    10–19, 22n.60, 57–8, 61–3, 65–7,
    70–5, 79–96, 97n.2, 98–107, 115,
    117–21, 168, 170, 216–22, 283
  without an original 14, 114–15,
    149–50
Trediakovskii, Vasilii 31, 33
Turgenev, Andrei 57–8, 60, 66–7, 69, 71
Turgenev, Ivan P. 57, 68–9, 71
Turgenev, Ivan Sergeevich 16, 77–96,
    97–115, 164
  'Faust' 89, 90, 100–02, 106
  'Gamlet i Don-Kikhot' ('Hamlet and
    Don Quixote') 97–8, 104–12
  Dvorianskoe gnezdo (*Liza*) 91–2
  Dym (*Smoke*) 80, 81, 90, 91, 92n.51
  Ottsy i deti (*Fathers and Sons*) 83, 90,
    92n.51, 107
  Rudin 92n.51, 101, 109, 112
Tynianov, Iurii 22, 117, 123–39, 159n.56

Ukraine 88, 144n.11, 164
  Ukrainian language 164
  Ukrainian writers 88–9
USSR (also Soviet Union) 2, 21–9, 133,
    135, 137, 145n.15, 151, 165, 186, 195,
    209, 235, 247, 254, 261, 263–4,
    266, 267, 280

Venuti, Lawrence 5, 8
Vestnik Evropy 66, 84, 87, 93, 94
Vesy 239

vol'nyi perevod see free translation
Vovchok, Marko 88–9, 98–100, 103
Vronchenko, Mikhail 101n.14, 102n.17,
    217, 221–2

Western Europe 61, 74, 77, 79, 80, 83, 84,
    86, 90, 93, 96, 113
  Western European literature 11,
    158n.53, 159, 283
Westernizer 5, 111
Whitman, Walt 20n.53, 26, 268, 271–3
Wilde, Oscar 20n.53, 24n.66, 88n.36,
    235–64
  Ballad of Reading Gaol 235, 238, 242,
    244, 248–50
  Salome 238–9, 257
Williams, William Carlos 266, 273
World Literature (*Vsemirnaia literatura*)
    21, 122, 249, 266
Writers Union 142, 144, 146n.18,
    150n.25, 158, 180, 184, 185–211,
    267, 268
  nationalities section 163, 180
  translators section 156

Young, Edward 13n.30, 68

Zenkevich, Pavel 156, 158, 161, 169, 200,
    204–5, 207–8
Zhirmunskii, Viktor 159n.56, 174,
    282
Zhukovskii, Vasilii 11–12, 14–15, 23,
    55–75, 103–5, 168, 194
Znamia 188, 192
Zola, Emile 86, 93–4
Zverev, A. 271–3

Russian Transformations: Literature, Thought, Culture

Series Editor:
Andrew Kahn, University of Oxford

Russian Transformations publishes studies across the entire extent of Russian literature, thought and culture from the medieval period to the present. The series gives special emphasis to the kinds of transformation that characterise Russian, Soviet and post-Soviet writing. Transformation has often been under the stimulus of (and resistance to) foreign traditions. Acts of cross-cultural and cross-literary reception mark Russia's sense of creative development and national identity. Transformation has often been the result of the on-going dialogues between writers working within the Russian literary tradition through polemic and subtle use of intertextuality. Similarly, the stunning political and social changes that have been characteristic of Russian history generated radical transformation in the institutions of literature and in forms of literature from Modernism to post-Perestroika as writers react to official policy on freedom of expression.

Proposals from established scholars, as well as more recent doctoral students, for single-author monographs and thematic collections are welcome. The series will publish works in English and Russian. For further information please contact Andrew Kahn (andrew.kahn@seh.ox.ac.uk).

Vol. 1   Andreas Schönle
The Ruler in the Garden. Politics and Landscape Design in Imperial Russia. 395 pages. 2007.
ISBN 978-3-03911-113-8

Vol. 2   Emily Lygo
Leningrad Poetry 1953–1975. The Thaw Generation.
374 pages. 2010.
ISBN 978-3-03911-370-5

Vol. 3   Emily Van Buskirk and Andrei Zorin (eds)
Lydia Ginzburg's Alternative Literary Identities. A Collection of Articles and New Translations. 457 pages. 2012.
ISBN 978-3-03911-350-7

Vol. 4   Muireann Maguire
           Stalin's Ghosts. Gothic Themes in Early Soviet Literature.
           343 pages. 2012.
           ISBN 978-3-0343-0787-1

Vol. 5   Leon Burnett and Emily Lygo (eds)
           The Art of Accommodation. Literary Translation in Russia.
           323 pages. 2013.
           ISBN 978-3-0343-0743-7